Unity for Professionals

A comprehensive guide for the Unity developer to connect, scale, and monetize

Josep Alemany i Fruitós

www.bpbonline.com

First Edition 2026

ISBN: 978-93-65892-475

Distributors:

BPB PUBLICATIONS
20, Ansari Road, Darya Ganj
New Delhi-110002
Ph: 23254990/23254991

DECCAN AGENCIES
4-3-329, Bank Street,
Hyderabad-500195
Ph: 24756967/24756400

MICRO MEDIA
Shop No. 5, Mahendra Chambers,
150 DN Rd. Next to Capital Cinema,
V.T. (C.S.T.) Station, MUMBAI-400 001
Ph: 22078296/22078297

To View Complete BPB Publications Catalogue Scan the QR Code:

Published by Manish Jain for BPB Publications, 20 Ansari Road, Darya Ganj, New Delhi-110002 and Printed by him at Repro India Ltd., Rewari.

www.bpbonline.com

Dedicated to

My beloved wife ***Remei***

and

my son ***Víctor***

About the Author

Josep Alemany i Fruitós is passionate about technology and began his journey in programming at the age of 12. His extensive professional background includes significant achievements early in his career, such as programming a game entirely in assembly language for the Commodore Amiga and participating in the deployment of the communications network for the 1992 Barcelona Olympic Games.

Throughout his career, he has played an active role in the technical community, with his programming blog leading him to serve as the president of the Lotus Notes User Group in Spain. His work has been recognized with multiple accolades, including an IBM award for Most Innovative Company for creating a management tool for public administrations, and the Samsung Spain Best App award for the Naval Museum of Madrid application.

In recent projects, he participated in the development of an AI system with emotion recognition that was contracted by FIFA during the Qatar World Cup. He currently works at the University of Valencia on a European project focused on the preservation of historical and cultural heritage through the development of tools (some in Unity 3D) and the use of AI.

About the Reviewers

- **Sergio Sebastián** is a Unity developer with a strong passion for interactive experiences and game development. He has extensive experience teaching Unity to computer science students, guiding them in areas such as 2D/3D gameplay, VR, and interactive applications.

  He holds a degree in multimedia engineering and currently works as a Unity teacher at Fempa, where he helps future professionals develop both technical expertise and creative confidence.

  Sergio also works as a developer at Minsait (Indra Group), contributing to enterprise projects in COBOL, while continuing to explore the creative and educational possibilities of Unity.

- **Chris West** is a senior software engineer with over 20 years of experience building web-based applications and services using C# and .NET technologies. In recent years, he has expanded his expertise into game development with Unity, focusing on gameplay programming, architecture, and design patterns.

  Chris is an active technical book reviewer who is passionate about helping developers evaluate learning resources and apply new concepts effectively. His professional engineering background allows him to assess technical accuracy, clarity, and real-world applicability from the perspective of a working developer.

  He is currently focused on advancing his skills in game development while continuing to build software professionally, and he regularly reviews books related to programming, Unity, and game design.

- **Steven Christian** is a medical researcher, Unity certified instructor, and XR engineer. He is currently focused on and working with spatial computing solutions and tools, including Unity 3D (C#), OpenXR, AR Foundation, Python, and cloud infrastructure like AWS. He is also focused on clinical neuroscience, integrating high-fidelity biometrics—such as eye, face, and head tracking—into virtual reality environments. With a passion for democratizing health education and establishing reproducible workflows, Steven specializes in building automated data pipelines that translate complex physiological signals into actionable insights. When he is not engineering new tools or studying as an MD/PhD candidate in integrative neuroscience at the University of Nevada, Reno, he runs Iltopia Studios, where he develops augmented reality graphic novels. He is an active reader, visual artist, and former division I collegiate athlete who enjoys comics, animation, and IT-related books, where he serves as a technical reviewer, consultant, and author for various publications about Unity, AR/VR development, and spatial computing.

Acknowledgement

First of all, I would like to thank my parents, who guided me to learn computer science and did everything they could to help me achieve my professional dream. It was not always easy.

I want to express my deepest gratitude to my family and friends for their unwavering support and encouragement throughout this book's writing, especially my wife Remei and my son Víctor.

I also thank BPB Publications for their guidance and expertise in bringing this book to fruition. The book's revision was a lengthy process, with the invaluable participation and collaboration of technical reviewers and editors who contributed greatly to its final approach. Thanks to their patience and perseverance.

I would also like to acknowledge the valuable contributions of my colleagues and coworkers during many years working in the tech industry, who have taught me so much and provided valuable feedback on my work.

Finally, I would like to thank all the readers who have taken an interest in my book and for their support in making it a reality. Your encouragement has been invaluable.

Preface

Today, creating professional games and apps involves much more than just being a great C# programmer or knowing all the tools in the Unity 3D editor. To bring your project to life, you need to understand the complete picture: the backend systems, the cloud infrastructure, and the advanced services that constantly elevate digital experiences. This is where **Unity Gaming Services** (**UGS**) comes into play, offering a powerful toolkit not just to develop your project, but to effectively scale and manage it from prototype to launch and throughout its entire lifecycle of continuous improvement.

This book is designed to serve as the definitive guide for professionals looking to master the entire lifecycle of game and app development using the Unity 3D environment. It covers everything from setting up cloud infrastructure and implementing multiplayer networks to leveraging the latest advancements in artificial intelligence. Throughout the book, you will learn how to integrate essential services, such as authentication, remote crash detection and resolution, analytics, and data-driven monetization, ensuring your projects are not only technically solid and robust, but also commercially viable.

This book is aimed at Unity developers, software engineers, and specialists who wish to expand their knowledge beyond simply making a game/app and publishing it on a store. It is for everyone who wants their development to be scalable, capable of continuous improvement, monetizable, and ultimately, a success. With this book, you will gain the knowledge to navigate the complexities of Unity's Cloud ecosystem and push the boundaries of what is possible in game development.

Chapter 1 - Frontend and Backend Development — We start with the essentials, refreshing key concepts like client/server architecture, authentication, REST APIs, and Game Metrics to lay a strong foundation.

Chapter 2 - Cloud Computing Services — Get a clear overview of the major players—AWS, Azure, GCP—and understand the different cloud models (IaaS, PaaS, SaaS) to make smart choices for your infrastructure.

Chapter 3 - Getting Starting with Unity Gaming Services — A practical, step-by-step guide to begin with UGS: creating projects, linking them to Unity, installing packages, and getting your first services up and running.

Chapter 4 - Unity Dashboard — Master the Unity Dashboard. Learn to manage projects, activate services, handle organization settings, roles, and billing—all from a single control center.

Chapter 5 - Exploring Data with Analytics System — Discover how to track and understand player behavior. Learn about events, environments, and how to use the Data Explorer and SQL to pull meaningful insights from your data.

Chapter 6 - Optimizing Player Lifecycle with Analytics — Move from data to action. Apply analytics to improve player journeys, using metrics like DAU and retention, audience segmentation, and funnels to boost acquisition and engagement.

Chapter 7 - Engagement, Gamification and Retention — Explore proven strategies to keep players coming back. We will look at storytelling tools, social features, user-generated content, and techniques like Cloud Content Delivery to keep your game feeling fresh.

Chapter 8 - Data Privacy and Consent — Navigate the crucial legal landscape. Understand regulations like GDPR and CCPA, and learn best practices for obtaining user consent and managing player data responsibly.

Chapter 9 - Unity Authentication for Multiple Platforms — Implement secure, cross-platform logins. We cover integrating sign-in with Facebook, Apple, and Google, and demystify the mechanics of tokens and sessions.

Chapter 10 - Scaling Multiplayer Games with Game Server Hosting — Dive deep into building multiplayer experiences that can grow. We focus on **Netcode for GameObjects** (**NGO**), network architectures, and using Relay servers to connect players seamlessly.

Chapter 11 - Enhance Your Game with Vivox — Add voice and text chat to foster community. Learn to configure Vivox, set up different channel types, and use moderation tools to create a safe space for players to connect.

Chapter 12 - Unity DevOps for Streamline Game Development — Streamline your workflow. Implement version control with Plastic SCM, set up CI/CD pipelines, and automate your build process to ship updates faster and more reliably.

Chapter 13 - Crash and Error Reporting with Cloud Diagnostics Advanced — Maintain stability and polish. Learn to use advanced diagnostic tools like the Unity Profiler and Cloud Diagnostics to quickly identify, debug, and resolve crashes and errors.

Chapter 14 - Strategies for Sustainable Monetization — Explore ethical and effective ways to generate revenue. We will walk through implementing **In-App Purchases** (**IAP**) and integrating various Unity Ads formats to build a solid business model.

Chapter 15 - Enhancing Your Projects with Unity — Polish your project's look and feel. Create complex animations with the Animator, integrate Mixamo characters, and use post-processing effects like Bloom to achieve a professional shine.

Chapter 16 - Stereoscopic Images in VR — Craft truly immersive VR. Understand the principles of stereoscopic vision and learn the techniques for implementing 3D images and 360-degree video directly within Unity.

Chapter 17 - Artificial Inteligence and Unity 3D — Bring the power of modern AI into your projects. We explore practical integrations with tools like ChatGPT for dynamic text, DALL-E for image generation, and Whisper for audio.

Chapter 18 - Last Features of Unity 6 — Stay ahead of the curve. We highlight the newest engine advancements, from AI tools like Muse and Sentis to rendering upgrades like the GPU Resident Drawer and support for emerging platforms.

Code Bundle and Coloured Images

Please follow the link to download the
Code Bundle and the ***Coloured Images*** of the book:

https://rebrand.ly/b0cfe6

The code bundle for the book is also hosted on GitHub at
https://github.com/bpbpublications/Unity-for-Professionals.
In case there's an update to the code, it will be updated on the existing GitHub repository.

We have code bundles from our rich catalogue of books and videos available at **https://github.com/bpbpublications.** Check them out!

Errata

We take immense pride in our work at BPB Publications and follow best practices to ensure the accuracy of our content to provide an indulging reading experience to our subscribers. Our readers are our mirrors, and we use their inputs to reflect and improve upon human errors, if any, that may have occurred during the publishing processes involved. To let us maintain the quality and help us reach out to any readers who might be having difficulties due to any unforeseen errors, please write to us at: **errata@bpbonline.com**

Your support, suggestions and feedback are highly appreciated by the BPB Publications' Family.

Piracy

If you come across any illegal copies of our works in any form on the internet, we would be grateful if you would provide us with the location address or website name. Please contact us at **business@bpbonline.com** with a link to the material.

If you are interested in becoming an author

If there is a topic that you have expertise in, and you are interested in either writing or contributing to a book, please visit **www.bpbonline.com**. We have worked with thousands of developers and tech professionals, just like you, to help them share their insights with the global tech community. You can make a general application, apply for a specific hot topic that we are recruiting an author for, or submit your own idea.

Reviews

Please leave a review. Once you have read and used this book, why not leave a review on the site that you purchased it from? Potential readers can then see and use your unbiased opinion to make purchase decisions. We at BPB can understand what you think about our products, and our authors can see your feedback on their book. Thank you!

For more information about BPB, please visit **www.bpbonline.com**.

Join our Discord space

Join our Discord workspace for latest updates, offers, tech happenings around the world, new releases, and sessions with the authors:

https://discord.bpbonline.com

Table of Contents

CHAPTER 1
Frontend and Backend Development

Introduction

For a few years now, the terms frontend and backend have been used to refer to the code that runs in the browser or the code that runs on the server in web programming, respectively. However, this architecture started much earlier and applies to developing games or apps for mobile devices in Unity.

In this chapter, we will review the history of computing and progress to see a few illustrations where one innovation or another is utilized. We aim to learn concepts that will allow us to better understand the following chapters.

Structure

The chapter covers the following topics:

- History of computing
- Authentication
- Game Metrics
    - Relational databases
    - SQL
    - NoSQL databases
    - Pros and cons
- REST API
- Cloud computing services
    - Capacity to make leaderboards with dashboard

Objectives

This chapter aims to establish fundamental vocabulary and concepts essential for developing the server-side architecture (backend) of games and applications built in Unity. Moving forward, we will go over the different ways of improving the projects to get better feedback on the app and detect problems faster.

Moreover, this chapter approximates the origin of computing and the client / server architecture. In the next chapters, we are going to dive deeper into the details and how to implement them in Unity 3D.

History of computing

At the dawn of computing, when there was no internet, and connections were measured in baud (bits per second), client/server architecture was used. The server stored all the data, generated a text-based interface, and transmitted it via serial cable to the terminals.

The terminals had no processing capacity. They were limited to showing what the server had generated for them on screen. They recorded the user's keystrokes and sent them to the server so that it could process them and generate the new interface.

It is a clear example of what the backend (server) and the frontend (terminals). It helps us to illustrate well the scope occupied by each one of them. Refer to *Figure 1.1*:

***Figure 1.1**: Sample of a console on a mainframe computer*

The client/server architecture is the initial basis of the web. When *Tim Berners-Lee* (refer to *Figure 1.2*) created HTML, a markup language, servers generated HTML pages by combining database content with templates and sent the resulting HTML text over the internet to the browser. This displayed the interface on the screen and sent the user's interactions back to the server. The server responded with an entirely new page after each interaction.

Over time, browsers were equipped with greater processing capabilities, and individual components of a webpage could update independently using technologies like AJAX. With the advent of Web 2.0, it was possible to avoid regenerating the entire page. Consequently, Frontend development improved significantly and became more interactive.

Figure 1.2: *Tim Berners-Lee creator of WWW on a NEXT computer*

Processor performance continued to improve steadily. Improvements to HTML-enabled browsers enable them to handle more interface-related tasks without relying on the server.

HTML5, CSS, and the significant improvements that have been made to the JavaScript language have enabled the development of rich, interactive web applications.

Frontend development on the web

Frontend development, on the other hand, alludes to the portion of web development that deals with what the client sees and interacts with, specifically. The frontend engineer is mindful of making the **user interface** (**UI**), which incorporates everything the client interacts with, such as buttons, shapes, menus, and design. The frontend designer employs languages like HTML, CSS, and JavaScript to construct the website's look and feel.

Backend development on the web

Backend development alludes to the portion of web development that deals with the server side of your application. Backend engineers are mindful of building and keeping up servers, application logic, and databases responsible for information handling and commerce logic. Compose the backend logic of your web application utilizing languages such as Python, Ruby, PHP, and Java.

Unity's developers usually tend to develop their game or app only in the editor (which would be the equivalent of the frontend), but usually, little or no attention is paid to all the development on the server side. A current game (where everything is hyperconnected) will not succeed if attention is not paid to the backend part.

In Unity, frontend usually refers to the in-game interface and behaviors, while backend refers to cloud services, authentication, databases, and analytics.

Client/server architecture examples in games and VR

Microsoft Flight Simulator (2020) is a large-scale example of client-server architecture in practice. The game streams detailed terrain and world data from cloud servers to the client in real-world, allowing for a realistic simulation of Earth's surface without storing the full dataset locally. This approach highlights the importance of backend services in supporting massive amounts of data and delivering it efficiently to players.

We begin by discussing one of the most important parts of recreation that works generally on the server side, that is, Microsoft Flight Simulator.

The adaptation of Microsoft Flight Simulator (2020) represents a major technical achievement in real-time simulation and cloud-based data streaming. Its special features are discussed as follows:

- The outline has more than 500,000,000 square kilometers. It reflects the entire Earth's surface.
- It features AI-generated renditions of real-world buildings, terrain, and trees.

All that colossal sum of information weighs 2.5 petabytes. No consumer-grade device could store or process the full dataset locally.

Indeed, the process of playing Flight Simulator on a computer can be quite straightforward. It primarily involves transmitting a relatively small subset of the pertinent data, especially when the player is employing the conventional client-server methodology. To better understand how client-server models function at scale, let us explore their application in a real-world example.

When Notre Dame Cathedral in Paris was rebuilt, the famous musician *Jean-Michel Jarre* decided to hold a concert in the metaverse. It was called *Welcome to the Other Side*. The engine chosen to stream the concert was: Unity 3D, as shown in *Figure 1.3*.

In this case, the server part had to store the information of all the users who were enjoying the concert and synchronize their position and movements in real-world so that the immersion was as realistic as possible.

The client side had to render the scene based on the user's location and the rotation of their field of view. Collect all user data and send it to the server.

Figure 1.3: *A concert on the metaverse needs a client/server architecture*

Authentication

According to NetworkWorld[1]:

Authentication using certificates is a feature of many internet security protocols, including the near-universal SSL/TLS, commonly used by web browsers to authenticate online transactions. However, while most SSL/TLS uses involve servers confirming their identities to client machines, the term certificate-based authentication usually denotes a situation where that scenario is reversed: an end user's device sends a certificate to prove its identity so the user can gain access to server or network resources.

While certificate-based authentication is not common in most games, secure authentication is still important, but it is necessary to identify and authenticate which user is connecting. When we launch new software development, it is important to monitor user behavior, such as level progression and game difficulty balancing. This helps personalize offers and detect potential fraud.

For example, by associating accounts with access rights based on purchase history or subscription status or restricts access to particular highlights, levels, etc.

For all this, it is necessary to be able to authenticate the user, and given the great ubiquity of social networks, in many cases, they are used for the user to confirm their identity. Using a social network as a means of authentication has two interesting values:

- Streamlines the sign-up process and simplifies content sharing for users, giving a frictionless sign-in and reducing account duplication.
- It empowers game designers to assemble client information from these stages.

A few platforms that permit us to verify are *Apple, Facebook/Meta, Google, Steam,* and *OpenID*.

Authentication implies obtaining personal data and, therefore, since authentication involves handling sensitive user data, legal compliance becomes essential. Since authentication involves personal data, legal compliance is a critical concern—one we will address later in the chapter.

Game Metrics

It is always considered that the developers are fully aware of the functioning of the games they develop. Players often behave in unexpected ways, revealing edge cases or design flaws that may cause bugs or unintended gameplay behavior. Metrics become a helpful tool by providing valuable insights into the game's performance for identifying areas for improvement and correcting bugs.

To assess the performance of the game, one needs to consider the following:

- **Player Count**: Tracks how many users are actively playing in the game, over a specific period. It provides an overall measure of the game's popularity and player retention and helps assess user engagement trends over time.

1 **https://www.networkworld.com/article/748294/infrastructure-management-simply-put-how-does-certificate-based-authentication-work.html**

- **In-Game Events**: This helps track daily active users, session duration, and monetization actions like purchases or invites.
- **Performance**: Measures how well the game runs across various hardware and platforms, identifying platform-specific issues.

All these measurements are stored in cloud databases and visualized later through analytics dashboards.

In later chapters, we will examine how these metrics can be used to improve the game and how each metric is used to help us make continuous improvements to our game.

Databases

Within the setting of game development, we utilize the databases as a central store for sorting and obtaining game-related data and the client profile with the game, levels, scores, and more.

The following are some critical concepts with regard to databases:

- **Data persistence**: This implies that the data related to the game is preserved, even when we uninstall it for a while and reinstall it, it maintains all the information, levels, and progress. There is data persistence.
- **Concurrency**: It refers to the ability of a system to handle multiple users accessing or modifying the same data simultaneously. For example, what happens when all players have to know where a Pokémon might be? If a group of users needs to access the same data (called concurrency), you should make the administration flexible upon request.

There are a few types of databases depending on their finalities. However, they are mostly classified as follows:

Relational databases

They have a predefined construction that manages the structure of the information. Schemas define the tables, columns, information sorts, and connections in development. Modifying the pattern frequently requires cautious planning and relocation forms.

Connections between tables are built by utilizing remote keys. This show implements information judgment and bolsters complex connections between substances.

SQL

The foremost critical distinction is the Inquiry Dialect. Relational databases utilize standard **Structured Query Language** (**SQL**). This dialect gives an effective set of explanatory commands for complex questions, joining tables, conglomerating information, and performing exchanges.

Scalability: Relational databases are vertically scalable, that is, they handle larger workloads by adding more resources to a single machine (upgrading hardware).

Some of the most used relational databases are MySQL, PostgreSQL, and SQL Server.

NoSQL databases

They do not have a predefined construction. They are named schema-less or schema-flexible. NoSQL databases allow flexible data models, such as document-based, key-value, or graph formats. They permit energetic and adaptable patterns, where distinctive records/documents within a collection can have distinctive structures. This adaptability empowers less demanding adjustment to changing information necessities and makes it less difficult to handle unstructured or semi-structured information.

NoSQL does not have SQL as a query language. NoSQL databases use non-SQL query languages that vary depending on the implementation. A few databases back SQL-like inquiry language to assist administration.

Scalability: NoSQL databases are evenly adaptable. They are built to handle large-scale conveyed frameworks and can effortlessly scale by including more servers or cloud frameworks. Now and then, this requires complex procedures like replication, dividing information, and dispersion.

Some of the most used NoSQL databases are MongoDB, Cassandra, or Redis.

Pros and cons

Depending on the needs of the application, a database model can be better or worse, as shown in the following points:

- **Relational databases**: They are well-suited for applications that require strong data consistency, complex relationships, and structured data. They are commonly used for transactional systems, financial applications, content management systems, and applications with complex business logic.
- **NoSQL databases**: NoSQL databases are suitable for applications with dynamic requirements, a large amount of unstructured or semi-structured data, and the need for high scalability and performance. They are often used in big data, real-time analytics, content management systems, IoT applications, and social networks.

REST API

Imagine you have important data or content from your application that needs to be accessed by external systems. In the past, this meant that a method must be established for the company desiring access. Further, the data must be structured in a way that the receiving system can understand.

Fortunately, the current systems allow a flexible approach to interoperate between different computer systems in a standard way: the REST API.

A web service based on **Representational State Transfer** (**REST**) is an architectural style for designing networked applications that use standard HTTP methods. API is a type of web service architecture that follows a set of principles and constraints for designing networked applications. RESTful APIs are commonly used in games to handle tasks like retrieving user data, submitting scores, or accessing leaderboards between systems over the internet using standard HTTP protocols.

RESTful APIs are widely used in web development due to their simplicity, scalability, and compatibility with existing web standards. They are platform-independent and can be accessed by various clients, including web browsers, mobile apps, and other systems. They have become the *de facto* standard for building web services and are commonly used for tasks such as data retrieval, data manipulation, authentication, and integration between different applications. Most web services and backend communication tasks are developed with them.

The information is interchanged in standard and open formats like XML or JSON.

Version control

If you are a developer, you have likely used version control systems like Git, GitHub, or TortoiseSVN to manage your project's code. These tools help track changes to your codebase over time, making it easier to collaborate, revert to earlier states, and identify when and where bugs were introduced.

In this section, we will look at two critical aspects of Unity development. First, Unity provides seamless deployment to a variety of online platforms, such as Google Play and the Apple App Store. While support for Windows deployment exists, it may involve more manual steps depending on the publishing platform.

Second, Unity includes tight integration with Unity Version Control (formerly Plastic SCM), a tool optimized for game development workflows. This system is especially well-suited for managing large binary assets and scenes common in Unity projects, and it integrates directly with the Unity Editor.

When crashes or errors occur in production, Unity's Cloud Diagnostics can help identify the cause. This tool collects real-time crash reports and exception data, enabling developers to diagnose and fix problems faster.

Version control systems also enable rollbacks to previous working states or seamless deployment of patches—critical when addressing bugs that affect users. This approach is central to modern development practices like **continuous integration and continuous deployment** (**CI/CD**), often implemented through DevOps workflows. DevOps is a collaborative approach that bridges development and operations, aiming to shorten feedback cycles and improve release quality.

Cloud computing services

A cloud computing service refers to a remote computing system or infrastructure that can run software or perform operations off-device. We can make requests to it when convenient for us.

There is another benefit of developing in the cloud, which is, **build automation**.

We can have several configurations. Therefore, cloud-based build automation allows cross-compilation for platforms you may not have direct hardware access to. For example, we can compile an application for *Linux* from a windows system.

If we compile it using build automation, we can have a configuration with a remote computer, for example, a *Mac,* and generate macOS builds using a cloud-based Xcode environment, this enables development for platforms you cannot natively build for on your local machine.

Another useful capability is executing code remotely in the cloud. You can write modular code libraries and deploy them to the cloud for remote execution.

We will be able to call this code module from our application. Cloud code modules typically return responses in formats like JSON or XML, making them easy to consume from client-side applications. This enables developers to offload processing, customize logic remotely, and fix issues without needing app updates.

The code is properly stored and managed in scripts and modules. The programming language is C#. It must be programmed to be reusable. Storing reusable cloud code in an online repository makes updates faster and provides flexibility across different client devices.

If the code were inside an application the device has installed, the change would not occur until each device is updated to the latest version. Some stores can take a long time to accept an application, so if the bug is critical, it could take weeks or months to be fully fixed. Refer to *Figure 1.4*:

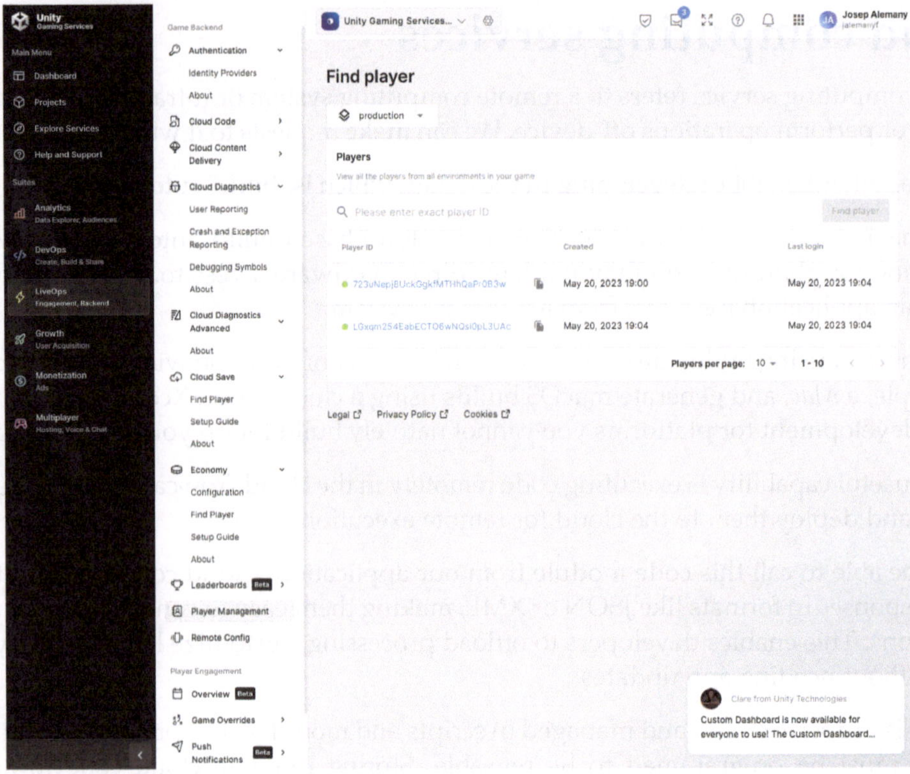

***Figure 1.4:** Unity Gaming Services console*

LiveOps is a Unity Gaming Services tool for real-time monitoring, configuration, and operational control of live game environments. Within the control panel, we find a section called LiveOps, as shown in *Figure 1.4*.

LiveOps allows for remote configuration changes, event scheduling, and reward distribution.

This is used to control the aspects of our projects in production (they are already in the store and on the users' devices) to be able to control and manage aspects such as player state, economy balancing, or feature flags in real-world.

Economy

Managing the in-game economy is a vital part of any live game or application. From a backend perspective, tracking user purchases and virtual goods enables developers to better understand monetization patterns, detect anomalies or fraud, and optimize item offerings.

Unity provides tools such as Unity **In-App Purchasing** (**IAP**) to handle transactions within the application. However, for security and analytics, it is a best practice to validate purchases on a secure backend. This often involves verifying receipts or transaction tokens with platform providers (e.g., Apple, Google Play) via a server-to-server API.

By integrating purchase validation and logging into your backend system, you can:

- Ensure that purchases are legitimate (protecting against spoofed receipts).
- Associate purchases with a unique user ID.
- Track revenue metrics like **average revenue per paying user** (**ARPPU**), conversion rates, and regional trends.
- Analyze which virtual goods perform best across player segments.

Data gathered from the backend can also feed into other systems like leaderboards (e.g., premium players vs. free players), reward systems, and LiveOps tools.

Monitoring economic data server-side allows developers to adjust pricing, bundles, and promotions without requiring a new game build—key for maintaining a responsive and successful in-game economy.

Since applications can be sold anywhere, it comes with a significant challenge. We must keep exhaustive control over each of the purchases made by each user, the currency, and the exchange in which the purchase is made. It is important to know which items are giving the best results and the ones not selling well, to improve or change them.

Monitoring the economy helps us to know what the return on investment is. We must know how much our application or game is generating.

Leaderboards

One of the common functions of the cloud is to centralize data about player results. All of this data is displayed on a leaderboard. For example, in a mobile racing game, players' best lap times are uploaded and ranked using Unity leaderboards. This shared data allows players to measure themselves by comparing results and creates greater competitiveness.

Here is a breakdown of the leaderboard's highlights.

Capacity to make leaderboards with dashboard

This includes permission to form and control leaderboards inside the Unity Dashboard, which could be a central interface for overseeing different viewpoints of your game. Key dashboard features include:

- **Oversee up to six million leaderboards**: You have the adaptability to handle a huge number of leaderboards within your venture, with a maximum of up to six million leaderboards.
- **Sort by most noteworthy to least or vice versa**: Leaderboards can be sorted in climbing (least to highest) or plummeting (most elevated to most reduced) levels and arranged, based on the scores accomplished by players.

- **Utilize best score, latest score, or add up to score methodologies**: You will select distinctive procedures to decide the score shown on the leaderboards. This could be based on the most excellent score accomplished by a player, the foremost, later score, or the entire aggregate score.
- **Resets of leaderboards, with archived versions available**: This feature permits you to reset the leaderboards at particular intervals, manually or with the help of the program. Furthermore, past forms of the leaderboards are chronicled, permitting you to keep track of verifiable information.
- **Bucketing to bunch players on a leaderboard into littler cohorts**: With bucketing, you will gather players into littler cohorts or categories based on certain criteria. This will help to make sub-leaderboards or divisions inside a leaderboard, empowering reasonable competition inside particular bunches.
- **Tiering to classify players based on their performance:** Tiering permits you to classify players into different categories or levels based on their execution. For example, players may well be classified as Gold, Silver, or Bronze based on their scores or rankings.
- **Preview release of the Unity Leaderboards SDK:** The Unity Leaderboards **Software Development Kit** (**SDK**) is presented in a preview discharge. This SDK gives engineers the tools and resources needed to execute leaderboards within Solidarity ventures effectively.
- **See the release of the Cloud Code JavaScript Leaderboards SDK**: Another SDK, particularly centered on Cloud Code and JavaScript, is additionally being released as a preview release. This SDK encourages the integration of the leaderboard's usefulness by utilizing Cloud Code and JavaScript inside Unity Applications.

REST API for in-game and organization

A **Representational State Transfer Application Programming Interface** (**REST API**) is used to interact with the leaderboard functionality. This API can be used for in-game operations, such as submitting scores, as well as authoritative tasks like making or resetting leaderboards.

Generally, these features aim to improve your game by giving comprehensive and customizable leaderboards, in turn permitting the developer to oversee rank, and display player scores, achievements, and rankings of successful players within their game.

Find player

As its name indicates, this function allows developers to locate a user. Each user is assigned a **unique identifier** (**user ID**), which allows developers to track user data accurately. This better aligns with technical terminology and standard practice. We will be able to know when the user registered for that application, assuming backend analytics or user metadata is being stored appropriately, and the last time they logged in. We will also be able to know all the inventory or purchases made by them if purchase tracking and inventory systems are implemented and integrated with user IDs.

Push notifications

Push notifications are messages or alerts that are sent to a user's devices, such as a smartphone, tablet, or computer, even when the user is not actively using an application or website.

Unity developers can use third-party services like **Firebase Cloud Messaging** (**FCM**) or OneSignal to implement push notifications, as Unity does not currently provide native push notification support.

These push notifications deliver relevant information directly to the users' devices or notification centers, usually in the form of a banner, pop-up, or badge. Push notifications serve as a way to engage and communicate with users by delivering timely and personalized information. They can be sent by mobile apps, web browsers, or other software platforms that can deliver notifications.

One of the issues that must be considered when sending a push notification is the time change. If we send a notice to a user and it is early morning in their country, they may find it intrusive or disruptive. Fortunately, most push notification platforms allow segmentation by region, timezone, or behavior to avoid this issue.

Conclusion

This chapter presents the concept of client/server engineering and its application in web development, games, and mobile apps. It clarifies the advancement of web development from the server-based approach to a better Frontend development empowered by progressions in HTML, CSS, and JavaScript. The chapter also discusses backend and frontend development, highlighting the significance of backend development in game development. It notes the illustration of the Microsoft Flight Simulator system to demonstrate the server-side preparation included in games.

The chapter digs into different points related to backend development, user authentication, metrics, databases (relational and NoSQL), REST API, version control, and cloud computing services. It clarifies the reason and noteworthiness of each subject, providing insights into their significance in application development.

The next chapter explores the major cloud computing service providers, offering a detailed comparison of the three market leaders: AWS, Microsoft Azure, and Google Cloud Platform. It breaks down essential cloud models such as IaaS, PaaS, and SaaS, analyzes specific services like storage and databases, and guides the reader through geographic coverage and pricing strategies.

Multiple choice questions

1. **In the context of web programming, which terms correctly describe the code running in the browser and the code running on the server?**
   a. Backend refers to the code running in the browser, and frontend refers to the code running on the server.
   b. Frontend refers to the code running in the browser, and backend refers to the code running on the server.
   c. Frontend refers to HTML and CSS, and backend refers exclusively to JavaScript.
   d. Frontend refers to servers, and backend refers to databases.
2. **What accurately describes the client/server architecture at the dawn of computing, when connections were measured in baud?**
   a. The terminals had significant processing capacity and generated interfaces locally.
   b. The server generated a text-based interface and transmitted it to terminals via a serial cable.
   c. The server was limited to recording the user's keystrokes.
   d. The client side (terminals) generated HTML pages to display the interface.
3. **According to the source, what are the primary responsibilities of backend engineers on the web?**
   a. Making the **user interface** (UI), including buttons, shapes, and menus, using HTML, CSS, and JavaScript.
   b. Building and keeping up servers.
   c. Managing databases responsible for information processing and commerce logic.
   d. Utilizing technologies like AJAX to update individual components of a webpage independently.
4. **Microsoft Flight Simulator (2020) serves as a large-scale example of client-server architecture in practice by highlighting which crucial backend function?**
   a. Utilizing Unity 3D to synchronize user positions and movements in a metaverse concert.
   b. Ensuring data persistence so that game progress is maintained even after uninstallation.
   c. Streaming the colossal sum of 2.5 petabytes of detailed terrain and world data from cloud servers to the client in real-world.
   d. Implementing certificate-based authentication to secure online transactions.

5. **What are the key benefits of using social networks as a means of user authentication for an application?**
   a. It streamlines the sign-up process, providing frictionless sign-in and reducing account duplication.
   b. It enables game designers to gather client information from these platforms.
   c. It guarantees better performance across various hardware and platforms.
   d. It ensures strong data consistency and complex relationships suitable for transactional systems.
6. **Regarding databases, what is a fundamental difference in how relational and NoSQL databases handle scalability?**
   a. Relational databases are evenly adaptable (horizontally scalable) by including more servers.
   b. NoSQL databases are vertically scalable, handling larger workloads by adding more resources to a single machine.
   c. Relational databases are vertically scalable.
   d. NoSQL databases are built to handle large-scale distributed frameworks and can scale evenly.
7. **Which of the following describes the nature and usage of a RESTful API? (Select all that apply)**
   a. It is an architectural style for designing networked applications that use standard HTTP methods.
   b. It is widely used in games to handle tasks like retrieving user data, submitting scores, or accessing leaderboards.
   c. It interchanges information in standard and open formats like XML or JSON.
   d. It is a feature used in LiveOps for real-time monitoring and event scheduling.
8. **What is the major advantage of executing modular code libraries remotely in the cloud (cloud code modules) rather than installing that code directly within the client application?**
   a. The code can only be programmed using the C# language.
   b. It automatically enables cross-compilation for platforms you may not have direct hardware access to, such as compiling for Linux from Windows.
   c. If a bug is critical, the developer can fix issues and update the logic remotely without needing to wait for each device to update to a new version via application stores.
   d. It allows the developer to utilize version control systems like TortoiseSVN or Git.

Answers

1	b
2	b c
3	b, c
4	c
5	a, b
6	c, d
7	a, b, c
8	c

Join our Discord space

Join our Discord workspace for latest updates, offers, tech happenings around the world, new releases, and sessions with the authors:

https://discord.bpbonline.com

CHAPTER 2
Cloud Computing Services

Introduction

Amazon Web Services (**AWS**), Microsoft Azure, and **Google Cloud Platform** (**GCP**) are the three major cloud computing providers in the market today. Each of them offers a range of services and tools to help organizations build, deploy, and manage their applications and infrastructure in the cloud.

AWS is the oldest and most established of the three, with a vast array of services covering everything from compute and storage to networking and **machine learning** (**ML**). It also has a strong community and a vast ecosystem of third-party tools and services. AWS is often the preferred choice for enterprises that require a high level of customization and control over their infrastructure.

Microsoft Azure, on the other hand, is known for its seamless integration with Microsoft's other products and services, such as Office 365 and Dynamics 365. It is particularly popular among enterprises that use Windows Server and Microsoft's development tools. Azure has a wide range of services similar to AWS, including compute, storage, networking, and AI/ML.

Google Cloud Platform is often considered to be the best choice for organizations leveraging Google's expertise in big data and analytics, as well as its powerful ML tools. It also has a strong focus on containerization and Kubernetes, making it a popular choice for organizations that want to build and deploy containerized applications. GCP has services similar to AWS and Azure, including compute, storage, and networking.

In summary, while all three cloud providers offer similar services and features, they differ in their strengths and focus areas. Organizations should consider their specific needs and goals when selecting a cloud provider.

Structure

The chapter covers the following topics:

- Cloud computing
- Cloud computing models
- Important cloud providers

  - o Amazon Web Services
  - o Microsoft Azure
  - o Google Cloud
- Geographical coverage
  - o Resource hierarchy
- Comparison of common cloud services
  - o Data storage
  - o Databases
  - o Networks and connectivity
  - o Authentication and security
  - o Tools for developers
- Pricing and cloud cost analysis

Objectives

In this chapter, we are going to see what cloud computing is, its advantages, and its models. The main objectives are to have an overview of the main platforms in the current market and to know what services and prices they offer. To do this, we are going to analyze and compare the main services and solutions that each of them offers, including storage, databases, connectivity, security, and development tools.

We will also see the deployment at the territorial level, which may be essential in some cases or markets.

Finally, we will see how to calculate the price we will have to pay. It is not trivial and, therefore, providers have developed calculators that will help us in the process.

Cloud computing

Cloud computing refers to the delivery of computing resources, including servers, storage, databases, networking, software, and analytics, over the internet on a pay-as-you-go basis. Instead of owning and managing physical infrastructure, users can access these resources from **cloud service providers** (**CSPs**) who maintain and operate data centers, housing the necessary hardware and software infrastructure.

Some of the key advantages are:

- **On-demand self-service**: Users can provision and manage computing resources, such as virtual machines or storage, without requiring intervention from the CSP. This enables agility and flexibility, allowing users to scale resources up or down based on their needs.

- **Broad network access**: Cloud services can be accessed from anywhere via the internet using various devices, including desktop computers, laptops, tablets, and smartphones. This accessibility promotes collaboration and remote work.
- **Resource pooling**: CSPs serve multiple users simultaneously, allowing them to pool and share resources across multiple customers. This multi-tenancy model maximizes resource utilization and provides cost savings.
- **Rapid elasticity**: Cloud resources can be quickly scaled up or down to meet changing demands. This elasticity ensures that users only pay for the resources they need and can easily accommodate spikes in traffic or workloads.
- **Measured service**: Cloud providers track and measure resource usage, providing transparency and enabling users to monitor and optimize their usage. Billing is typically based on actual resource consumption, allowing for cost control and optimization.

Cloud computing models

Based on the architecture, you have the following models:

- **Infrastructure as a service (IaaS)**: The CSP provides virtualized computing resources such as virtual machines, storage, and networks. Users control the operating systems, applications, and configurations deployed on the infrastructure.
- **Platform as a service (PaaS)**: In addition to the infrastructure, the CSP also provides a platform that includes an operating system, development tools, and runtime environments. Users can focus on building and deploying applications without managing the underlying infrastructure.
- **Software as a service (SaaS)**: Users access software applications hosted on the cloud infrastructure. The CSP manages the infrastructure, platform, and application, while users only need a web browser or a thin client to use the software.

Cloud computing offers numerous benefits, including cost savings, scalability, flexibility, increased efficiency, and access to advanced technologies. It has transformed the way businesses and individuals consume and deploy computing resources, enabling innovation and accelerating digital transformation across industries.

Important cloud providers

In 1943, *Thomas Watson*, the president of IBM at the time, delivered this famous phrase:

I think there is a world market for maybe five computers.

-Thomas Whatson, President of IBM (1943)

At present, it might appear like an exaggeration, but the truth is that when it comes to cloud computing, the market is divided among very few. We are going to assess the main players in the market. We will also attempt to compare their solutions in order to comprehend what they have to offer, as well as their advantages and disadvantages.

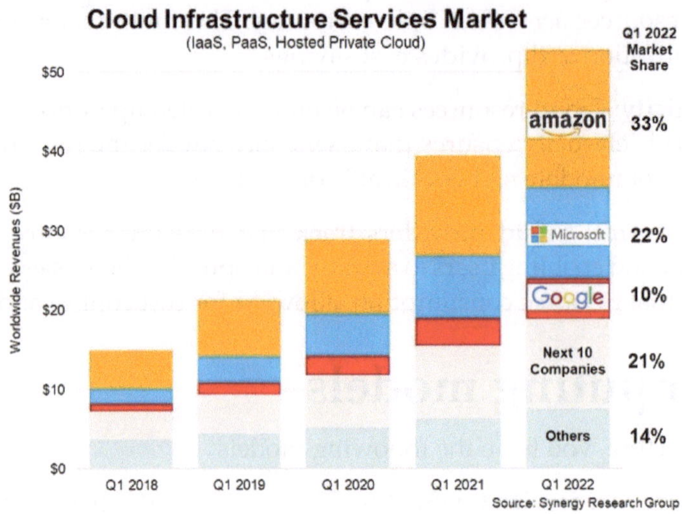

***Figure 2.1**: The more important cloud providers of recent years*

***Source:** https://digitalcloud.training/comparison-of-aws-vs-azure-vs-google/*

As seen in *Figure 2.1*, the market is divided between three dominant companies and then some others, including IBM, VMware, and Alibaba (very present in the Chinese market). We do not want to give you the impression that these three cloud providers are the only options. There is a significant number of them out there, but for the purpose of this survey, we focused on these three. They are often discussed in conjunction with each other, so it made sense to compare them. Moreover, the information about them is readily available.

Amazon Web Services

AWS is the oldest provider on the market and has been in operation since 2006. As the cloud industry's first provider, the company has gained a special edge over its competitors with a vast array of services covering everything from compute and storage to networking and machine learning. It also has a strong community and a vast ecosystem of third-party tools and services. AWS is often the preferred choice for enterprises that require a high level of customization and control over their infrastructure. Some of the most famous clients are:

- Netflix
- Expedia
- Airbnb

- Coursera
- Coca-Cola

Microsoft Azure

Microsoft's Azure started in 2010, four years after AWS. However, it became a competitor quickly. Azure is Microsoft's public Cloud platform, known for seamless integration with Microsoft's other products and services, such as Office 365 and Dynamics 365. It is particularly popular among enterprises that use Windows Server and Microsoft's development tools. Azure has a wide range of services similar to AWS, including compute, storage, networking, and AI/ML. Some of its prominent clients include:

- 3M
- HP
- Asus
- Mitsubishi
- Starbucks
- **National Health Service** (**NHS**) United Kingdom

Google Cloud

Google Cloud was also launched in 2010. The number of its cloud services is relatively small compared to AWS and Azure. It offers more than 100 services (instead of the 200 offered by AWS or Azure). GCP is often considered to be the best choice for organizations that want to leverage Google's expertise in big data and analytics, as well as its powerful machine learning tools. It also has a strong focus on containerization and Kubernetes, making it a popular choice for developers and companies that want to build and deploy containerized applications. Some of his notable clients include:

- UPS
- PayPal
- Spotify
- Twitter
- Toyota

Geographical coverage

One of the huge benefits of employing a huge public cloud provider is that you simply pick up and get to their worldwide framework. Moreover, you can effectively make virtual servers in places near your group of onlookers (or near yourself). These three suppliers all have different information centers spread over the world, but as you may see underneath, they are not all rise in terms of scope.

You can consult the locations of the data centers worldwide in the following links:

- **AWS: https://aws.amazon.com/about-aws/global-infrastructure/**
- **Azure: https://azure.microsoft.com/en-us/regions/**
- **Google Cloud Platform: https://cloud.google.com/about/locations/**

In the following figure, you can see the main data centers, their interconnections, and capacities. It is important to take this into account if your app is going to require a lot of resources. The map is as follows:

Figure 2.2: *Global geographical coverage*

Source: *https://www.atomia.com/2016/11/24/comparing-the-geographical-coverage-of-aws-azure-and-google-cloud/*

The following illustration shows a map of where AWS data centers are located around the world. This page is very interesting because it can be consulted interactively and is always up to date. You can consult the following cloud providers:

- Amazon Web Services
- Google Cloud
- IBM Cloud
- Microsoft Azure
- Oracle Cloud

- Alibaba Cloud
- Tencent Cloud
- Huawei Cloud

The map of AWS data centers is as follows:

Figure 2.3: Global internet connections

Source: *https://www.cloudinfrastructuremap.com/#/cloud-service-provider/amazon-web-services*

Resource hierarchy

Even if we do not know, we are using a hierarchy; all cloud platforms have one. From the first moment we start using a cloud service, we are using its structure. Understanding and planning to use this hierarchy becomes extremely important as cloud volume increases. The first interaction you have with a cloud platform is related to its hierarchy of resources. Once the hierarchy is understood, it is crucial to design how the resources will be organized. This can be done using a variety of methods or by combining them, listed as follows:

- By arranging the organization's resources according to their lifecycle so that they can all be generated or destroyed at once.
- Organizing by type is ideal for services not connected to an application.
- When all resources have the same policies and lifecycle, organizing by application is suitable.
- Planning according to the environment development, testing, and production enables a bigger distance between them.
- Departmental grouping, regional grouping, or cost center grouping are some examples of grouping.

Although uncommon, these grouping techniques can be helpful in certain circumstances.

Generally speaking, it is advisable to combine several organizational techniques, as shown in the following figure:

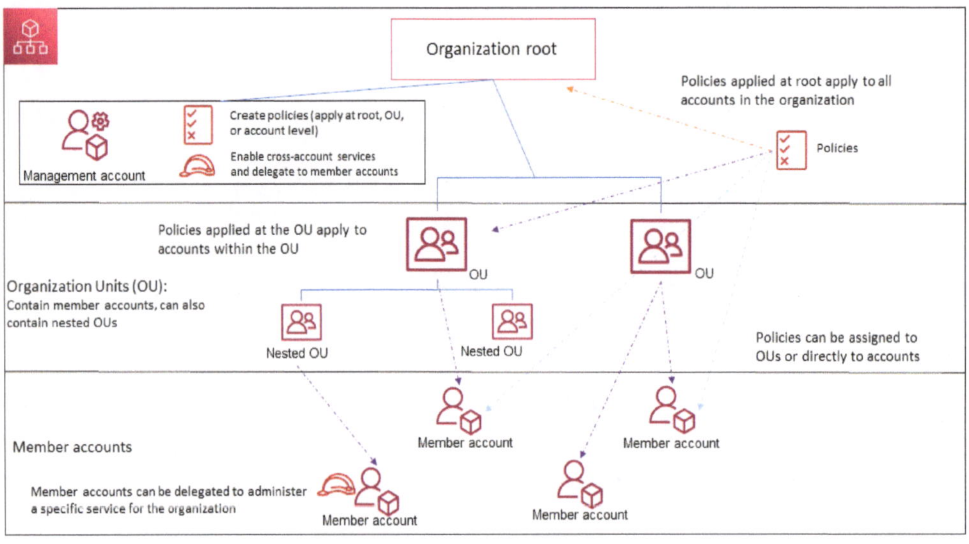

***Figure 2.4**: AWS Organizations terminology and concepts*

***Source:** https://docs.aws.amazon.com/organizations/latest/userguide/orgs_getting-started_concepts.html?ref=enmilocalfunciona.io*

You can learn more about the hierarchy of the cloud providers on the following pages:

- AWS: **https://docs.aws.amazon.com/organizations/latest/userguide/orgs_getting-started_concepts.html?ref=enmilocalfunciona.io**

- **Azure**: **https://learn.microsoft.com/en-us/azure/cloud-adoption-framework/ready/azure-setup-guide/organize-resources?ref=enmilocalfunciona.io**
- **GCP**: **https://cloud.google.com/resource-manager/docs/cloud-platform-resource-hierarchy?ref=enmilocalfunciona.io**

Comparison of common cloud services

Compute refers to the ability to compute or process a basic yet essential cloud service. Any of the *big three (Amazon Web Services, Microsoft Azure, and Google Cloud Platform)* provides a variety of Linux and Windows-based instances, some with GPUs, others with huge, high-performance configurations.

Managed Kubernetes and serverless services are now available to everyone. Kubernetes Engine stands out in the first due to its level of development. The serverless service, called Lambda, supports a broader range of programming languages (Java, Go, PowerShell, Node.js, C#, Python, and Ruby).

Two of the best-known computer services that have been added recently:

- **AWS Outposts** allows you to use Amazon Cloud technology locally.
- **GKE On-Prem** enables you to use Kubernetes Engine in your data center.

The following table compares cloud services offered by the three major cloud providers, specifically the service models: **infrastructure as a service** (**IaaS**), **platform as a service** (**PaaS**), container services with Kubernetes, and serverless computing:

Service	AWS	Azure	Google
IaaS	**Elastic Compute (EC2)** **https://aws.amazon.com/es/ec2/**	Azure Virtual Machine https://azure.microsoft.com/es-es/products/virtual-machines/	Google Compute Engine **https://cloud.google.com/compute/**
PaaS	AWS Elastic Beanstalk **https://aws.amazon.com/es/elasticbeanstalk/**	App service **https://azure.microsoft.com/en-us/products/app-service/**	Google App Engine **https://cloud.google.com/appengine/docs/standard/**
Container with Kubernetes	AWS Elastic Container Service for Kubernetes EKS **https://aws.amazon.com/es/eks/?nc2=type_a**	**Azure Kubernetes Service (AKS)** **https://azure.microsoft.com/es-es/products/kubernetes-service/**	Google Kubernetes Engine **https://cloud.google.com/kubernetes-engine/**

Service	AWS	Azure	Google
Serverless	Lambda **https://aws.amazon.com/es/lambda/**	Azure Functions **https://azure.microsoft.com/es-es/products/functions/**	Google Cloud Functions **https://cloud.google.com/functions/**

Table 2.1: Comparison of computing cloud services

Data storage

Storage capacity is another crucial feature of the cloud. They all provide a wide array of highly dependable services for all forms of storage, including object-based, file, and disc, for instance, backup, and others.

All three companies offer services for moving massive amounts of data to the cloud, including sending equipment to the client's location to copy the data and transporting it to their data center to transfer it quickly and securely.

The largest and most impressive of all is Snowmobile, which transports data to your facilities on an Amazon truck that is nearly 20 m. Azure is the only provider of managed disaster recovery services.

While the cost may fluctuate depending on factors such as storage type, data volume, and geographical region, a general observation can be made that these services tend to be more cost-effective in Azure when compared to Google, and in Google when compared to Amazon, as shown in the following table:

Service	AWS	Azure	Google
Object storage	**Simple Storage Service (S3)** **https://aws.amazon.com/es/s3/**	Blob Storage **https://azure.microsoft.com/es-es/products/storage/blobs**	Google Cloud Storage **https://cloud.google.com/storage/**
Cold storage	AWS Glacier	Archive Blob Storage	Google Cloud Storage Nearline
File storage	EFS	Azure file storage	ZFS / Avere
Block level storage	**Elastic Block Storage (EBS)**	Managed disks	Google Compute Engine Persistent Disks

Table 2.2: Comparison of data storage

Databases

The catalog of databases available in the cloud is vast: relational databases, NoSQL, caches, data warehouses, etc.

All three providers support managed services for databases. They also offer NoSQL as well as document-based databases. AWS also offers a proprietary RDBMS named *Aurora*, a fast and highly scalable database for MySQL and PostGreSQL.

There are only two relational database engines supported by Google: MySQL and PostgreSQL. Azure also supports MariaDB and SQL Server, and Amazon adds Oracle to all of these.

With BigQuery, Google shines out particularly well in this segment.

Graph-based databases and services for database replication and migration are only available through Azure and AWS.

Here is a brief comparison of the three providers as shown in *Table 2.3*:

Service	AWS	Azure	Google
RDBMS	AWS RDS	**Structured Query Language** (**SQL**) Database	Google Cloud SQL
NoSQL—key value	DynamoDB	Table storage	Bigtable, Cloud Datastore
NoSQL—indexed	AWS SimpleDB	Cosmos DB	Google Cloud Datastore

***Table** 2.3: Comparison of databases*

Networks and connectivity

Each provider uses a different set of technologies and approaches each demand differently.

However, we can handle the networks of our cloud infrastructure, set up subnets, load balancers, configure the **network address translation** (**NAT**), set up firewalls, create **virtual private networks** (**VPNs**), make direct connections with business data centers, or set up a **content delivery network** (**CDN**) with any of them.

Since each cloud service provider names the technology according to their own criteria, it can sometimes be difficult to compare different types of solutions.

In the following table, you can see the networking and connectivity services by the technique used by each provider, so that you can compare them based on the equivalent service:

Service	AWS	Azure	Google
Isolated virtual network environments	Virtual Private Cloud	Virtual Network	Virtual Private Cloud
Connection with on-prem environments	AWS Managed VPN	VPN Gateway	Cloud VPN
Managed DNS to manage names and records	Route53	Azure DNS	Google Cloud DNS

Service	AWS	Azure	Google
Global Content Delivery Network	CloudFront	Content Delivery Network	Cloud CDN
Dedicated private network to connect Cloud and local environments	Direct Connect	ExpressRoute	Cloud Interconnect
Load balancing: Automatically distributes incoming traffic	Elastic Load Balancing	Load Balancer	Cloud Load Balancing

Table 2.4: Comparison of connectivity

Authentication and security

There are many security services, but we will focus only on those that can be used the most when developing an app/video game, such as authentication or protection against DDoS.

Identity management is done through **identity and access management** (**IAM**). Although natively the IAM of Google and Azure are highly oriented to Gsuite and Active Directory, respectively, they all offer cross-platform integration solutions.

With the recent addition of Cloud Armor by Google, they all have a service to protect against DDOS attacks.

It is strongly recommended that you explore the rest of the services that may be useful in a certain project:

Service	AWS	Azure	Google
Authentication and authorization	IAM	Active Directory Active Directory Premium	Cloud IAM Cloud Identify-Aware Proxy
Multifactor authentication	Multifactor authentication	Multifactor authentication	Multifactor authentication
Protection against distributed denial of service (**DDoS**) attacks	AWS Shield	DDoS Protection Service	Cloud Armor

Table 2.5: Comparison of authentication and security

Tools for developers

Today, we have the necessary tools to build, deploy, diagnose, debug, and manage scalable services and applications in a cross-platform mode.

This wide and varied offer seems aimed at making it easier for the cloud to be our development environment. They include the most common services (code repositories, construction tools, deployment managers) to the most specific (queue services, messaging, API management, or search engines).

As of today, all three have their service mesh services available.

The following table names the tools that the different cloud service providers provide so that developers can manage and create applications in their environments:

Service	AWS	Azure	Google
Git repositories	AWS Source Repositories https://github.com/aws	Azure Source Repositories	Cloud Source Repositories
Code repositories	CodeCommit	Azure Repos	Cloud Source Repositories
Templates	Quick Start	Quickstart Templates	
Command line interface (CLI)	Command Line Interface	CLI PowerShell	Cloud Tools for Powershell Cloud SDK
Cloud code build	CodeBuild	Visual Studio Team Services	Cloud Build
API management	API gateway	API management	Cloud endpoints Apigee API management
Tools for development	Developer Tools[1]	Developer Tools	
Mobile development	Amplify	Mobile Apps Xamarin Apps	
App deployment	CodeDeploy CodePipeline	Azure DevOps Azure Pipelines	
App test devices	Device Farm	AppCenter	Cloud Endpoints Cloud Test Lab
Mobile apps analysis	Mobile analytics	Hockey App Application Insights	
Notifications Service	**Simple Notification Service (SNS)**	Notification Hubs	Firebase Cloud Messaging
Payment Service	Amazon Dev Pay		Google Pay API
Mesh Service	App Mesh	Service Fabric Mech	Istio

1 **https://aws.amazon.com/es/developer/tools/**

Service	AWS	Azure	Google
Queue Service	**Simple Queue Service (SQS)**	Azure Queue Storage	Cloud Pub/Sub
Video Streaming and transcode	Elastic Transcoder	Media Services	
Worfkflow	**Simple Workflow Service (SWF)**	Logic Apps	

Table 2.6: Comparison of developer's tools

This table is particularly interesting because it allows each service to be identified on the three platforms, something that is not always obvious. The following figure shows the same (or very similar) infrastructure implemented on the three Cloud platforms and each of the services that have been used:

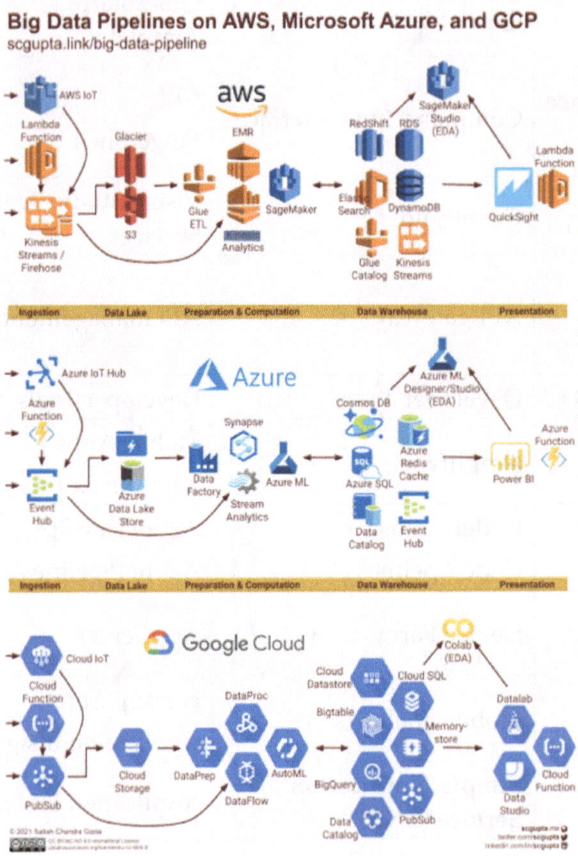

Figure 2.5: Services side by side

Source: *https://www.reddit.com/r/Cloud/comments/mkfyn2/big_data_pipeline_on_aws_microsoft_azure_and/*

The following figure is especially interesting because it compares the three platforms, looking at their strengths and weaknesses, market share, and why we should or should not choose each of them:

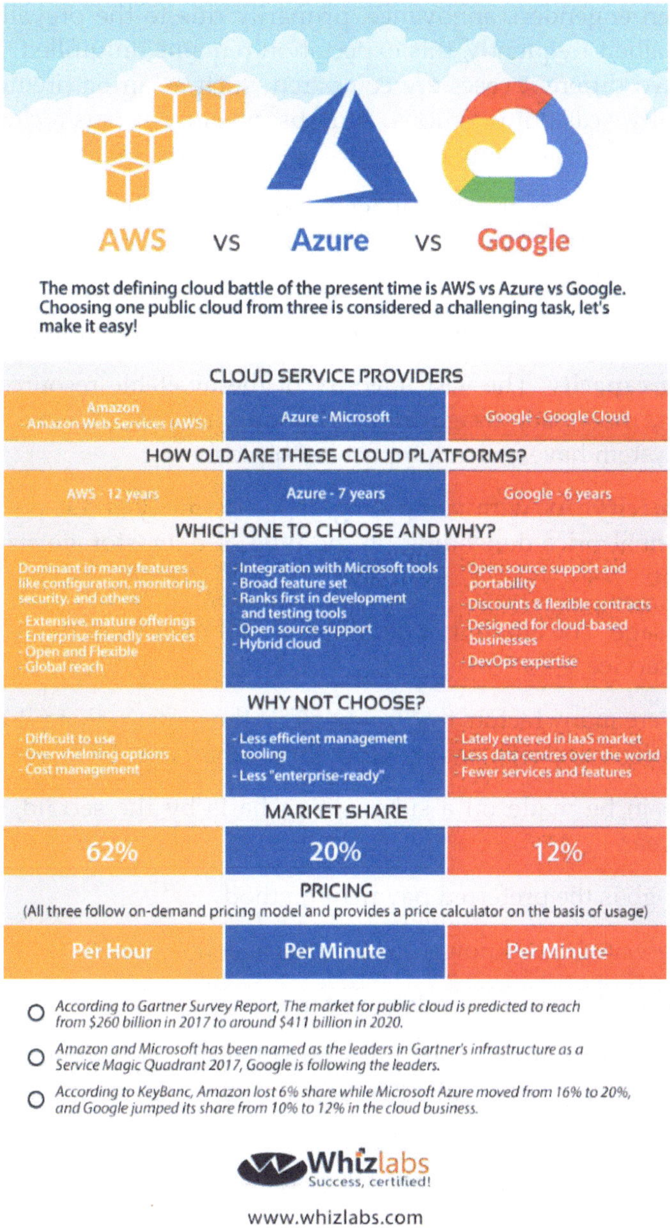

***Figure 2.6**: Comparison of cloud providers*

Source: *https://www.whizlabs.com/blog/aws-vs-azure-vs-google/*

Pricing and cloud cost analysis

When using the cloud, cost is a factor that assumes a lot of significance. Indeed, it holds true that this factor often engenders annoyance, primarily due to the prevailing anticipation of reduced expenses, albeit frequently, this expectation remains unfulfilled. A cost difference is acceptable when two different cases are compared, such as an on-premise installation that lacks high availability, scalability options, and observability versus a cloud installation that offers the necessary high availability, scalability based on demand, and high observability.

It is important to conduct correct cost management, because when a multitude of services are available for use that can start to be used quickly and easily, there is a risk of unexpected costs that exceed the planned budget.

There are three main factors that determine the cost of cloud computing services:

- **Computing capacity**: The vast majority of the available resources need computing capacity and necessary usage time, in addition to the number of CPUs, GB, and operating system have a direct impact on the cost.
- **Storage capacity**: As with computing capacity, many resources require storage. It affects the final price depending on the type of data, storage size, and redundancy requirements.
- **Network usage**: The amount of data transferred to or from the service influences the cost of the service.

Additionally, there are many factors that might affect the price, making it difficult to compare prices directly between suppliers, among other things that must be taken into account:

- Purchases can be made on a subscription basis by the second, minute, hour, day, month, or year.
- Pay-as-you-go is the preferred payment method.
- Instances reserved, also known as a long-term contract mode.
- **Location**: The address of your data center.
- **Service level**: In addition to what was already said, each service is offered at various levels, with variable costs and advantages, so it is necessary to evaluate the expected use before choosing the best level.

The three suppliers each give a separate set of tools that can be used to properly control expenditures to acquire the desired advantages at a reasonable cost. Using resources as efficiently as possible is made possible through cost management.

These resources can be divided into cost management and pricing calculators.

To facilitate the estimation of costs, the different platforms have developed tools that, once the necessary resources have been specified, give us a very approximate price of the real costs:

- GCP Pricing Calculator
- Azure Pricing Calculator
- AWS Pricing Calculator

In addition to these price calculators, there are specific tools for cost management, listed as follows:

- Azure Cost Management tool
- AWS Cost Explorer
- GCP Cost Management

Through these tools and calculators, you can study the cost of the different services and compare them between the three cloud platforms, indicating how to optimize costs:

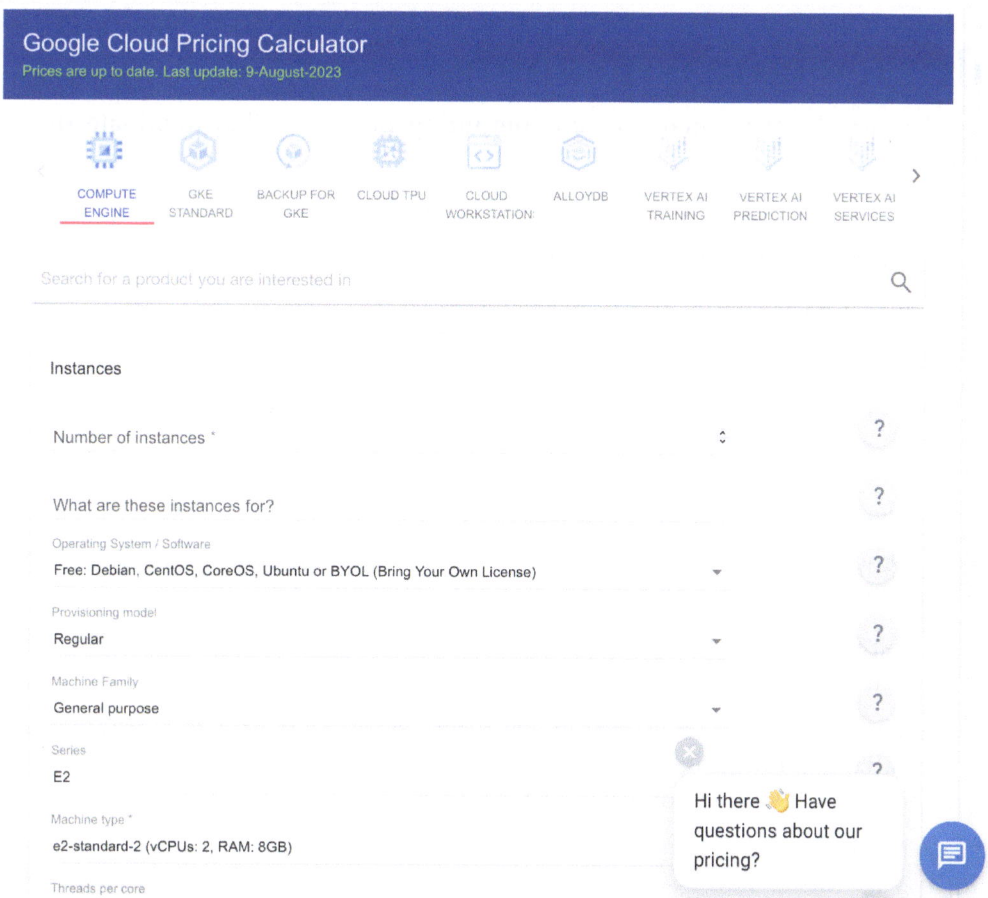

Figure 2.7: Google Cloud Pricing Calculator

Conclusion

In this chapter, we have explored generic cloud services (those not explicitly developed for Unity but for any platform). AWS, Microsoft Azure, and GCP are the three leading cloud service providers, and each has its advantages and strengths.

We learned that AWS offers a vast and mature set of services that cover a wide range of cloud computing needs, and Azure's strengths in hybrid cloud, enterprise support, and integration with Microsoft technologies make it a valuable choice for businesses already using Microsoft products and for those with complex enterprise IT requirements.

We also learned GCP is another major cloud service provider, with strengths in data analytics, ML, and its global network infrastructure, making it particularly attractive for organizations with data-intensive workloads, AI and ML needs, and cloud-native application development.

In the next chapter, we will see that Unity Enterprises has developed a specific platform for developers that offers many advantages.

Multiple choice questions

1. **What are the three major cloud computing providers that dominate the market today?**
   a. AWS, Unity Gaming Services, and Microsoft Azure
   b. Microsoft Azure, GCP, and AWS
   c. IBM, Oracle Cloud, and Alibaba Cloud
   d. AWS, Microsoft Azure, and VMware
2. **What characteristics define the advantages of cloud computing?**
   a. Ownership and management of physical infrastructure
   b. Measured service, where billing is based on actual resource consumption
   c. On-demand self-service, allowing users to provision resources without CSP intervention
   d. Rapid elasticity, allowing resources to quickly scale up or down to meet changing demands
3. **Which cloud computing model describes services where the provider delivers virtualized computing resources, but the user controls the operating systems and applications deployed on that infrastructure?**
   a. PaaS
   b. SaaS

c. IaaS

d. DaaS

4. **Which of the following is a key characteristic of Microsoft Azure's market position, making it particularly popular among certain enterprises?**

a. Its powerful ML tools and focus on containerization and Kubernetes.

b. Its seamless integration with Microsoft's other products and services, such as Office 365 and Windows Server.

c. Being the oldest provider on the market with the largest community and third-party tool ecosystem.

d. Offering the proprietary RDBMS named Aurora.

5. **When comparing storage options, which statement is generally true regarding the cost-effectiveness of the three major providers?**

a. Costs tend to be more effective in Google Cloud when compared to Azure.

b. Costs tend to be more effective in Amazon when compared to Google.

c. Costs tend to be more effective in Azure when compared to Google.

d. Costs tend to be similar across all three platforms, regardless of storage type or region.

6. **What are the three main factors that determine the cost of cloud computing services? (Select all that apply)**

a. Service level, defining variable costs and advantages.

b. Computing capacity, including usage time and number of CPUs.

c. Storage capacity, including data type and redundancy requirements.

d. Network usage, based on the amount of data transferred to or from the service.

7. **In the category of developer tools, what is the name of the serverless computing service provided by AWS that supports a broader range of programming languages?**

a. Azure Functions

b. Google Cloud Functions

c. Lambda

d. Elastic Beanstalk

8. **Which organization method is suitable for cloud resources when all resources have the same policies and lifecycle?**
    a. Organizing by lifecycle
    b. Organizing by department
    c. Organizing by application
    d. Organizing by type

Answers

1	b
2	b, c, d
3	c
4	b
5	c
6	b, c, d
7	c
8	c

References

1. **https://cloud.google.com/cost-management?ref=enmilocalfunciona.io**
2. **https://aws.amazon.com/es/aws-cost-management/aws-cost-explorer/?ref=enmilocalfunciona.io**
3. **https://azure.microsoft.com/en-us/products/cost-management/?ref=enmilocalfunciona.io**
4. **https://calculator.aws/#/?ref=enmilocalfunciona.io**
5. **https://azure.microsoft.com/en-us/pricing/calculator/?ref=enmilocalfunciona.io**

Chapter 3
Getting Starting with Unity Gaming Services

Introduction

Unity Technologies has developed a platform designed to streamline game development by assisting developers in creating, launching, and growing their games while managing the underlying infrastructure. This platform provides tools for monetization, data analysis, cloud-based deployment, multiplayer functionality, performance monitoring, user management, and support for virtual and augmented reality.

The services offered by **Unity Gaming Services** (**UGS**) enable developers to concentrate on creating immersive gameplay experiences while ensuring optimal performance and scalability across multiple platforms, including Windows, Mac, iOS, Android, and others. By utilizing UGS, developers can save time and resources, facilitating their ability to reach a broader audience effectively.

This chapter provides an introduction to UGS, guiding readers through the process of integrating it into their projects. It covers essential steps such as configuring existing Unity projects, installing necessary packages, initializing services, and utilizing features like event tracking for analytics. The text also emphasizes creating custom events to gather comprehensive insights into user engagement.

Upon completing this chapter, readers will gain a comprehensive understanding of how to effectively utilize UGS to make data-driven decisions, enhance player experiences, and scale their games across platforms. This platform serves as a valuable resource for developers seeking to create high-quality games while ensuring a broad reach.

Structure

The chapter covers the following topics:

- First steps with Unity Gaming Services
- Creating a dashboard project
- Linking your Unity project

- Installing Unity Gaming Services packages
- Initializing Unity services
  - The use of code
  - Events
  - Validating that the event is successfully sent
- Creating a custom event
  - Validating the custom event as successfully registered
- Utilizing UGS Analytics for Game Growth case study
  - Monitoring user retention
  - Comparing tutorial mission completion rates
  - Segmenting behavior by region and platform

Objectives

UGS provides a range of solutions for game developers, all in one place. These tools can work together as a cohesive set or as modular components that complement your existing technology. The suite includes a cloud-based backend, analytics that provide a comprehensive view of players, and multiplayer solutions for all game genres. All of these solutions are integrated with a monetization platform that can help power your success.

You will learn how to install the package, initialize the data recollection, and link your projects to start using UGS. Let us start!

First steps with Unity Gaming Services

First, there is great news for you. You can start for free!

Of course, Unity charges for the services it provides, but to test in development, you will not need to make any payment, and when you have to, it will be because your game already has a significant number of users.

Go to the main page: **https://unity.com/solutions/gaming-services** and click on the **Get started for free** button.

If you already have a Unity account, you can use it to authenticate yourself. Otherwise, you will need to create one by filling out a form. This typically requires providing your name, email address, and creating a password. You may also be asked for information about your game development project, such as its genre and target platform. You might also need to provide payment details (credit card or other method) even though you won't be charged initially; this is often required for account verification purposes.

Once authenticated, you will land on the UGS dashboard, where you can enable and configure various services for your project. The following figure shows the main screen:

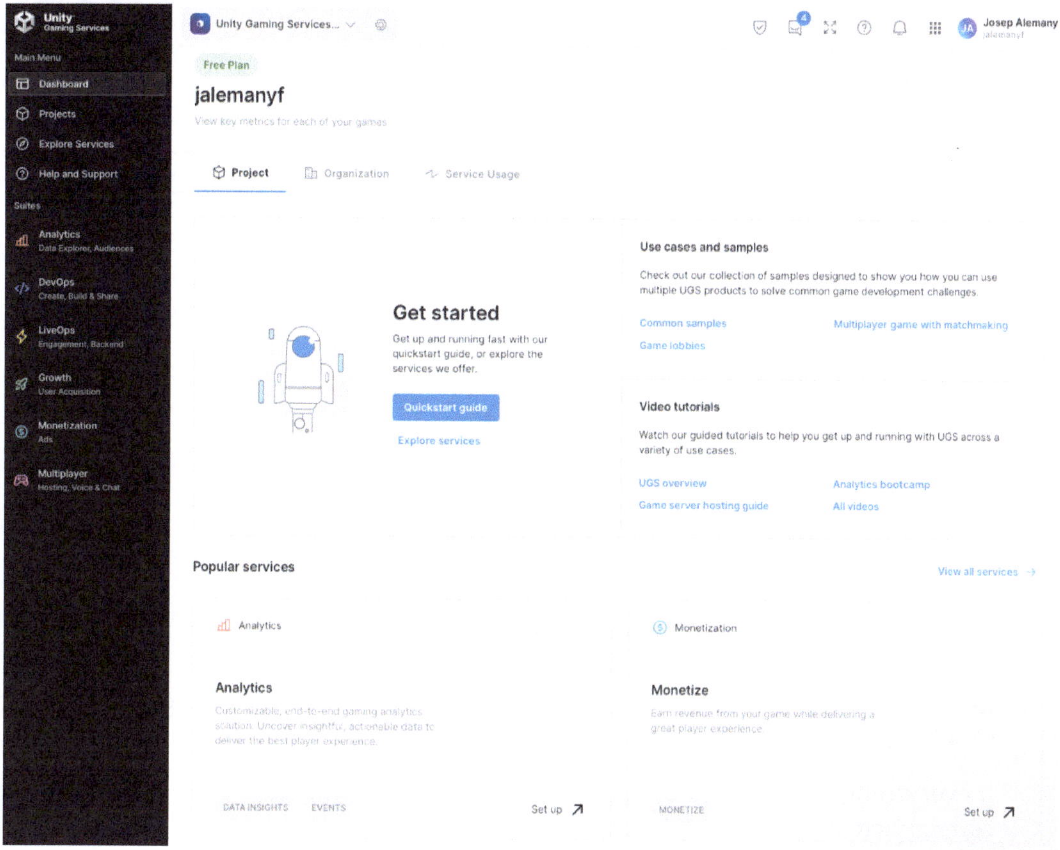

Figure 3.1: Unity Gaming Services main dashboard

In the UGS dashboard, you can enable and configure the services for your project. In the following steps, the simplest way to setup a Unity project to use UGS is described.

Creating a dashboard project

In the UGS dashboard, you can enable and configure the services for your project. You can perform the following simple steps to set up a Unity project to use UGS:

1. Click on the **Projects** button in the upper-left navigation menu. This will open a page with all the projects you have created on Unity. (You can add the functionality to any project you have, but we are going to create a new one to do it easier).
2. You would see a blue button on the top-right of the screen with the text **Create project**:

Figure 3.2: Create project button

3. Click it, and a window will appear:

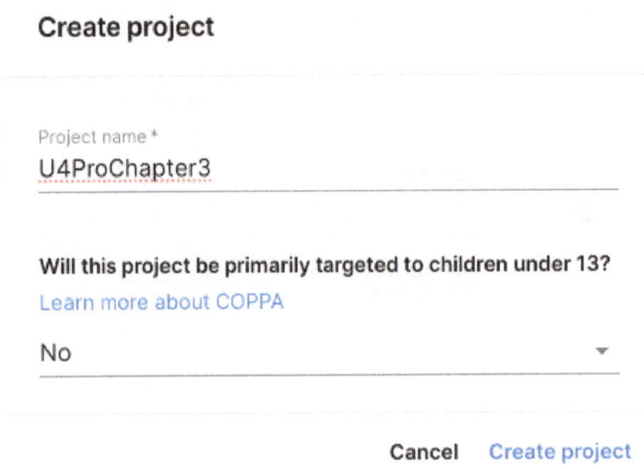

Figure 3.3: Create Project Form

4. Enter the name of your project (U4ProChaper3) and click on **Create project** (let the COPPA option to No).

   If everything went well, a window should appear indicating that the project has been correctly created. Congratulations! You just created your first project in UGS:

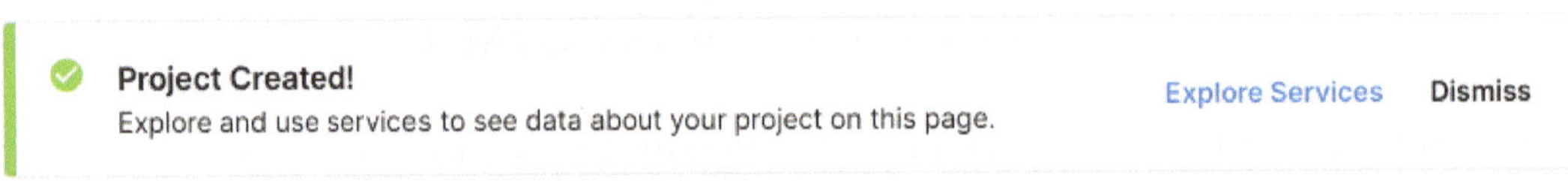

Figure 3.4: Confirmation message of the created project

Now, you can explore the services. Some of the services that can be activated are:

- Analytics
- LiveOps - Authentication
- LiveOps - Cloud Code
- LiveOps - loud Save
- LiveOps - Economy
- Multiplayer – Lobby

In this first project, we are going to make it easy and start by activating the Analytics service through the following steps:

1. Click on **Setup** to start configuring the service, as shown in the following figure:

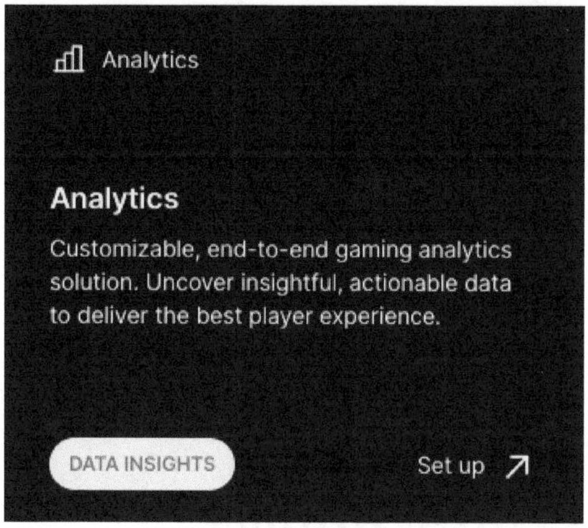

***Figure** 3.5: Analytics service on the Unity Cloud*

   Clicking the **Setup** button initiates a guided configuration process within the Unity Gaming Services dashboard. This process is designed to walk you through enabling and integrating various aspects of the selected service—in this case, Analytics. The setup wizard will present a series of options and settings that need to be configured before the service can be fully operational. It is crucial to understand each setting thoroughly to ensure proper data collection and functionality. We will delve into these settings in more detail shortly.

2. In the next window, click on the **Set up Analytics** blue button:

   - **Analytics service overview**: The analytics service provides comprehensive data tracking and reporting capabilities, allowing developers to monitor player behavior, identify trends, and make informed decisions about game development and marketing strategies. It allows you to track custom events, user properties, and other relevant metrics.

   - **Data privacy considerations**: Before enabling analytics, carefully review Unity's privacy policy and ensure compliance with all applicable data protection regulations (e.g., GDPR, CCPA). Transparency with players regarding data collection practices is essential for building trust and maintaining a positive reputation. Consider implementing consent mechanisms to obtain explicit user permission before tracking their activity.

   - **Setting up data collection**: After clicking the **Set up Analytics** button, you will be presented with several configuration options:

- **Data sampling rate**: This setting determines how much data is collected and stored. A higher sampling rate provides more detailed insights but consumes more storage space and processing power. Start with a lower sampling rate during development to minimize costs and gradually increase it as your game gains traction.
- **Event filtering**: Define which events should be tracked by the Analytics service. You can filter out irrelevant or sensitive data to reduce noise and improve performance.
- **User properties**: Track user-specific attributes, such as player level, game difficulty, or subscription status. User properties allow you to segment your audience and gain a deeper understanding of their behavior.

Now, we are going to go to the Unity Editor and add the package. You can do this in a new project or one that you have previously created. To make it simple, in the examples, it is done in a newly created project.

Linking your Unity project

Note: To all these operations, your user must belong to an organization and be authenticated on Unity's servers. If you have not met this requirement, you can find very useful information at this address: https://docs.unity.com/cloud/en-us/organizations.

If you already have a Unity user and need to register for one of the services in Unity Cloud, the address is: https://cloud.unity.com/home/login?redirectTo=Lw==.

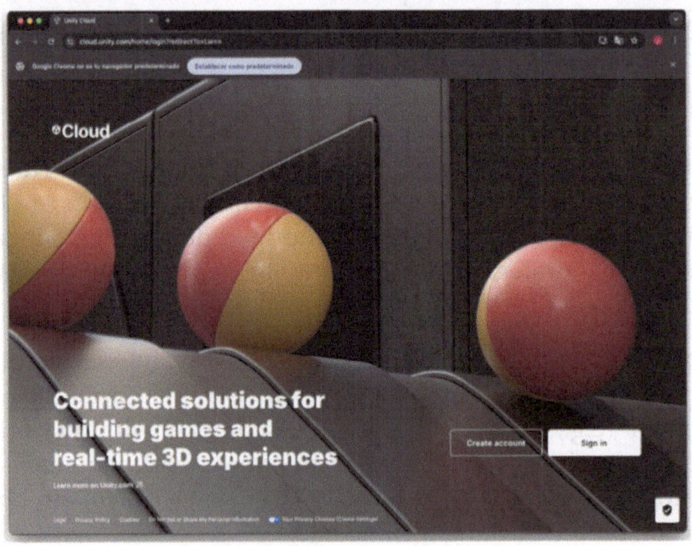

Figure 3.6: Unity Cloud's main page

Currently, when we create a new project, we can connect it directly to the Unity Cloud, but let us see how it is possible to add the connection to UGS in a project that did not have that functionality previously:

1. In the Unity Editor, open **Project Settings** menu and select **Services** option.

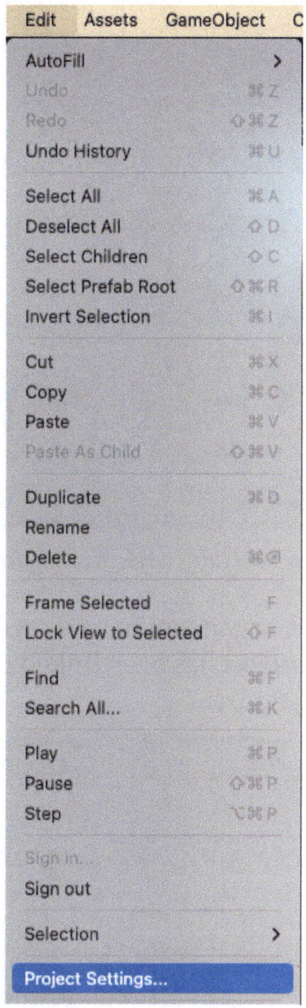

***Figure 3.7**: Activate services in an existing project*

Refer to the following figure additional context:

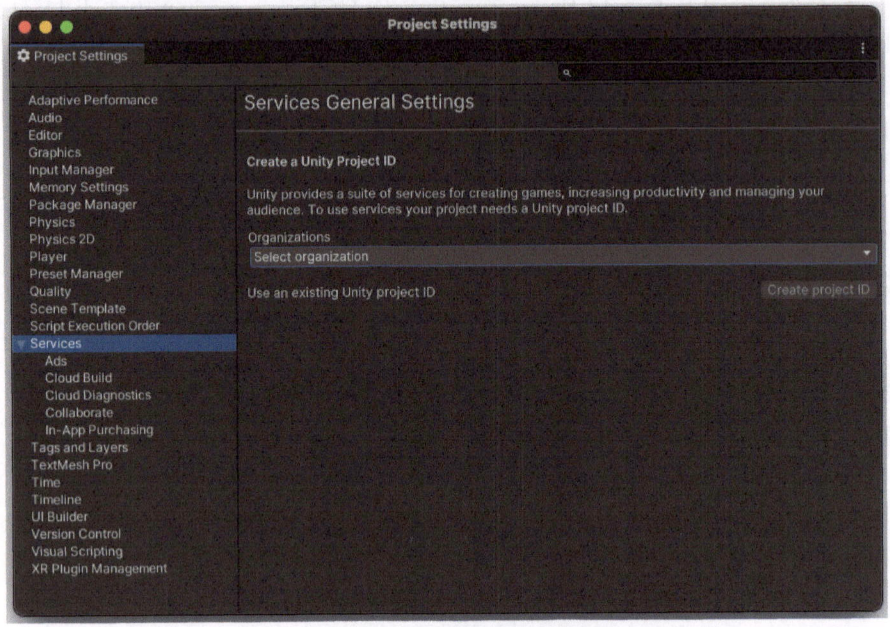

Figure 3.8: Unity services configuration

2. In the dropdown, choose the organization and create a project ID or use one that you have already created. If the project has been linked correctly, you can see it in a window that looks like the following figure:

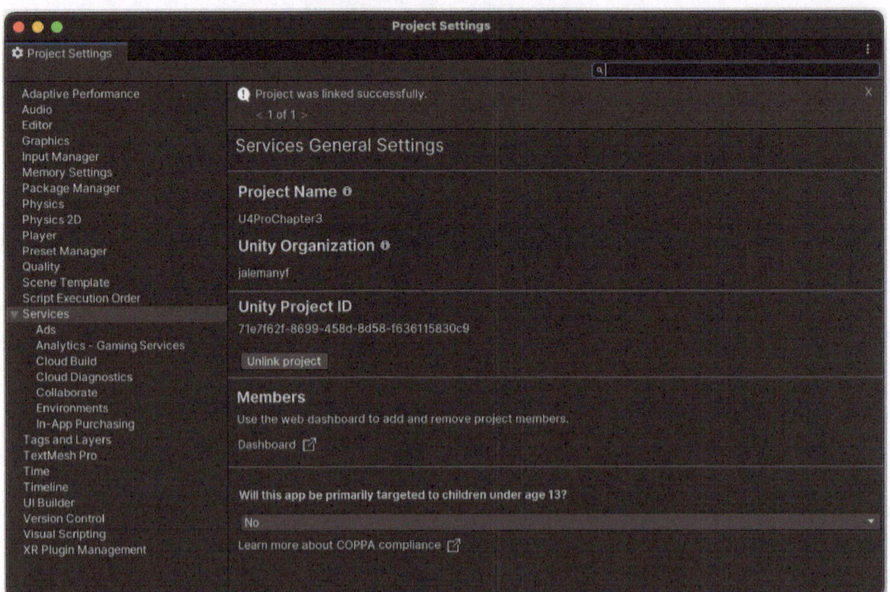

Figure 3.9: Project Settings configuration detail when the project is linked to Unity Cloud

Now that we have linked the project, we must install a package that allows us to activate the different services by code.

A Unity package is a collection of assets, scripts, and tools bundled together to extend the functionality of Unity projects. These packages provide pre-built components or libraries that developers can import into their Unity projects to enhance features without having to build everything from scratch. Unity packages are used to add or modify features such as physics systems, rendering tools, UI components, or specific platform support.

Unity packages are managed via the *Unity Package Manager*, which allows developers to install, update, and remove packages.

Installing the Unity Gaming Services package

In order to use Unity Gaming Services, the corresponding package must be installed. The following are the necessary steps:

1. Open the package manager window in Unity's Editor **Window** | **Package Manager**:

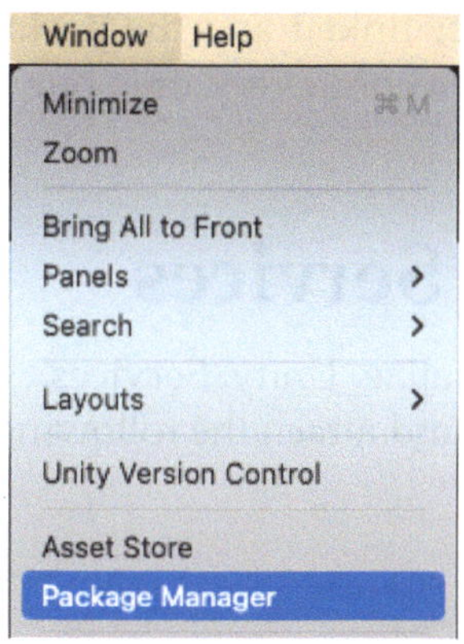

Figure 3.10: Open the window Package Manager from the menu

2. When you are in the **Package Manager** window, select **Packages: Unity Registry** from the dropdown:

Figure 3.11: Make sure to select the Unity Registry option

3. Type **`com.unity.services`** in the search field to bring up all available services. Locate the package called **Analytics**, select it, and click install:

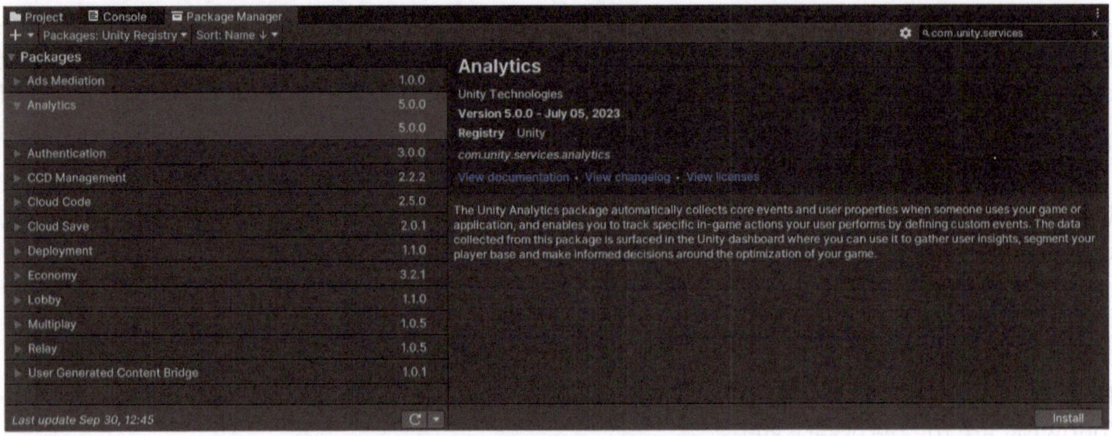

Figure 3.12: Analytics package's installation

Alright, now you have your service linked and the package to start using it. Now, we will create the first code where we will record every time our app starts and send the data to the cloud to create statistics.

Initializing Unity Services

This is the simplest code to initialize Unity Services. In Unity Editor, create an empty **`GameObject`** on the hierarchy view and attach the following C# Script to it:

```
using System;
using UnityEngine;
using Unity.Services.Core;

public class InitUnityCloudGS : MonoBehaviour
{
    async void Awake()
    {
        try
        {
            await UnityServices.InitializeAsync();
        }
        catch (Exception e)
        {
            Debug.
```

```
        LogException(new Exception("The following error occurred: " + e.Message ));
            }
        }
}
```

Verifying initialization: After running your game, check the Unity Gaming Services dashboard to confirm that data is being collected. Navigate to the **Analytics** section and look for recent events. If no data appears, double-check your initialization code and network connection.

The use of code

When the GameObject is initialized, an asynchronous call is made to initialize the services.

If any error occurs, it raises an exception, which will give an error message in the console window.

Now, you just need to prove that everything works. Save the script and hit the play button in the Unity Editor. If everything goes well, absolutely nothing will happen, and no message will appear on the console, but an event will have already been registered in the cloud.

Events

An event is an action or occurrence that happens within your game/app, such as when the game starts or when the player performs activities such as discovering a treasure or purchasing an item.

Events contain contextual information about the action, such as the item that was obtained, how much money the player had, and how the item was acquired.

They can also contain important information about the user: what platform they are playing on, what country they are playing from, and what their playing patterns are (casual, intensive, weekends).

These events can be customized to fit your game and send you useful information. Through the Data Explorer and Funnels, you can measure player engagement, spending, and conversion.

Validating that the event is successfully sent

First of all, we must warn you that you will have to be a little patient; the data does not appear immediately, and if you have come this far, it is possibly the ideal time to take a short break.

After a few minutes, the data will begin to appear within the UGS interface. Let us see how they appear. On the UGS website, select **Analytics** | **Event Browser** and then select the project you are analyzing from the dropdown (`U4ProChapter3` on the image). The following figure showcases the screen that should appear:

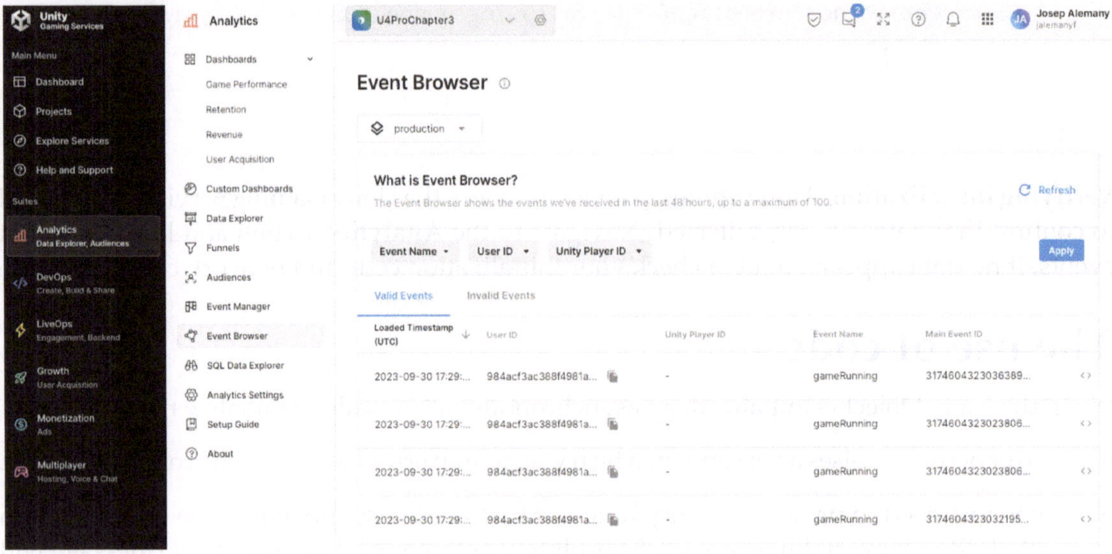

***Figure 3.13**: Event Browser with some events registered*

The table you can see in the preceding figure is recorded every time our app has been started (it has been started many times, so that enough data could be seen).

Just by initializing the service, two events are logged: **`gameStarted`** and **`gameRunning`**. At first glance, it does not seem much, but it would allow us to know how many times our app is being used and in what time slots our users prefer to use it!

Let us now see a graph of our fantastic event log. To do this, you must go to **Analytics** | **Data Explorer** in the menu on the left:

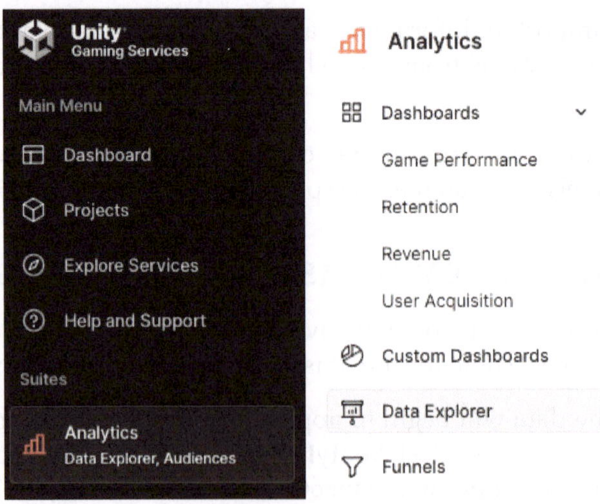

***Figure 3.14**: Select Analytics on the side menu*

Now, we are going to add the conditions so that our graph can be seen. Press the **+ Add Event** button.

A drop-down menu will open where you can choose which event we want to measure. In this case, it is **`gameStarted`**:

> **Note: All standard events are already sold by default, and we will only need to choose them.**

The metrics bar looks like the following figure:

***Figure 3.15**: Metrics bar page*

> **Note: This is the simplest example possible, but I recommend that you look at the functions and groupings to dig deeper into the capabilities of the system.**

Finally, for the results to take effect, we must press the **Apply** button and voila, we have our first usage graph for the app created automatically with data sent by Unity Clients, as shown in the following figure:

***Figure 3.16**: Peak for the data collected*

Let us now look at some of the functionalities that **Data Explorer** offers us:

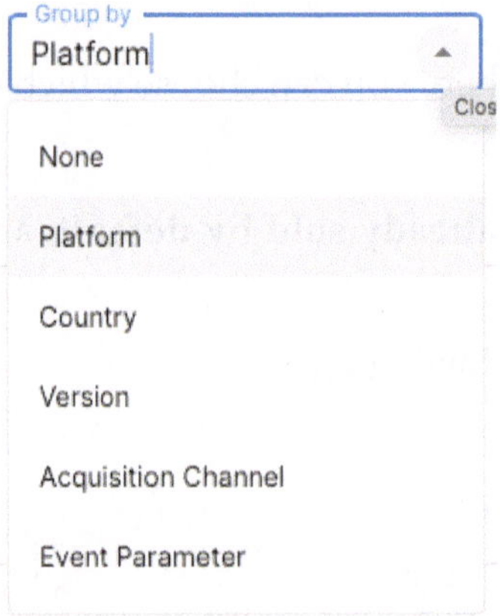

***Figure 3.17**: Various options of Data Explorer*

Firstly, you can change the metric grouping by selecting the dropdown under **Group by**. Grouping by Platform will allow us to know if our app is more used on Android or iOS, on PlayStation or XBox. Grouping by country will allow us to know in which countries we have the most users. The combination of both filters gives us a real market study and helps us make important decisions.

It is also important to highlight the Version filter that will allow us to know how many of our users are still using an old version, and if we should force them to update or give them maintenance service.

Creating a custom event

The metrics we have seen are quite interesting, but the events we have used are generic (gameStart and gameRunning). Now, let us see how it is possible to register a custom event, such as mission 3 completed, holy chalice found, through h the following steps:

1. To create a new event, go to the **Analytics | Event Manager** menu and press the blue **Add New | Custom Event** button (on the right side of the screen):

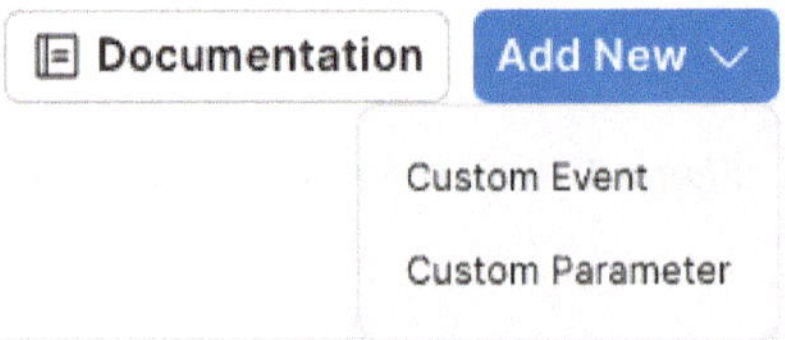

***Figure 3.18**: Button to create a Custom Event or a Custom Parameter*

2. Entering on the Analytic's menu with all the following options available:

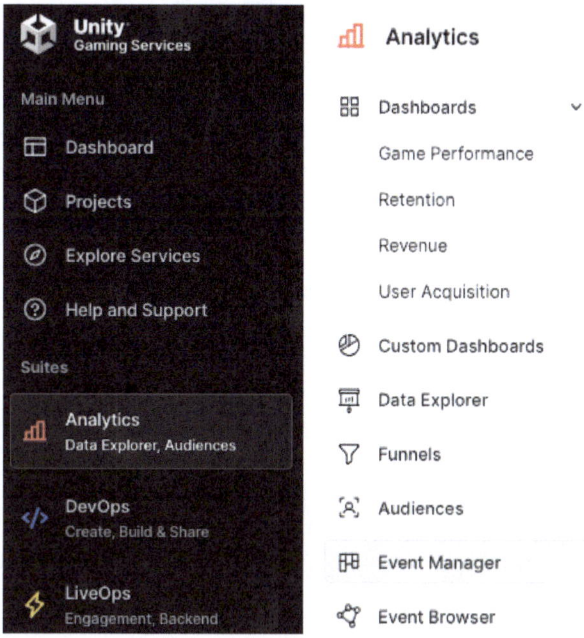

***Figure 3.19:** Analytic's menu options*

3. A right-side form will appear where you are required to enter the name of the event and a description.
4. The name must consist only of English alphanumeric and underscore characters. For this sample, **`mission3_completed`** was used.
5. When you **Confirm**, the event is created but not enabled.

Note: Parameters can be edited but not deleted. Data types include string, integer, float, and bool. You can add up to 1,500 parameters to the environment.

After creating the custom event on the cloud side, we need to modify our code to send the new event. The following is the modified code:

```
using System;
using System.Collections.Generic;
using Unity.Services.Analytics;
using UnityEngine;
using Unity.Services.Core;

public class InitUGS : MonoBehaviour
{
```

```
    async void Start()
    {
        try
        {
            await UnityServices.InitializeAsync();
        }
        catch (Exception e)
        {
            Debug.LogException(new Exception("The following error occurred: " + e.Message ));        }
    }

    public void SendCustomEvent()
    {
        AnalyticsService.Instance.StartDataCollection();
        AnalyticsService.Instance.RecordEvent("mission3_completed");
        AnalyticsService.Instance.Flush();
        Debug.Log("Sending Custom Event");
    }
}
```

As you can see, you must add the code **`using Unity.Services.Analytics;`** to call the event function.

Be careful to put the event name **`("mission3_completed")`** exactly the same as you typed it before. If not, it will never be found.

The simplest way to call the **`SendCustomEvent`** method is to create a single button UI interface and call the function when it is clicked.

After completing Mission 3, it is time to set up a custom event in Unity Analytics to record this milestone. The following figure shows the example found in the book's code:

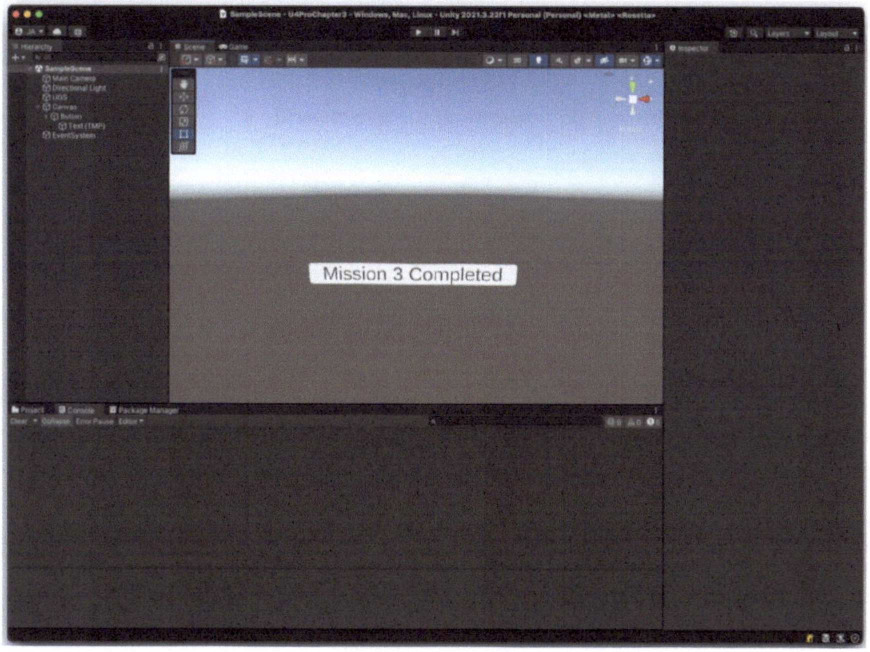

Figure 3.20: Minimum interface with a button that creates the event

Validating the custom event as successfully registered

Run the Unity project and click the button two or three times. Then, go to your UGS console, to menu **Analytics** | **Event Browser**:

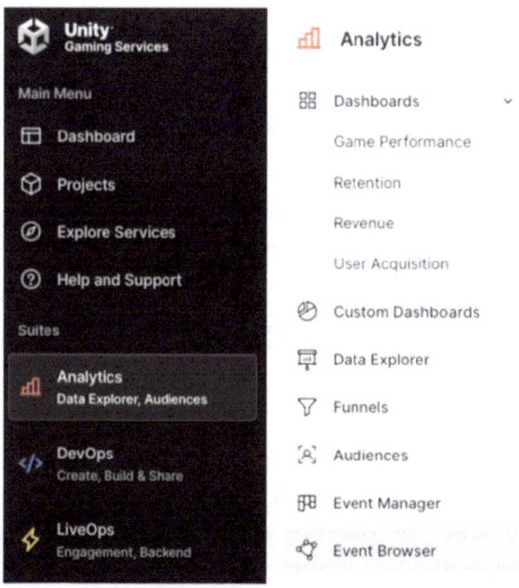

Figure 3.21: Select Event Browser inside the Analytics options

Now, we must indicate the name of the event by which it is going to be filtered. In the first drop-down menu, enter the name of your event and then click **Apply**:

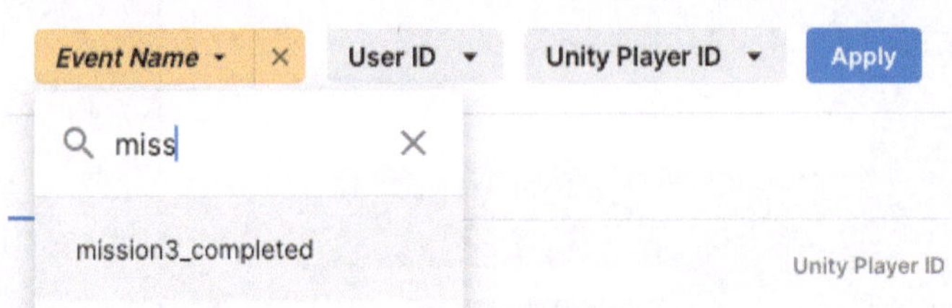

Figure 3.22: Filtering by event's Name

If everything is correct, a window will appear with several rows of the event that we have created, which we can now use to make our own statistics, as shown in the following figure:

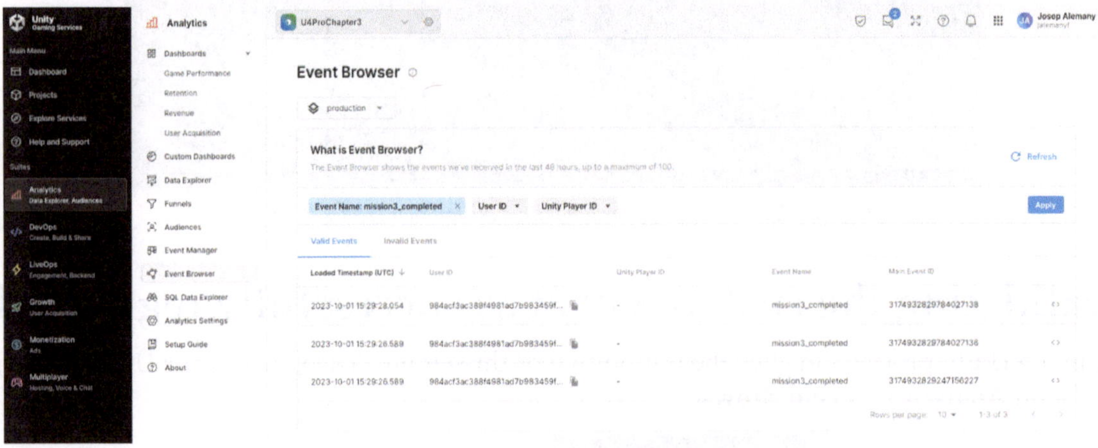

Figure 3.23: Image of event browser with some data collected

Note: In the code, we have added a line (`AnalyticsService.Instance.Flush();`) which is not recommended for use in a production App.

This line speeds up sending the events more immediately. Liberties were taken to put it so that the data arrives sooner when the tests are done, but it is not advisable to abuse it.

Utilizing UGS Analytics for Game Growth case study

Unity Gaming Services (UGS) offers a platform designed to assist developers in creating, launching, and growing their games. Crucial to this platform are the analytics tools, which provide a comprehensive view of players and facilitate data-driven decision-making to enhance player experiences and scale games across various platforms, including Windows, Mac, iOS, and Android.

This case study demonstrates how a hypothetical game studio, developing a cross-platform fantasy RPG, *Aethelgard Legends*, leverages UGS Analytics to monitor user retention, analyze tutorial completion rates, and segment player behavior by region and platform.

Monitoring user retention

For *Aethelgard Legends*, monitoring user retention is paramount to long-term success. UGS Analytics automatically begins tracking key metrics upon initialization of the services.

By default, UGS registers standard events such as **gameStarted** and **gameRunning**. These events allow the developers to immediately gather essential data. By analyzing the registered instances of the gameStarted event using the Analytics Data Explorer, the studio can determine *how many times* the app is being used and identify the time slots when users prefer to engage with the game. The frequency of these logged events is a direct indicator of player activity and retention over time.

This data is further enhanced by using the grouping features available in the Data Explorer. By grouping the gameStarted events by attributes like playing patterns (e.g., casual or intensive), the studio can identify if specific segments of their player base exhibit poor retention and require focused updates or engagement efforts. Measuring player engagement is a core capability provided through the Data Explorer and Funnels.

Comparing tutorial mission completion rates

To ensure that new players are successfully learning the core mechanics and converting into long-term users, *Aethelgard Legends* requires detailed data on its tutorial completion funnel.

Analytics are used to measure specific in-game activities. Since the standard events are generic (like game start/run), the studio must utilize **custom events** to track the tutorial progression. An event is an action or occurrence within the game, such as discovering a treasure or purchasing an item. The studio defines custom events for critical steps in the tutorial process, for example:

- tutorial_start
- mission1_completed
- mission2_completed
- mission3_completed (similar to the sample custom event **`"mission3_completed"`** mentioned before, in the source).

Custom events are first configured in the UGS Event Manager. Subsequently, the developers modify the game code to call the custom event function, such as **`AnalyticsService.Instance.CustomData("mission3_completed")`**, ensuring the event name exactly matches the one set in the cloud.

Once the data is collected and verified in the Event Browser, the developers use Funnels in UGS to visualize player flow and measure conversion rates through the tutorial. By comparing the rates of completion between **`mission1_completed`** and **`mission3_completed`**, the studio can pinpoint exactly which mission causes the largest player drop-off, allowing them to make targeted design decisions to improve that specific part of the onboarding experience.

Segmenting behavior by region and platform

To effectively manage marketing and server infrastructure, *Aethelgard Legends* utilizes UGS for powerful audience segmentation. Events tracked by UGS contain contextual information about the user, including the country they are playing from and the platform they are using.

In the Data Explorer, developers can use the Group by function to segment key metrics:

1. **Grouping by Platform**: This allows the studio to understand if *Aethelgard Legends* is used more frequently on certain operating systems or consoles. For instance, grouping by platform may reveal that iOS users have a higher rate of completing the tutorial (derived from the custom events) than Android users. This information may prompt the studio to investigate performance issues or UI/UX differences on the less successful platform.
2. **Grouping by Country (Region)**: This grouping reveals in which countries the game has the most users. This information is crucial for localized marketing efforts and content updates.
3. **Combined Filters**: The ability to combine Platform and Country filters provides a **real market study**. For example, the studio could segment the completion rate of **`mission3_completed`** specifically for players in the United Kingdom using PlayStation, thereby gaining a deeper understanding of localized, platform-specific player behavior.

Aethelgard Legends uses Unity Gaming Services to track custom events, measure engagement, and segment user properties, enabling data-driven decisions for game development and marketing.

Conclusion

This chapter has provided a foundational understanding of UGS, elucidating its pivotal role in optimizing game development from conception to expansion. UGS provides a comprehensive toolkit designed to facilitate backend infrastructure management, enabling developers to focus on crafting immersive gameplay experiences across platforms such as Windows, Mac, iOS, and Android. The chapter has detailed the initial steps for engaging with UGS, encompassing the creation of a dashboard project, its linking with a Unity project, and the installation of requisite packages. A primary focus was placed on data analytics, demonstrating the initialization of services and the tracking of both standard events like game starts and custom events tailored to specific in-game activities. The Event Browser and Data Explorer were introduced as indispensable tools for visualizing and interpreting player data, facilitating data-driven decisions regarding player engagement and game performance. Furthermore, the modularity and scalability of UGS were discussed, emphasizing its cost-free accessibility during the development process.

Moving forward, the next chapter will introduce the Unity Dashboard, the central interface for managing all facets of your Unity projects and UGS services. You will acquire knowledge on navigating its diverse sections, controlling project settings, and overseeing your organization and billing.

Multiple choice questions

1. **What is the core benefit of utilizing UGS in the development process, as stated in the source?**
   a. To exclusively support VR and AR development using C#.
   b. To enable developers to concentrate on creating immersive gameplay experiences while ensuring optimal performance and scalability across multiple platforms.
   c. To require manual configuration for every service to reduce cloud cost.
   d. To limit platform support only to Windows and Mac devices.
2. **What is stated regarding the initial cost and access to Unity Gaming Services?**
   a. A paid annual subscription is mandatory before any services can be configured.
   b. Developers can start for free, and charges are only applied when the game already has a significant number of users.
   c. Developers must immediately provide full payment details, which are charged instantly for activation.
   d. Access is only granted after verifying an existing Unity Pro license.
3. **Within the Unity Editor, what is the correct process to link an existing local Unity project to a project created in the UGS dashboard?**
   a. Run the command AttachUGS.exe from the Unity project root folder.
   b. Open the Project Settings menu, select the Services option, and then choose the organization and link the Project ID.
   c. Modify the Assets/Settings.json file manually with the Project ID.
   d. The project must be created from scratch in the Editor; existing projects cannot be linked.
4. **What is the name of the package that must be installed via the Unity Package Manager to enable the recording of events and send them to Unity Cloud?**
   a. The com.unity.analytics package (or simply the Analytics package).
   b. The com.unity.cloud.core package.
   c. The UGS.Event.Recorder package.
   d. The LiveOps package.

5. **When defining a custom event in the UGS Event Manager, what character types must the event name consist of?**
   a. Any Unicode character, including spaces and symbols.
   b. Only English alphanumeric and underscore characters.
   c. The name can only contain numbers but must start with a letter.
   d. Only C# variable names are accepted.
6. **In C# scripting, which asynchronous method call is necessary to start the core Unity Services within the application's lifecycle?**
   a. Debug.Log("Sending Custom Event");
   b. AnalyticsService.Instance.Flush();
   c. await UnityServices.InitializeAsync();
   d. AnalyticsService.Instance.StartDataCollection();
7. **Which two fundamental methods can developers use within the Analytics Data Explorer to categorize data about their player base and gain insights? (Select two)**
   a. Filtering by network latency.
   b. Grouping by country.
   c. Grouping by CPU architecture.
   d. Grouping by platform.
8. **Which event is automatically logged by UGS immediately upon initializing the Analytics service within the application, providing instant usage data?**
   a. mission3_completed
   b. gameStarted
   c. adImpression
   d. transactionFailed

Answers

1	b
2	b
3	b
4	a
5	b
6	c
7	b, d
8	b

Chapter 4
Unity Dashboard

Introduction

Developing a professional app/game requires some important challenges, such as multiplayer services, user acquisitions, engagement, remote deployment, and growth. In the previous chapter, we saw the main cloud computing operators and the services they provide, but none of them are tailor-made for Unity.

Unity Technologies has developed its own cloud services to provide solutions to most of the problems that developers may encounter. These cloud services are called **Unity Gaming Services** (**UGS**)

The main advantages of using UGS are the ease of integration into your development and the support of the entire development lifecycle. UGS provides a range of solutions for game developers, all in one place. These tools can work together as a cohesive set or as modular components that complement your existing technology. The suite includes a cloud-based backend, analytics that provide a comprehensive view of players, and multiplayer solutions for all game genres. These solutions are integrated with a monetization platform that can help power your success.

In the UGS dashboard, we have an interface from which we can control all our Unity-connected projects, their status, statistics, and the services that we have active or those that we can add. The dashboard allows us to see, at a glance, all the projects and services that we have in operation, as well as see statistics of their operation, or activate new services.

In this chapter, you will learn how to navigate the dashboard effectively and understand the different sections, such as Preferences, Sidebar, Main Window, and more. You will discover how to work with projects, set up projects, and understand the Administration section, which includes managing Unity Organizations, Members, and Roles, Finance and Billing, and Budget Alerts. Additionally, we will explore the Organization settings. You will also learn how all members are categorized under User Type and Role.

Additionally, this chapter will cover the Service Usage submenu within the Organization, where you can check how much each service is used. We will also discuss the Unity Cloud Personal Plan, which offers 10 GB of completely free storage that can be used for various purposes.

Throughout this chapter, you will gain a deeper understanding of the Unity Dashboard and its features, allowing you to work more efficiently with your projects and data.

Structure

The chapter covers the following topics:

- The Unity Dashboard
- Dashboard navigation
  - Discover section
- Administration
  - Roles in Unity Cloud
  - Benefits of roles in Unity Cloud
  - Best practices for role management in Unity Cloud
  - Managing invoices
  - Make payments
  - Managing credit card information
  - Configuring payment settings

Objectives

By the end of this chapter, you will be able to navigate the Unity Dashboard interface, locate and understand the information about your active projects, including their statistics, and add new services to existing projects. You will also learn create, edit, and configure projects in the dashboard, enable and disable services on a project, transfer projects between organizations, assign roles to organization members and archive projects

The Unity Dashboard

The Unity Dashboard is the control center of the platform, a Swiss army knife that allows access to products and services, organizes projects, and manages subscriptions.

First, we are going to see the graphical aspect of the dashboard, its interface, and how we can navigate to access the different menus and sections.

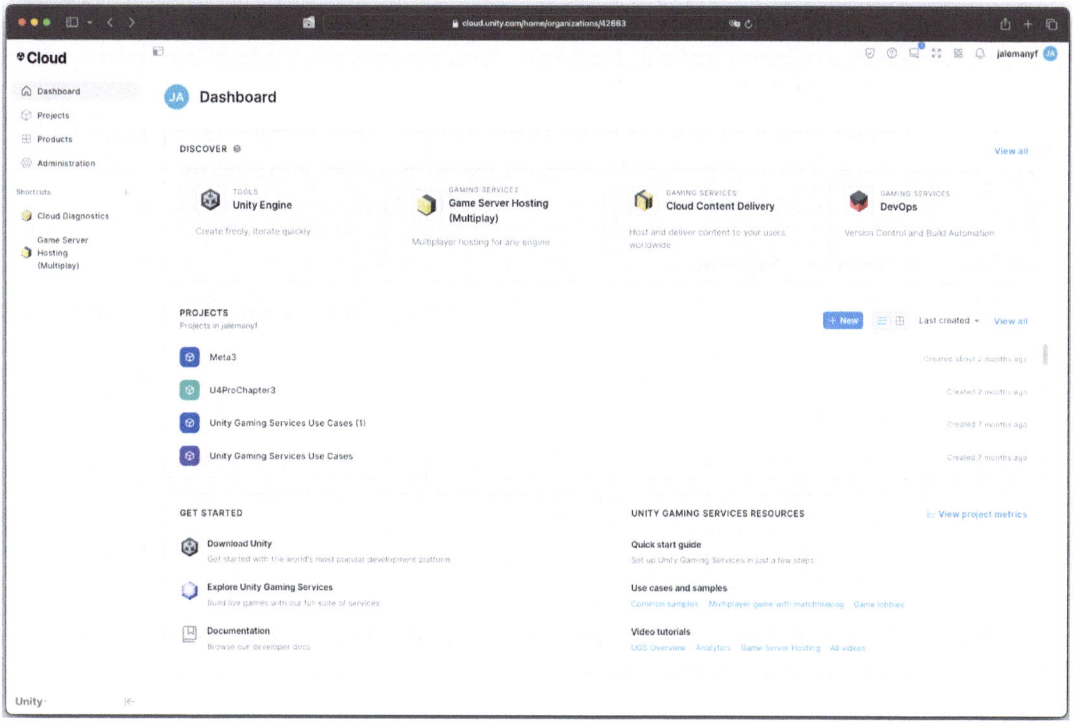

Figure 4.1: Dashboard overview

Dashboard navigation

Next, we are going to see each of the parts that make up the dashboard, the different menus, and the navigation system, so that it is easy for us to locate each functionality in the navigation.

Preferences: In the upper right part of the web, we can find a series of icons that manage the environment preferences. They are available at all times, in case we wish to change them.

Figure 4.2: Environment Preference´s menu

Each of the icons has the following functionality:

	**Privacy Preference Centre** Unity provides tools and services to help developers manage user privacy within UGS. The Unity Privacy Preferences Centre is a feature that allows developers to enable/disable all cookies they wish to share to prevent unwanted access.
	**Help and Support** This icon is a shortcut that directly opens the help documentation on the operation of Unity Gaming Services.
	**Conversations** This option opens a chat window where you can receive technical support as well as notifications of new features that are being added. On occasion they also ask for a survey.
	**Enter/Exit focus mode** Enable or disable focus mode by closing any window other than the central one to avoid distractions.
	**Quick access** Enable or disable focus mode by closing any window other than the central one to avoid distractions.
	**Notifications** By clicking, the notifications window will open where we will receive notices when we use the system more intensively.
	**Show/Hide sidebar** Lastly, there is an icon that is not inside the bar. At the same height but on the left side is the icon that allows us to show or hide the left sidebar. In this bar, there is a navigation menu but, sometimes, it is useful to hide it to focus on the central part or simply because the screen size is small.

***Table 4.1**: Table of icons and functionalities on preferences menu*

In the following figure, you can see in detail the Privacy Preference Centre, where you choose the Cookies you want to better preserve privacy:

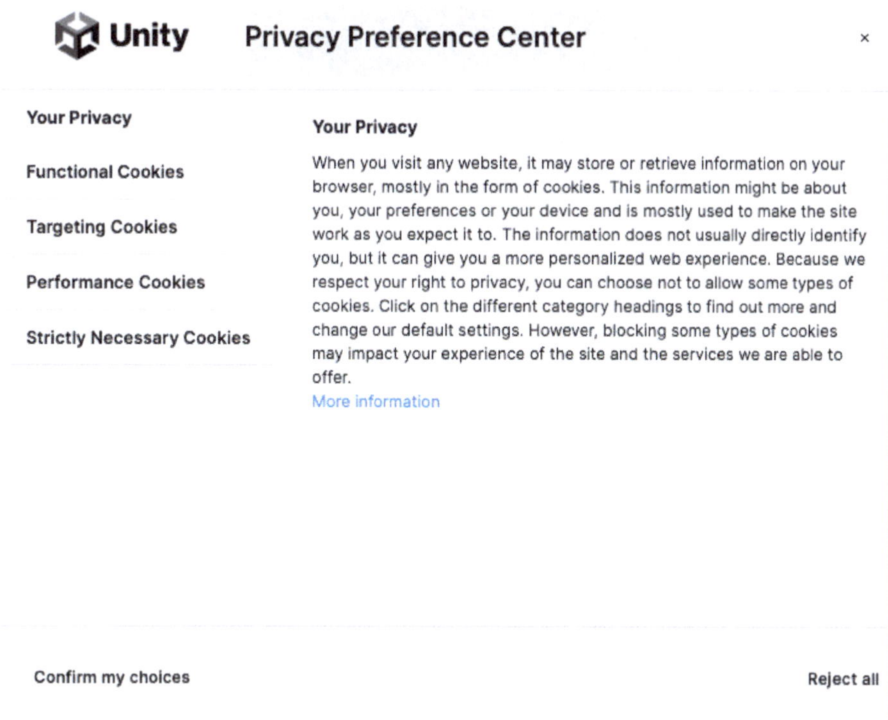

Figure 4.3: *Privacy Preference Centre's window*

In the conversation center, we will receive notifications and support from Unity technicians, as shown in the following figure:

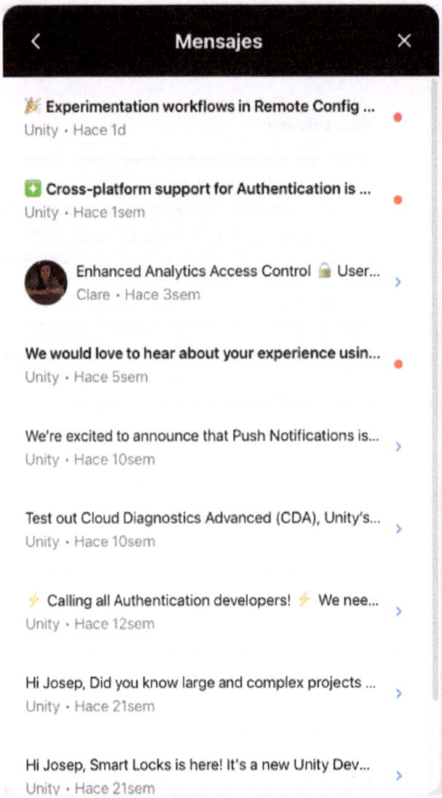

***Figure 4.4**: Detail of the Message´s window*

On some occasions, they suggest we do a survey to improve the service or find out what we think of it.

Sidebar

Let us look at some details in the following points:

- In the sidebar, we find navigation menus that will allow us to access the main sections of Unity Gaming Services, as shown in the following figure, much faster.

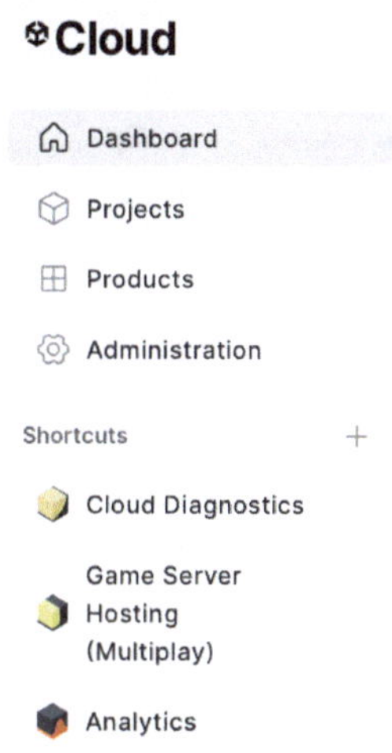

Figure 4.5: Sidebar menu

- The Products menus are especially important, from where you access all the services offered by the platform, and **Administration**, where the organizations, billing and more administrative aspects are controlled.
- The shortcuts take us directly to some of the services we use the most. It is a quick way to access them.

Main window

When we select the **Dashboard** option in the left side menu, four different areas appear on the main screen:

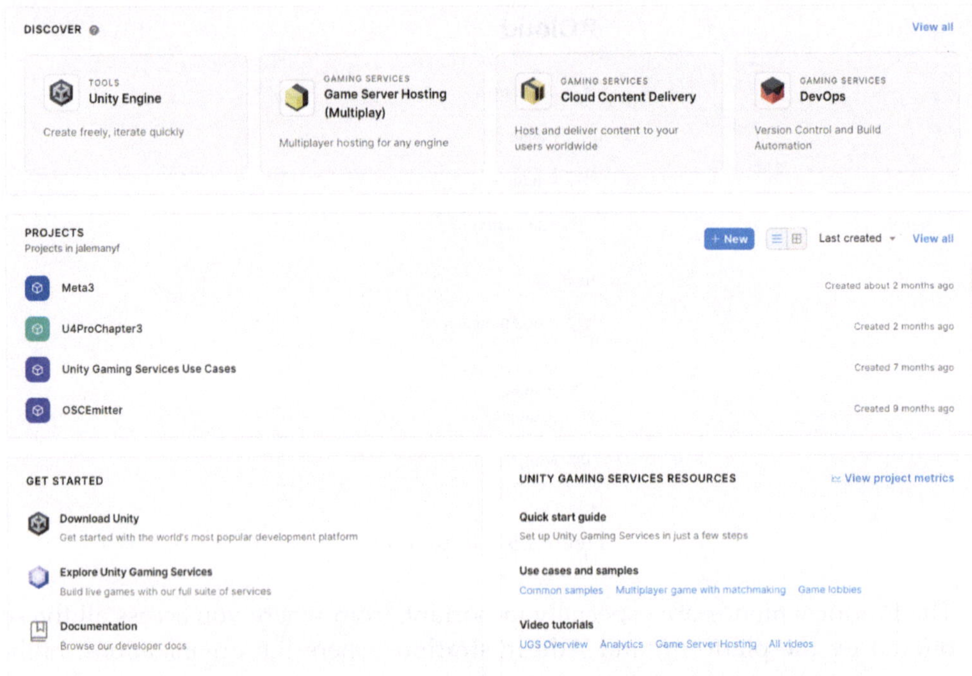

***Figure 4.6**: Detail of the discovery section with the current project*

Discover section

The **Discover** section is one of the most important sections. From this window, we can access many services that we can discover. They are classified into the following categories:

- **Gaming service**:
  - Accounts
  - Devops
  - Engagement and analytics
  - Content management
  - Crash reporting
  - Game economy
  - Community
  - Multiplayer
- **Grow**:
  - User acquisition

- Monetization
- Tools
- Unity Weta tools

- **Education**
    - Education licenses and benefits
- **Unity AI**

In the next chapters, we will see how to use some of these services.

In the **Projects** section, we will find the projects that we have carried out with Unity, even those that are not connected to cloud services. At the top right, we have some icons that help us better organize the content. The icons are as follows:

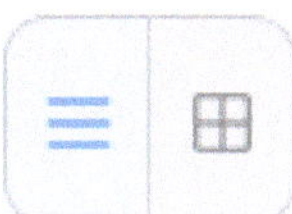	**List or table** With this icon we can select how we see the list of projects, whether in a list (with more space for the name) with a single project per row or as a table.
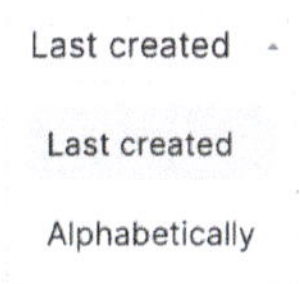	**Sort order** Select to sort projects alphabetically or by creation date.
	**View all** Opezns a window with all the projects we have created, not just some of them.
	**New** From here, we can also create a new project for the Unity 3d editor. When we do so, it will ask us for the name and age classification (to avoid apps that are not suitable for minors, it is mandatory to meet this requirement).
	Project metrics At this time, we still do not have metrics for our projects, but it is important to know that from each of the projects we can access their metrics directly if we hover the mouse pointer over it and click on View project metrics.

***Table 4.2:** Explanation of the icons of the Projects section*

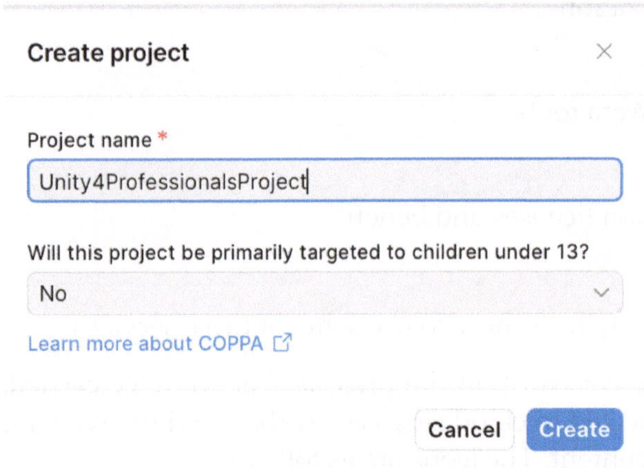

Figure 4.7: Creating a New Project

Working with projects

Apart from creating new projects, you can modify existing projects. Double-click on a project, and it will take you to a window where you can control the following features:

- **Name**: You can edit and modify the project name.
- **Icon**: You must upload `.jpg`, `.png` or `.webp` files to be the new project's icon. A 1:1 ratio is recommended.
- **Project ID**: This field is readable only, but you can copy it.
- **Google License Key**: If you develop with Google's Cloud platform, you can associate your license with the project directly, facilitating connections for in-app purchases.
- **Children's Online Privacy Protection Act (COPPA) designation**: This is the category assigned for minors. We will see the regulations in future chapters.

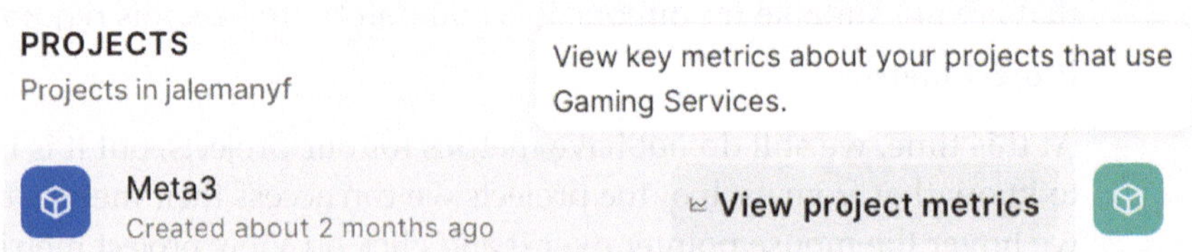

Figure 4.8: This is what the projects look like before we open them

The following figure shows the window with the preceding features:

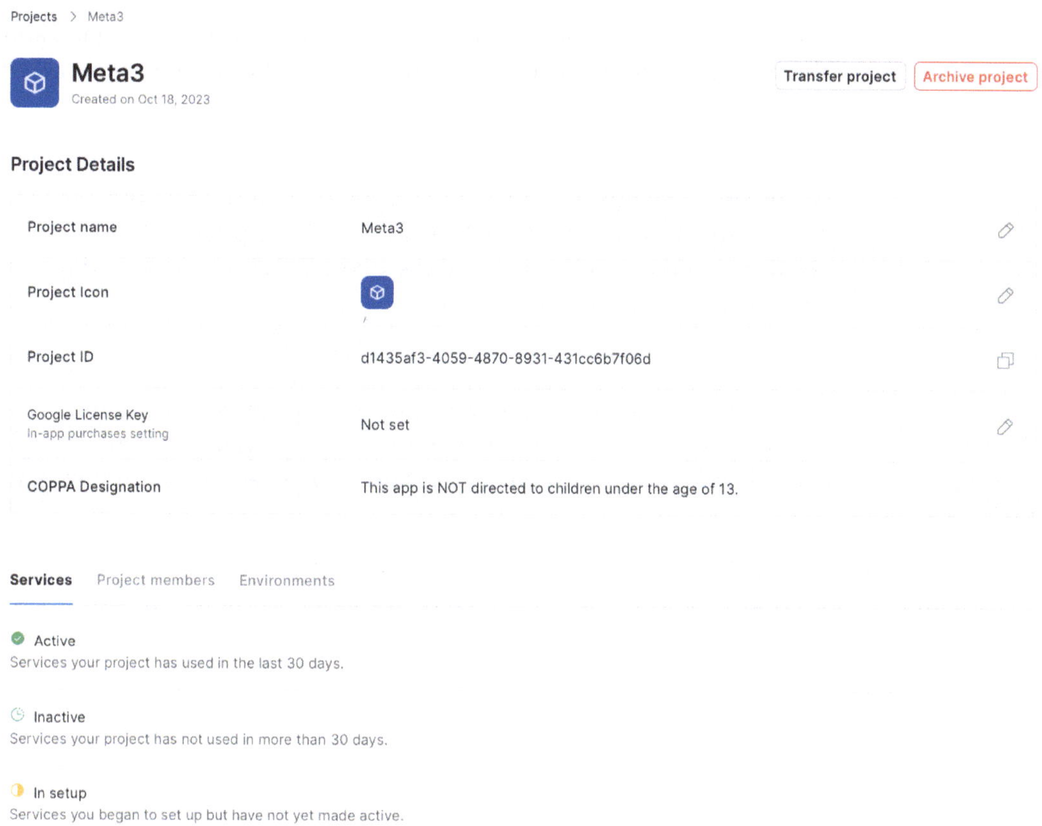

***Figure 4.9**: Inside the Project´s form*

Apart from the form with the fields at the bottom, we have three tabs, as seen in *Figure 4.9*, with the following maintenance:

1. **Services**: All UGS can be activated/deactivated for the project we are editing. This way, we have absolute control over what is working and what is not.
2. **Project members**: People who can work on the project can be added, modified, or removed here. It is an access control list to control who is allowed and who is not. Members must belong to the organization (we will see this later in this chapter, in the section, *Unity Organization*.
3. **Environments**:
    - **Unity Environment**: Environments allow you to save and segregate content from the development stage to the production stage. They are logical divisions for UGS data related to your project. The environments are isolated. This means that if you change data in one environment, data in other environments will not be affected.

At the top right, we have two buttons with important functions as seen in the following table:

Transfer project	You can transfer a Project from one organization to another organization but, you must be also an owner or manager. Users who are not part of the destination organization will lose access to the project. *Be Careful with this function!*
Archive project	If the previous function must be performed with caution, this section is surely much more dangerous. When we archive a project, the project will be deactivated for all Unity Services, and any associated files, data, and information might be lost forever.

***Table 4.3:** Options when you finish a project*

The **GET STARTED** section is designed to help newcomers or beginners quickly understand and begin using Unity. Here, we will find the projects we have carried out with Unity. Its primary purpose is to provide a clear and concise pathway for users who are just getting started.

This section, as shown in the following figure, should guide you through the initial steps and provide enough information to start using it effectively. It can significantly enhance the user experience for beginners:

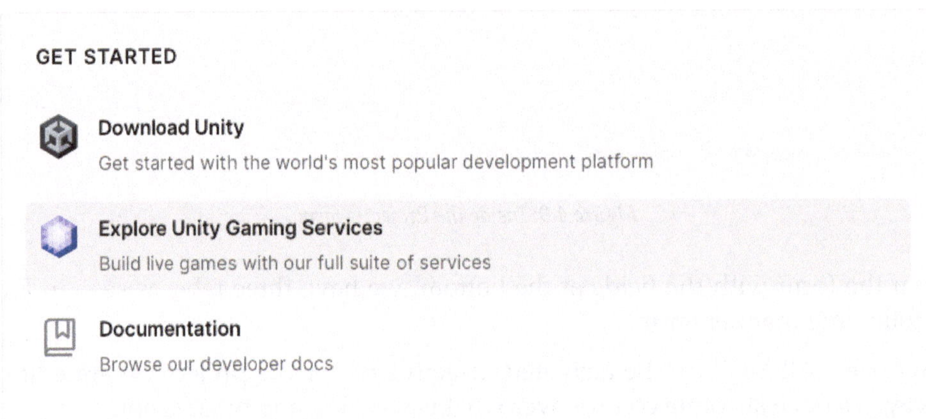

***Figure 4.10:** Section to help you START a new Project. Access to the Documentation*

In the **Unity Gaming Services Resources**, *Unity Technologies* has grouped all kinds of resources to make our tasks easier and help us be productive as soon as possible. For example, guides, samples, and some video tutorials, as shown in the following figure:

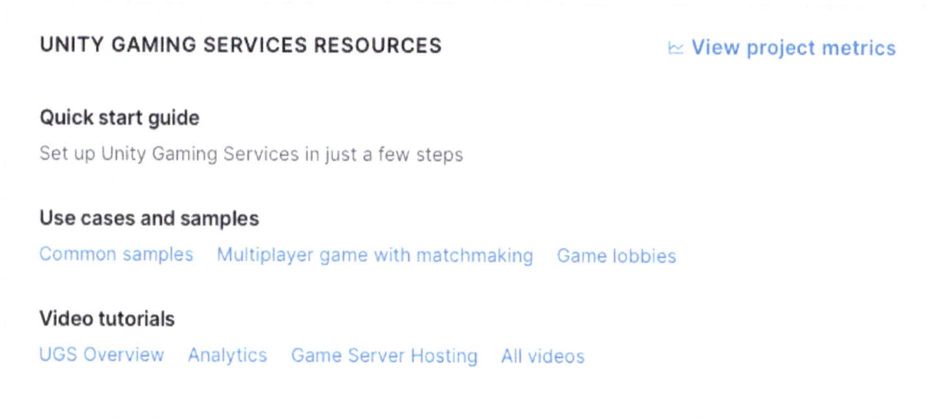

***Figure 4.11**: Detail of the resources, really useful to start quickly or consult*

The examples are in a GitHhub repository that we can clone and access a large amount of fully functional code. Each tries to show one of the functionalities separately so that it is easy to follow and implement. Additionally, the GitHub repository is updated regularly.

The videos are on YouTube and are quite interesting.

It is highly recommended to use these resources to see how to use the different services.

Administration

The next option in the sidebar is Administration. This section is especially important since it is where Unity registers organizations and developers and where billing data, costs, and payment methods are kept.

Unity organizations

An organization in Unity typically represents a collective entity that can include individual developers, teams, or even entire companies working on Unity projects.

Unity organizations may include tools for managing Unity licenses within a team. This is crucial for ensuring that all team members have the necessary licenses to use Unity features and services.

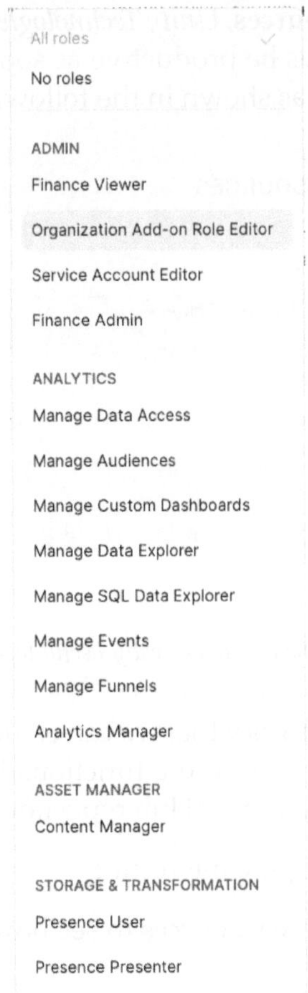

Figure 4.12*: All roles you can assign*

The *Organization settings* are basically records with a unique ID, and basic data, like, name, industry (what you do), and address.

All members hang from that organization and are classified into **User type** and **Role**, as shown in the following figure:

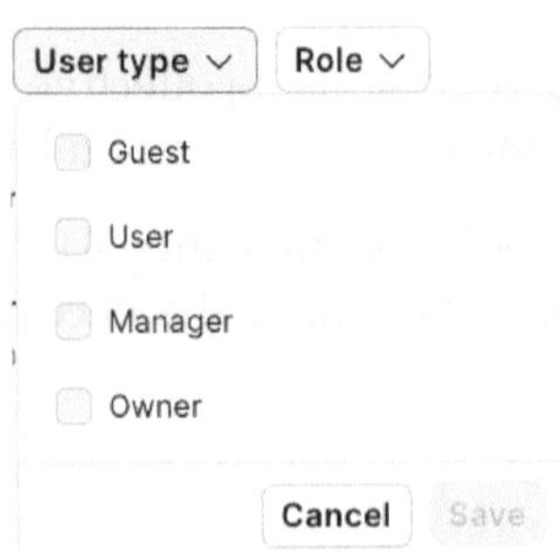

Figure 4.13*: User type*

When we have services active and running, we can check how much they are used in the *Service Usage* submenu within the organization.

For registering, Unity offers 10 Gigabytes completely free, which can be used in the Unity Cloud Personal Plan. The percentage of use of that storage can be consulted in the Unity Cloud Storage submenu. Such cloud storage is especially useful to use with a tool called **Asset Manager**. Asset Manager is a central place to find and store assets that the members of an organization share. Asset Manager is a secure space where you can collaborate using your favourite tools.

The cloud storage is also useful to work as a team on the same project or when doing version control using Plastic (Unity's version control tool).

Members and roles

In Unity Cloud, membership and roles are essential components that determine how users interact with the platform and manage their resources:

- **Memberships**: A membership is a type of user account that represents an individual or organization using Unity Cloud. Memberships can be free or paid, depending on the plan chosen by the user.

  There are two types of memberships in Unity Cloud:

  - **Free membership**: A free membership provides limited access to Unity Cloud features and resources.
  - **Paid membership (also known as a Subscription)**: A paid membership offers advanced features and resources, including support and priority services.

- **Roles**: A role is a set of permissions that determine what actions a user can perform within a specific part of the Unity Cloud platform. Roles are assigned to users based on their membership level and job function.

  There are two types of roles in Unity Cloud:

  - **User role**: A user role defines the permissions and access an individual has to Unity Cloud features and resources.
  - **Group role**: A group role is a set of permissions that can be applied to multiple users or groups within a Unity Cloud organization.

Roles in Unity Cloud

Here are some common roles found in Unity Cloud:

- **Admin**: An admin has full control over the entire Unity Cloud platform, including user accounts, settings, and features.

- **Manager**: A manager has control over a specific area of the platform, such as projects, teams, or resources.
- **Contributor**: A contributor can create and edit content, but may not have full access to all features.
- **User**: A standard user can view and interact with Unity Cloud features and resources, but is limited by their role.
- **Role-based access control (RBAC)**: Unity Cloud uses **RBAC** to manage user permissions and access. RBAC defines the relationships between roles, users, and features, ensuring that each user only has access to the resources they need to perform their job function.

Here is how it works:

- **Role hierarchy**: Roles are organized in a hierarchical structure, with more advanced roles inheriting the permissions of less advanced roles.
- **Permission sets**: Permissions are assigned to specific roles or groups, defining what actions users can perform within Unity Cloud features and resources.
- **User assignment**: Users are assigned to roles based on their membership level and job function.

Benefits of roles in Unity Cloud

Roles provide several benefits in Unity Cloud, including:

- **Improved security**: Roles ensure that sensitive information is only accessible to authorized individuals.
- **Efficient resource management**: Roles help manage resources more efficiently by limiting access to specific features and areas.
- **Simplified user onboarding**: Roles simplify the onboarding process for new users by assigning them to a specific role based on their job function.

Best practices for role management in Unity Cloud

To get the most out of roles in Unity Cloud, follow these best practices:

- **Create clear and concise roles**: Define roles that accurately reflect user responsibilities and permissions.
- **Use a hierarchical structure**: Organize roles in a logical hierarchy to ensure that users only have access to necessary resources.
- **Regularly review and update roles**: Periodically review role permissions and update them as needed to reflect changes in job functions or platform features.

By understanding membership, roles, and RBAC in Unity Cloud, you can manage user access and permissions more efficiently, ensuring that each user only has access to the resources they need to perform their job function.

Finance and billing

The Unity Cloud financial administration dashboard is designed to help you manage your invoices, payments, and credit card information. This dashboard is divided into four main sections:

- **Invoices**: View and manage all outstanding invoices.
- **Payments**: View and make payments on outstanding invoices.
- **Credit card**: Manage your credit card information, including payment due dates and credit limits.
- **Settings**: Configure payment and billing settings.

Managing invoices

To manage your invoices in Unity Cloud, follow these steps:

1. Click the **New Invoice** button to create a new invoice.
2. Enter the required information, such as the payment due date and total amount.
3. Select how you want taxes to be applied (if applicable).
4. Accept or reject the invoice.

Make payments

To make payments for outstanding invoices in Unity Cloud, follow these steps:

1. Click the **New Payment** button to create a new payment.
2. Enter the required information, such as the payment date and amount paid.
3. Select how you want taxes to be applied (if applicable).
4. Accept or decline the payment.

Managing credit card information

To manage your credit card information in Unity Cloud, follow these steps:

1. Click the **My Cards** button to view a list of all your credit cards.
2. Select the credit card you want to manage.
3. Enter the required information, such as the payment due date and credit limit.
4. Accept or decline the credit card.

Configuring payment settings

To configure payment settings in Unity Cloud, perform the following steps:

1. Click the **Settings** button to access the settings section.
2. Select the option you want to configure (e.g., tax application).
3. Enter the required information.
4. Accept or reject the changes.

Budget alerts

Many of the services have a relatively small cost that is normally zero when we develop, but when we start to have many users, it becomes something to consider.

In order to prevent unpleasant surprises when you receive your bill from UGS, you can create a budget. Quotes are simply intended as notice. When budgetary objectives are reached, services will remain active and billed at the relevant rates.

Conclusion

This chapter has explored the UGS platform and its dedicated dashboard. Unity Technologies has developed UGS as a comprehensive suite of tools and services specifically designed to address the challenges faced by game and app developers using Unity. UGS offers a compelling alternative to traditional cloud service providers, offering streamlined integration and support tailored for the Unity development process.

It provided a detailed examination of the Unity Dashboard, highlighting its role as the central control hub for managing Unity projects and services. You have learned how to navigate the dashboard interface, including its various sections and menus. We explored key functions such as creating and configuring projects, managing project members and environments, and understanding project metrics. Additionally, the administrative features of the dashboard were covered, including managing Unity Organizations, handling finance and billing, and setting budget alerts. By mastering the concepts and skills presented in this chapter, you are well-equipped to harness the power of the Unity Dashboard to streamline your development workflow and maximize the potential of your Unity projects.

In the next chapter, you will delve into the Analytics System to learn how to collect, store, and analyze user data effectively. You will explore the concept of isolated environments for safe testing and learn to record essential user actions through both automatic and custom events. Furthermore, you will discover how to generate meaningful reports using the Data Explorer and perform advanced analysis by writing SQL queries to uncover deeper insights into player behavior and game performance.

Multiple choice questions

1. **What is the stated role of the Unity Dashboard in managing Unity projects?**
   a. It is solely the interface used for coding and compiling C# scripts.
   b. It is the control center of the platform, allowing access to products and services, organizing projects, and managing subscriptions.
   c. It is a feature used primarily for generating text-based interfaces.
   d. It functions exclusively as a repository for Unity Editor code assets.
2. **What are the key advantages of using UGS**?
   a. The ease of integration into your development and the support of the entire development lifecycle.
   b. Its exclusive reliance on proprietary SQL databases.
   c. Offering 2.5 petabytes of detailed terrain data streaming.
   d. Managing certificates for online transaction authentication.
3. **When navigating the Unity Dashboard, which two menus in the Sidebar are highlighted as being especially important for controlling platform services and administrative aspects?**
   a. The Quick access menu and the Notifications menu.
   b. The Discover Section and the Get Started section.
   c. The Products menu and the Administration menu.
   d. The Privacy Preference Centre and the Help and Support menu.
4. **What is the functionality of the Enter/Exit focus mode icon found within the environment preferences?**
   a. It opens a chat window for receiving technical support.
   b. It is used to show or hide the left sidebar.
   c. It enables or disables focus mode by closing any window other than the central one to avoid distractions.
   d. It manages the cookies the developer wishes to share to better preserve privacy.
5. **When modifying an existing project's features, which specific field is identified as being readable only (but copyable)?**
   a. The Project Name.
   b. The Project ID.
   c. The Project icon.
   d. The COPPA designation.

6. **Regarding project management, what critical consequence occurs when a developer archives a project?**
   a. The project is automatically transferred to a new organization.
   b. The project is deactivated for all Unity Services, and any associated files, data, and information might be lost forever.
   c. The ability to assign roles to organization members is temporarily locked.
   d. The project's billing method is automatically reset to pay-as-you-go.
7. **What is the primary function and key characteristic of Environments within a project?**
   a. They are solely responsible for managing payment processing and credit card information.
   b. They are used to assign different User roles (Admin, Manager, Contributor).
   c. They are isolated logical divisions for UGS data, allowing content segregation from the development stage to the production stage.
   d. They represent the geographic location of the nearest data center.
8. **In the Administration section, what is the amount of completely free storage offered under the Unity Cloud Personal Plan?**
   a. 1 GB of storage.
   b. 5 GB of storage.
   c. 10 GB of completely free storage.
   d. 100 GB of free storage.

Answers

1	b
2	a
3	c
4	c
5	b
6	c
7	c
8	c

CHAPTER 5
Exploring Data with Analytics System

Introduction

As a game/app developer, gaining insights into how players interact with your creation is paramount. This chapter will guide you through the powerful Analytics System, a suite of tools designed to collect, store, and analyze significant amounts of data about your users. By the end of this chapter, you will understand how to record essential user actions as events, differentiating between those automatically captured and the custom events you can define to track specific in-game behaviors. You will explore the concept of isolated environments for your data, enabling safe testing and development practices. Furthermore, you will learn to harness the power of the Data Explorer to generate meaningful reports and visualize your data through various metrics and events, allowing you to quickly grasp user trends. The chapter will also introduce you to Funnels, a visual method to understand the journey players take through your game and identify potential drop-off points. You will discover how to categorize your players into audiences based on their behavior and characteristics, enabling targeted engagement strategies. Finally, you will be introduced to **Structured Query Language** (**SQL**) Data Explorer, a feature that allows for advanced data analysis by writing and executing SQL queries to uncover deeper insights into player behavior and game performance.

Structure

The chapter covers the following topics:

- Enviroments
    - Creating an environment
- Events
    - Custom events
    - Events Browser
- Data Explorer

- Creating a report
- Creating a funnel
- Audiences
- Creating an audience

- SQL Data Explorer
  - Structured Query Language
  - Programming SQL queries

Objectives

The objectives of this chapter are to learn how to record information about how our app is used and understand how to represent it. To do this, we will learn concepts such as environments, events, and triggers. We will see how to develop the necessary code to store all that information in the cloud and then be able to ask for it using SQL. Finally, we will begin to generate graphs that will help us understand the behavior of our clients more quickly and easily.

First, we are going to explain some concepts that will be necessary.

Environments

According to Unity technical documentation:

Environments are logical partitions for Unity Game Services that contain data associated with your project.

The main characteristic of the environments is that they are isolated. In other words, you can change data in one environment, and the data in other environments is not affected.

Usually, at least two environments are created: one for development and one for production. In this way, tests can be carried out in the development environment without affecting in any way a product that our clients already have installed. It is like a sandbox to test before releasing to the market.

Environments are applied at the project level.

Creating an environment

Follow these steps in the Unity Game Services Dashboard:

1. Select **Projects** on the left menu; you can see your projects in the center part of the screen. Click on the `projects` where you want to modify the environment.

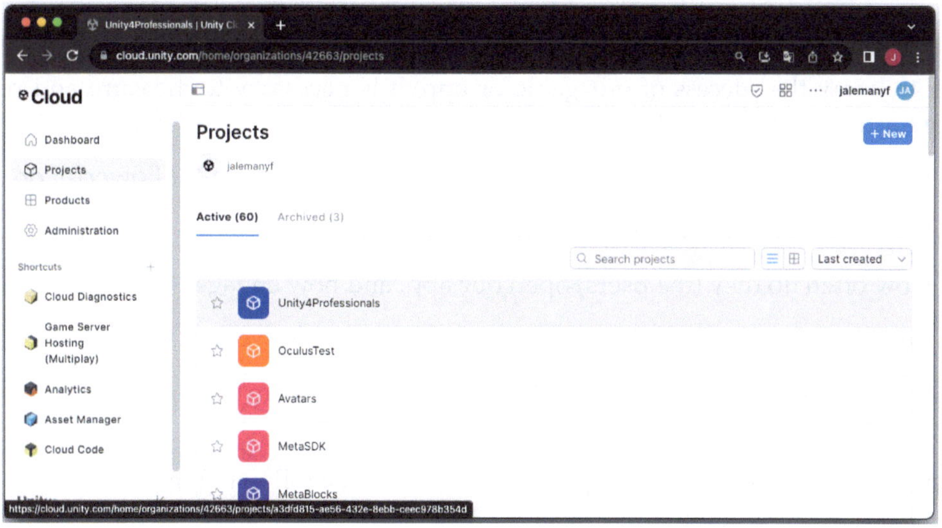

***Figure 5.1**: Select the Project to change the environment*

2. When the project is selected, you can view an environment tab with the **Add Environment** button:

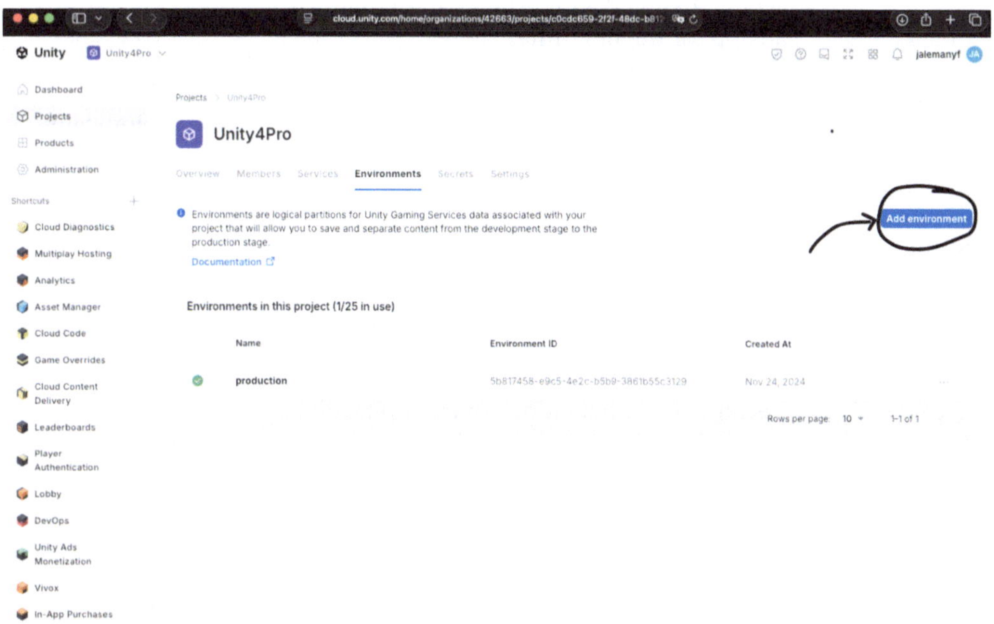

***Figure 5.2**: You can add a new environment to the project*

By default, all projects start with a production environment (It does not have to be created). A project can have a maximum of 25 environments.

Events

In order to know the success of our game or app, it is necessary to measure and record all important actions that users take:

- What type of cell phone do your players have? Android or iOS? Powerful or not?
- Which countries have the best results for you?
- How often do they (the users) open our app, and how engaged are your players?
- Which audiences are underperforming? Where should we focus to improve?

Each of these incidents/happenings is called *Events*. Some of them are registered automatically, and others are not.

The events that are automatically logged can be seen in the following table:

Event name	Description	Trigger type
newPlayer	Sent upon a new player installing the application on their device.	Automatic
gameStarted	A new session begins when the user launches an app for the first time.	Automatic
gameEnded	Sent upon a player's departure from the game.	Automatic
gameRunning	Sent periodically while the application is operational to monitor session activity.	Sent periodically while the application is operational to monitor session activity. Automatically every 60 seconds, if no other events have been sent since the last check.
clientDevice	Records the initial launch of an application by a user and any subsequent changes in device information.	Automatic
ddnaForgetMe	Logs the date and time when a player elects to opt out of data collection.	Automatic
sdkStart	Sent upon initialization of the SDK.	Automatic
notificationOpened	Sent upon opening a push notification or receiving a notification while the game is in progress.	Automatic
notificationServices	Records the player's push notification tokens.	Automatic

Event name	Description	Trigger type
outOfGameSend	This is sent when a push notification reaches a player.	Automatic
userAssignment	Automatically assigns a player to a campaign for reporting purposes.	Automatic

Table 5.1: *Just by activating automatic data recording, we will be able to know our customers' habits much better*

The following table contains a series of other events that are not automatically launched but can be very useful. It is important to know that they already exist on the platform and that we only need to launch them using a trigger:

Event Name	Description	Trigger type
aquisitionSource	Record information about the channel from which the user was acquired. This data should be populated using the attribution provider's SDK.	Requires manual triggering
adImpression	Players can manually send an ad when they have been shown one within the game.	Requires manual triggering
transaction	When a player makes an in-app purchase, this message is sent to track the purchase amount. Transaction validation can be performed using the Unity IAP.	Requires manual triggering
transactionFailed	When a player makes an unsuccessful in-app purchase transaction, a transaction event is recorded. Successful transactions are tracked separately.	Requires manual triggering

Table 5.2: *The following events require us to do some programming in order for them to be registered*

Custom events

These events are very interesting, but they are of a general nature (when the game starts, how long you are in it, when it ends.). However, if it is necessary to record specific information, you can create *Custom Events* where we will record that the user has passed the first and second level, for example.

Refer to the following steps in the Unity Game Services Dashboard:

1. To create a new custom event, click on **Products / Analytics / Event Manager** and then press the blue right button labeled **Add New/Custom Event**.

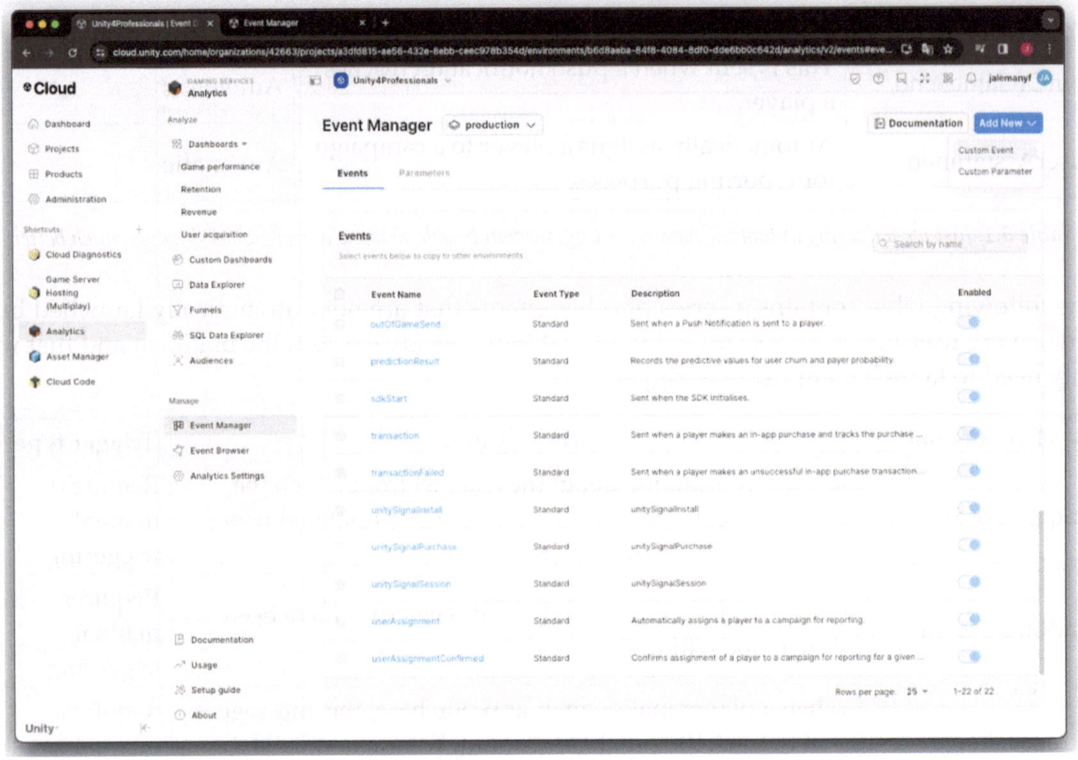

Figure 5.3: *In the Event Manager panel, we can manage all types of events*

2. Assign a name and provide a description to the Custom Event. Remember that names must be composed solely of English alphanumeric characters and commence with a letter. Custom Events can be enabled or disabled, but they cannot be deleted. When we create a custom event, a form like the following will appear:

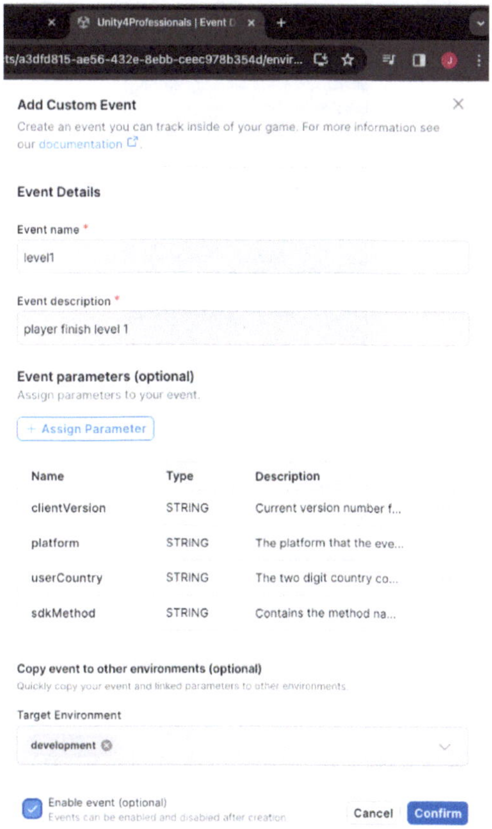

***Figure 5.4**: Detail of the form to create a Custom Event*

3. Parameters can be assigned from the Event Manager creation window. To create your own, select **Assign Parameter** and then **Create New Parameter**. Parameters need a name, description, and data type. The first character of your parameter name must be a letter. The name can only contain English alphanumeric and underscore characters. You can edit parameters, but not delete them. The data types encompass string, integer, float, and bool. You are permitted to add up to 1,500 parameters to the environment.

Let us see how we should prepare a Unity Project to be able to register events automatically, and the code that we will have to write:

1. Create a New Unity Project (it does not matter if URP or HRP).

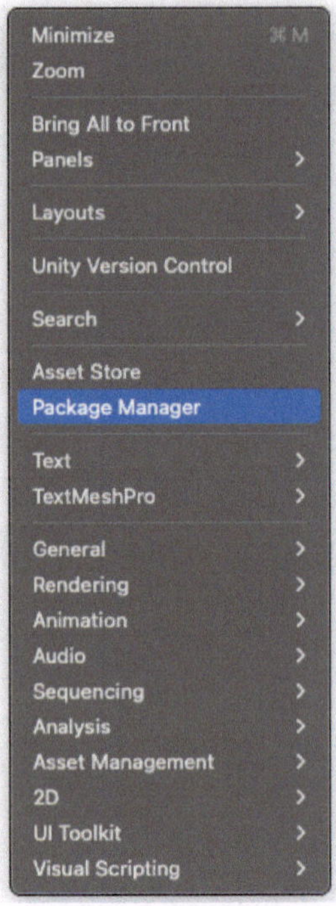

***Figure 5.5**: Open the Package Manager Window to install the Analytics package*

2. Import and install the **Analytics** package from Unity Register packages. This system allows us to record events and send them to Unity Cloud:

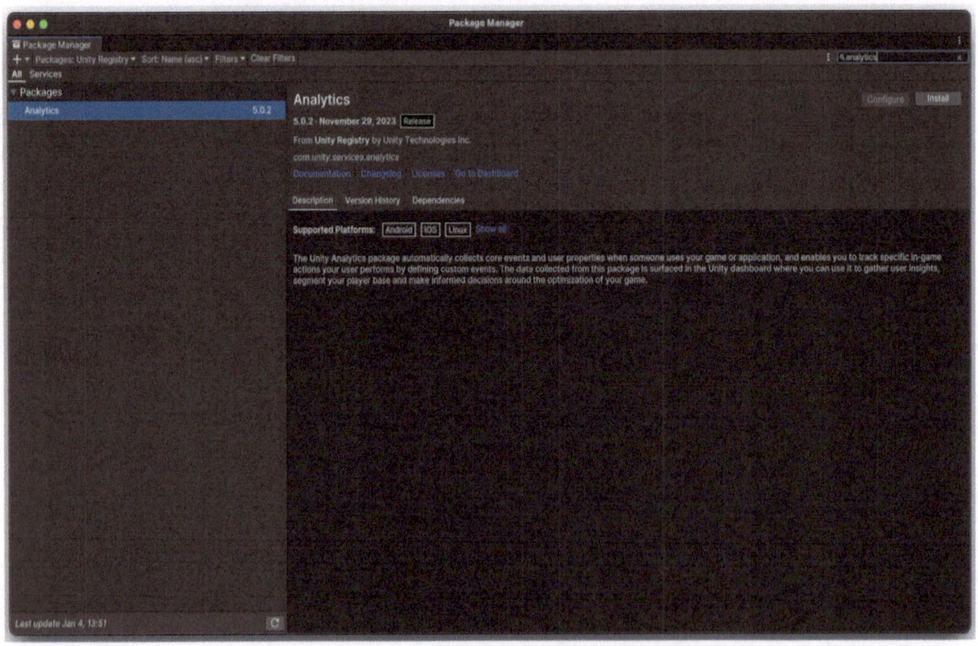

***Figure 5.6**: Analytics package installation screen*

3. Create an Empty Object on the hierarchy Window of the Editor:

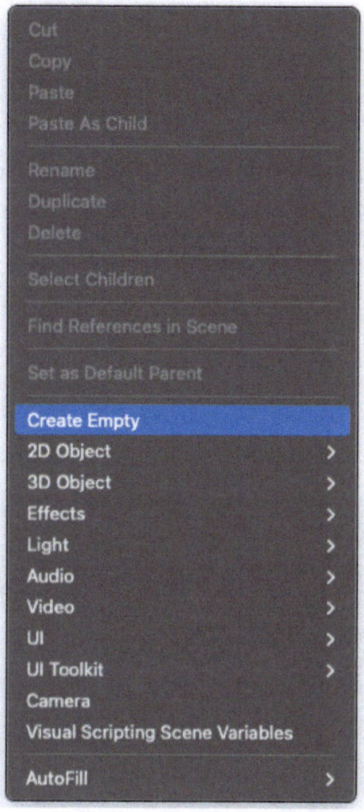

Figure 5.7: *We create an empty object where we will add the code*

4. Attach a new script to the Empty Object as a Component. We have called the class **`GamingServices`**.

   The following is the simplest code:

```
using UnityEngine;
using Unity.Services.Core;
using Unity.Services.Analytics;
using Unity.Services.Core.Environments;

public class GamingServices : MonoBehaviour
{

    async void Awake()
    {
        var options = new InitializationOptions();
       options.SetEnvironmentName("production");
        await UnityServices.InitializeAsync(options);
```

```
            AnalyticsService.Instance.StartDataCollection();
        print("Initializing UGServices...");
        }
}
```

The script basically initializes Unity Services, specifically configuring the environment as production (*line 11*), initializing services asynchronously, and starting data collection for analytics (*line 13*).

5. The last step left so we can send data to the server is to initialize the services in the Project. To do this, we will go to the menu **Edit** | **Project Settings** | **Services**.

   To manage the project's online services, we can access them through the Services menu in **Project Settings**, as shown in the following figure:

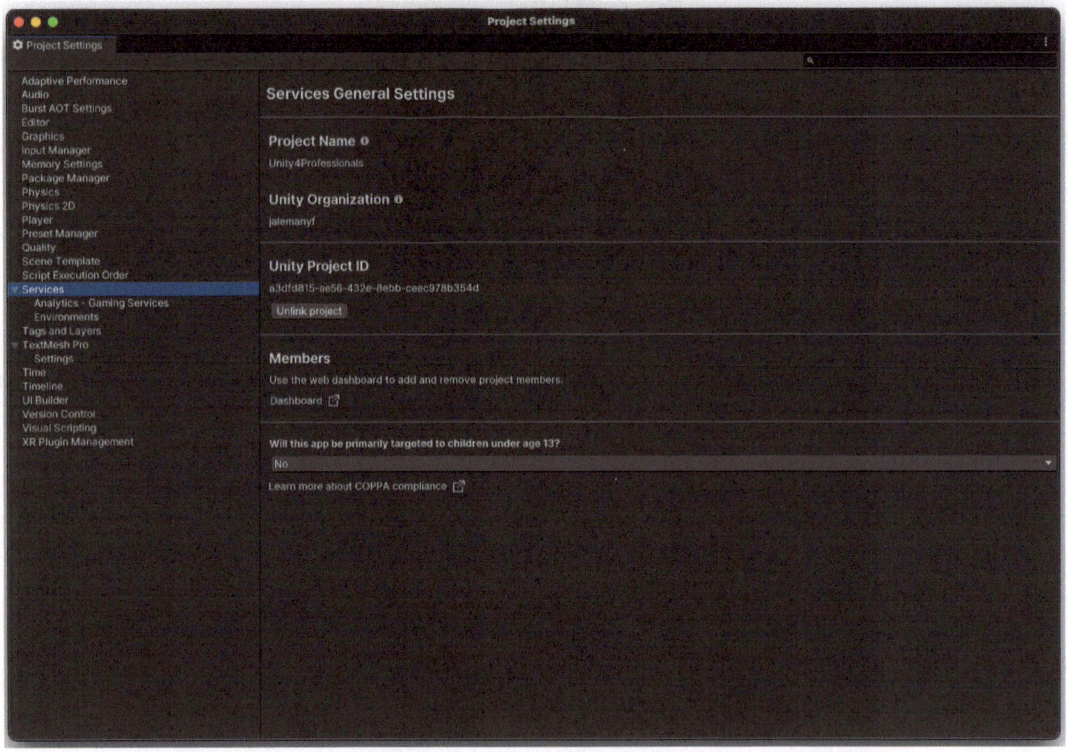

Figure 5.8: *Project Settings where we can check which services are activated*

To manage the cloud services that our project has, you can access "Project Settings" from the following menu:

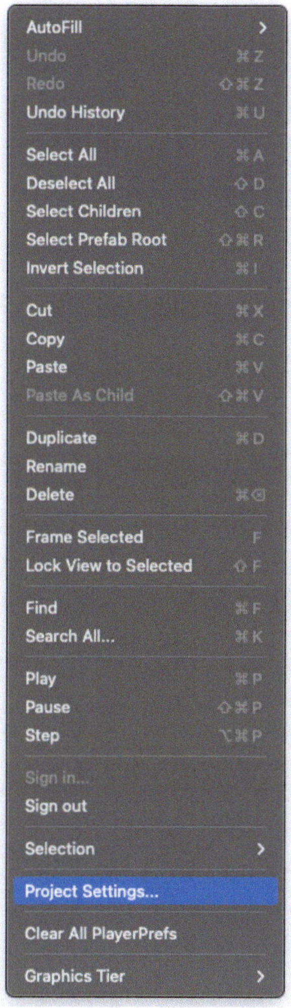

Figure 5.9: *To access the Project Settings, you must access it with the Edit/Project Settings menu*

If this project is executed in the editor, data is already beginning to be recorded, although it is not something immediate. Normally, it can take two or more hours, depending on the network connection and its status, for information to start appearing on the Dashboard.

The first graph that appears will probably look something like the following figure. A graph with a single peak indicates that a timely recording has already taken place. Congratulations! You have now successfully recorded data in the cloud.

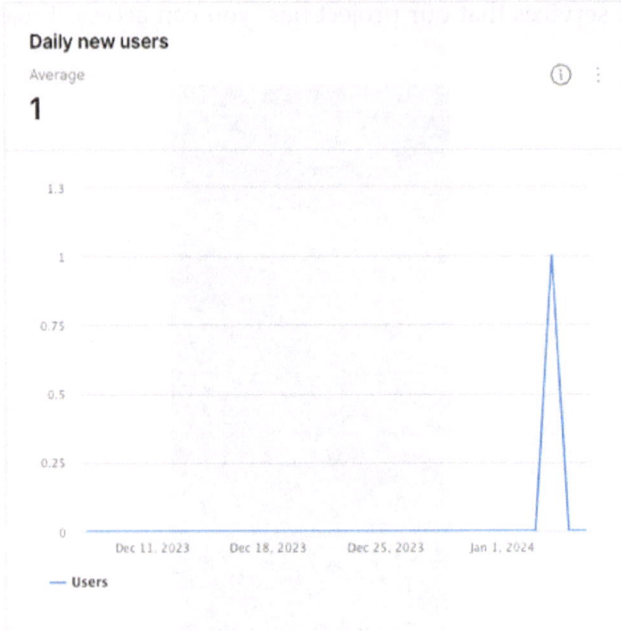

***Figure 5.10**: The first activity log*

The following code goes a step further and logs Custom Events to know when a user finishes levels 1 and 2 of the game:

```
using UnityEngine;
using Unity.Services.Core;
using Unity.Services.Analytics;
using System.Collections.Generic;
using Unity.Services.Core.Environments;
using System;

public class GamingServices : MonoBehaviour
{
    private Dictionary<string, object> levels = new Dictionary<string, object>();

    /// <summary>
    /// Initialize and instantiate UGS asynchronously
    /// </summary>
    async void Awake()
    {
```

```
        var options = new InitializationOptions();
        options.SetEnvironmentName("production");
        await UnityServices.InitializeAsync(options);
        AnalyticsService.Instance.StartDataCollection();
        print("Initializing UGServices...");
    }

    /// <summary>
    /// Level1 is completed
    /// </summary>
    public void Level1Finished()
    {
        try
        {
            levels.Add("level1", true);
            AnalyticsService.Instance.CustomData("levels", levels);
            AnalyticsService.Instance.Flush();
            Debug.Log("Registering Custom Event Level 1 finished");
        }
        catch(Exception e)
        {
            Debug.Log("The level one is finished before");
        }
    }

    /// <summary>
    /// Level2 is completed
    /// </summary>
    public void Level2Finished()
    {
        try
        {
            levels.Add("level2", true);
            AnalyticsService.Instance.CustomData("levels", levels);
            AnalyticsService.Instance.Flush();
            Debug.Log("Registering Custom Event Level 2 finished");
        }
```

```
54.         catch (Exception e)
55.         {
56.             Debug.Log("The level two is finished before");
57.         }
58.     }
59. }
```

Two public functions have been added to be launched from a button in an interface.

The normal process is that the events are stored in a memory buffer and are sent to the server from time to time.

To force them to be sent immediately, the Flush command has been used on lines 33 and 51, but this should not be used in a real environment because it can slow down other processes.

With all the data we store, we can make reports with graphs. The tool to create reports is called Data Explorer.

An event is a JSON file that contains fields other than the ones we define:

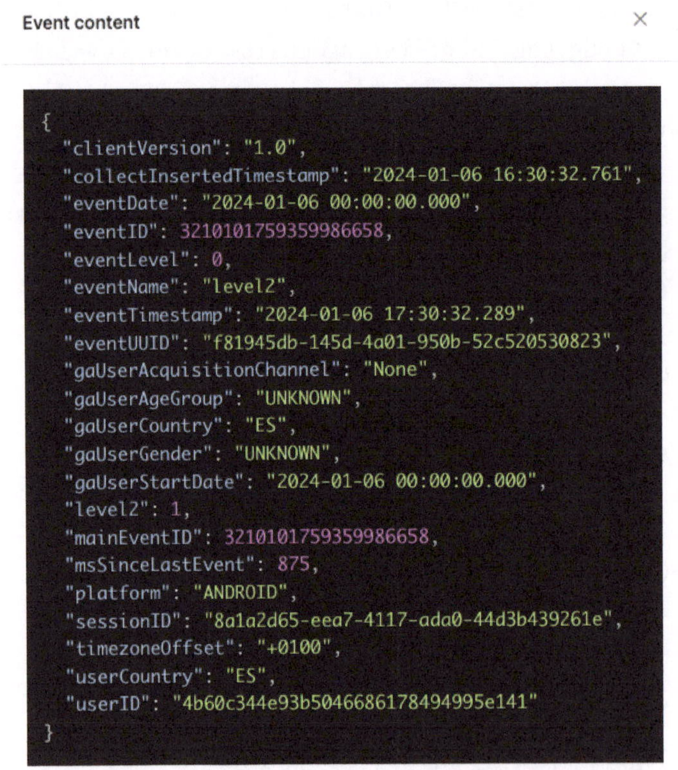


```
{
  "clientVersion": "1.0",
  "collectInsertedTimestamp": "2024-01-06 16:30:32.761",
  "eventDate": "2024-01-06 00:00:00.000",
  "eventID": 3210101759359986658,
  "eventLevel": 0,
  "eventName": "level2",
  "eventTimestamp": "2024-01-06 17:30:32.289",
  "eventUUID": "f81945db-145d-4a01-950b-52c520530823",
  "gaUserAcquisitionChannel": "None",
  "gaUserAgeGroup": "UNKNOWN",
  "gaUserCountry": "ES",
  "gaUserGender": "UNKNOWN",
  "gaUserStartDate": "2024-01-06 00:00:00.000",
  "level2": 1,
  "mainEventID": 3210101759359986658,
  "msSinceLastEvent": 875,
  "platform": "ANDROID",
  "sessionID": "8a1a2d65-eea7-4117-ada0-44d3b439261e",
  "timezoneOffset": "+0100",
  "userCountry": "ES",
  "userID": "4b60c344e93b5046686178494995e141"
}
```


***Figure 5.11**: Sample JSON from the level2 event*

Events Browser

To debug events coming in from your game, use the Event Browser feature in Analytics. One can view up to the last 100 events sent by their game within the last 48 hours.

In the following figure, you can see the list of events within the online platform:

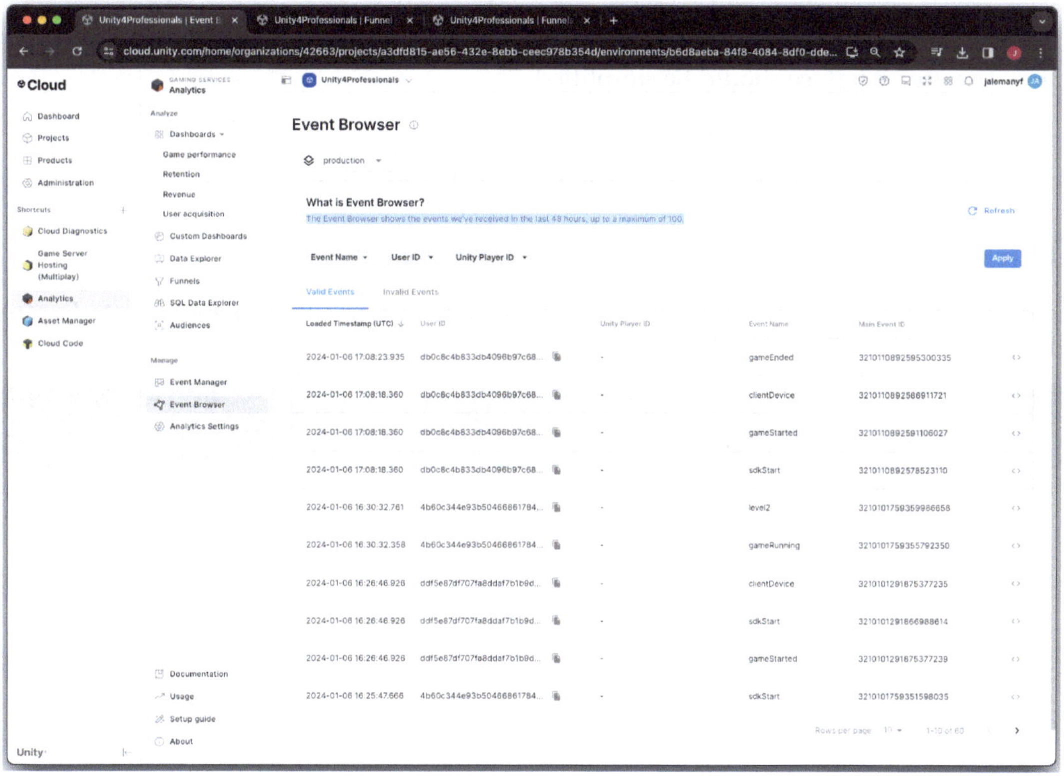

Figure 5.12: Panel where we can follow and maintain all the events that our project records

Note: Event processing time varies. Legacy Analytics events should be available in UGS within two hours after being sent.

Data Explorer

Data Explorer empowers you to manipulate and analyze your data by applying filters and events, and grouping it by platform, country, or version. You can query your game data based on predefined metrics or events, apply dimension filters, and group the series by dimension. The visualization options include bar charts, line graphs, area graphs, pie charts, and stacking bar charts.

Unity Analytics has been enhanced with the following features and enhancements in comparison to its predecessor:

- The data is refreshed at a minimum of every two hours subsequent to the installation of the SDK.
- Filters with multiple dimensions and tailored filter values.
- You can categorize them by dimension.
- The user interface should be simplified.
- The data visualization has been improved.
- The concept of transparency in relation to metric definitions.

Creating a report

To create a report, within Unity Gaming Services, go to the **Analytics** menu | **Data Explorer** and push the **+New Report** button (at the top right):

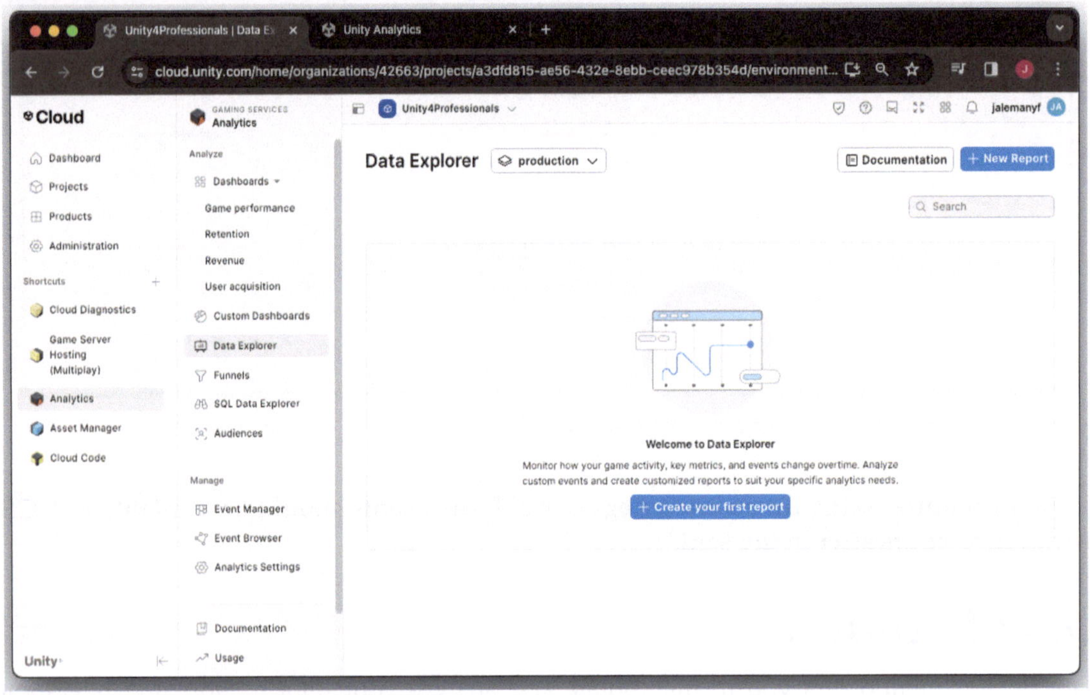

Figure 5.13: Analytics | Data Explorer menu and panel when you start

A new window will open where we can add metrics or events to start. After clicking on Add Event, a long list will appear with all the available events (to the right of the event, there is an icon with a question mark; if you hover your mouse over it, an explanation of what that event is will appear).

Currently, clicking the button displays a pop-up window asking, *Do you want to create a Data Explorer report in the new or old experience?*

The new experience simplifies the data entry process, but the underlying concepts are exactly the same.

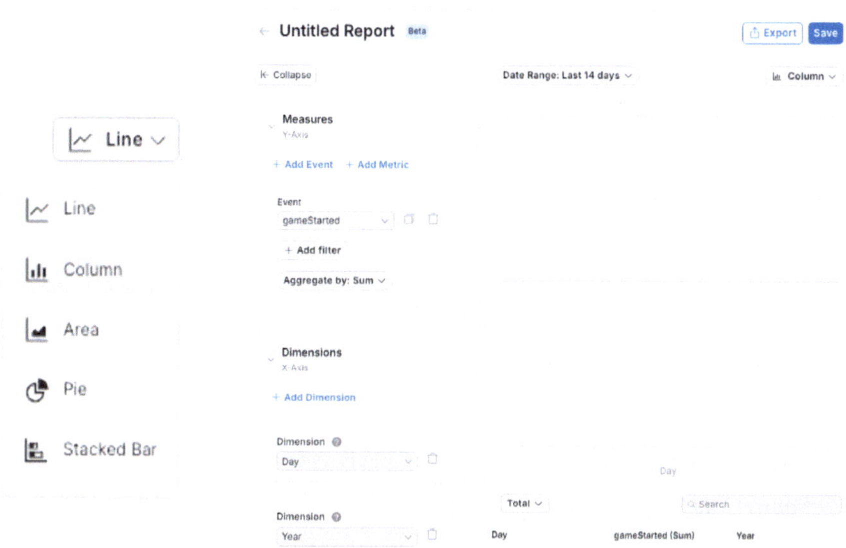

Figure 5.14: Chart type selector and the new report creation experience

Select the event **gameStarted**. Let all the other parameters and click on the **Apply** button, as shown in the following figure:

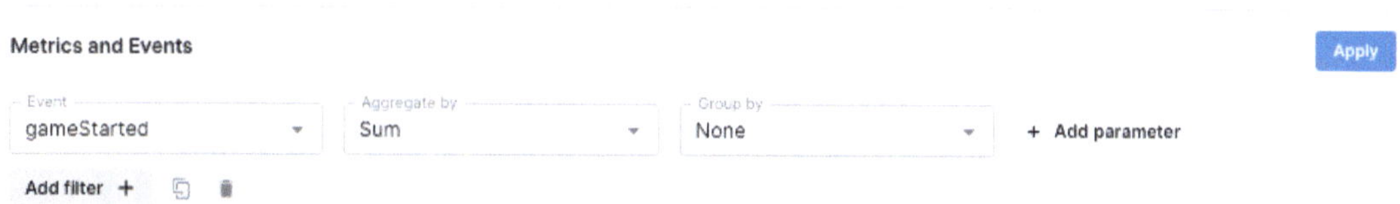

Figure 5.15: Selecting the gameStarted event in the Data Explorer

In the following figure, you can see the graph of different events that have been recorded over time in a project:

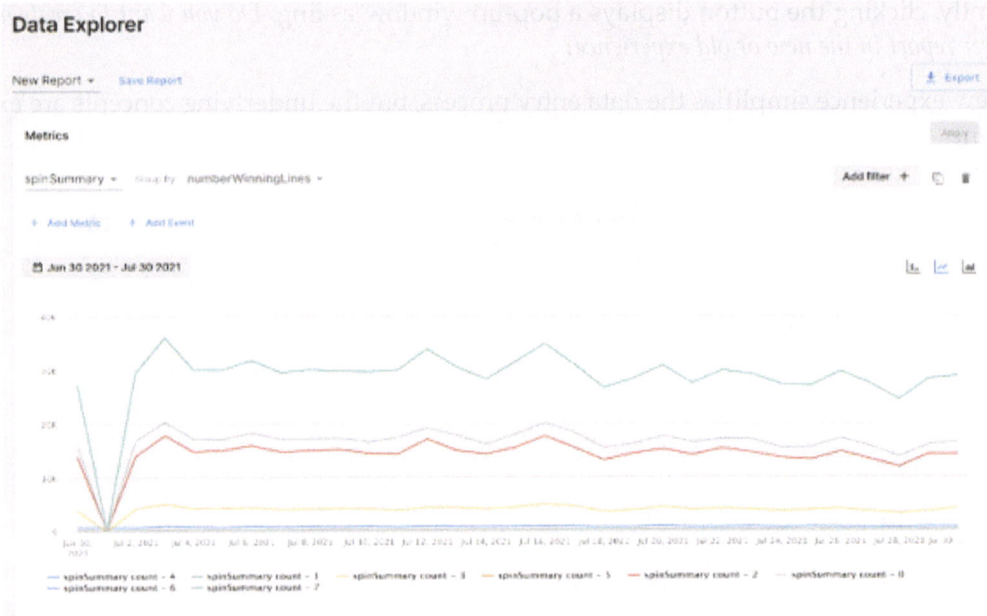

***Figure 5.16**: Example of what the graph of events looks like over a period of time*

***Source:** https://docs.unity.com/ugs/en-us/manual/analytics/manual/data-explorer*

The graph editor is very versatile and allows you to create different styles of metrics, allowing you to create a dashboard of what interests you most, as shown in the following figure:

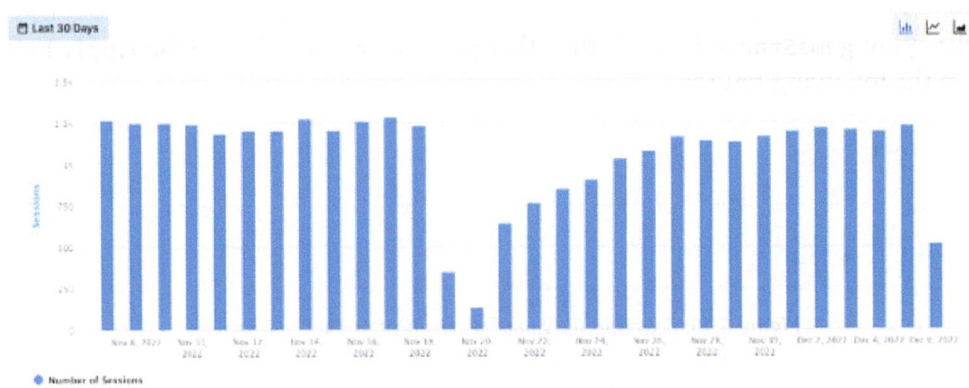

***Figure 5.17**: Simple report created in the Data Explorer*

You have now created your first report. Even a simple report can already yield valuable insights. Play around with the chart type button. Notice that at the bottom, you have the total number of times your App has been run since it started recording data. As you record more data, your reports will contain much more information, and you will be able to apply filters and statistical measurements, as shown in the following figure:

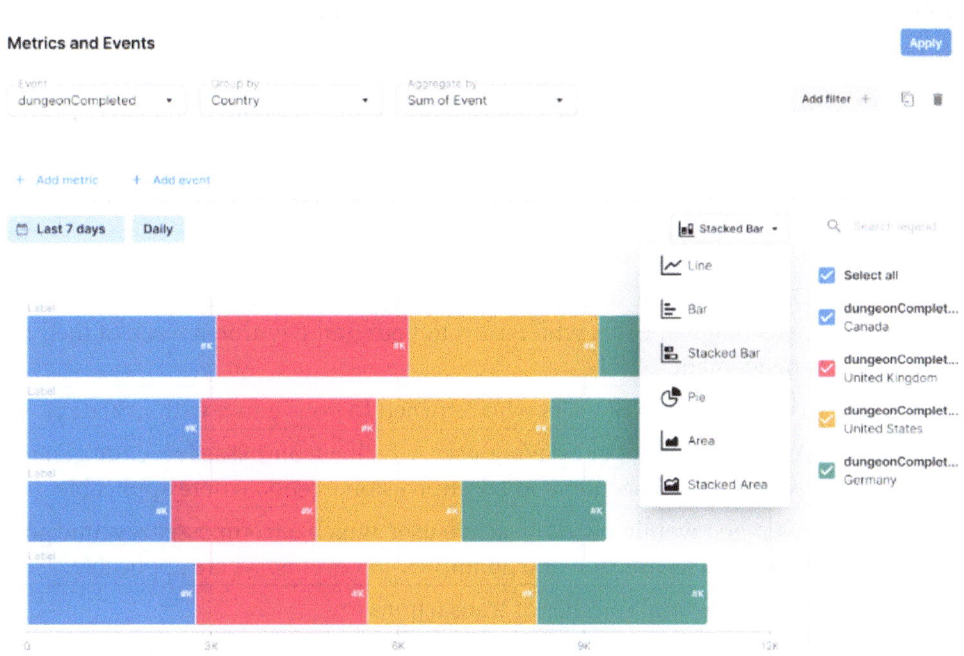

***Figure 5.18**: Sample of the metrics available in the Data Explorer*

If instead of adding an event, you select add metric, another very long list appears with some acronyms that are difficult to understand. Fortunately, Unity Technologies has published the following list of each of the metrics:

Metric	Description
DAU	The number of distinct players who participate in the game each day.
DAU (new vs. returning)	What percentage of **daily active users** (**DAU**) were new on that particular day
WAU	The number of distinct players who participated in the previous seven days.
MAU	Stands for the number of unique players who have played the game in the past 30 days.
DAU per MAU	The percentage of MAUs who played on a specific day DAU and **monthly active users** (**MAU**).
New users	Daily users who are new to the platform on that particular day.
Session length	The time elapsed between the user's initial app launch and their subsequent exit.
Number of sessions	The number of sessions played on that particular day.

Metric	Description
Sessions per user	The average number of sessions per user.
Total daily play time	The total playing time of all players on that particular day.
Daily play time per DAU	The average playing time of users who played on that particular day.
Day 1 retention	The percentage of users who returned to your game within a day.
Day 7 retention	Day 7 retention, also known as the one-week retention rate, represents the percentage of users who return to your game within a week of their initial engagement.
Day 30 retention	The percentage of users who returned to your game within 30 days.
ARPPU	Average revenue per paying user, which encompasses revenue generated from both transaction and ad impression events, where applicable.
ARPDAU	Average revenue per daily active user, which encompasses revenue generated from both transaction and ad impression events, where applicable.
Transactions	Count the total number of transactions.
Paying users	Paying users refer to the number of DAUs who made purchases on a specific day.
Revenue per transaction	Transaction amount divided by the number of transactions.
Total revenue	Total amount of all transactions.

***Table 5.3**: List of acronyms for metrics provided by Unity Technologies*

Creating a funnel

A funnel refers to a series of steps or stages that players go through in your game, from the initial engagement to a specific desired outcome, such as making a purchase or completing a level. A way to visualize and analyze the player's journey within your game.

Understanding a funnel helps game developers understand where players might be dropping off and optimize the gaming experience to improve retention and encourage desired actions.

The Unity Gaming Services may provide tools or analytics features to track and analyze player behavior throughout these funnel stages, helping developers make informed decisions to improve the overall gaming experience.

Click on **Analytics** | **Funnels** | **+ New Funnel** button:

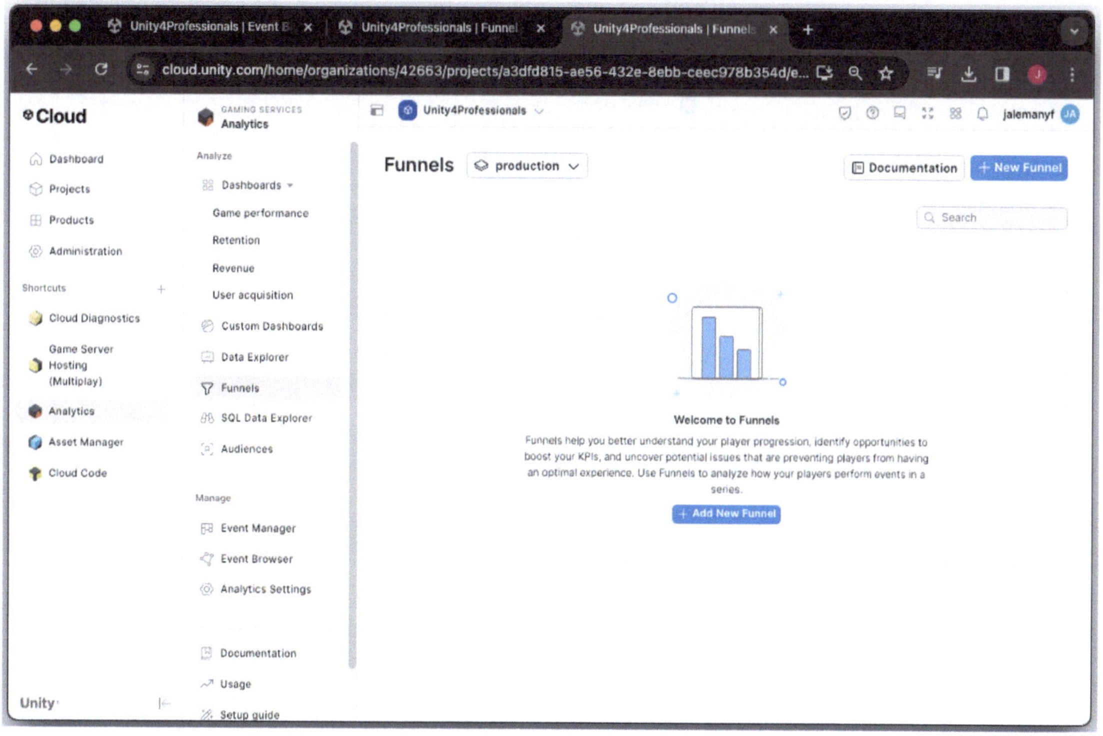

***Figure 5.19**: Creating a funnel*

Let us create the simplest funnel possible. It will only take two steps:

1. Display the options and choose **gameStart**.
2. Scroll down to the last options and select **level2** (the custom event).

Push the Apply button, and the first funnel will appear with the data you have registered:

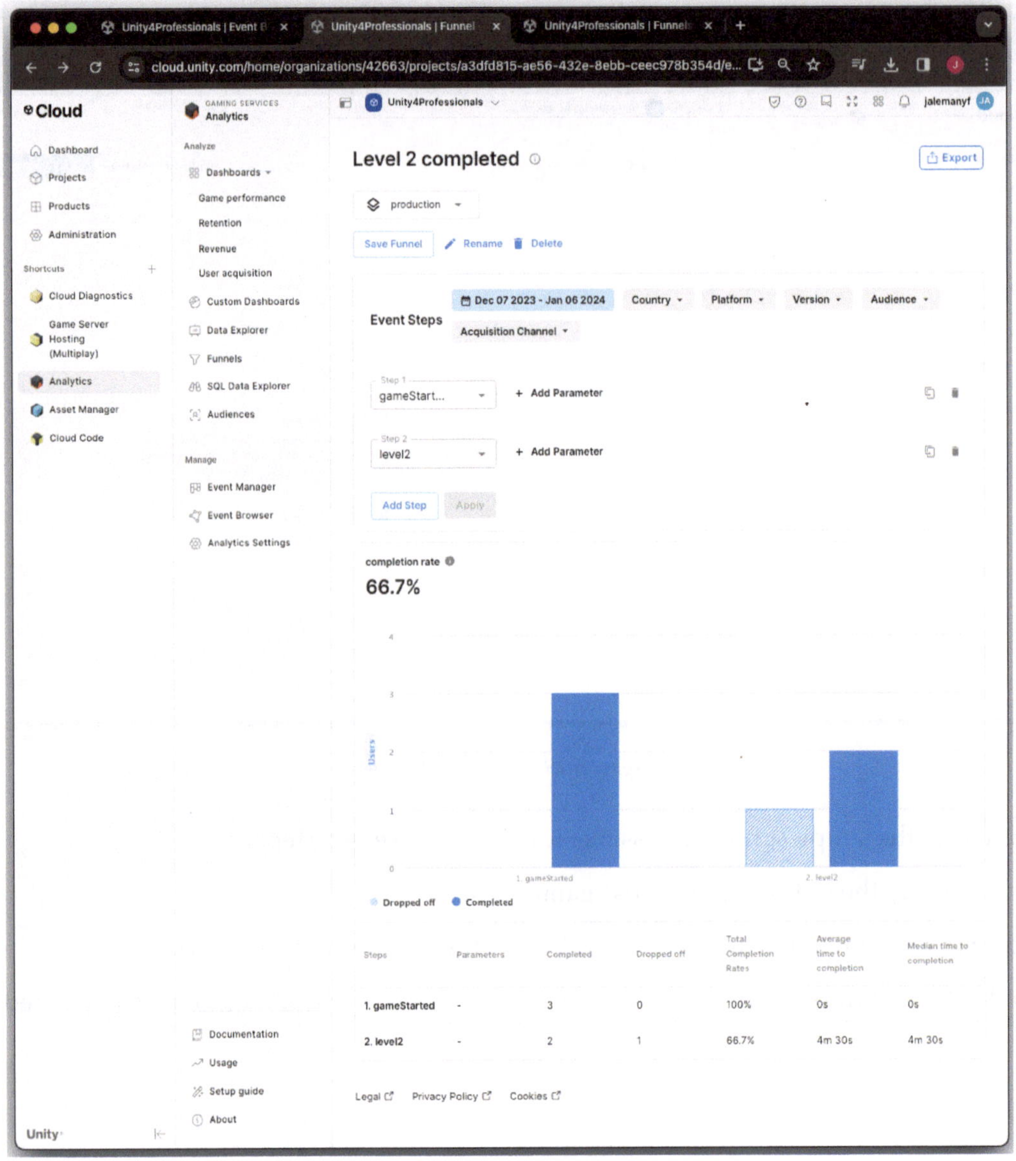

Figure 5. 20: A Funnel of the Custom Event level2

Once we have recorded a lot of data, we can extract very valuable information from it. Normally, a database is used to store the information. Unity Gaming Services has ensured that we do not have to deal with the complexity of creating a database from scratch (creating tables and relationships). It is much easier to work with events and funnels, but to make queries if you have used a language typical of relational databases.

Audiences

Audiences are categorized based on specific criteria, such as player behavior or geographical location. This allows for the targeting of audiences to personalize their gaming experience.

One can segment their Audience based on in-game behaviors, such as a recent purchase within the last few days. One can conduct an analysis of groups of players and identify potential engagement opportunities.

Predefined user metric segments can be used to filter and target players. For instance, to target a Remote Config Campaign, you can create custom Audiences based on predefined user metrics.

The standard audience includes players who are recently active, those who are just starting out, and those who have been churning. The players share their experiences with your game. You can, for instance, target unengaged gamers who only play occasionally (say, once or twice a week) with specialized game content to entice them to play more often.

The following table defines the criteria used for segmentation:

Name	Description	Criteria
Recently Active Players	Recently Active Players: This feature identifies players who have engaged in the game within the past 30 days. It encompasses the entire current player base and serves as a versatile tool for implementing generic Game Overrides, such as communicating updates to the game. The lastGameSessionEventTimestamp represents the date of the most recent player session, and it is limited to days less than or equal to 30.	lastGameSessionEventTimestamp days <= 30
All Spenders	Players who have spent real money in-game are the primary direct revenue generators for the player base. These players can be targeted for special offers or premium content. They are also useful for sweeping premium effects, such as turning off full-page ads.	Total Real Currency Spent > 0
Non-Spenders	Non-Spenders are players who have used your app but have not made any real-money purchases. You can encourage them to spend by offering targeted first-time conversion offers or displaying in-app advertisements. Their total real currency spent is zero.	Total Real Currency Spent = 0

Name	Description	Criteria
Recent Spenders	Players who have made a real money purchase within the past seven days are potential targets for repeat purchase offers or special content for recent spenders.	Last payment timestamp < 7 days
Lapsed Spenders	Players who have previously spent real money but have not made another purchase in more than 30 days may be targeted with personalized offers that provide additional value to encourage repeat business.	Last payment timestamp > 30 days
New Players	Players who have recently begun playing the game might find it helpful to receive introductory messages about the game's content, events, and time-limited in-app purchases, such as starter packs.	firstGameSessionEventTimestamp <= 2 days
Existing Players	Existing players are those who have played the game for at least two calendar days. They are ideal for sending messages about current and upcoming events, as well as time-limited offers. The lastGameSessionEventTimestamp must be less than two days old for this purpose.	lastGameSessionEventTimestamp < 2 days
Engaged Players	Players who are highly active in your game (played every day in the past week) are the core of the playerbase who are most likely to respond to calls to action messaging and offers.	Days Played Last 7 Days >= 7
Unengaged Players	Players who have shown low activity in your game (played for two or fewer days in the past week) are not completely churned, but they likely need some intervention to prevent them from completely leaving the game.	Days Played Last 7 Days <= 2
Dormant Players	Players who have been active in the game but have not played for the past 14 days are encouraged to return by receiving re-engagement calls through out-of-game messaging.	lastGameSessionEventTimestamp falls between 7 and 14.
Churned Players	Players who have not played the game for more than 14 days are likely inactive and can be re-engaged through out-of-game messaging.	lastGameSessionEventTimestamp >=l 14

Name	Description	Criteria
Veteran Players	Players who have played more than 100 sessions in their lifetime are the most likely to continue playing and promote the game. They serve as effective targets for encouraging players to rate the game and fostering social interactions.	Total Sessions Played > 100

***Table 5.4**: Predefined Audiences*

If needed, custom audiences can be created from the Audience view. Normally, the easiest way is to start with an initial audience and add conditions to filter the information.

Creating an audience

To create an audience, follow these steps in the Unity Game Services Dashboard:

1. Go to **Analytics** | **Audiences** menu and click on the top-right blue button **Create Audience**:

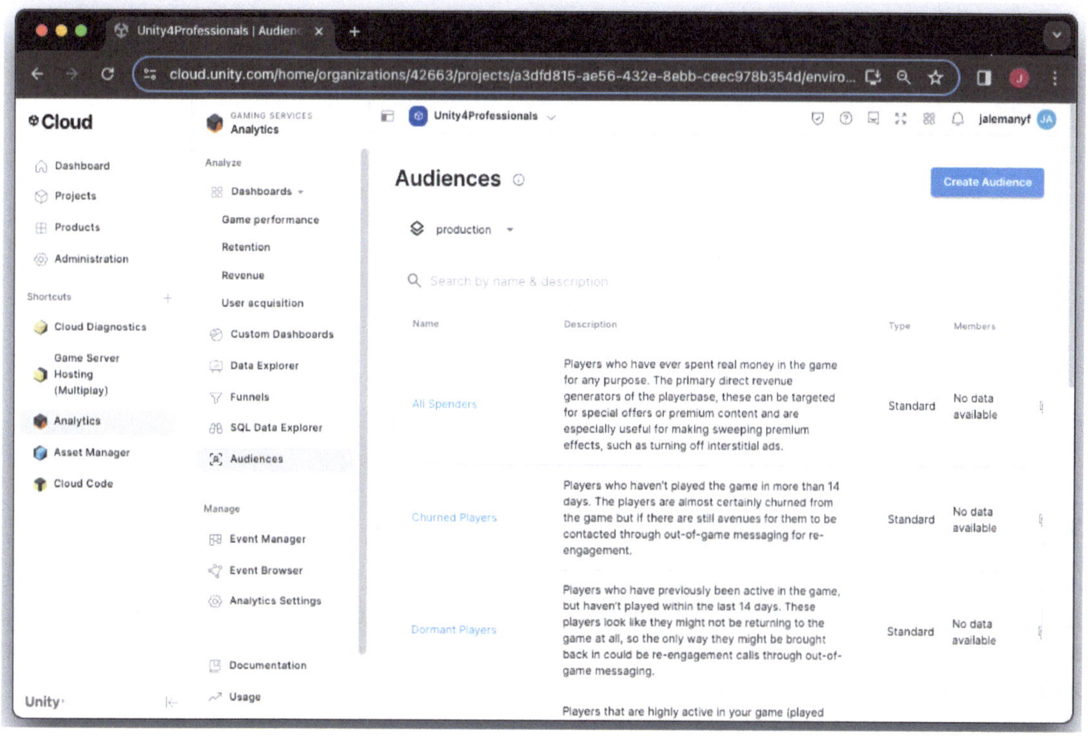

***Figure 5.21**: Analytics/Audiences panel*

An audience is a way to group users with one or more common characteristics.

In the next step, we will create an audience by filling out a form that defines the characteristics that should determine the selection.

2. Go to **Analytics | Audiences** menu and click on the top-right blue button **Create Audience.** Fill in the fields and create an audience:

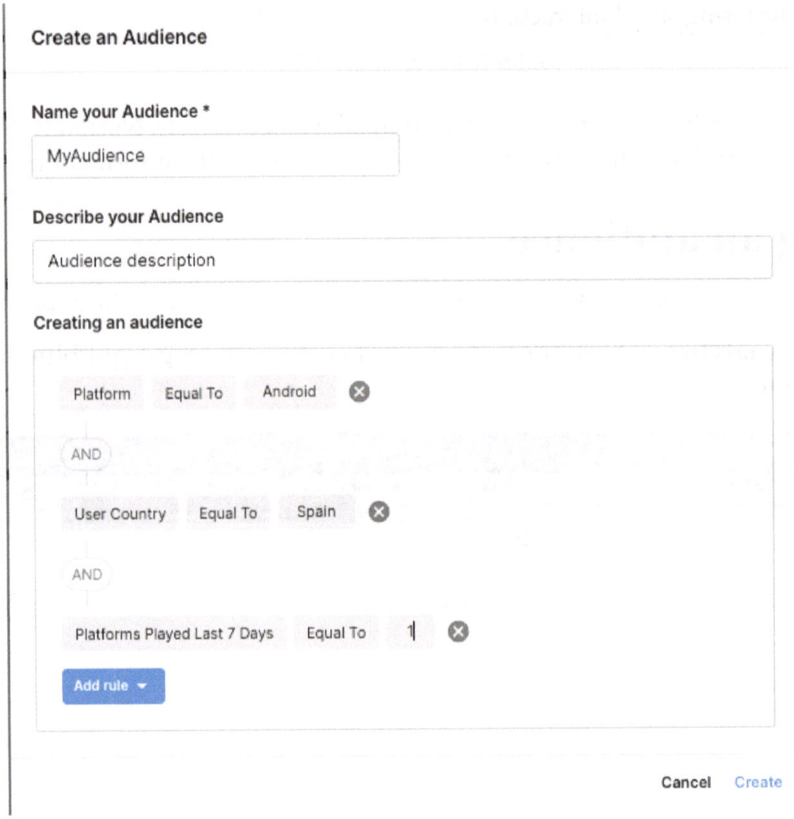

Figure 5.22: Form to fill in the fields and create an audience

SQL Data Explorer

Utilize SQL Data Explorer to generate and execute read-only SQL queries on your data, display the results in various visualizations, and incorporate them into a dashboard. You will gain insights that might not be available from other Analytics products. To get started using the query editor, follow these steps:

1. Go to **Analytics | SQL Explorer** menu.
2. Be sure that the data is updated and then click the **Run** button on the up-right of the query window:

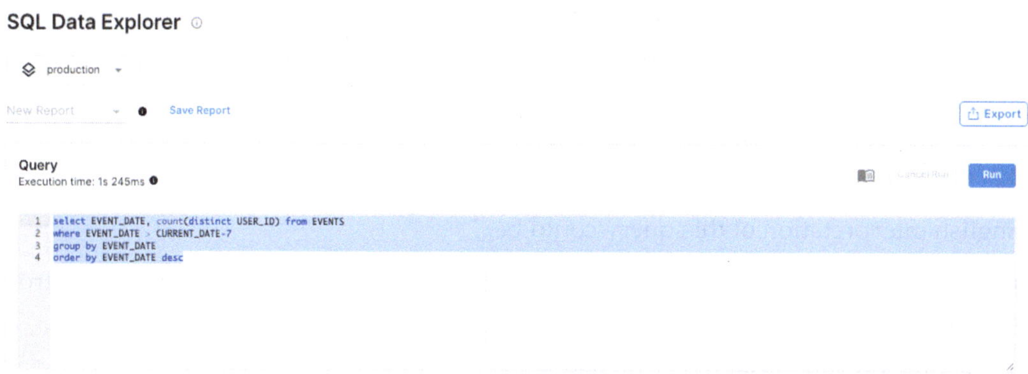

***Figure 5.23**: SQL Explorer with a query and the Run button*

3. In the **Chart Setup** select what value will be seen in each of the axes of the graph and click on the **Apply** button.

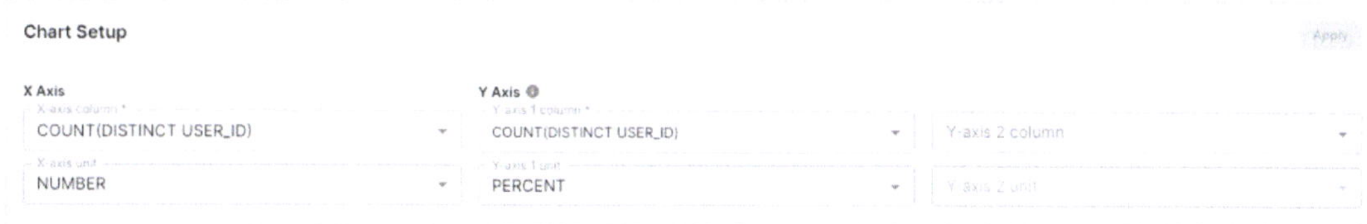

***Figure 5.24**: Selecting what value will be seen in each of the axes of the graph in the Chart Setup*

4. Finally, you will be able to see a graph of the processed data and also a table with the required information:

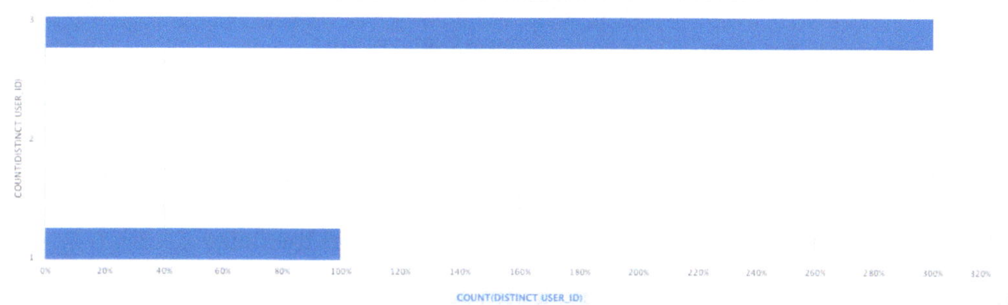

***Figure 5.25**: A graph of the processed data and a table with the required information from the SQL Data Explorer*

Structured Query Language

Structured Query Language (SQL), is a programming language designed for managing and manipulating relational databases. It is used by developers, database administrators, and analysts to interact with databases in a wide range of applications, from websites to business applications.

Let us see what a simple query looks like:

```
select EVENT_DATE, count(distinct USER_ID) from EVENTS
where EVENT_DATE > CURRENT_DATE-7
group by EVENT_DATE
order by EVENT_DATE desc
```

An English interpretation of this query could be:

- Select the **EVENT_DATE** and **USER** fields (count the number of different users) from the **EVENTS** table.
- Events must be from the last week.
- grouped by event date.
- Sorted in descending order by the date of the event.

As you can see, SQL is a high-level language that is very easy to understand (although it can get complicated with complex queries).

Unity Gaming Services uses an SQL dialect called Snowflake. You can find all the documentation here:

https://docs.snowflake.com/en/guides-overview-queriesExporting results

The data obtained by the queries can also be exported in two formats: PNG and CSV:

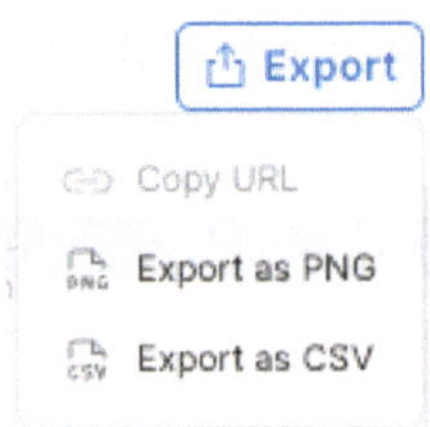

Figure 5.26*: Illustrates the button to export the data in the SQL Data Explorer*

Above the Query window on the right is the button to export the data.

If exported as PNG, the graph will be saved on your computer as an image (this can be useful to put it in a report without having to take screenshots and crop).

If exported as CSV, it will be saved as a text file separated by commas. Normally, this type of file is used to later import that information into spreadsheets or external databases.

Programming SQL queries

The objective of this book is not to teach SQL programming, but here are some references to other interesting books to learn this language from our publisher. There are more books, like the following, but they usually use some proprietary database engine:

- *SQL in 7 days* (**https://bpbonline.com/products/sql-in-7-days?_pos=2&_sid=ed846c30f&_ss=r**)
- *SQL and NoSQL Interview Questions* (**https://bpbonline.com/products/sql-and-nosql-interview-questions?_pos=7&_sid=ed846c30f&_ss=r**)
- *Learn SQL with MySQL* (**https://bpbonline.com/products/sql-with-mysql-relational-database-book-ebook?_pos=5&_sid=ed846c30f&_ss=r**)

We are going to see some query examples that are very useful when you have a very successful game:

- Added players per hour in local time zone:

```
SELECT DATE_PART('hour', EVENT_TIMESTAMP) AS localHour,
    COUNT(DISTINCT USER_ID) AS UniqueUsers
FROM EVENTS
GROUP BY localHour
ORDER BY localHour
```

  The environment is very versatile. The following figure shows how we apply the SQL query and then adjust which data we prefer to see on each of the axes:

***Figure 5.27**: Pie Chart of the average session length by session number*

- Median and average session length:

```
--Gets session data
WITH data AS (
    SELECT MIN(EVENT_DATE) AS eventDate,
        EVENT_JSON:sessionID::STRING AS sessionID,
        USER_ID,
        SUM(EVENT_JSON:msSinceLastEvent::INTEGER) AS sessionDurationMs,
        COUNT(*) AS eventCount
    FROM EVENTS
    GROUP BY sessionID, USER_ID
),

--Aggregates for median value
medianValues AS (
    SELECT *,
        MEDIAN(sessionDurationMs) OVER (PARTITION BY eventDate) AS medianSessionTime
    FROM data
    WHERE eventCount > 1
)

--Further aggregates data
SELECT eventDate,
    ROUND(AVG(sessionDurationMs)/1000, 2.0) AS "Mean session time in seconds",
    ROUND(medianSessionTime/1000, 2.0) AS "Median session time in seconds",
    COUNT(DISTINCT USER_ID) AS "Sample size users",
    COUNT(DISTINCT sessionID) AS "Sample size sessions"
FROM medianValues
GROUP BY eventDate, medianSessionTime
ORDER BY eventDate DESC
```

- Average session length by session number:

```
-- Gets session data
-- Conditional change event pulls out the sessionID only when it has changed from the last occurrence
WITH sessions AS (
```

```
    SELECT USER_ID,
        EVENT_JSON:sessionID::STRING AS sessionID,
        EVENT_TIMESTAMP,
        EVENT_NAME,
        EVENT_JSON:msSinceLastEvent::INTEGER AS msSinceLastEvent,
        -- Conditional change event pulls out the session-ID only when it has changed from the last occurrence
        CONDITIONAL_CHANGE_EVENT(EVENT_JSON:sessionID) OVER (PARTITION BY USER_ID ORDER BY EVENT_ID) + 1 AS sessionCounter
    FROM EVENTS
    WHERE sessionID IS NOT NULL
        AND msSinceLastEvent IS NOT NULL
),

-- Aggregates session data
session_aggregates AS (
    SELECT MAX(USER_ID) AS userID,
        MIN(EVENT_TIMESTAMP),
        sessionID,
        sessionCounter,
        SUM(msSinceLastEvent) AS msSessionLength,
        COUNT(*) AS eventCount
        FROM sessions
        GROUP BY sessionID,
                sessionCounter
)

-- Further aggregates data
SELECT
    sessionCounter AS sessionNumber,
    COUNT(*) AS sessionsCounted,
    ROUND(AVG(msSessionLength) / 60000, 2.0) :: FLOAT AS avgSessionLengthMinutes
FROM session_aggregates
GROUP BY sessionCounter
ORDER BY sessionCounter
```

The following figures aim to illustrate the many possibilities that the platform has to show us information in a simple and, above all, highly configurable way:

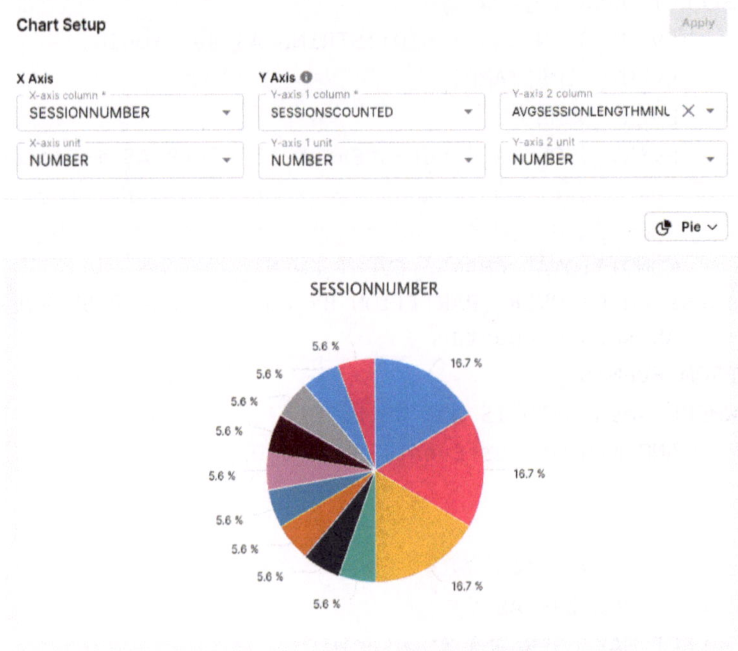

Figure 5.28: Pie chart of the Query

The following figure shows additional information:

Figure 5.29: Area chart of the Query

- New player retention matrix:

```
-- Gathers user activity data and calculates user retention.
WITH days_data AS (
    SELECT
        USER_ID,
        PLAYER_START_DATE AS install_date,
        EVENT_DATE
    FROM FACT_USER_SESSIONS_DAY
    WHERE PLAYER_START_DATE >= CURRENT_DATE - 30
)
SELECT
    install_date,
    COUNT(DISTINCT CASE WHEN EVENT_DATE = install_date THEN USER_
ID END) AS installs,
    COUNT(DISTINCT CASE WHEN EVENT_DATE = install_date + 1 THEN USER_
ID END) AS day_1,
    COUNT(DISTINCT CASE WHEN EVENT_DATE = install_date + 2 THEN USER_
ID END) AS day_2,
    COUNT(DISTINCT CASE WHEN EVENT_DATE = install_date + 3 THEN USER_
ID END) AS day_3,
    COUNT(DISTINCT CASE WHEN EVENT_DATE = install_date + 4 THEN USER_
ID END) AS day_4,
    COUNT(DISTINCT CASE WHEN EVENT_DATE = install_date + 5 THEN USER_
ID END) AS day_5,
    COUNT(DISTINCT CASE WHEN EVENT_DATE = install_date + 6 THEN USER_
ID END) AS day_6,
    COUNT(DISTINCT CASE WHEN EVENT_DATE = install_date + 7 THEN USER_
ID END) AS day_7,
    COUNT(DISTINCT CASE WHEN EVENT_DATE = install_date + 8 THEN USER_
ID END) AS day_8,
    COUNT(DISTINCT CASE WHEN EVENT_DATE = install_date + 9 THEN USER_
ID END) AS day_9,
    COUNT(DISTINCT CASE WHEN EVENT_DATE = install_date + 10 THEN USER_
ID END) AS day_10,
    COUNT(DISTINCT CASE WHEN EVENT_DATE = install_date + 11 THEN USER_
ID END) AS day_11,
```

```
    COUNT(DISTINCT CASE WHEN EVENT_DATE = install_date + 12 THEN USER_
ID END) AS day_12,
    COUNT(DISTINCT CASE WHEN EVENT_DATE = install_date + 13 THEN USER_
ID END) AS day_13,
    COUNT(DISTINCT CASE WHEN EVENT_DATE = install_date + 14 THEN USER_
ID END) AS day_14,
    COUNT(DISTINCT CASE WHEN EVENT_DATE = install_date + 21 THEN USER_
ID END) AS day_21,
    COUNT(DISTINCT CASE WHEN EVENT_DATE = install_date + 30 THEN USER_
ID END) AS day_30
FROM days_data
WHERE EVENT_DATE BETWEEN install_date AND install_date + 30
GROUP BY install_date
ORDER BY install_date DESC;
```

D28 Churn versus D28 Rolling Retention

Rolling retention, a more nuanced and dynamic metric, highlights continuous user engagement. Unlike traditional user retention, which measures users over fixed time frames, rolling retention calculates the percentage of users who remain active from a specific point in time, irrespective of their initial usage duration.

The formula for calculating rolling retention is as follows:

*Day N rolling retention = (Number of users who opened the application on day N or later / Number of users who installed the application N days ago) * 100%*

The following SQL code allows us to group users who have played in the last 28 days. This way, we can separate those who are registered from those who are still playing:

```
-- Participates in active player days and compiles activity data for the team.
WITH activity_data AS (
    SELECT
        PLAYER_START_DATE,
        EVENT_DATE,
        EVENT_DATE - PLAYER_START_DATE AS n,
        USER_ID
    FROM FACT_USER_SESSIONS_DAY
```

```
    WHERE PLAYER_START_DATE > CURRENT_DATE - 60 AND EVENT_DATE > CURRENT_
DATE - 60
)
SELECT
    PLAYER_START_DATE,
    COUNT(DISTINCT USER_ID) AS installs,
    COUNT(DISTINCT CASE WHEN n >= 28 THEN USER_ID END) AS d28Retained,
    COUNT(DISTINCT CASE WHEN n >= 28 THEN USER_
ID END) * 100.0 / COUNT(DISTINCT USER_ID) AS d28RollingRetention,
    100.0 - (COUNT(DISTINCT CASE WHEN n >= 28 THEN USER_
ID END) * 100.0 / COUNT(DISTINCT USER_ID)) AS d28Churn
FROM activity_data
GROUP BY PLAYER_START_DATE
ORDER BY PLAYER_START_DATE;
```

When you see the SQL code, you probably wonder how you can know the names of the fields that are defined in the tables. To know the exact name, you must do the following steps:

1. Click on the button with a red circle, shown in the following figure:

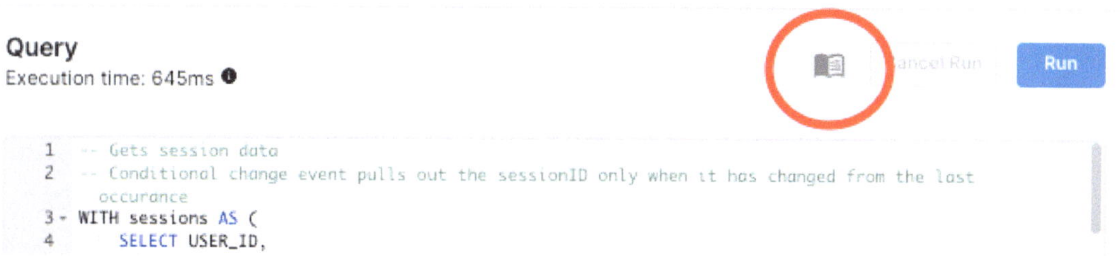

Figure 5.30: *Button (with a red circle) to see the defined tables and their fields in the SQL Data Explorer*

2. This will open a window where each of the defined tables can be displayed with all its fields and the type of data that each field contains. It helps a lot when we create our own queries:

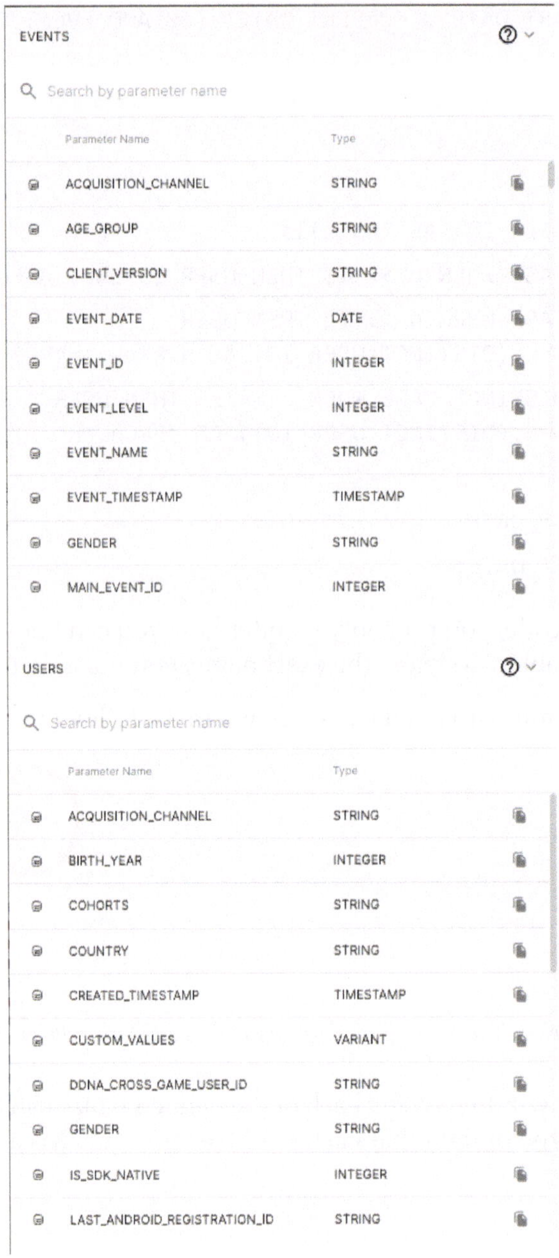

***Figure 5.31:** Defined tables with their fields and their data types in the SQL Data Explorer*

Conclusion

This chapter, which equipped you with the skills to collect, store, and analyze game data using the Analytics System. The next chapter will explore how these analytical capabilities can be applied to understand and improve the journey of your players from their initial discovery of the game to becoming loyal customers. This will involve examining key stages of the player lifecycle, including acquisition, engagement, monetization, retention, churn, and reactivation. The chapter will also delve into how analytics enables data-driven decisions for user experience improvement, covering topics such as retention strategies, understanding audiences for targeted experiences, different monetization approaches, the use of funnels to visualize player progression, and the importance of engagement data. Ultimately, the next chapter will provide methods for applying player data and feedback to positively evolve the user's experience within your game.

Multiple choice questions

1. **What is the primary characteristic and purpose of Environments in the Analytics System?**
    a. They define the hardware specifications of the cloud servers.
    b. They are logical partitions that are isolated from each other, allowing developers to test changes in development without affecting the production data.
    c. They are used to manage billing and cost allocation for different regions.
    d. They are essential for activating standard automated events like gameEnded.
2. **Which two events are automatically logged by UGS upon the initialization of the Analytics service within the application?**
    a. mission3_completed and transactionFailed
    b. newPlayer and ddnaForgetMe
    c. gameStarted and gameRunning
    d. adImpression and aquisitionSource
3. **When defining a Custom Event or its Parameters, what are the restrictions regarding the naming convention?**
    a. The name must be unique globally and contain only numeric characters.
    b. The name must be composed solely of English alphanumeric characters and underscore characters, and must commence with a letter.
    c. The name can include spaces, but must not exceed 25 characters.
    d. Only C# variable names are accepted, regardless of character type.

4. **What is the maximum number of parameters a developer is permitted to add to an environment?**
   a. 30 parameters
   b. 100 parameters
   c. 500 parameters
   d. 1,500 parameters
5. **What is the primary function of the Data Explorer tool in UGS Analytics?**
   a. To create and manage SQL tables and relationships.
   b. To run asynchronous code modules in the cloud.
   c. To manipulate and analyze game data by applying filters and events, and grouping the data by dimension for visualization (e.g., using bar charts, line graphs, or pie charts).
   d. To manually send ad impressions to the server.
6. **In the Data Explorer, what information can a developer determine by using the Group by function with the Platform and Country filters combined?**
   a. The server latency of their nearest data center.
   b. A real market study regarding user behaviour in specific geographical regions and on certain platforms.
   c. The total revenue generated by all paying users (ARPPU).
   d. The list of users who have been categorized as Churned Players.
7. **What is the specific analytical purpose of utilizing Funnels in the Analytics System?**
   a. To execute SQL queries on the data.
   b. To manage the in-game economy and reward distribution.
   c. To visualize and analyze the player's journey within the game and identify potential drop-off points between stages.
   d. To export data in PNG or CSV format.
8. **When performing advanced data analysis, what SQL dialect is used within the SQL Data Explorer tool?**
   a. **Transact-SQL (T-SQL)**
   b. Oracle PL/SQL

c. MySQL

d. Snowflake

9. **What is the definition of the predefined audience All Spenders?**

   a. Players who have played every day in the past week (Days Played Last 7 Days >= 7).

   b. Players who have spent real money in-game (Total Real Currency Spent > 0).

   c. Players who have made a purchase within the last seven days.

   d. Players who have played for at least two calendar days.

10. **In the simplest C# script used to initiate UGS Analytics, what is the correct sequence of asynchronous calls necessary to start collecting data?**

    a. Call AnalyticsService.Instance.Flush() followed by print("Initializing UGServices...").

    b. Call AnalyticsService.Instance.StartDataCollection() followed by await UnityServices.InitializeAsync().

    c. Call await UnityServices.InitializeAsync() followed by AnalyticsService.Instance.StartDataCollection().

    d. Call Debug.LogException followed by AnalyticsService.Instance.CustomData.

Answers

1	b
2	c
3	b
4	d
5	c
6	b
7	c
8	d
9	b
10	c

Join our Discord space

Join our Discord workspace for latest updates, offers, tech happenings around the world, new releases, and sessions with the authors:

https://discord.bpbonline.com

CHAPTER 6
Optimizing Player Lifecycle with Analytics

Introduction

Analytics is a critical component of game development, providing game developers with the insights they need to understand their players and improve their games. In this chapter, we are going to explore how analytics can help game developers to optimise the player lifecycle, from acquisition to retention and monetization.

The player lifecycle is a key concept in game development, describing the journey that players take from discovering a game to becoming a loyal customer. Analytics can help game developers to optimise each stage of the player lifecycle, from understanding how players discover their game to identifying which features keep players engaged and which ones cause them to churn.

One of the key advantages of analytics is that it enables game developers to make data-driven decisions. By analyzing player behavior and engagement data, game developers can discern patterns and trends that guide their development decisions. For instance, they can ascertain which features are most favored by players and accordingly prioritize their development.

Analytics can aid game developers in pinpointing and resolving player experience issues, such as high churn rates or low conversion rates. By comprehending the underlying causes of these problems, game developers can make necessary modifications to enhance the player experience, thereby boosting player retention and monetization.

Overall, analytics is a potent tool that empowers game developers to optimize the player lifecycle and enhance their games. By offering game developers the necessary insights, analytics enables them to make data-driven decisions, leading to the creation of captivating and immersive games that retain players' engagement and loyalty.

Structure

The chapter covers the following topics:

- Player lifecycle
- Analytics
- Retention

- Audiences
- Monetization
- Funnels
    - o Sample funnels
    - o Reasons funnels are important
- Engagement data
- User experience improvement
- Data-driven decisions for user experience improvement
- Sample Dashboard

Objectives

The objectives of this chapter are to learn specific methods for applying player data and feedback to improve the user experience within the game.

We are going to tailor game offerings to different demographic groups and player preferences, develop a detailed understanding of how to guide players from initial acquisition to long-term retention, demonstrate how to use the obtained information to make informed decisions, and optimize the player experience.

First, we are going to explain some concepts that will be necessary.

Player lifecycle

The foremost step is to understand how users interact and use our game. The whole process is called the **player lifecycle**.

It is the various stages or phases that a player goes through during their interaction with a game. These stages typically include the following:

- **Onboarding** or installation is the initial phase in which players download and install the game. The process encompasses the creation of an account, the configuration of preferences, and comprehending the fundamental principles of the game.
- The **engagement** phase involves players actively participating in the game. They may be completing levels, achieving goals, or interacting with different features. The goal of the game is to keep them interested and engaged.
- **Monetization** involves any interactions related to in-game purchases or ads. Players are free to spend money on virtual items, upgrades, or other premium features.
- The retention strategy focuses on maintaining players' interest and ensuring their continued engagement with the game over time. Developers often implement features such as new content, rewards, or events to keep the experience fresh and enjoyable.

- **Churn or attrition** refers to the stage where players stop playing a game. Developers must understand why players leave and address those issues to improve player retention.
- If a player has stopped playing, the **reactivation** phase involves attempts to bring them back into the game. This could encompass updates, novel content, exclusive events, or individualized incentives.

Now that we know the stages a player goes through, we will have to measure how many players we have in each stage and try to maintain the maximum number of players for as long as possible.

Analytics

In the previous chapter, we looked at how analytics allows events to be recorded in the cloud and stored in a database. The following information is very valuable and explains how our project is working in the market:

- How many users have registered?
- How many of them opened the app again afterward?
- Do they really use it, or was it just a one-day curiosity?

One of the most used measures to know how well a game performs is called **daily active users** (**DAU**). As we have seen in the stages, there are many users who register but then do not play or who only play a few times and then abandon the game. For this reason, it is important to know how many users really play daily.

Analytics provides a series of pre-built reports that help a lot to obtain the information. Navigate to **Analytics** | **Dashboards** | **Game Performance**:

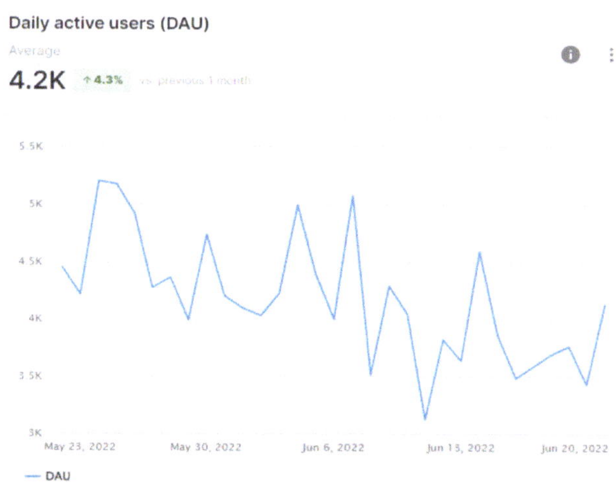

***Figure 6.1**: The best way to know how many users play every day*

These reports are:

- **Daily new users**: The number of players who have transmitted data from your game for the initial time on each calendar day. You can see from this chart how many new players have started playing your game. This data is not available through the app stores, since it is only available through the app stores.
- **Daily active users (DAU)**: The number of players in your game. A player who initiates a session is an active player. The number of players present on each calendar day is the DAU.
- **Monthly new users**: Number of players who have sent data from your game for the first time each calendar month. You can find this chart to see how many new players have started playing your game.
- **Weekly and monthly active users (WAU and MAU)**: The number of players who have transmitted data from your game for the first time, in each calendar month. Utilize this graph to determine the number of new players who have commenced playing your game.

In addition to knowing if the user enters each day, it is very important to know how long they stay in our app (in a free-to-play model, this means more ads and, therefore, more income):

- **Session length**: The average duration that players spend in a single gameplay session. Use this chart to see how long players are playing your game and how those changes over time.

  For example, in the following figure, you can see that the average session duration is about 6 minutes and is experiencing a decrease of -14.3% (approximately one minute) compared to the previous month:

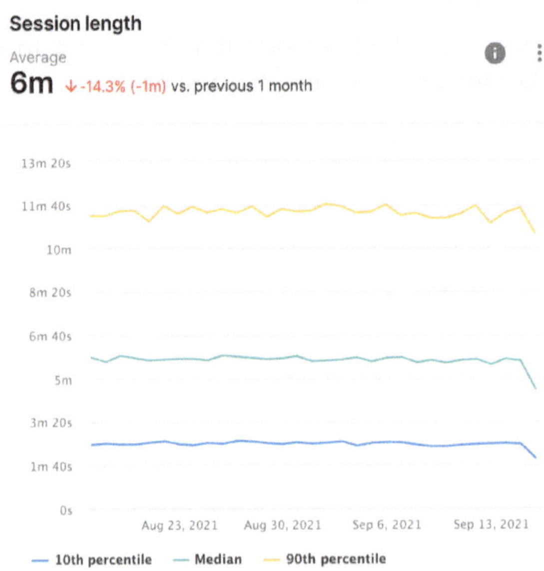

***Figure 6.2:** The session length to know how much time the users spend on your app*

When making statistics of this type, it is important to eliminate sessions that last too short (for example, less than three seconds) and those that last too long (for example, more than four hours) to avoid the average being biased by improbable durations of the sessions.

- **Session per DAU**: The number of sessions per DAU. Utilize this graph to determine the average number of sessions played by your players on a daily basis.

  For example, an average number of sessions per DAU of fifteen users on May 13th means active players played an average of fifteen times each day.

There are more default reports to explore on the Analytics Dashboard's navigation menu. They provide detailed information on revenue, retention, and user acquisition. The Data Explorer, Custom Dashboard, funnels, and SQL Data Explorer tools let you create your own charts.

Retention

Retention refers to the ability of a game to keep players engaged and returning for an extended period of time. It is a key performance indicator in the gaming industry, reflecting sustained player interest and overall game success. High retention rates suggest that players enjoy the game and play it regularly, while low retention rates indicate problems that require attention. If your active install count starts to decline, as shown in the following figure, you will need to introduce incentives to keep players playing your game.

Note: It is important to act before users stop using your app.

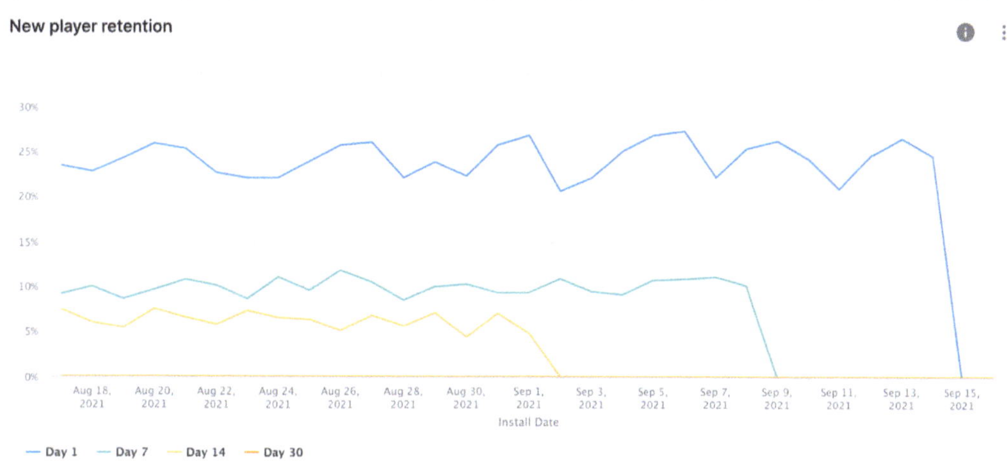

***Figure 6.3**: Number of segmented installations achieved*

The following figure visualizes the duration of player interaction within the app over time. Our goal should be to retain the player as long as possible.

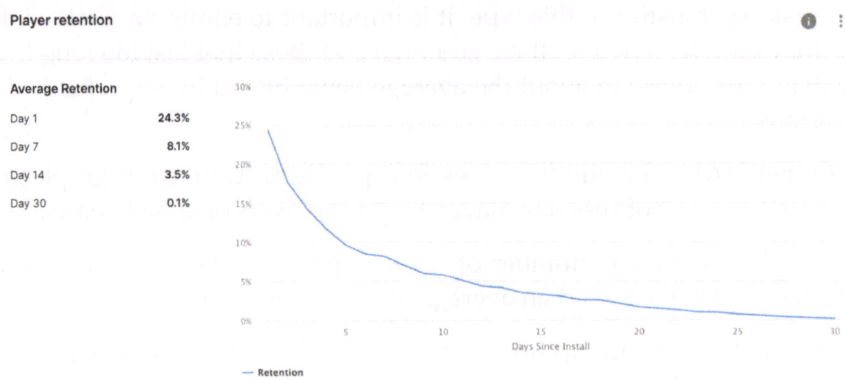

***Figure 6.4**: The retention shows how many users are active over the time*

In order to keep players interested, game developers often implement retention strategies. Several strategies may include introducing new content, running special events, offering rewards, providing social features, and addressing player feedback to enhance the overall gaming experience.

Audiences

Audiences are individuals who are categorized based on certain criteria, such as player behavior or geographical location. The ability to target audiences to personalize their gaming experience is available.

We had seen what audiences are previously, but now we want to highlight how audiences are used for the segmentation of active users.

It is possible to categorize audiences based on factors like player behavior or location. This allows for personalized game experiences by targeting specific audiences.

One can segment their audience based on in-game behaviors, such as recent purchases made within the past seven days. By analyzing groups of players, you can identify potential opportunities for engagement.

Unity has some pre-made audiences that are very useful. The standard audiences are detailed as follows:

Name	Description	Criteria
Recently active players	This group together all players who have joined the game in the last 30 days. This is an easy way to contact current players. It is often used to inform players about changes to the game.	lastGameSessionEventTimestamp days <= 30

Name	Description	Criteria
All spenders	Players who have spent real money in the game are the main direct income generators. They are ideal for offering them premium content or some special offer.	Total Real Currency Spent >0
Non-spenders	Players who, although they play, have never spent real money. They should be offered deals to get them to make their first purchase or to allow ads within the App in order to avoid paying.	Total Real Currency Spent = 0
Recent spenders	Players who have made a real-money purchase in the past seven days are potential targets for repeat or complementary purchase offers to their previous purchase.	Last payment timestamp < 7 days ago
Lapsed spenders	Players who spent real money more than 30 days ago may receive personalized offers that provide additional value to encourage repeat purchases.	Last payment timestamp > 30 days ago
New players	Players who have just started playing may find it helpful to receive introductory messages about in-game content, events, and limited-time in-app purchases such as starter packs.	firstGameSessionEventTimestamp <= 2 days ago
Existing players	Players who have been playing the game for the past two days. This feature is very useful for sending messages about current and upcoming events, trying to get them engaged in the game.	lastGameSessionEventTimestamp < 2 days ago
Engaged players	Players who are highly active in their game (played every day last week) are the core of the player base that is most likely to respond to call-to-action messages and offers.	Days Played Last 7 Days >= 7
Unengaged players	Players who have shown low activity in your game (playing for two days or less in the last week) are not completely abandoned, but they likely need some intervention to prevent them from leaving the game and turning back.	Days Played Last 7 Days <= 2

Name	Description	Criteria
Dormant players	Players who have been active in the game but have not played for the past 14 days are encouraged to come back by receiving reactivation calls through out-of-game messages such as push notifications.	lastGameSessionEventTimestamp between 7 and 14 days
Churned players	Players who have not played the game for more than 14 days are likely inactive and can be contacted again via out-of-game messages.	lastGameSessionEventTimestamp >= 14
Veteran players	Players who have played more than 100 sessions are the most likely to continue playing and promoting the game. They are effective targets to encourage players to rate the game and invite friends to play as well.	Total Sessions Played > 100

***Table 6.1**: Predefined audiences*

The predefined audiences are really useful but cannot be edited. If you need a different audience, it must be created with **custom audiences**:

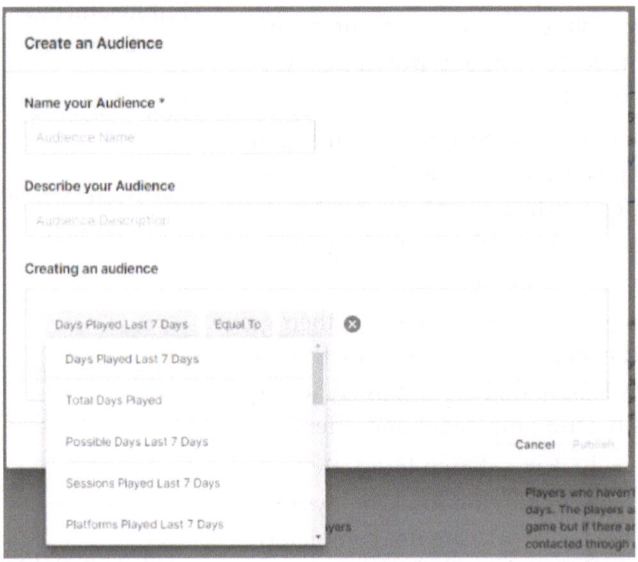

***Figure 6.5**: Interface for creating custom audiences within Unity Analytics*

The following figure shows the form where you can select the criteria for generating the chart. Multiple conditions can be added graphically (without having to program them in SQL). The power and versatility of the dashboard will allow you to customize it with all types of queries:

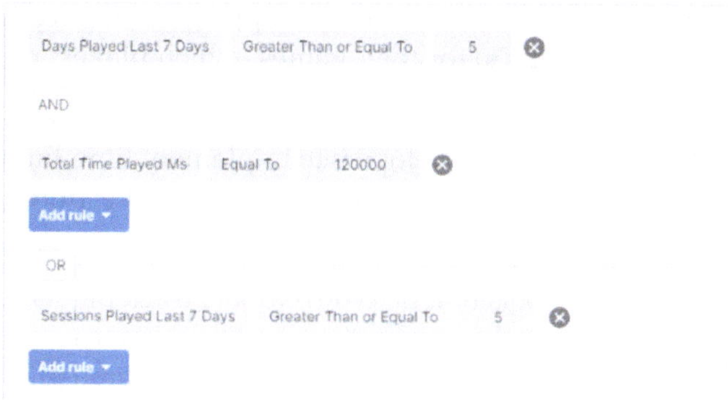

***Figure 6.6**: Detailed view of custom audience creation options and filters in Unity Analytics*

Monetization

The process of generating revenue from a game. Game developers employ a variety of strategies and mechanisms to contribute to the financial success of their games.

Unity Gaming Services provide a range of tools and features that enable developers to employ diverse monetization strategies. The following are some key aspects of monetization in Unity Gaming Services:

- One common form of monetization involves enabling players to make in-game purchases. This can include purchases of virtual items, power-ups, cosmetic enhancements, or other premium content. Unity provides a framework for seamlessly implementing in-app purchases.
- Ad integration is an alternative method of monetizing games, which involves the utilization of advertisements. Developers are able to integrate advertising networks into their games, displaying video, banner, or interstitial ads. Unity provides support for various ad networks, making it easier for developers to implement and manage ad monetization.
- Several games offer subscription-based models, where players pay a regular fee to access premium features, exclusive content, or other benefits. Unity supports the implementation of subscription-based marketing strategies.
- Unity Gaming Services permit developers to incorporate rewarded advertisements, wherein players can opt to view an advertisement on their own initiative in exchange for in-game rewards. A non-intrusive way to monetize while also offering something valuable to players.
- Games often have their own virtual currency systems, which players can purchase with real money. Using these virtual currencies, you can then purchase in-game items or upgrades.

- Developers have the ability to create supplementary content or expansions **Dowloadable Content** (**DLCs**) for their games, which players can acquire to enhance their gameplay experience.
- Unity Gaming Services enable developers to implement time-limited offers, discounts, and promotions in order to encourage players to make purchases during specific periods.
- Unity provides analytics tools that help developers track player behavior and analyze spending patterns. These tools can also be used to optimize monetization strategies. It is possible for developers to experiment with different monetization approaches and determine which ones are more effective.

Funnels

In the context of game development and analytics, a funnel refers to a series of steps or stages that players go through from the initial engagement with the game to achieving a specific goal or conversion. Each step in the funnel represents a key interaction or event in the player's journey, and the funnel as a whole provides a visual representation of how players move through these stages.

The funnels tool contains:

- A bar graph that shows how far you have fallen as you move.
- Table showing the number of users in each step, the percentage of users dropping off, and the average time users spend between each step.
- The ability to export the table and chart.

Sample funnels

The completion of a tutorial is one of the most common funnel types. Since the tutorial is one of the first things players see in the game, your players will decide if the core gameplay is what they want out of your game. This funnel helps you identify which tutorial steps may be confusing, too hard, or take too long to complete. It is usually a sequence of the *tutorial step started* event with the *step ID* as a parameter. To go deeper, this can be a sequence of *tutorial step started*, and *tutorial step ended* to collect information on how the player handled this tutorial step. This is done using parameters in *tutorial step ended*, for example, the time to equip the weapon, the number of tries to hit the enemy, and if the player uses a mechanic shown in a previous step:

- The level progression funnel is a basic visualization to see how players flow through your main progression mechanic. This can be a player level (role-playing game), a level completion (puzzle), or what suits your game design. This funnel will help you understand if a level is too difficult or long to complete, and where you lose most of your players. This is usually a simple sequence of your *level up* or *level completed* event.

- The feature discoverability and use of funnels challenge UX assumptions, from characters' abilities used, gear equipped, and achievements page visited. Though some features might be presented in tutorials, some players might forget about them or find them unhelpful to progress. Funnels can check if players use the features regularly.
- The first and subsequent purchases will help you understand how many players convert from non-paying to paying users and how many players are ready to pay again in your game. You can check if players received enough value from the first purchase to buy again. This is usually a sequence of transactions where the'real Currency' parameter is greater than 0. This funnel can also be used to consume ads with a sequence of adImpression events.
- Use the audience conversion funnel to target audiences with specific offers to understand how sequences of offers are converting. Tune your offer campaigns and adjust the price and rewards of each offer, identified by their names, to optimize conversion rates. This funnel is a sequence of your offer names that you expect your audience to buy.

Reasons funnels are important

Funnels are crucial in understanding and optimizing user experiences, and they are particularly important in the Unity Gaming Services framework. Here is why funnels are so important:

- **Visualizing player flow**: Funnels provide a clear and concise visual representation of how players navigate through various stages of the game. This helps developers identify potential impediments, drop-off points, or areas for enhancement.
- **Understanding player behavior is crucial for developers**: Analyzing funnel data provides valuable insights into player behavior and preferences. Understanding how players progress through various stages of the game allows us to tailor the gaming experience to meet their expectations.
- **Finding conversion points**: Funnels highlight specific conversion points or objectives, like making an app purchase, completing a challenge, or achieving a certain level. It is paramount to comprehend the manner in which players engage with the game's user interface and the revenue generation strategies employed.
- **Enhancing user initiation/user onboarding**: Funnels are particularly useful for optimizing the onboarding process. Developers can analyze how players progress from downloading the game to completing essential tutorial stages, ensuring a smooth and engaging introduction to the game.

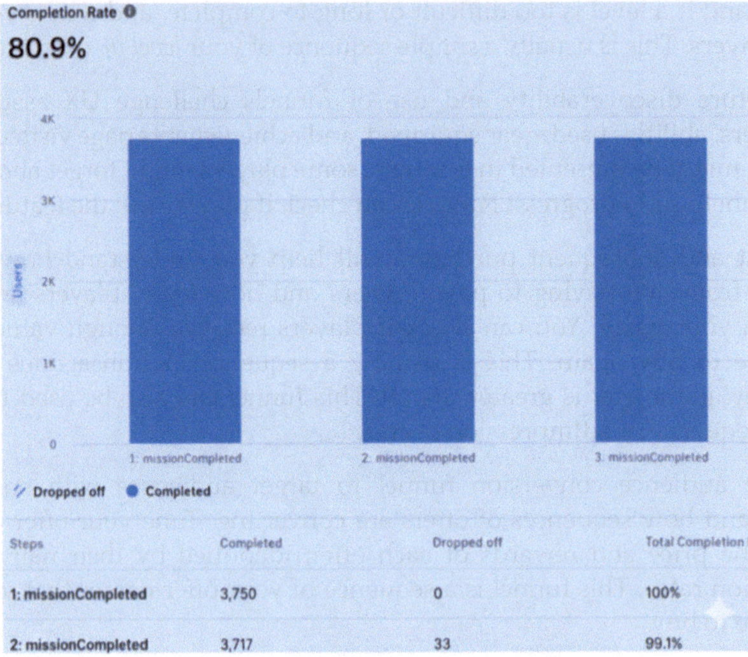

Figure 6.7: Funnel metrics sample

Engagement data

Engagement data, which encompasses information and metrics, offers valuable insights into user interactions and participation within a specific application, service, or platform. It plays a pivotal role in comprehending player behavior, preferences, and the overall user experience. This information helps developers, publishers, and analysts make informed decisions to enhance the game and optimize its performance. Of course, some of the metrics that we have already seen before are used (session duration, frequency of use, retention), but it is important not to neglect even the last detail to get the user hooked on our game. Here are some crucial aspects of engagement data:

- **Monetization analytics**: For games with monetization strategies, Unity Gaming Services provides data on in-app purchases, virtual currency transactions, and other revenue-related activities. This provides developers with an opportunity to evaluate the effectiveness of their monetization models.

- **Player feedback and ratings**: Unity Gaming Services may incorporate functionalities for gathering feedback and ratings from users. This information aids developers in assessing player satisfaction and identifying areas for enhancement.

- **User progression monitoring**: There are various game elements, such as levels, achievements, and quests. allow developers to track player progression. This data facilitates the comprehension of players' progression through the game and the potential obstacles or obstacles that may arise.
- **Social interaction metrics**: Unity Gaming Services may provide insights into social interactions within games, including features such as multiplayer interactions, guild memberships, and collaborative gameplay or social network publishing.

By utilizing engagement data within Unity Gaming Services, developers can gain a comprehensive understanding of player behavior, enabling them to make data-driven decisions to enhance gameplay experiences, optimize monetization strategies, and continually improve their games.

User experience improvement

In video games, improving player experience involves enhancing a player's satisfaction, enjoyment, and engagement over time. To quantify this improvement, two pivotal metrics are commonly employed: engagement and retention.

Engagement quantifies the level of activity and frequency with which players interact with the game. It encompasses metrics such as:

- **Session length**: The duration of a single player session.
- **Session frequency**: The regularity with which players return to play.
- **Number of actions per session**: The count of actions performed during a session, including quests completed and levels played.
- **Social interactions**: Metrics related to player communication, such as messages sent and multiplayer activity.

An increase in engagement often signifies that players are finding the game more enjoyable or rewarding.

Retention measures the percentage of players who return to the game after their initial session. Common retention metrics include the following:

- **Day 1, Day 7, and Day 30 retention**: The percentage of players who return on these specific days.
- **Churn rate**: The percentage of players who discontinue playing.

Improving retention indicates a consistent return of players, which typically indicates an overall enhancement of the player experience.

By analyzing trends in engagement and retention over time, developers can ascertain whether updates, features, or design modifications are genuinely enhancing the player experience.

Data-driven decisions for user experience improvement

The utilization of engagement data in Unity Gaming Services for data-driven decision-making necessitates a meticulous methodology for scrutinizing the gathered data and implementing enhancements to the user experience. Here is a comprehensive guide that provides a step-by-step approach to utilizing engagement data to enhance user experience within the Unity Gaming Services framework:

1. **Establishing key performance indicators (KPIs)**: Identify the KPIs that align with your game's objectives. This could include metrics such as player retention, in-app purchases, completion rates, and social interactions.
2. **Collect and analyze data**: Use Unity Analytics or other analytics tools integrated into Unity Gaming Services to collect data on player behavior, events, and interactions. Analyze this data in order to identify patterns, trends, and areas for improvement.
3. **Identify pain points**: It is imperative to identify specific aspects of the user experience that may be posing challenges for players. Look for areas where engagement is low or where player feedback highlights issues.
4. **Ensure that the onboarding process is optimized**: Use engagement data to understand how players are progressing through the onboarding process. It is a must to streamline tutorials, furnish precise instructions, and ensure that novice players are able to swiftly grasp the fundamental principles of the game.
5. **Enhance game balancing**: To identify any imbalances or difficulty spikes, analyze player progression data. Adjust the game mechanics, levels, or challenges to ensure a more seamless and pleasurable progression path.
6. **Improve player experiences by personalizing them**: Utilize player segmentation based on engagement data to deliver personalized experiences. To improve overall engagement, tailor in-game offers, rewards, and challenges to specific player segments.
7. **Optimize your monetization strategies**: Utilize monetization analytics to improve your in-app purchase strategies. Identify successful monetization strategies and adjust pricing or offerings in accordance with player behavior and preferences.
8. **Ensure timely updates are implemented**: Regularly update the game based on the insights gleaned from engagement data. To maintain player interest over time, we must address player concerns, introduce new content, and keep the gaming experience fresh.
9. **Engage in social interaction**: Utilize social interaction metrics to enhance multiplayer experiences or collaborative gameplay. Introduce features that encourage player interaction and collaboration to encourage community engagement.

10. **Collecting and acting on feedback**: Use user feedback and ratings to understand player sentiment. We must utilize constructive feedback to address our concerns and prioritize enhancements to features that align with player expectations.

11. **Iterate and conduct an A/B test**: Implement modifications incrementally and utilize A/B testing to evaluate the impact of specific modifications. This ensures that you can validate the effectiveness of changes before applying them universally.

12. **Continually monitor key metrics**: Establish a systematic approach for monitoring crucial engagement metrics over a period of time. This ensures that you remain responsive to changing player behavior and can quickly address emerging issues.

Sample Dashboard

When you have the metrics activated and parameterized (the standard ones and the customized ones), you can create a Dashboard similar to the one that appears in the following figure and obtain the following information:

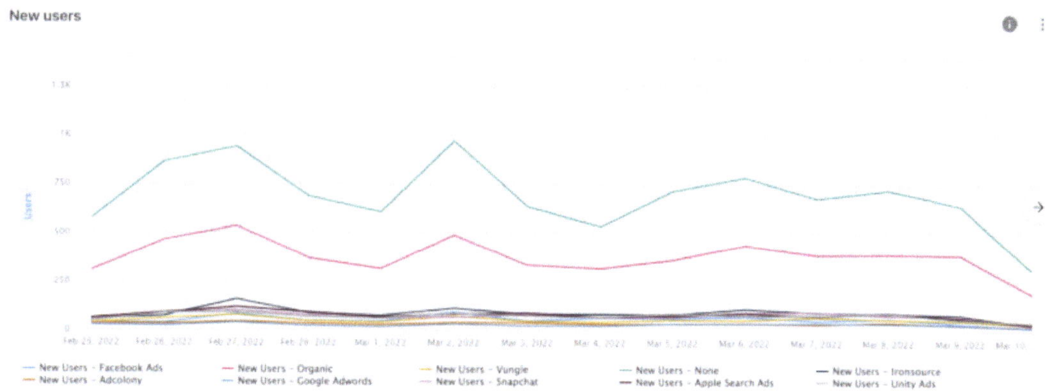

See the DAU (daily active users) and MAU (monthly active users) filtered by acquisition.

Figure 6.8*: Example of a graph showing the acquisitions of active users on a daily and monthly basis segmented*

It is important to know who your customers are, what platforms they use, and how they interact with your game or app. The following figure shows daily active users segmented by acquisition channel, allowing you to analyze which channels are most effective:

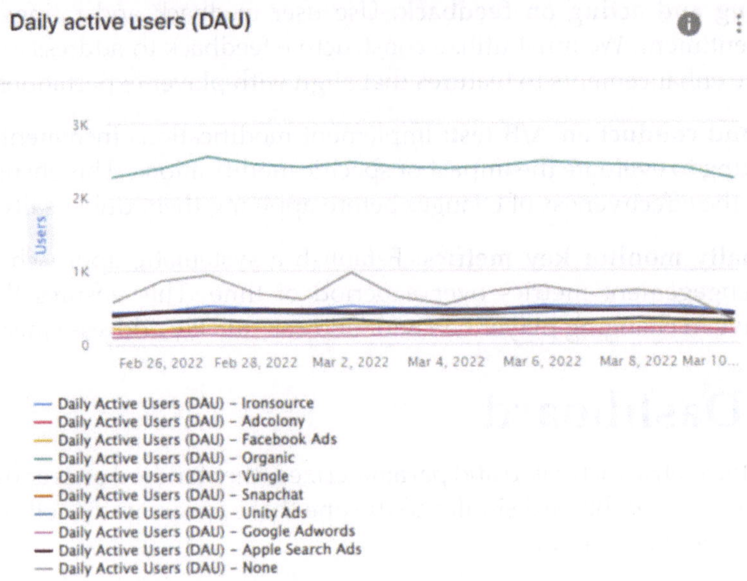

***Figure 6.9**: Chart of the DAU segmented by channels*

Which channel has the most players, and which players generate the most money?

Thanks to the Unity Cloud system, you will be able to sort them by country, platform, version, audience, and how they got there. You can see how many new users there are each day, how many people use each channel, how much money each channel generates daily, and how long it remains active:

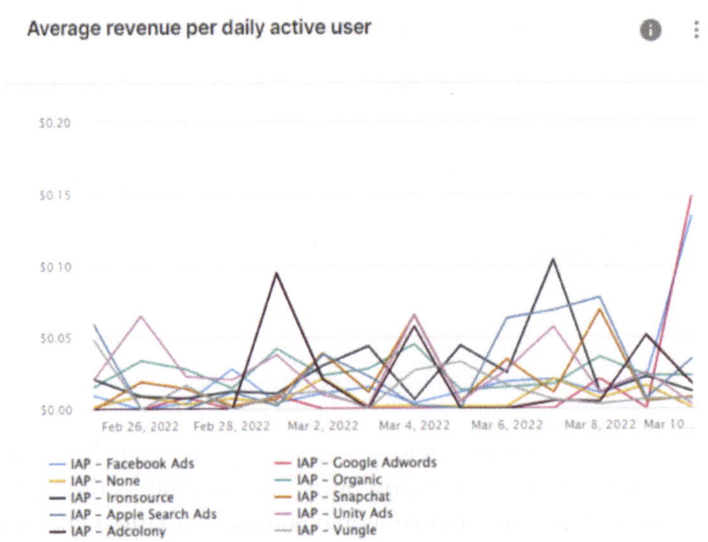

***Figure 6.10**: Complete view of user acquisition channel performance within the sample dashboard*

Conclusion

In conclusion, this chapter explored the multifaceted world of Unity Gaming Services, examining key components that contribute to a holistic gaming ecosystem. Unity Gaming Services provides a comprehensive toolkit for developers to create immersive and sustainable gaming experiences, encompassing the understanding and targeting of specific audiences, the utilization of retention strategies, monetization avenues, and engagement data.

A pivotal aspect of the funnel concept was the importance of guiding players through a seamless journey from discovery to long-term engagement. Using Unity Gaming Services' ability to analyze and interpret player behavior through data empowers developers to refine and enhance player experiences continuously.

Moreover, the emphasis on enhancing the player experience highlights the company's unwavering commitment to not only meet but also surpass player expectations. By utilizing Unity Gaming Services, developers have the capability to create dynamic, responsive, and captivating games that resonate with their intended audience.

The insights and strategies discussed in this chapter provide a roadmap for developers to create successful games and foster lasting connections with their player communities. Unity Gaming Services is a catalyst for innovation and growth in the gaming industry, promising an exciting future where player satisfaction and developer success converge.

In the next chapter, we will look at some techniques to try to retain players. We will use various techniques to make the user experience as enriching and rewarding as possible. This way, we will see our charts increase, both in terms of user numbers and profits.

Multiple choice questions

1. **What is the primary characteristic and purpose of Environments in the Analytics System?**
   a. They define the hardware specifications of the cloud servers.
   b. They are logical partitions that are isolated from each other, allowing developers to test changes in development without affecting the production data.
   c. They are used to manage billing and cost allocation for different regions.
   d. They are essential for activating standard automated events like gameEnded.
2. **Which two events are automatically logged by Unity Gaming Services (UGS) upon the initialization of the Analytics service within the application?**
   a. mission3_completed and transactionFailed
   b. newPlayer and ddnaForgetMe
   c. gameStarted and gameRunning
   d. adImpression and aquisitionSource

3. **When defining a Custom Event or its Parameters, what are the restrictions regarding the naming convention?**
   a. The name must be unique globally and contain only numeric characters.
   b. The name must be composed solely of English alphanumeric characters and underscore characters, and must commence with a letter.
   c. The name can include spaces, but must not exceed 25 characters.
   d. Only C# variable names are accepted, regardless of character type.
4. **What is the maximum number of parameters a developer is permitted to add to an environment?**
   a. 30 parameters
   b. 100 parameters
   c. 500 parameters
   d. 1,500 parameters
5. **What is the primary function of the Data Explorer tool in UGS Analytics?**
   a. To create and manage SQL tables and relationships.
   b. To run asynchronous code modules in the cloud.
   c. To manipulate and analyze game data by applying filters and events, and grouping the data by dimension for visualization (e.g., using bar charts, line graphs, or pie charts).
   d. To manually send ad impressions to the server.
6. **In the Data Explorer, what information can a developer determine by using the Group by function with the Platform and Country filters combined?**
   a. The server latency of their nearest data center.
   b. A real market study regarding user behaviour in specific geographical regions and on certain platforms.
   c. The total revenue generated by all paying users (ARPPU).
   d. The list of users who have been categorized as Churned Players.
7. **What is the specific analytical purpose of utilizing Funnels in the Analytics System?**
   a. To execute **Structured Query Language** (**SQL**) queries on the data.
   b. To manage the in-game economy and reward distribution.
   c. To visualize and analyze the player's journey within the game and identify potential drop-off points between stages.
   d. To export data in PNG or CSV format.

8. **When performing advanced data analysis, what SQL dialect is used within the SQL Data Explorer tool?**
   a. T-SQL (Transact-SQL)
   b. Oracle PL/SQL
   c. MySQL
   d. Snowflake
9. **What is the definition of the predefined audience All Spenders?**
   a. Players who have played every day in the past week (Days Played Last 7 Days >= 7).
   b. Players who have spent real money in-game (Total Real Currency Spent > 0).
   c. Players who have made a purchase within the last seven days.
   d. Players who have played for at least two calendar days.
10. **In the simplest C# script used to initiate UGS Analytics, what is the correct sequence of asynchronous calls necessary to start collecting data?**
   a. Call AnalyticsService.Instance.Flush() followed by print("Initializing UGServices...").
   b. Call AnalyticsService.Instance.StartDataCollection() followed by await UnityServices.InitializeAsync().
   c. Call await UnityServices.InitializeAsync() followed by AnalyticsService.Instance.StartDataCollection().
   d. Call Debug.LogException followed by AnalyticsService.Instance.CustomData.

Answers

1	b
2	c
3	b
4	d
5	c
6	b
7	c
8	d
9	b
10	c

Join our Discord space

Join our Discord workspace for latest updates, offers, tech happenings around the world, new releases, and sessions with the authors:

https://discord.bpbonline.com

CHAPTER 7
Engagement, Gamification and Retention

Introduction

This chapter dives into key aspects of game development, focusing on using data and player feedback to improve the user experience. It covers methods to guide players from their initial onboarding to long-term engagement, all while optimizing their overall enjoyment.

Some key topics covered are **storyline development**, learning how to craft compelling narratives using tools like Cinemachine and Timeline, **gameplay strategies**: Discover techniques for setting clear goals, balancing difficulty, and introducing rewarding mechanics that keep players engaged, **social interactions**: Explore features like multiplayer modes, leaderboards, in-game chat, and social group creation, p**rogression and rewards**: Understand how to design systems that allow players to advance through levels or categories, ensuring a sense of achievement and motivation. Some more topics of learning would be **personalization**: See how **user-generated content** (**UGC**) can be integrated and adapted to player preferences, creating a more tailored and engaging experience**, challenges**: Dive into designing challenges with a progressive difficulty curve to keep players motivated without overwhelming them, **new content**: Learn how to use **Cloud Content Delivery** (**CCD**) to roll out regular updates and new features, extending the lifespan of your game and push notifications: Get insights into creating effective push notifications , including best practices for timing, audience segmentation, and regulatory compliance.

The chapter emphasizes using the right tools and techniques to make informed decisions based on player data and feedback. The ultimate goal is to create a dynamic and evolving game that keeps players engaged and ensures their experience continues to improve.

Structure

The chapter covers the following topics:

- Storyline
    - Cinemachine
    - Post-processing

  - Timeline
- Gameplay
- Social interactions
- Personalization
  - User Generated Content
- New content
- Cloud Content Delivery
- Push notifications
  - Analytics and performance monitoring

Objectives

This chapter aims to provide readers with the tools and knowledge to enhance their game development process by using player data and feedback. It focuses on practical skills that will help in creating more engaging and successful games.

Readers will also learn how to analyze player behaviour to understand their journey from initial acquisition to long-term retention. The goal is to enable informed decisions that will optimise the player experience. The ultimate aim is to provide readers with the skills needed to adapt their games based on player feedback and data analysis.

Ultimately, identify specific methods to apply data and player feedback to the positive evolution of the game.

Storyline

Developing a compelling narrative is an essential component for enhancing gaming. The right story can get players involved in the game, making it more fun and engaging. Using a storyline to enhance gaming is a good idea.

To be sure that the story engages, you must take into account some rules:

- **A clear purpose should be defined**: Set up a compelling and specific objective for the players to attain. They feel like they are moving in the right direction.

  Unity has a wonderful tool called Cinemachine that allows you to use the graphics engine as if you were the director of a movie. Together with a timeline, it allows you to make professional productions, as shown in the following figure:

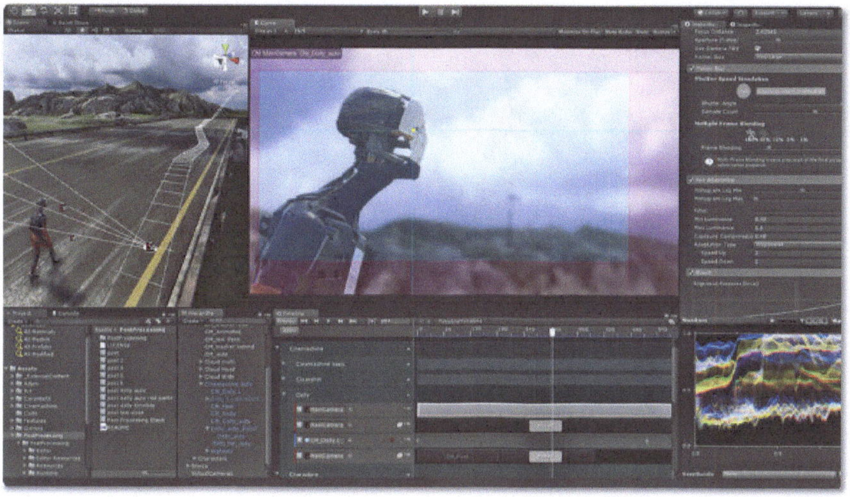

Figure 7.1: *Adam is a very impressive piece of art created with Unity*

You can find the documentation about CineMachine on: **https://docs.unity3d.com/Packages/com.unity.cinemachine@2.3/manual/index.html**

The Adam project is a short film made by OAK Studios using Unity. It has won numerous prestigious international awards and is proof that Unity is an excellent platform for audiovisual production:

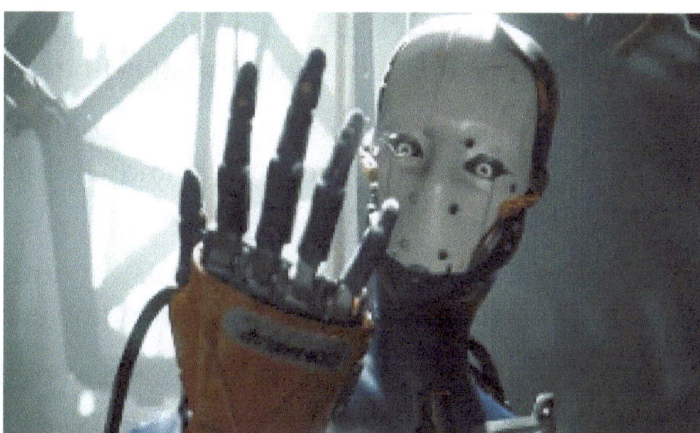

Figure 7.2: *A frame of the great Adam project*

- **Make the characters in the story relatable and engaging**: To get emotionally involved, players should feel a connection to the characters, be they friends or foes.
- **Create a cohesive and engaging gaming environment**: You can do this with your own tales, lore, and sagas. A well-defined world provides context for players' choices and actions.

Another frame from the Adam project that makes us empathize with the character:

Figure 7.3: Be sure to create an engaging environment

- **Allow players to make meaningful choices**: This adds a layer of personalization and encourages replayability as players explore different paths.

  Introduce tension and obstacles that propel the story forward. Overcoming obstacles keeps players involved in the plot and makes them feel accomplished.

- **You must use timing efficiently**: Maintain player interest by controlling the pacing of the story. You want to mix up the tension, excitement, and chill time to make it fun and interesting (remember, you can create custom events).
- **Tie the narrative progression to rewards, achievements, or unlockable content**. This incentivizes players to continue engaging with the storyline and the overall game.
- **Using timing efficiently**: Maintain player interest by controlling the pacing of the story. You want to mix up the tension, excitement, and chill time to make it fun and interesting (remember, you can create custom events).
- **Tie narrative progression to rewards, achievements, or unlockable content**: This incentivizes players to continue engaging with the storyline and the overall game.
- **Give feedback and consequences**: Show the consequences of the player's choices by offering feedback on their actions. This encourages players to feel empowered and accountable in the gaming world.
- **Integrate narrative elements into the gameplay mechanics**: Puzzles or stumbling blocks could be tacked onto the narrative, enhancing the link between the game's story and its engaging elements.
- **Elicit emotions through the storyline**: Whether it is humor, drama, or suspense. Emotional involvement enhances the gaming experience and makes the story stick in your mind.

Sherman is another project with exceptional characters and animation that demonstrate the great capabilities of Unity:

***Figure 7.4**: Sherman[1], a short Unity animation, showcases the platform's potential for high-quality content*

- **Use multimedia components**: Text, music, sound effects, images, and even video, particle emitters all work together to tell a story. Various media formats enhance immersion and accommodate different learning and engagement styles.

  Whenever possible, include online or communal elements in the narrative. This can foster a sense of belonging and competition among players.

  Remember that gamification's success hinges on figuring out your audience and crafting a tale that catches their interest. Gather feedback and tweak your story often to keep it fresh and fun.

  A more recent human character animation project, The Heretic, demonstrated the capabilities of Unity 2019's graphics engine by utilizing the **High Definition Render Pipeline** (**HDRP**). This pipeline, along with the integrated post-processing stack and Visual Effect Graph, enabled the project to achieve its visual goals:

***Figure 7.5**: The Heretic is a short to show HDR capabilities*

1 You can see the short on youtube: **https://www.youtube.com/watch?v=JFtCHvyul-I**

Other short films made with Unity to demonstrate the capabilities of its graphics engine and tools are:

- **The Heretic**: This short was made to demonstrate the great graphic capabilities and creation of digital humans. The entire project is in the Unity store and is very interesting. It is recommended to download and install it to see what techniques have been used. A blog explaining the making of is also available at this address: **https://unity.com/the-heretic**.
- **Enemies**: This serves as a tech demo of the advanced capabilities of **real-time 3D (RT3D)**. It builds on the work done on the previous demo, *The Heretic*, which introduced Unity's first realistic digital human.

  The team behind Enemies is made up of experienced game professionals, led by writer, director, and cinematographer Veselin Efremov.

  Enemies introduced several cutting-edge systems and enhancements to achieve photorealistic results, all rendered in real-world and at 4K resolution.

  You can obtain more info at his address: **https://unity.com/demos/enemies**.
- **Time Ghost**: The video was developed using an unmodified Unity 6 engine and was officially unveiled at Unite 2024 in Barcelona. The primary goal of *Time Ghost* is not only to entertain but also to demonstrate what can be achieved with Unity 6, specifically highlighting advancements in visual quality, project complexity, and the practical use of machine learning workflows.

  Time Ghost pushes the engine to its limits by integrating several advanced **real-time 3D (RT3D)** features, leveraging advancements across all of Unity 6's graphics capabilities.

  Time Ghost is an invaluable resource for developers, providing direct access and insight into the capabilities and workflows associated with the latest engine version, Unity 6. You can find the project at this address: **https://unity.com/demos/time-ghost**

  - **Exploring Complex Workflows**: The demo validates Unity 6's ability to handle unprecedented project complexity. Developers can learn how to efficiently manage massive scenes (up to 12 million vegetation instances) with DOTS ECS, which is key to creating large-scale or highly detailed open-world environments.
  - **Practical AI/ML implementation**: Time Ghost is a model for integrating machine learning into real-time rendering. By examining the example character package, you can see how Unity's runtime AI, the Inference Engine, is implemented to achieve high-fidelity cloth simulation with minimal performance overhead (0.8 ms per frame). This provides a clear and practical example of how to apply AI models in your own projects
- **WiNDUP**: It is an emotional short film with a Pixar aesthetic that has won many awards. In the following figure, you can see the high technical level of Unity for the creation of human characters with their facial expressions:

***Figure 7.6**: Graphics engines aim for metahumans: indistinguishable digital actors*

Cinemachine

Cinemachine offers exactly what its name suggests, that is, being able to use Unity as if we were a film director.

This tool allows you to create several virtual cameras to show a sequence from different points of view. That way, we can do the work of a filmmaker and change the camera to improve the narrative of the story and make it much more spectacular and enjoyable. We can do an introductory tracking shot of the stage, follow a character while he moves or fights, change the Depth of Field, and see an explosion from various angles. If all this is accompanied by appropriate music and good visual effects, we will achieve a wow effect that will mark the user experience.

You can install Cinemachine like any other package: open Window/Package Manager, find Cinemachine on Unity Registry and Install.

The following figure shows how to install the Unity package Cinemachine. It is used to create cinematic scenes with multiple virtual cameras:

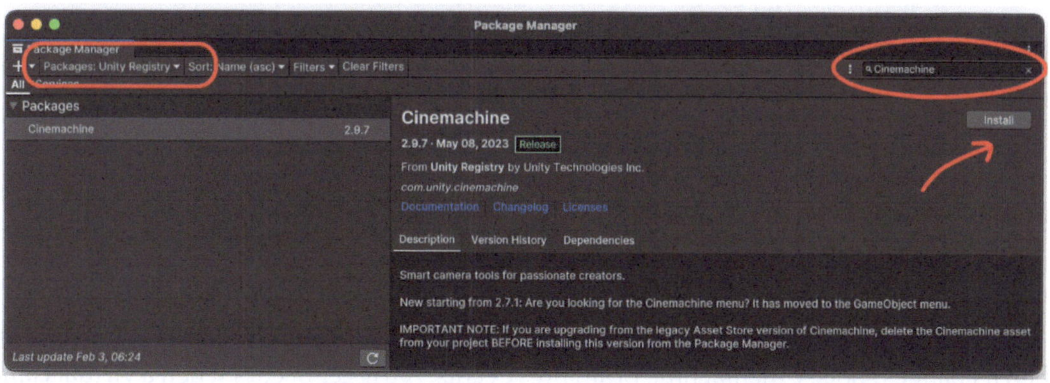

***Figure 7.7**: Import and install Cinemachine package*

Virtual cameras

Cinemachine does not invent or create fresh cameras. For multiple shots, it directs a single Unity camera. These shots were composed with virtual cameras. Control the Unity camera's settings by moving and rotating it. If your scene is performance-sensitive, you must know that the virtual cameras are designed to consume very little processing power. The developer creates the virtual cameras from which they want to take the different shots in the scene. Cinemachine only stores the transform (position and angles in 3D space) to relocate the Unity camera to the virtual camera position when necessary.

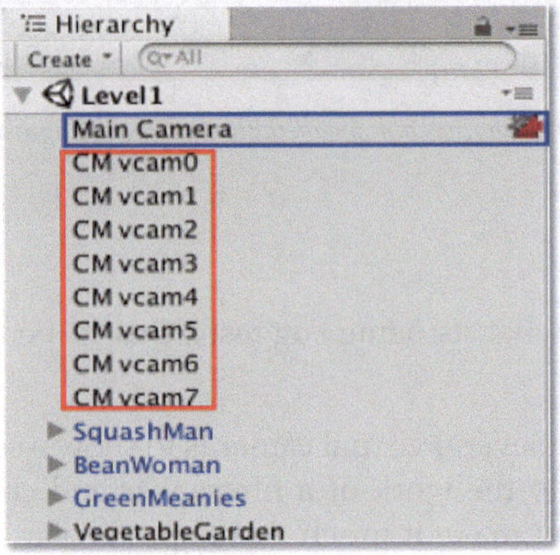

Figure 7.8: Detail of virtual cameras

To monitor and control all active virtual cameras, Cinemachine has a component called Cinemachine Brain. You will need to add this component to the main camera to define how to perform blending between virtual cameras.

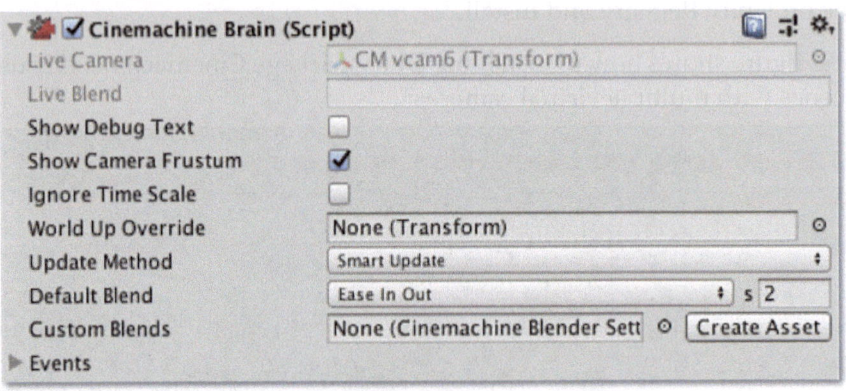

Figure 7.9: The component cinemachine brain is added

When it changes shots, Cinemachine Brain fires events. A trigger occurs when a virtual camera goes live. An event is fired when it cuts from one virtual camera to another. Reset temporal effects with the latter one. These events can be especially useful for timing with special visual effects at the right moment (when the camera is well-focused).

The virtual camera component has the following two important parameters:

- **Follow**: This will be a gameobject on your scene. It could be a car, a character, or whatever you want. This virtual camera will move with the gameobject.
- **LookAt**: Similar to the **Follow** option, but instead of moving, the camera only rotates to keep the assigned object in view.

So that the camera movement is not mechanical and robotic, the system simulates the real behavior of a human camera, leaving some tolerance zones when focusing and making smooth and fluid movements to track.

One of the coolest features of Cinemachine is character tracking with the camera. This feature can be used to track characters as they walk, run, or jump:

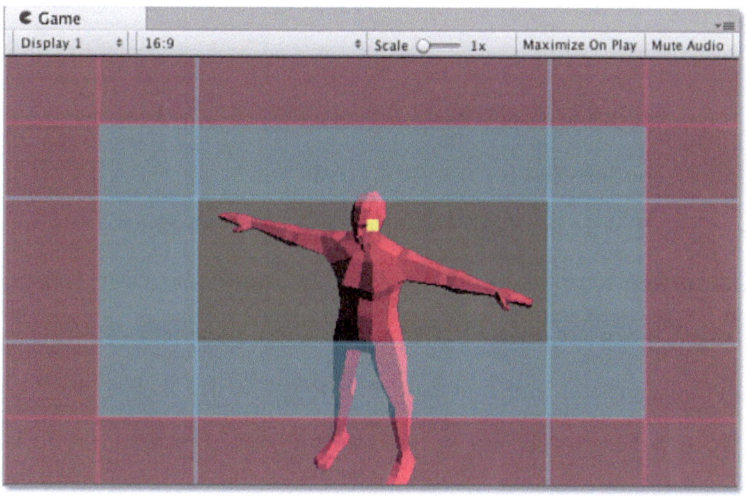

***Figure 7.10**: Some zones let the cameras track a GameObject*

These algorithms are used to move a virtual camera in Cinemachine:

- The transposer moves in a fixed relationship to the target.
- Do Nothing does not move the virtual camera.
- Framing Transposer Moving in a fixed screen-space relation to the target.
- The Orbital transposer varies with the following target, optionally taking player input.
- Dolly is tracked, following a set of instructions, following a predefined path. It is, basically, a journey.
- Hard lock to target uses the same position as the target.

To specify how to rotate the virtual camera when it looks at a specific GameObject, use the aim properties:

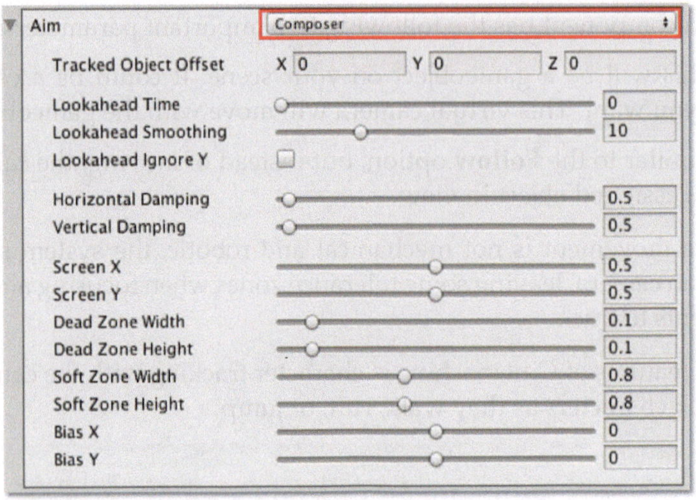

***Figure 7. 11**: Detail of the Aim to track objects*

The properties that can be selected for the Aim are as follows:

- **Composer**: The look at the target should be kept in the camera frame.
- **Group Composer**: Keep multiple sights in the frame for group composition.
- **Do Nothing**: Do not procedurally rotate the virtual camera.
- **POV**: Rotate the virtual camera based on the user's input.
- **Same as Follow Target**: The camera's rotation should match that of the target you are following.
- **Hard Look At**: The look at the target should be in the center of the camera frame.

Post-processing

A Post-Processing Profile asset is held by the Cinemachine Post Processing extension when it is activated. The blend weight is applied to the Post Process effects if the camera is blending with another virtual camera.

Perform the following steps to set up Post Processing with Cinemachine on the main camera:

Install the Post Processing V2 package using the habitual procedure on package manager window.

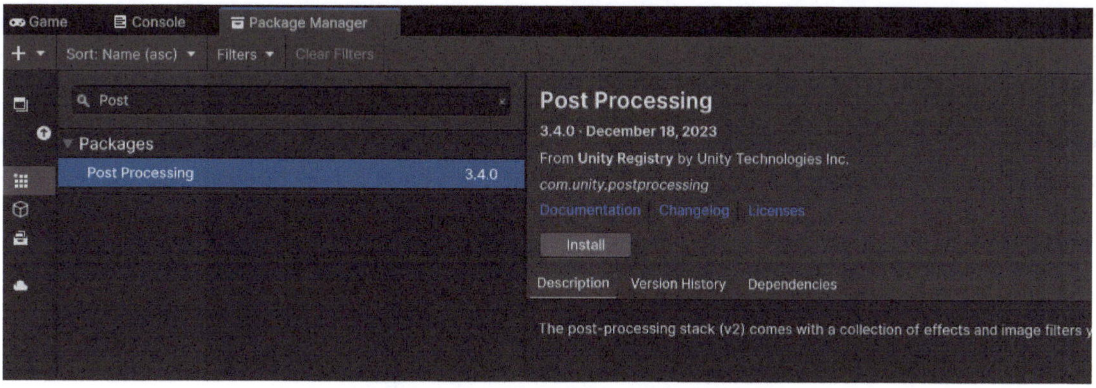

Figure 7.12: *Install the Post Processing Unity package*

Select the main camera, where you previously installed CinemachineBrain, and add a new Component called Post-process Layer:

Note: You will need to select a layer other than Everything.

The following figure shows the camera with the Cinemachine Brain component already added, to which we will now add the Post-process Layer:

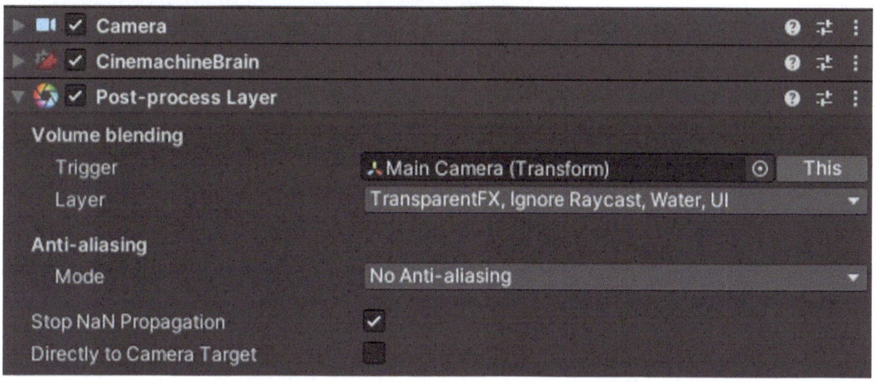

Figure 7.13: *Be sure to trigger the correct camera to do the Post-process*

Timeline

Another plugin called Timeline[2] is usually used in conjunction with Cinemachine. Timeline allows us to do the assembly process. In traditional film production, after having recorded the scenes on celluloid, they were visualized, the scenes the director wanted were selected, and the final master was edited.

2 You can find all the information about Timeline at website: **https://docs.unity3d.com/Packages/com.unity.timeline@1.8/manual/index.html**

Thanks to the combination of Cinemachine and Timeline, we have a film studio that we can modify in real-world and repeat the scenes as many times as necessary, from all points of view and with infinite cameras.

As you can see in the following figure, we will use Timeline as a non-linear video editing system, where we can switch between the different animations to create our scenes using different tracks:

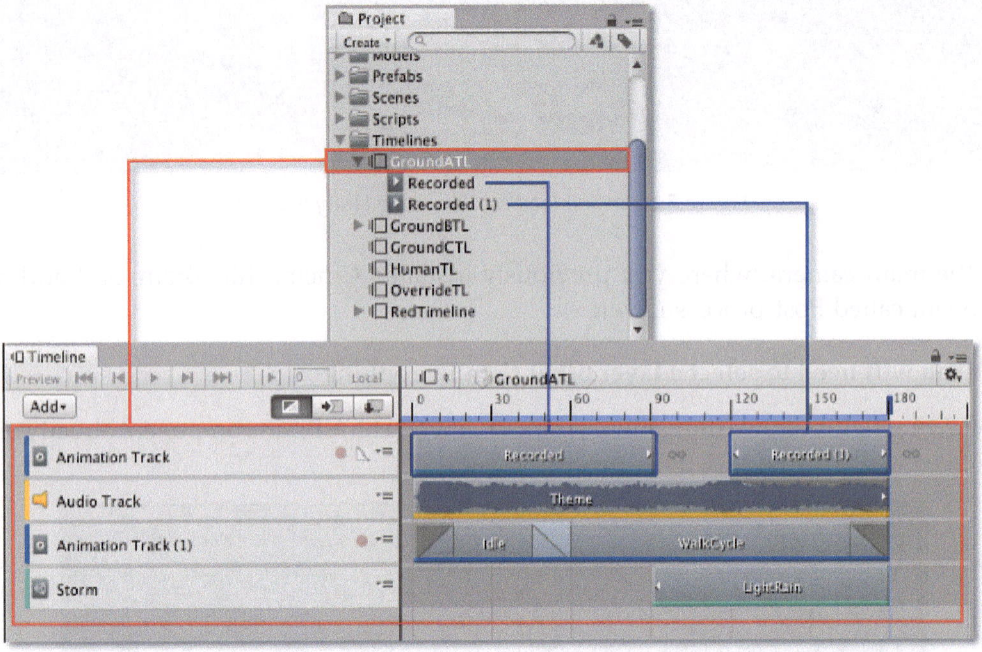

***Figure 7.14**: Timeline lets you create complex storylines*

The timeline supports non-linear editing, which allows for branching storylines and adaptive narratives based on player choices.

You can use Timeline to trigger various events and actions in your game, like spawning enemies, solving puzzles, or altering environmental conditions.

Gameplay experiences should be dynamic and responsive to the narrative and tailored to player decisions.

Gameplay

Utilizing gameplay wisely is crucial for crafting an engaging and enjoyable gaming experience. Some ways to make gaming more fun are as follows:

- **Clear objectives and goals should be defined**: Define the goals and objectives of the game in detail. The experience becomes more meaningful when players feel a sense of direction and purpose.

- **Make a well-balanced difficulty curve**: Make sure you design a sequence of challenges that progress in difficulty. A complete challenge path keeps players excited and avoids hassle.

  Implement rewards programs that provide immediate feedback on achievements and progress. Points, badges, levels, or in-game items can be used to earn rewards, creating a cycle of positive reinforcement.

- **Facilitate the improvement of skills**: Opportunities must be integrated for players to develop and demonstrate new skills. Players should get better and better as they improve.
- **Allow player freedom and agency**: Give players choices that matter and affect the game. This can be achieved through a variety of plots, character individualization or tactical choices, giving players the feeling of being in charge.
- **Introduces competition and collaboration**: Incorporate elements of competition and cooperation to attract different preferences. The social aspect of the game can be enhanced through leaderboards, challenges, and online multiplayer options.
- **Implement feedback mechanisms**: Provide timely and constructive feedback on the game. This could be done with visual cues, sound effects, or other messages that help players weigh the consequences of their choices.
- **Encourage curiosity**: Create an environment that encourages exploration. Hidden benefits, additional content, or alternate routes can entice players to delve deeper into the game.
- **Make sure your user experience is seamless**: A fluid and intuitive user interface and user experience should be prioritized. A well-thought-out interface improves player engagement and makes the game more accessible.
- **Increases replayability**: Create features that entice players to return to the game, such as multiple endings, random events, or unlockable content. This extends the fun element of the game.
- **Implement progression mechanisms**: A progression system must be designed that allows players to advance through levels or categories. This makes you feel accomplished and encourages greater participation.
- **Real-world rewards can be integrated**: Consider incorporating tangible rewards or incentives to attract players. This could include discounts, special access, or tangible items related to the game.

One of the games that can be considered one of the best examples of gameplay and engagement is Pokémon Go:

Figure 7.15: Pokémon Go was a successful game using augmented reality

- **Continuous improvement**: Adapt to the player's contributions. Collect player feedback frequently and use it to improve the gaming experience. This continuous revision keeps the game fresh and relevant. Remember to adapt the elements of your game to the preferences and motivations of your target audience. Periodically analyze player behavior and adjust game dynamics to improve the overall gamification experience

> Note: **Remember, you can analyze data with analytics to segment your audiences.**

To keep players engaged, Pokémon Go changed the content on special dates such as Christmas or Halloween, as shown in the following figure:

Figure 7.16: Creating new content ensures that users want to play

In short, prioritize the fun factor. A game that is fun and entertaining will naturally lead to higher engagement and a positive gamification experience.

Social interactions

Including social interactions in gaming can significantly enhance the overall experience, fostering a sense of community and involvement. Here are some strategies for leveraging social interactions for better gamification:

- **Multiplayer features are included**: Implement multiplayer options that allow players to work together or compete against each other. This can include cooperative tasks, team challenges, or game-based competitions.
- **Rankings and leaderboards**: Establish ranking lists to showcase players' accomplishments and standings. This bolsters the competitive aspect and encourages friendly competition among those involved.

  https://docs.unity.com/ugs/en-us/manual/leaderboards/manual/leaderboards
- **Social sharing**: Social media sharing options should be integrated into the game. Sharing progress, accomplishments, or top scores with friends and family helps spread the word about the game and build a sense of camaraderie.
- **Talk and chat in-game**: To facilitate communication between players, include in-game chat or messaging features. They can plan, share tricks, or just hang out with other gamers. UGS has a tool called Vivox SDK, a voice and text chat system that brings in-app communications to your project. In future chapters, we will see this tool in more depth, but its main characteristics are:
  - Cross-platform functionality.
  - Directed voice and text communication services.
  - Group voice and text communication services.
  - Buddy and presence services.
- **Clans[3]or families/friends tool**: Establish a mechanism for players to join groups, clans, or teams. It makes it easier to make friends, encourages teamwork, and makes you feel part of something bigger.

  To accomplish this feature, UGS has a tool: Friends.

  The Friends service facilitates player engagement by providing players with a social system that seamlessly integrates with other Unity services. With Friends, your players can do the following:
  - Send and receive friend requests.
  - Build and manage friend lists.
  - Block and remove other players.
  - The user communicates with a friend.

3 Friends Information: **https://docs.unity.com/ugs/en-us/manual/friends/manual/welcome**

Friends facilitates the creation and maintenance of relationships with ease and provides the necessary tools to effectively integrate standard Friends functionality into your game. Presence features allow your players to announce their current in-game status to other players, and support for custom presence metadata. This allows games to easily support features like joining in progress or spectating.

The term *relationship* refers to the status between two users. Certain relationship statuses necessitate the consent of both users, while others only require the consent of one user. The Friends SDK automatically categorizes the various relationships and presents a collection for each type of relationship. The relationship types are friend requests, friends, and blocks, as shown in the following figure:

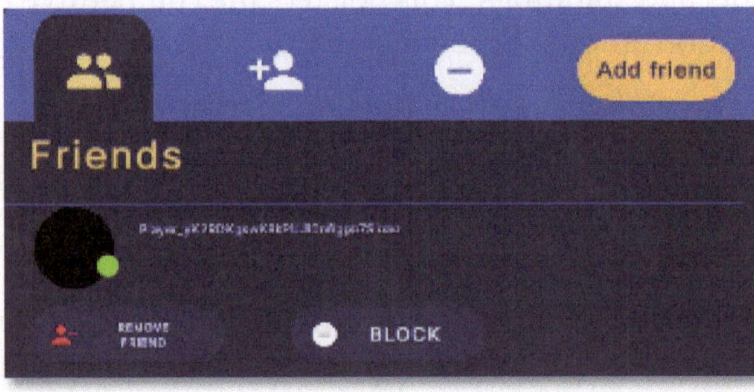

***Figure 7.17**: Detail of the list of friends that appears in the example app*

The Friends Service provides an HTTP API for managing user relationships of various types and regulating user presence.

In order to facilitate use with apps created using Unity or any other development environment, an HTTP API has been chosen. We are currently supporting the following types of relationships:

- **FRIEND_REQUEST**: This is an incoming or outgoing friend request.
- **FRIEND**: An active friendship between two users that has been mutually accepted.
- **BLOCK**: A one-way relationship that allows a user to block a different user in order to prevent gaming experiences with that user.

- **Collective challenges**: Design challenges or quests that require collaboration between players. Working together to achieve common objectives can foster cooperation and encourage social interactions. Introduce tasks or quests that require interaction with other players. Helping each other complete tasks or collaborating on larger objectives could be involved.

If there are collective challenges, there must also be social rewards and recognition.

Establish incentives and recognition tied to social interactions. Helping others or participating in community activities could get you special badges or extra cash.

Another tool that makes development much easier for us, offered by Unity Cloud, allows us to improve competitiveness in a very simple way. These are *Leaderboards*.

Try using leaderboards to increase competition. With customizable real-time leaderboards, players can compare their performance in real-time to boost engagement and competition.

It is possible to interact with leaderboards using the following interfaces:

- Utilize the Unity Cloud Dashboard to create and oversee your leaderboards and access your entries.
- Implement Leaderboards for games that are not **made with Unity** (**MWU**) by utilizing REST APIs:
- Execute player actions through the Client REST API.
- Execute administrative actions by utilizing the Admin REST API.
- Utilize the command line interface to initiate calls to the Leaderboards service.
- Utilize the Unity SDK to incorporate leaderboards into your application.

You can implement the Leaderboard functionality using the Cloud Code service. Deployments are supported for the Unity Editor and the command-line interface.

This option allows you to configure Leaderboards using files, instead of the Unity Cloud Dashboard UI.

Please include these files as part of the version control system to minimize the Unity Cloud Dashboard context switching.

Here is a code example on how you can record results on a leaderboard by adding metadata to it (the Barcelona Dragons team in this case):

```
public async void AddScoreWithMetadata()
{
    var metadata = new Dictionary<string, string>() { {"team", "Barcelo-
na Dragons"} };
    var playerEntry = await LeaderboardsService.Instance
        .AddPlayerScoreAsync(
            leaderboardId,
            150,
            new AddPlayerScoreOptions { Metadata = new Dictionary<string, s
tring>(){{ "team", "Barcelona Dragons" }}});
    Debug.Log(JsonConvert.SerializeObject(playerEntry));
}
```

- **Events and tournaments**: Organize in-game activities, competitions, or contests that bring players together. These gatherings can create a sense of camaraderie and exhilaration, enticing active involvement, as shown in the following figure:

Figure 7.18: Minecraft is the game par excellence, where players create and share their own content

Let us consider some social elements that can be included in your game:

- **Real-time teamwork**: Implement real-time collaboration tools if possible. This could include simultaneous gameplay, cooperative missions, or collaborative endeavors that require cooperation from all involved.
- **Social feedback**: Allow players to offer feedback and suggestions on each other's achievements or contributions. Rewarding your peers can boost energy and commitment.
- **Community forums or platforms are listed**: Establish outside gaming communities or platforms where players can discuss the game, discuss tactics, and connect with others who share the same interests.
- **Responsive community management**: Have a responsive community management team to address player concerns, moderate interactions, and foster a positive and inclusive gaming environment.

By incorporating these social elements into your gamification strategy, you can create a more dynamic and socially engaging experience for players. Always consider the preferences and motivations of your target audience to tailor the social features to their needs.

First, we must understand how users interact and use our game. The whole process is called Player LiveCycle.

Player livecycle is a cycle of various stages or phases that a player goes through during their interaction with a game. These stages typically include the following:

- **Onboarding** or installation is the initial phase in which players download and install the game. The process encompasses the creation of an account, the configuration of preferences, and comprehending the fundamental principles of the game.

- The **engagement** phase involves players actively participating in the game. They may be completing levels, achieving goals, or interacting with different features. The goal of the game is to keep them interested and engaged.
- **Monetization** involves any interactions related to in-game purchases or ads. Players are free to spend money on virtual items, upgrades, or other premium features.
- The **retention** strategy focuses on maintaining players' interest and ensuring their continued engagement with the game over time. Often, developers implement strategies to ensure that players continue to find the game enjoyable and do not lose interest quickly.
- **Churn or attrition** refers to the stage where players stop playing a game. Developers must understand why players leave and address those issues to improve player retention.
- If a player has stopped playing, **reactivation** involves attempts to bring them back into the game. This could encompass updates, novel content, exclusive events, or individualized incentives.

Now that we know the stages a player goes through, we will have to measure how many players we have in each stage and try to maintain the maximum number of players for as long as possible.

Personalization

Minecraft is a clear example of a game where users can create personalized content (called mods). Precisely, this feature has significantly extended the game's lifespan and greatly improve its playability, always offering new content and functionalities.

Until now, if we wanted to incorporate user-generated content, we had to create our own system to manage it.

User Generated Content

Thanks to a new functionality from UGS, called **User Generated Content** (**UGC**), we will have a comprehensive solution to create and manage content.

One of the greatest exponents of a game that supports user-generated content is Minecraft, where you can make all kinds of mods that personalize and improve the experience, as can be seen in the following figure:

***Figure 7.19**: Example of Minecraft customization by users with content from another game: Portal*

In some cases, the improvements created by users are of surprising quality and add a lot of value to our game. The following figure shows a water customization in Minecraft with dynamic reflections and realistic wave behavior:

***Figure 7.20**: Improved the quality of some textures (such as water) through user customization*

The creator's process is as follows:

- Game developers create content that players contribute to your game.
- Search, evaluate, moderate, and interact with this content.
- This creates an incremental spiral of in-game content production driven by your most engaged creators.
- Content quality improves with time, thanks to sophisticated moderation.

One of the features of UGS is that it offers a one-stop solution for creating and managing content. The wide range of creative options available to players allows user-generated content in games to cover virtually anything from JPEGs to asset packs. Such user-generated content is considered unlicensed.

When users upload content, it is important to adapt to player input/contributions: Collect player feedback frequently and use it to improve the gameplay experience. This constant updating keeps the game fresh and relevant. Remember to adapt your game to fit the needs and motivations of your target audience. You can use data analysis to segment your audience by analyzing player behavior and adjusting game mechanics to improve the overall gameplay experience. You can find more information about this at: **https://docs.unity.com/ugs/en-us/manual/ccd/manual/UnityCCD.**

In the following figure, we can see the appearance of the Unity Creator Center tool that allows us to manage and control the content created by users before implementing it in our development. It is necessary to keep strict control in case someone tries to upload content that is not appropriate for our audience (for example, adult content in a children's game):

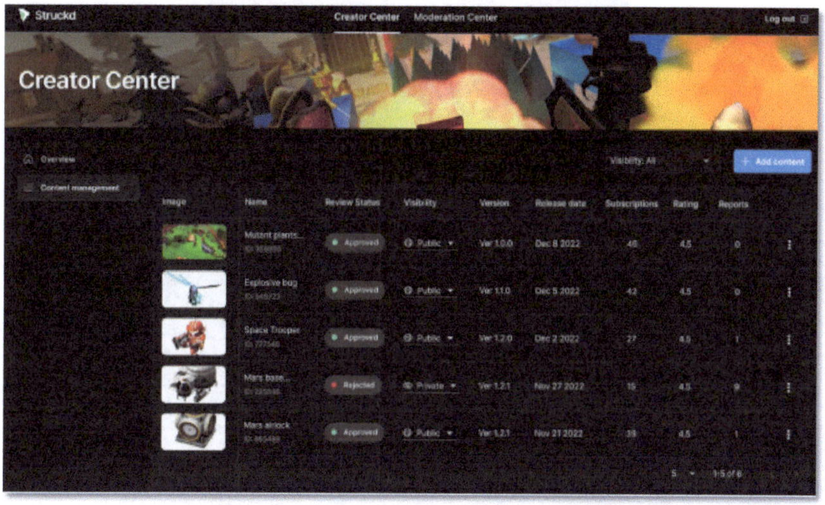

***Figure 7.21**: Example of a content manager created by users thanks to the UGS tool*

Viewing and editing content is done in the creator center. Content creators can check out stats about their work and how it is doing, like moderation, feedback, and evaluations. They are also capable of altering, removing from the list, or removing their content altogether.

Tools for moderation aid in assessing the content that has been uploaded. Game studios have the option of controlling themselves or soliciting help from others. Tag your content for advanced discovery with both automated and manual methods.

Set up rules for content moderation and get the tools you need to check and curate it. You can also give staff or community members moderation permission to help review content efficiently.

New content

One of the most interesting functions valued by app and game users is that new content is always generated.

A very clear example is the game *Angry Birds*, which has managed to release new versions for festivities and events, as shown in *Figures 7.22* and *7.23* (such as Christmas or Halloween) that enrich the ecosystem created with its players:

***Figure 7.22**: Angry Birds with special content for Christmas*

***Figure 7.23**: Angry Birds with special content for the Halloween holiday*

Unity has some tools that have traditionally helped us with these tasks (Unity Bundles and currently addressables fulfill this function) but UGS has a service that is better and more scalable.

Cloud Content Delivery

The Unity-managed cloud service hosts and delivers content to your application's users worldwide without having to reinstall a fresh version. Creating and maintaining your own similar service is a snap with the Unity development platform. **Cloud Content Delivery** (**CCD**) is especially useful for high-quality games or applications that require regular content updates.

More information about Unity CCD could be found at the following website: **https://docs.unity.com/ugs/en-us/manual/ccd/manual/UnityCCD**

CCD lets you divide up your content into groups called buckets to establish a streamlined project path. A bucket is a single context for publishing content.

A typical workflow example could be:

Have different environments (one for development and one for production). Within each environment, have separate repositories for different platforms, with names like iOS and Android.

A repository can be private or public to control which users can access it:

***Figure 7.24:** CCD-based cross-platform configuration example*

There is a whole control system to manage the content we publish. The content that is inside the buckets is called **entries,** and each time we make a delivery, it is called a **release**.

In the following figure, we see what the form for creating a Bucket looks like and how we should choose whether it will be open to everyone or only to a few users, depending on their profile:

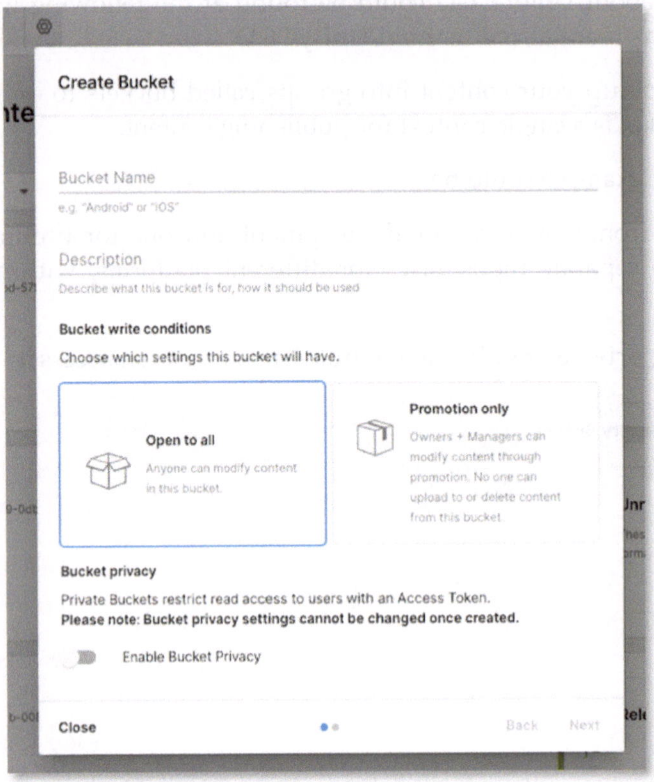

***Figure 7.25**: Detail of creating a container to publish new content*

Exhaustive control, similar to version control in programming, can be carried out from UGS in the CCD dashboard.

Normally, the CCD is a process very much intended for the backend, which is why it ends up being convenient to use the command line, which allows more agility for developers and is always much more parameterizable.

For this reason, CCD is usually used via the **command line interface** (**CLI**). CCD CLI can be found here: **https://docs.unity.com/ugs/en-us/manual/ccd/manual/UnityCCDCLI**.

In the following figure, you can see how three metadata files containing graphics have been uploaded using CCD commands:

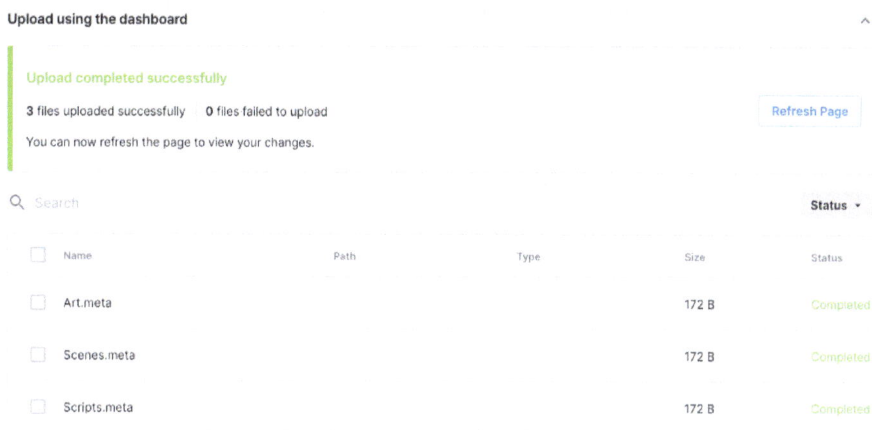

Figure 7.26: *Sample of CCD commands executed*

Push notifications

Push notifications can be used to send messages to players who are not actively playing your game, as shown in the following figure:

Figure 7.27: *Push notification on a mobile device*

Push notifications are available for iOS and Android mobile devices, and messages can be scheduled to go out at a specific time in the future or on a regular basis. You can track how many people downloaded them and jumped into your game as a result.

When we want to send push notifications, we must be clear about several concepts:

- We will have to make a different configuration for Android and another for iOS.
- It is important to **segment your audience** and send notifications only to those who are important. We can create a rejection effect if we are too insistent.
- Segment your audience based on demographics, behavior, or preferences to deliver targeted messages.

- Make sure your push notifications match the user's interests, habits, and preferences.
- Do it at the right time:
- Pick the best time to notify your followers, taking into consideration their routines and regional differences.
- Communicate topeople when they are less likely to interact, like at night.
- Use persuasive language to encourage action or interaction: Craft clear, concise, and compelling messages that grab the user's attention.
- Allow users to alter/ customize the types of notifications they receive.

Analytics and performance monitoring

Once sent, it is important to measure the impact and its effectiveness to ensure we are doing it in the best possible way.

Compliance with rules and regulations:

- Ensure compliance with data protection and privacy regulations, such as the General Data Protection Regulation or the Consumer Privacy Act.
- Respect privacy preferences and get user consent before sending push notifications.
- Once a push notification is launched, it is important to monitor the impact it has on the target and segment it is aimed at. In the following figure, we see an example:

Figure 7.28: Measuring the impact of push notifications once launched for a specific segment

The use of push notifications is included with Unity Analytics as it is considered a premium service, but it is strongly recommended not to exceed 10 monthly notifications per active user (MAU). You can start with push notifications at: **https://docs.unity.com/ugs/en-us/manual/push-notifications/manual/get-started**

If this amount is exceeded, Unity will contact you to learn more about your use case and make sure everything is configured correctly. If exceeded on a regular basis, a usage fee may apply. The surcharge is reflected on your monthly bill, and these fair usage limits reset at the beginning of each calendar month.

When launching a campaign using push notifications, it is important to make a forecast of how many we will need based on the number of active users:

Number of active players (MAU)	Fair usage notifications
1,000	10,000
50,000	500,000
100,000	1,000,000
1,000,000	10,000,000

Table 7.1: *Approximate calculation per month (MAU)*

In the following figure, you can see the entire workflow in creating and planning a push notification:

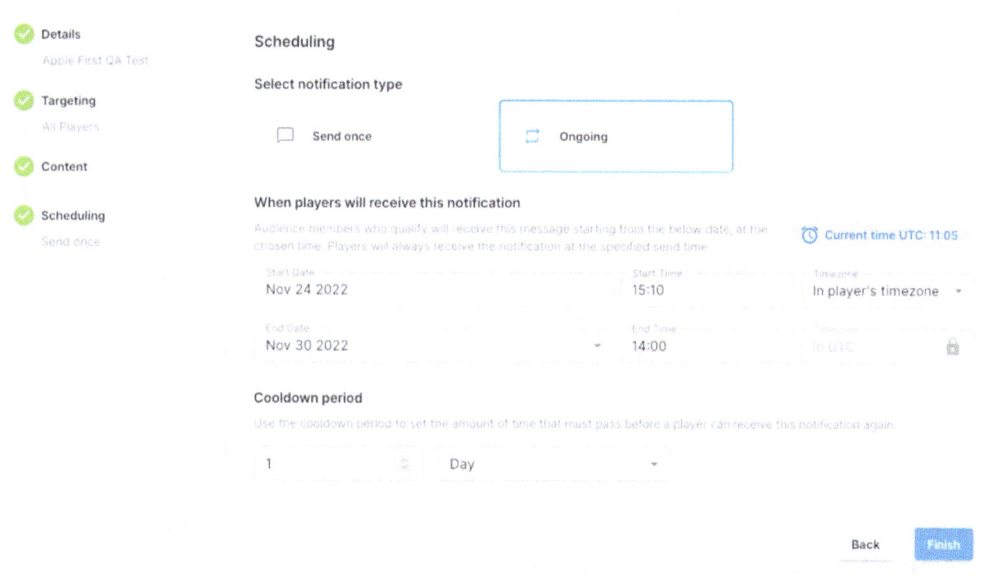

Figure 7.29: *Push notification publishing process*

Conclusion

In conclusion, this chapter serves as a comprehensive guide to learn about some of the many tools we have in Unity to make our creations much more enjoyable.

Tools for creating multimedia and storytelling content, such as Cinemachine and Timeline, have greatly enhanced our abilities to tell stories. If we possess the proficiency in utilizing these tools effectively, we can concentrate more effectively on the creation of the narrative and its characters.

Subsequently, we devoted our attention to the gameplay itself, encompassing concepts such as the difficulty curve, the creation of challenges and rewards, and examining how the social component can significantly enhance the user experience.

Finally, we addressed one of the biggest issues that every developer faces when they have already created a game: how to keep the content alive for longer. We have seen how a system can be used to add new content in a clean and easy way, as well as how users can help us with their own creations.

Hopefully, this chapter will encourage you to use and delve much deeper into them to improve the quality of your developments. In the next chapter, we will learn about the legal obligations concerning game developers.

Multiple choice questions

1. **What is the primary role of the Cinemachine Brain component when setting up cinematic sequences in a Unity project?**
   a. To automatically install the PostProcessing V2 package into the project.
   b. To manage the blending and transition events between multiple Virtual Cameras.
   c. To generate the final rendered movie file after the Timeline sequence is complete.
   d. To automatically adjust the character's facial expressions during dialogue scenes.
2. **Which of the following elements is fundamental to designing an engaging gameplay experience that enhances player retention?**
   a. Maintaining a high, static difficulty level throughout the game to reward only the most dedicated players.
   b. Implementing a system of clear objectives supported by a well-balanced, progressive difficulty curve.
   c. Removing explicit visual and sound feedback to promote player self-discovery.
   d. Limiting player agency to ensure the narrative follows a strictly linear plot.
3. **What UGS tool is specifically designed to integrate in-game voice and text communication services into a project?**
   a. UGS Cloud Content Delivery
   b. UGS Friends Service

   c. Vivox SDK
   d. UGS Leaderboards

4. **Which feature is recommended when crafting a compelling narrative to incentivize players to continue engaging with the storyline?**
   a. Creating randomized difficulty spikes to introduce tension and unpredictability.
   b. Tying narrative progression directly to rewards, unlockable content, or achievements.
   c. Utilizing the same single camera angle throughout the story to maintain visual consistency.
   d. Developing characters who are intentionally unrelatable to encourage critical
   e. distance.

5. **A developer intends to update in-game advertisements and offer a new seasonal currency pack to all players globally without forcing them to download a full application update from the app store. Which UGS solution is ideal for deploying this new content?**
   a. Utilizing the UGS Friends service to share asset updates directly between clients.
   b. Integrating the CCD service to deliver assets post-installation.
   c. Managing the new content solely through the Unity Editor's asset bundling system.
   d. Deploying the update using the Vivox SDK for real-time asset transmission.

6. **To prevent push notifications from being perceived as intrusive or disruptive, developers must adhere to which of the following best practices?**
   a. Utilizing persuasive language and ensuring messages are highly concise.
   b. Restricting the frequency to no more than 10 monthly notifications per active user (MAU).
   c. Employing audience segmentation to schedule messages based on regional differences and user routines.
   d. Using the default system notification time zone setting for universal consistency.

7. **In the context of Cinemachine, which properties determine how a Virtual Camera rotates to keep an assigned object in view?**
   a. Follow
   b. LookAt
   c. POV
   d. Dolly is tracked

8. **Which methods are generally recommended as techniques for integrating social interactions to enhance the player experience and foster community involvement?**
   a. Establishing ranking lists and Leaderboards to encourage friendly competition.
   b. Providing social rewards and recognition tied to participating in collective challenges.
   c. Implementing UGC features to allow players to create and share custom items.
   d. Centralizing all community discussions in an external, unmoderated forum platform.

9. **What key strategy enables developers to increase replayability and extend the enjoyment derived from a game?**
   a. Implementing progression systems that allow players to advance through levels or categories.
   b. Incorporating features that entice players to return, such as multiple endings or unlockable content.
   c. Ensuring a single, linear storyline that is strictly followed without player choice.
   d. Continuously collecting player feedback and adapting game dynamics accordingly.

10. **In the context of the UGC solution, why is robust moderation control critical for content uploaded by players?**
   a. To ensure content creation is limited exclusively to veteran players (over 100 sessions).
   b. To rigorously manage the complexity and file size of content for optimal performance.
   c. To prevent users from uploading unlicensed content or material inappropriate for the target audience (e.g., adult content).
   d. To automate the conversion of user-uploaded assets into Addressables and Bundles.

Answers

1	b
2	b
3	c
4	b
5	b
6	b
7	a, c
8	c
9	a, b, d
10	c

Chapter 8
Data Privacy and Consent

Introduction

This chapter examines the legal obligations that game developers must adhere to when handling user data, especially **personally identifiable information** (**PII**), with the goal of enhancing the player experience. The chapter highlights that while analytics are valuable for improving games, the collection of personal data is strictly governed by various data privacy laws. Developers will discover the necessity of obtaining consent for data collection under regulations such as GDPR and PIPL, and the requirement to provide notice and opt-out options as mandated by laws such as CCPA. Understanding and implementing the correct mechanisms for consent and opt-out across different regions is presented as crucial for developers who use analytics, as a user's decision to opt-out can directly affect analytics and key metrics.

In the previous chapters, we saw how we stored all types of data (events, session time, ranking of scores, content, etc.). All this information must meet legal requirements that also vary depending on the location from which the users are from or where our server is located. In this chapter, we are going to try to look at the legal aspects of having our content stored in the cloud.

Structure

The chapter covers the following topics:

- Declarations before publishing
  - Privacy policy
  - Advertisements
  - Target audience and content
  - Requesting permissions
- Juristiction privacy
  - Unity rules
  - Important laws and regulations

- Age restrictions
- Scope
- Publishing store models
- Best practices
    - Save user data locally
    - Let the users take control
    - Intellectual property rights

Objectives

In the previous chapters, we saw how we stored all types of data (events, session time, ranking of scores, content, etc.). All this information must meet legal requirements that also change depending on the area of the planet where the users are from or where our server is located. In this chapter, we are going to try to look at the legal aspects of having our content stored in the cloud. By the end of this chapter, you will gain a comprehensive understanding of the legal landscape surrounding user data in the context of game development and how to ensure your applications comply with diverse data privacy and consent requirements across different jurisdictions.

Declarations before publishing

When publishing an app to the Google Play or App Store, developers are required to make certain declarations to ensure compliance with various policies and regulations. These declarations are important since they help maintain the integrity of the store ecosystem, protect users, and ensure that apps meet certain standards.

Privacy policy

The inclusion of a privacy policy in your application's store listing facilitates transparency regarding the manner in which you handle sensitive device and user personal data.

The privacy policy, along with any in-app disclosures, must provide a comprehensive explanation of how your application collects, uses, and shares user data. This includes the entities with whom it shares this information.

Note: **Please consult your legal advisor to determine the specific requirements.**

It is mandatory to link to a privacy policy on your app's store listing page and within your application. Ensure that your privacy policy is accessible via an active URL and applies to your app.

For applications targeting children, it is imperative to include a link to a privacy policy on your app's store listing page and within your application, regardless of whether your application has access to sensitive permissions or data. Ensure that your privacy policy is accessible via an active URL and applies to your app. It is noteworthy that even applications that do not access any personal or sensitive user data are required to submit a privacy policy.

Advertisements

It is mandatory for developers to disclose whether their application incorporates advertisements. This encompasses advertisements delivered through third-party advertising **software development kits** (**SDKs**), display advertisements, native advertisements, and banner advertisements. Applications that contain advertisements will be marked with the **Contains ads** label on their Play Store listing. This tag will be accessible to all users of the Play Store.

Of course, it must be taken into account that the ads displayed comply with the other policies. It would be absurd for an app intended for children to show violent content or content directly for adults.

Target audience and content

You must specify the target age group of your application. Any app that includes children in its target audience must comply with the requirements of the Google Plays family policy.

It is essential to provide accurate information about your application. Depending on your target audience selection, your app may be subject to additional policies. In the section *International age rating coalition* in this chapter, we will detail the PEGI classification for minors.

Requesting permissions

After adding your app, permission requests will be evaluated during the release process. If your application requests the utilization of highly risky or sensitive permissions, such as SMS, microphone, camera, contacts local database, or call log, it may be necessary to complete the Permissions declaration form and obtain approval from the store.

Jurisdiction privacy

When storing so much user information, it is necessary to comply with data protection regulations, such as the **General Data Protection Regulation** (**GDPR**) in the European Union or the **California Consumer Privacy Act** (**CCPA**) in the United States. This includes obtaining user consent for data collection, ensuring the secure processing of personal information, and facilitating access to user data.

It is also mandatory to provide a mechanism for players to retrieve and delete their data in accordance with the guidelines of the GDPR. After the request is processed, the player data will be available for download for seven days.

Unity rules

Apart from international laws, we are using Unity Gaming Services to store information. We must be clear about the conditions under which we must proceed so as not to incur any legal problems.

These are the two documents that define the terms of use and privacy policies for Unity Gaming Services:

- Unity Terms of Service[1]
- Privacy Policy Hub[2]

From the content of these preceding documents, pay special attention to the following sentence:

We (Unity Technologies) do not determine your legal basis for processing. Instead, it is your responsibility as the controller to determine such a legal basis.

This means that Unity leaves it up to developers to implement client-side decisions about whether or not end-user consent is required to store information. So, you should keep in mind that, as a developer, this is your responsibility.

Important laws and regulations

The digital app market is growing very rapidly across all devices and around the world. With just one click, developers can publish their games and apps virtually anywhere, but each region has its own standards and/or laws. It is very important that you know what legislation is applicable in each case. Depending on the geographic area and the subject matter, the following are the main laws you must take into account when developing an app or game:

- **GDPR**: The GDPR came into effect in the **European Economic Area** (**EEA**). The term GDPR also includes the UK GDPR, which is the UK's version of GDPR and applies after Brexit.
- **CCPA**: The **California Consumer Privacy Act** (**CCPA**) as amended by the **California Privacy Rights Act** (**CPRA**).
- **PIPL**: In November of 2021, the **Personal Information Protection Law** (**PIPL**) took effect in China.
- **LGPD**: The Brazilian General Data Protection Law.

1 https://unity.com/es/legal/terms-of-service
2 https://unity.com/es/legal/privacy-policy

- **VCDPA**: The Virginia Consumer Data Protection Act.
- **CPA**: The Colorado Privacy Act
- **CTDPA**: The Connecticut Data Protection Act
- **UCPA**: The Utah Consumer Privacy Act
- **PIPEDA**: The Canadian Personal Information Protection and Electronic Documents Act.
- **DPA**: A Data Processing Addendum (or Data Processing Agreement) is a component of a contract that outlines the rights and responsibilities of each party regarding the processing of personal data.
- **PDP**: It is an Argentine Law 25.326 on the Protection of Personal Data.

Penalties

Talking about penalties is always awkward, but it is necessary. The following table shows the sanctions for violating the main laws. Actual consequences may vary depending on the severity of the breach, intent, and role of the individual involved:

Law	Max penalties (Company)	Individual developer liability	Notable cases/Notes
GDPR	€20 million or 4% of global turnover (whichever is higher)	Possible fines if acting as data controller or negligent	Meta fined €1.2 billion (2023)
CCPA/ CPRA	$2,500 per violation or $7,500 if intentional	Civil lawsuits in case of data breaches by negligence	Consumers can sue for data leaks
PIPL	¥50 million (~$7M) or 5% of annual revenue	Criminal liability possible in severe violations	Law includes personal accountability in some cases

Table 8.1: Summary of maximum legal and financial penalties

Let us look at one of the largest software stores, which maintains an enviable content control system, as an example:

App Store and Apple[3]: If there is a company that prides itself on being secure with privacy, it is, without a doubt, Apple. Even now, when other stores other than the Palo Alto company will be able to publish apps for iOS, it imposes its rigorous control.

This is based on two major pillars: ATT or Apple Tracking Transparency

3 You can fine more about App privacy details here: https://developer.apple.com/app-store/app-privacy-details/

Since iOS 14 and its subsequent versions mandate publishers to obtain explicit consent for tracking the user's device across applications, this feature is known as **App Tracking Transparency** (**ATT**):

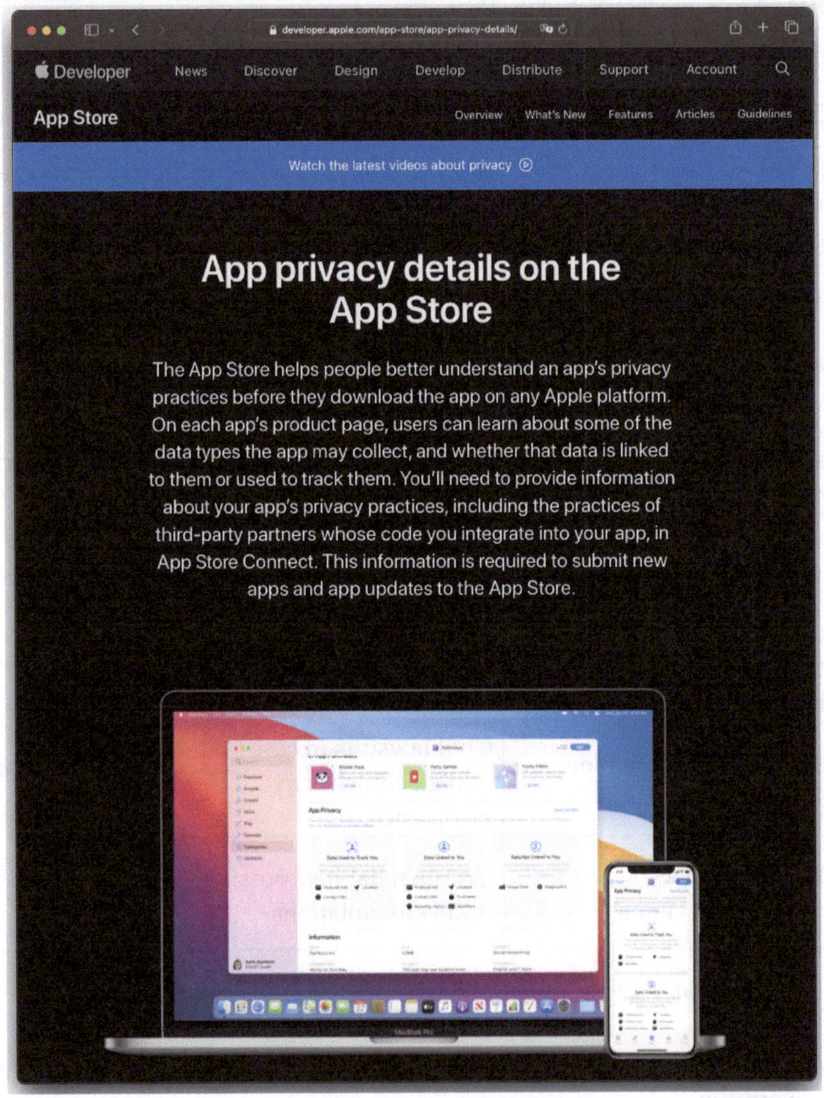

Figure 8.1: *Apple as one of the main companies that ensures the security of its users*

Age restrictions

Ensure compliance with laws regulating the collection of personal information from minors. Implement age verification mechanisms if your game is intended for adults only. Some of the laws provided for the protection of minors are:

- **COPPA**[4]: The **Children's Online Privacy Protection Act** (**COPPA**) prohibits the collection and utilization of data from children under the age of 13.

  As the law is quite complex to understand, if you want to delve deeper into this law, you can refer to the following guide:

  https://www.ftc.gov/system/files/ftc_gov/pdf/coppa_sbp_1.16_0.pdf

- **PEGI**[5]: The **Pan-European Game Information** (**PEGI**) age rating system was established to assist European parents in making informed decisions regarding the purchase of computer games.

  The following figure shows the complete age-based rating offered by PEGI:

Figure 8.2: *PEGI is one of the controls with the most age ranges*

According to Google's classification, the characteristics by age should be the following:

- **PEGI 3**: The content of the apps included in this category is considered suitable for all age groups. A certain degree of violence in a comic context is acceptable (i.e., the forms of violence typical of cartoons such as *Bugs Bunny* or *Tom and Jerry*). These apps include, for example, *WhatsApp* or *Agar.io*.
- **PEGI 7**: Any application that is normally classified as suitable for three-year-olds, but contains scenes or sounds that could scare them, can be included in this category. Some of the most popular are *Minecraft* or *Clash of Clans*.
- **PEGI 12**: This age category includes games or applications that show more explicit acts of violence with fantasy characters or non-explicit manifestations of violence with animals or characters with human features, as well as more explicit nudity and simulations of games of chance. Cursed language in this category should be moderate and not include sexual profanity. Here, we can find applications like *Game of War* or *Epic Heroes War*.
- **PEGI 16**: This category is used when the representation of violence or sexual activity reaches a level where it is completely assimilated into the real world. Apps rated as suitable for a 16-year-old audience may use more inappropriate language, encourage drug and tobacco use, and depict criminal activities. We find *Hungry Shark Evolution*.

4 You can consult COPPA at this address: https://www.ftc.gov/legal-library/browse/rules/childrens-online-privacy-protection-rule-coppa

5 You can consult PEGI at: https://pegi.info/page/pegi-organisation

- o **PEGI 18**: Applications in which violence reaches a level where it becomes a manifestation of brutality or that include elements of specific types of violence (for example, killing without reason or shows scenes of violence towards defenseless or sexual characters). These applications may also include explicit sexual content and displays of discrimination or idealization of drug use. With *GTA: Chinatown Wars* or *Talking Ted*.

It is important that games clearly intended for an adult audience are properly classified to protect minors, as shown in the following figure:

Figure 8.3: Grand Theft Auto is a well-known game for adults

- **CARU**: A self-regulatory organization dedicated to promoting responsible privacy practices for children under the age of thirteen.

International Age Rating Coalition

With so many laws and regulations, it was to be expected that there would be some supranational organization that would help classify and put in order the classification system at a global level.

The International Age Rating Coalition is a global association of content rating authorities from across the world. The primary objective of this project is to establish a unified system for age ratings and content descriptors for digital games and mobile applications. The coalition is made up of rating authorities from several countries and regions, including the Entertainment Software Rating Board in the United States, the **Pan European Game Information** (**PEGI**) in Europe, and others from countries such as Australia, Brazil, and South Korea.

One of the largest international organizations for age-based content classification is the IARC:

***Figure 8.4**: International Age Rating Coalition*[6]

The functions of IARC are as follows:

- IARC has developed a standardized questionnaire that developers can use to receive age ratings for their games and apps in multiple regions simultaneously. This quiz encompasses diverse aspects of content, including but not limited to violence, language, sexuality, and gambling.
- Using the IARC classification system, developers can streamline the process of obtaining age ratings for their digital content. Instead of submitting separate applications to each qualification authority in distinct countries, developers can submit a single questionnaire through the IARC system, thereby reducing time and effort.
- IARC allows developers to reach a global audience by obtaining age ratings from multiple regions. This is especially important for digital distribution platforms like app stores, where content can be accessible to users worldwide.
- The IARC's age ratings aid consumers, particularly parents and guardians, in making informed decisions about the suitability of digital content for diverse age groups. By prominently displaying age ratings and content descriptors, users can gain a better understanding of the nature of content prior to downloading or purchasing it.
- The IARC system is designed to be adaptable to technological and content changes. IARC continuously updates its questionnaire and rating criteria to ensure that they remain relevant and effective.

Overall, the International Age Rating Coalition plays a critical role in promoting responsible consumption of digital content, supporting the global gaming and app development industry, and protecting users, especially children, from inappropriate content.

6 https://www.globalratings.com/for-developers.aspx

Scope

The following world map shows the data protection regulations in each country/region:

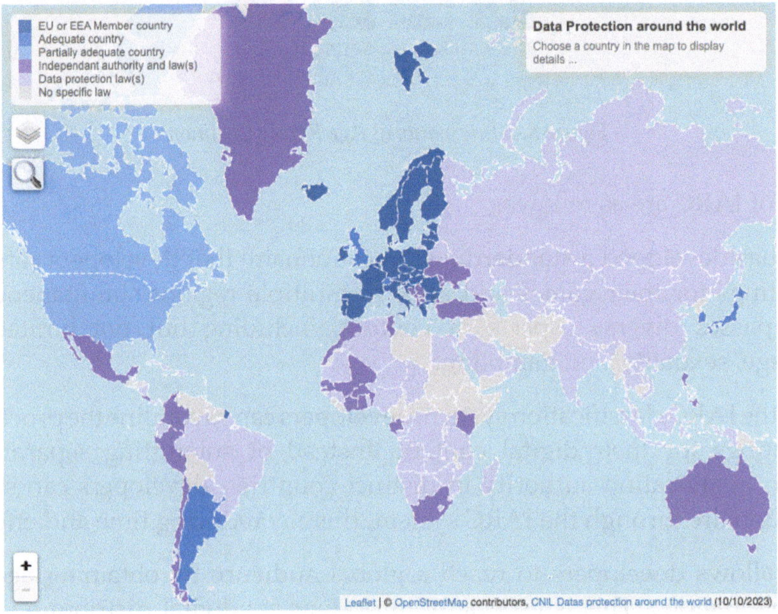

Figure 8.5: Interactive world map of data protection seen from France
Source: *https://www.cnil.fr/en/data-protection-around-the-world*

This is an interactive map showing the different data protection laws around the world. It is a map from a French organization called **Commission Nationale de l'Informatique et des Libertés (CNIL)**[7]. As such, your information is relevant to how the European Union sees it, but since it is one of the most restrictive legislations, it is interesting to take it into account so that our apps are approved.

Publishing store models

The control models of Apple and Android are very different from each other: Apple does exhaustive control of all aspects of an App before its publication. The process is carried out by experts, and nothing is published that escapes this rigorous control. Publishing an app in the Apple Store can take several weeks.

Google, for its part, is more permissive (at least in the initial phase). The control is done in an automated way and is much faster (just hours or a couple of days). The responsibility falls more on the developer, who decides, for example, whether the content is suitable for minors.

7 https://www.cnil.fr/en

If, once the app is published, any complaint is received about its content or classification, it is evaluated and may be removed from the store if it fails to comply with the regulations (with the corresponding economic or criminal sanction depending on the degree of violation).

Best practices

To try to preserve user data as much as possible and avoid problems, we are going to take into account some practices that can help us.

Save user data locally

To avoid legal problems, it is very important to try to have as little personal data as possible. That is to say, *try to limit the amount of personal information about users.*

If it is still necessary for us to obtain your preferences, we kindly request that you store as much information as possible on your own device, either in cookies, preferences, or a local database.

In order to carry out the monitoring of metrics that we have observed in previous chapters, it is imperative that we obtain solely statistical data, and not personal data. For example, we can determine if a new level we have added is difficult by the number of people who have been able to overcome it and those who have not. It is unnecessary to retain the name and surname of those who have passed it in the cloud. It is generally preferable to store all statistical data in the cloud and user preferences locally. This adds some complexity to the development, but if we are clear from the beginning, we will create the database infrastructure complying with all legal requirements.

This will avoid many legal problems and those that may arise from sending *sensitive* data over the internet. We can also avoid some attacks by malicious hackers:

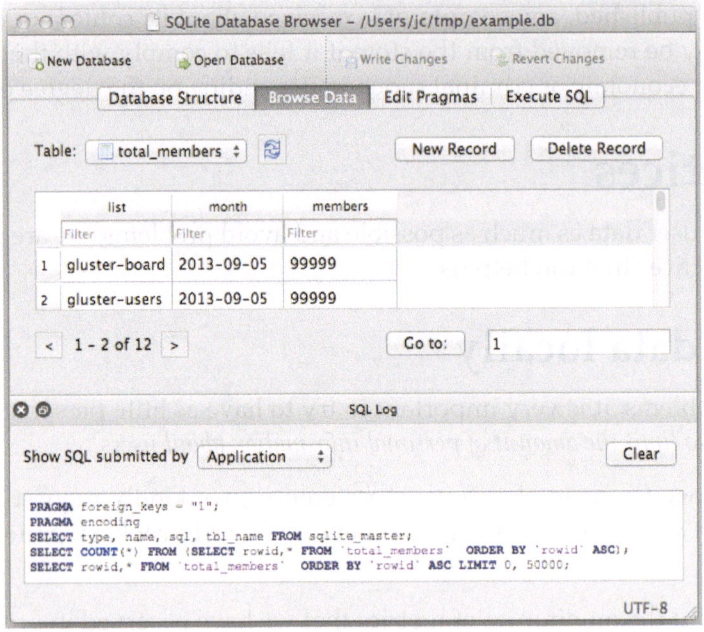

Figure 8.6: SQLite is a single-user local database commonly used to store local data

Finally, it is advised that data that is stored locally be encrypted, which adds extra security.

Let us look at some of the most used encryption algorithms:

- **Advanced Encryption Standard (AES)**: AES is a widely used symmetric encryption algorithm. It encrypts data using a symmetric key, which is shared between the parties involved. AES is efficient and provides strong encryption.
- **Rivest-Shamir-Adleman (RSA)**: RSA is an asymmetric encryption algorithm commonly used for secure data transmission and digital signatures. It uses a public-private key pair, where data encrypted with the public key can only be decrypted with the corresponding private key.
- **Secure Hash Algorithm 256 (SHA-256)**: SHA-256 is a cryptographic hash function that generates a fixed-size hash value from input data. It is commonly used for data integrity verification and password hashing. While it is not reversible like encryption, it is useful for securely storing passwords or checking data integrity.
- **MD5 message-digest**: This algorithm is a widely used hash function that produces a 128-bit hash value.

Although MD5 was originally designed to be a cryptographic hash function, it has been found to suffer from extensive vulnerabilities.

This is the cryptographic security example code we provide in the GitHub repository. It is recommended to encrypt data before writing it to the database. When content is retrieved, it can be decrypted. This way, even if someone were to get hold of our databases, they would not be able to use the information stored in it.

The code defines a class called **CryptoMethods,** which contains functions for encrypting and decrypting data. One of the primary cryptographic methods included is AES, which is a widely used symmetric encryption algorithm. Symmetric encryption means the same key is used for both encrypting and decrypting the data:

```
namespace CryptoNamespace
{
    using System;
    using System.Text;
    using System.Security.Cryptography;

    /// <summary>
    /// This class provides cryptographic methods for AES encryption/decryption
    /// and a simple XOR-based encryption.
    /// </summary>
    public class CryptoMethods
    {
        // AES Key: Must be 32 characters (256-bit key) for AES encryption
        private const string aesKey = "b28a74327a1b20b4311a3976acf096cd";

        // AES Initialization Vector (IV): Must be 16 characters (128-bit block size)
        private const string aesIv = "unity4profession";

        /// <summary>
        /// Encrypts a plaintext string using AES encryption.
        /// </summary>
        /// <param name="inputData">The plaintext string to encrypt.</param>
        /// <returns>The encrypted string encoded in Base64 format.</returns>
        public static string AESEncrypt(string inputData)
        {
            // Use a disposable AES crypto provider to manage encryption
            using (AesCryptoServiceProvider aes = new AesCryptoServiceProvider())
```

```
{
            aes.BlockSize = 128; // The block size for AES (128 bits)
            aes.KeySize = 256; // The key size for AES (256 bits)
            aes.Key = Encoding.ASCII.GetBytes(aesKey); // Convert key to byte array
            aes.IV = Encoding.ASCII.GetBytes(aesIv); // Convert IV to byte array
            aes.Mode = CipherMode.CBC; // Use Cipher Block Chaining (CBC) mode
            aes.Padding = PaddingMode.PKCS7; // Use PKCS7 padding to handle block size alignment

            // Convert the input string into a byte array
            byte[] inputBytes = Encoding.ASCII.GetBytes(inputData);

            // Create an encryptor using the specified key and IV
            ICryptoTransform encryptor = aes.CreateEncryptor();

            // Perform the encryption and get the encrypted byte array
            byte[] encryptedBytes = encryptor.TransformFinalBlock(inputBytes, 0, inputBytes.Length);

            // Convert the encrypted bytes into a Base64 string and return it
            return Convert.ToBase64String(encryptedBytes);
        }
    }

```

The **AESDecrypt** method performs the reverse operation. It takes the Base64 encoded encrypted string, decodes it back into bytes, and uses the same AES key, IV, mode, and padding to transform it back into the original plaintext string. This allows the data to be securely stored or transmitted and then retrieved in its original form:

```

    /// <summary>
    /// Decrypts a Base64-encoded string using AES decryption.
    /// </summary>
    /// <param name="inputData">The Base64-encoded string to decrypt.</param>
```

```
        /// <returns>The decrypted plaintext string.</returns>
        public static string AESDecrypt(string inputData)
        {
            // Use a disposable AES crypto provider to manage decryption
            using (AesCryptoServiceProvider aes = new AesCryptoServiceProvider())
            {
                aes.BlockSize = 128; // AES block size (128 bits)
                aes.KeySize = 256; // AES key size (256 bits)
                aes.Key = Encoding.ASCII.GetBytes(aesKey); // Convert key to byte array
                aes.IV = Encoding.ASCII.GetBytes(aesIv); // Convert IV to byte array
                aes.Mode = CipherMode.CBC; // Use Cipher Block Chaining (CBC) mode
                aes.Padding = PaddingMode.PKCS7; // Use PKCS7 padding

                // Convert the Base64-encoded string into a byte array
                byte[] encryptedBytes = Convert.FromBase64String(inputData);

                // Create a decryptor using the specified key and IV
                ICryptoTransform decryptor = aes.CreateDecryptor();

                // Perform the decryption and get the decrypted byte array
                byte[] decryptedBytes = decryptor.TransformFinalBlock(encryptedBytes, 0, encryptedBytes.Length);

                // Convert the decrypted bytes into a string and return it
                return Encoding.ASCII.GetString(decryptedBytes);
            }
        }

        /// <summary>
        /// Encrypts a plaintext string using a simple XOR cipher and encodes the result in Base64.
        /// </summary>
        /// <param name="input">The string to encrypt.</param>
        /// <param name="key">The key used for XOR encryption.</param>
```

```
        /// <returns>The encrypted string encoded in Base64 format.</returns>
        public static string XorEncrypt(string input, string key)
        {
            // Create a character array to store the XOR result
            char[] output = new char[input.Length];

            // XOR each character of the input string with the corresponding character from the key
            for (int i = 0; i < input.Length; i++)
            {
                output[i] = (char)(input[i] ^ key[i % key.Length]);
            }

            // Convert the result to a Base64-encoded string and return it
            return Convert.ToBase64String(Encoding.UTF8.GetBytes(new string(output)));
        }

        /// <summary>
        /// Decrypts a Base64-encoded string that was encrypted using XOR cipher.
        /// </summary>
        /// <param name="encrypted">The Base64-encoded string to decrypt.</param>
        /// <param name="key">The key used for XOR encryption.</param>
        /// <returns>The decrypted plaintext string.</returns>
        public static string XorDecrypt(string encrypted, string key)
        {
            // Decode the Base64-encoded string back into its original XOR-encrypted form
            string decoded = Encoding.UTF8.GetString(Convert.FromBase64String(encrypted));

            // Create a character array to store the XOR result
            char[] output = new char[decoded.Length];

            // XOR each character of the decoded string with the corresponding character from the key
```

```
            for (int i = 0; i < decoded.Length; i++)
            {
                output[i] = (char)(decoded[i] ^ key[i % key.Length]);
            }

            // Convert the result back to a plaintext string and return it
            return new string(output);
        }
    }
}
```

XOR encryption is an encryption method used to encrypt data and is hard to crack by the brute-force method, i.e, generating encryption keys to match the correct one. This operation is sometimes called the modulus 2 addition (or subtraction) process.

The logic is a string of text can be encrypted by applying the bitwise XOR operator to every character using a given key. To decrypt the output, merely reapplying the XOR function with the key will remove the cipher.

This algorithm is quite simple to implement and quite effective. Following is a code example:

```
using UnityEngine;
using CryptoNamespace;
/// <summary>
/// This class demonstrates how to use XOR encryption and decryption.
/// Note: The namespace `CryptoNamespace` contains additional encryption methods, including AES encryption.
/// </summary>
public class Crypto : MonoBehaviour
{
    /// <summary>
    /// Unity's Start method is called when the script is first executed.
    /// Here, it demonstrates the process of encrypting and decrypting a message using XOR.
    /// </summary>
    private void Start()
    {
        // The message to be encrypted
        string message = "Encrypt this message";

        // The encryption key. Ensure the key is long and
```

```
complex enough for security.
        string key = "Unity4Professionals";

        // Encrypt the message using XOR encryption
        var xorencryptsample = CryptoMethods.XorEncrypt(message, key);

        // Log the original and encrypted messages to the Unity console
        Debug.Log("Original message = " + message + " - XOR Encrypted message: " + xorencryptsample);

        // Decrypt the message using the same key
        var decrypted = CryptoMethods.XorDecrypt(xorencryptsample, key);

        // Log the encrypted and decrypted messages to the Unity console
        Debug.Log("Encrypted message = " + xorencryptsample + " - Decrypted message: " + decrypted);
    }
}
```

Let the users take control

When the app uses the camera, GPS, microphone, etc., the user must be informed at all times. Please make sure they give your express consent.

It is imperative that any modifications made to the privacy policies are adequately communicated and that explicit consent is sought.

To enhance the assurance that no issues are generated, it is advisable to permit the user to modify everything from a preferences menu.

Intellectual property rights

It is imperative that you possess the necessary licenses or clearances for any third-party assets, such as music, images, or trademarks, used in your games. This includes Unity assets purchased from the online Unity Asset Store. So, be careful about the licenses of each asset you acquire.

Furthermore, it is imperative to safeguard your own intellectual property by acquiring copyrights, trademarks, and patents.

The following list describes the most common copyright licenses for digital content, each offering different levels of permission and restrictions. It is essential for creators and users alike to understand these licenses in order to ensure that they comply with copyright law and respect the rights of content creators:

- **All Rights Reserved (ARR)**: This is the default copyright status for most content. It means that the copyright holder retains all rights granted by copyright law, and others are not allowed to use, distribute, or modify the work without explicit permission.
- **Public Domain (CC0)**: Works in the public domain lack copyright protection and can be freely used by anyone for any purpose. The **Creative Commons Zero (CC0)** license is a tool used to dedicate works to the public domain, waiving all copyright and related rights.
- **Attribution (CC BY)**: This license permits others to distribute, remix, modify, and build upon the work, even for commercial purposes, provided that they acknowledge the original creator(s) for their original creation. This is the most permissive Creative Commons license.
- **Attribution-ShareAlike (CC BY-SA)**: This license grants others the right to remix, modify, and build upon the work, even for commercial purposes, provided that they acknowledge the original creator(s) and license their new creations under the same terms. This license is often used for collaborative projects and open content initiatives.
- **Attribution-NonCommercial (CC BY-NC)**: This license permits others to remix, modify, and build upon the work without commercial gain, provided they acknowledge the original creator(s). New creations based on the original work must not be used for commercial purposes.
- **Attribution-NoDerivatives (CC BY-ND)**: This license permits others to redistribute the work, both commercially and non-commercially, provided that it remains unchanged and in its entirety with proper credit to the original creator(s).
- **Attribution-NonCommercial-ShareAlike (CC BY-NC-SA)**: This license allows others to remix, tweak, and build upon the work non-commercially as long as they credit the original creator(s) and license their new creations under the same terms.
- **Attribution-NonCommercial-NoDerivatives (CC BY-NC-ND)**: This is the most restrictive Creative Commons license. It permits others to download and share the works with others, provided they credit the original creator(s). However, they cannot modify the works in any way or use them commercially.

Conclusion

In this chapter, we looked at the critical legal obligations that game developers face when handling user data, particularly PII. It was emphasized that the fundamental necessity of a transparent privacy policy, readily accessible to users, that clearly outlines the collection, use, and sharing of their data. The importance of accurately declaring advertisements within applications and precisely defining the target audience, especially when developing for children, was underscored, requiring adherence to platform policies and age regulations such as COPPA and PEGI. Furthermore, the necessity of complying with various global data protection laws, including GDPR, CCPA, PIPL, and LGPD, was explored. This entails securing explicit user consent for data collection and ensuring the secure processing of that information. It is crucial to remember that as the developer, you are the controller responsible for implementing these client-side consent decisions. While Unity provides the necessary tools, it does not determine your legal basis for processing data. Best practices were shared, including minimizing personal data collection, utilizing local storage where feasible, and employing encryption to enhance security. Additionally, empowering users with control over their data and respecting intellectual property rights, both for assets used and their own creations, were emphasized. Equipped with the essential knowledge to manage user data legally and ethically, the logical next step is to comprehend how to securely manage the identities of your players.

In the next chapter, we will demonstrate how Unity Authentication provides a secure and reliable service for player identity management within your game. You will learn how this service integrates with various external providers, such as Facebook and Google, along with built-in email and password options. We will illustrate how Unity Authentication facilitates seamless progress preservation across devices by integrating with services like Cloud Save and offering advanced security features, including multi-factor authentication, passwordless login, and account linking. You will discover the process for setting up the Authentication service within the **Unity Gaming Services** (**UGS**) dashboard and configuring specific providers. Additionally, we will clarify the fundamental concepts of tokens and sessions that underpin the authentication process.

Multiple choice questions

1. **Who is primarily responsible for determining the legal basis for processing end-user data when utilizing UGS?**
   a. The user, by providing explicit consent upon installation.
   b. Unity Technologies, as the data processor.
   c. The developer, acting as the controller.
   d. The hosting server's geographical location.
2. **Which of the following data privacy regulations applies specifically to the protection of personal information within the European Economic Area (EEA) and the United Kingdom?**
   a. CCPA
   b. PIPL
   c. GDPR
   d. VCDPA

3. **What U.S. law specifically prohibits the collection and utilization of data from children under the age of 13?**
   a. Pan-European Game Information (PEGI)
   b. California Consumer Privacy Act (CCPA)
   c. Children's Online Privacy Protection Act (COPPA)
   d. International Age Rating Coalition (IARC)

4. **When is a developer generally required to include a link to a privacy policy on their application's Store Listing page?**
   a. Only if the application processes highly risky or sensitive permissions (e.g., camera or microphone).
   b. Only if the application targets children as part of its audience.
   c. Only if the application collects any personal or sensitive user data.
   d. Regardless of whether the application accesses any personal or sensitive user data.

5. **Which of the following cryptographic methods are described in the chapter as providing functionalities for securing user data?**
   a. Advanced Encryption Standard (AES)
   b. Rivest-Shamir-Adleman (RSA)
   c. MD5 message-digest
   d. Secure Hash Algorithm 256 (SHA-256)

6. **According to the Pan-European Game Information (PEGI) classification described in the chapter, which category includes games that show more explicit acts of violence with fantasy characters or non-explicit manifestations of violence with animals or characters with human features?**
   a. PEGI 3
   b. PEGI 7
   c. PEGI 12
   d. PEGI 16

7. **How do the typical application publishing models of Apple (App Store) and Google (Play Store) differ regarding pre-publication review?**
   a. Apple employs automated control, allowing rapid publishing (hours/days), while Google relies on extensive expert control (weeks).
   b. Apple relies on automated control, placing responsibility primarily on the developer, while Google requires expert review.
   c. Apple employs exhaustive control by experts (weeks), whereas Google uses automated and faster control (hours/days), placing more initial responsibility on the developer.
   d. Both stores use the International Age Rating Coalition (IARC) system exclusively for content review and verification.

8. **To mitigate potential legal and security issues related to user data, what is the recommended best practice regarding data storage for metrics tracking?**
   a. Obtain consent through the Firebase SDK before storing PII on the server.
   b. Store only statistical data in the cloud and attempt to store personal preferences locally.
   c. Encrypt all data using the same key for both encryption and decryption (symmetric encryption).
   d. Retain the name and surname of all users who successfully complete a difficult level.
9. **Scenario: A developer in China publishes a new game that collects player email addresses. To ensure compliance with required regulations regarding personal data protection, which specific law should the developer prioritize implementing robust consent mechanisms for?**
   a. California Consumer Privacy Act (CCPA).
   b. Children's Online Privacy Protection Act (COPPA).
   c. Brazilian General Data Protection Law (LGPD).
   d. Personal Information Protection Law (PIPL).
10. **If a creator uses the Creative Commons license type known as Attribution-NoDerivatives (CC BY-ND) for their asset, what usage restriction must others adhere to?**
    a. They are permitted to use the asset only for non-commercial purposes.
    b. They are allowed to modify the work, provided they license the new creation under the same terms.
    c. They can redistribute the work commercially, but it must remain unchanged and in its entirety.
    d. They are prohibited from sharing the work with others, even non-commercially.

Answers

1	c
2	c
3	c
4	d
5	a, b, c
6	c
7	c
8	b
9	d
10	c

Chapter 9
Unity Authentication for Multiple Platforms

Introduction

By utilizing Cloud Save with Unity Authentication, players can authenticate with multiple platform accounts, thereby ensuring seamless progress preservation across their devices.

This chapter focuses on Unity Authentication for multiple platforms. It offers a secure and safe method to authenticate your players and manage their identities within your game. The chapter covers the authentication service itself, including the simplest authentication methods. You will learn about the Unity Gaming Services Authentication setup, showing you how to configure the service. Furthermore, it details how to implement sign in with Apple and Google Sign in. While not included in UGS directly, Firebase as another authentication option from Google is also discussed. By the end of this chapter, you should be able to understand the different authentication providers available and know how to integrate some of the main ones into your Unity project using UGS.

Unity Authentication provides a dependable and secure means of managing player identities within your game, thereby enabling you to concentrate on crafting engaging gameplay experiences.

Structure

The chapter covers the following topics:

- Authentication service
    - Variety of suppliers
    - Amazon Cognito
    - Microsoft Azure Active Directory
    - Auth0
    - Google Sign in

- The simplest Authentication
- Working of Authentication
    - Concept of a token
    - Understanding session
- Unity Gaming Services Authentication setup
    - Facebook authentication
- Sign in with Apple
- Google Sign in
- Firebase
- Oculus
- Steam
- Open ID

Objectives

In the previous chapters, we saw how we stored all types of data (events, session time, ranking of scores, content, etc.). All this information must meet legal requirements that also change depending on the area of the planet where the users are from or where our server is located. In this chapter, we are going to try to look at the legal aspects of having our content stored in the cloud.

Authentication service

An authentication service refers to a system or component of a software application that verifies the identity of individuals or entities attempting to access the system. It ensures that users are the person they claim to be before granting them access to resources or functionalities within the application.

Authentication services typically involve the use of credentials, such as usernames and passwords, but they can also include more advanced methods like biometric data (fingerprint, facial recognition), security tokens, or multifactor authentication.

The main objective of an authentication service is to securely validate the identity of users, thereby protecting sensitive information and resources from unauthorized access. It plays a pivotal role in safeguarding the security and integrity of digital systems and is frequently a fundamental component of contemporary software architectures, particularly in web applications, mobile applications, and enterprise systems.

Variety of suppliers

One of the first surprises regarding authentication is the large number of service providers that exist. Each company has developed its own system, since it is the gateway to obtaining user data. This information is tremendously valuable for big data, data science, and advertising, which generate profits.

Since there are so many different systems, programming is extremely complicated, since different development must be carried out for each platform. Large platforms have also created tools with which we can use different types of authentication with a single code.

The primary factors contributing to the proliferation of diverse providers are:

- Numerous systems originate from diverse social networks or online services that, upon their creation, were required to develop their own systems. Among them are the following:
    - *Meta, Facebook*, and *WhatsApp* (Meta is the parent company, but since the companies were previously different, the system for identifying users is not always the same).
    - *X* was formerly *Twitter*.
    - *Google* offers various services such as Gmail, Google Drive, Youtube, Google Maps, and other similar services.
    - *Apple*: iCloud, the App Store, and Apple Pay.
- When it comes to authentication, users possess distinct preferences and habits. Some users may opt to sign in with their Google account, while others may opt to utilize their Facebook credentials. By providing multiple authentication options, services can meet the diverse preferences of their user base.
- Partnerships and ecosystems are distinct strategies employed by numerous organizations to implement authentication services as a component of their broader ecosystem strategy. For example, the Google Sign in is closely integrated with other Google services, such as Gmail, Google Drive, and YouTube. Apple authentication services are intricately intertwined with the Apple ecosystem, comprising iCloud, App Store, and Apple Pay.
- Large user bases, such as Google and Facebook, offer authentication services that are widely recognized and used on numerous platforms and websites. This accessibility allows users to log in without having to create new accounts for each service they use.
- Some users may have a greater trust in certain companies when it comes to managing their authentication credentials. For example, users may feel more comfortable using authentication services provided by well-established tech giants such as Google, Apple, or Microsoft, given their reputation for strong security measures.

- Different authentication services are able to provide specialized functions or integration capabilities tailored to specific use cases or industries. Oculus, for example, offers custom authentication services for virtual reality applications and experiences.
- In some cases, companies may be required to comply with specific regulations or standards related to user authentication or data privacy. Multiple authentication options allow them to meet these requirements while also providing flexibility to users.

In the **Authentication** section, you can configure your project and the different authentications:

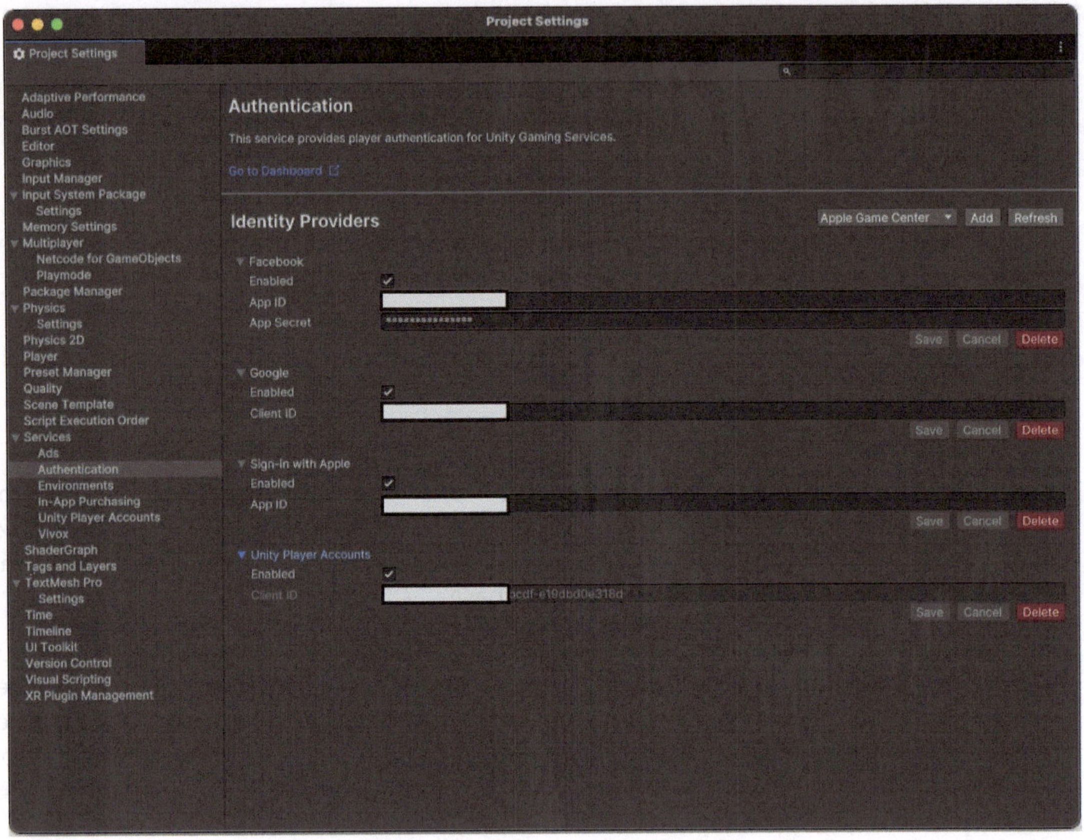

***Figure 9.1**: Your project settings with the different authentications*

Amazon Cognito

Amazon Cognito is a comprehensive identity management solution also offered by Amazon Web Services. It provides authentication and authorization for web and mobile applications.

Compared to other services, Amazon Cognito offers tight integration with AWS services, making it ideal for applications hosted on AWS infrastructure.

It provides features like user pools for authentication, federated identities, multifactor authentication, and user data synchronization across devices. The following figure details the AWS workflow that ensures a user's data is accessible and available to all AWS services once they have authenticated:

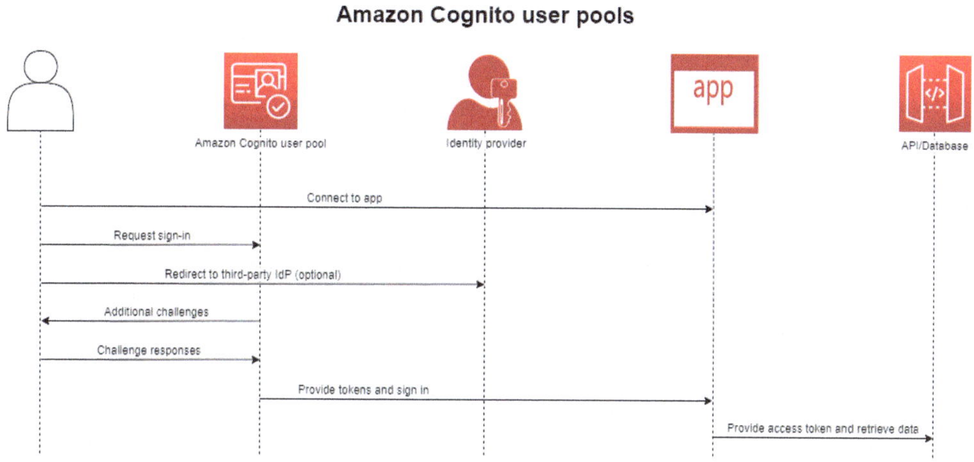

Figure 9.2: *Amazon Cognito centralizes authentication across the entire AWS infrastructure*

Microsoft Azure Active Directory

Azure AD is a Microsoft cloud-based identity and access management service. It provides authentication and authorization services for applications and resources hosted on the Azure platform and on-premises environments.

Azure Active Directory provides seamless integration with Microsoft's ecosystem of products and services, including Office 365, Azure services, and Windows devices.

It supports a variety of authentication methods, including username/password, multi-factor authentication, social logins, and integration with on-premises Active Directory environments.

Microsoft Azure Active Directory provides seamless integration with Microsoft's ecosystem of products and services. The following figure shows how Azure Active Directory is used to authenticate users and grant them access to their subscribed services (some from Microsoft itself, but also from third parties):

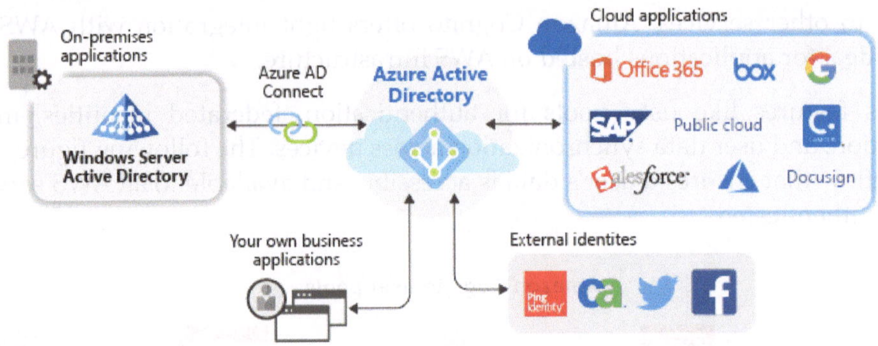

Figure 9.3: Microsoft leverages Active Directory for Azure, adding value to corporate networks

Auth0

Auth0 is a globally recognized **identity as a service** (**IDaaS**) platform that offers authentication and authorization solutions for web and mobile applications, and single-page applications.

The software offers a range of functionalities, including user management, social logins, multi-factor authentication, and custom authentication workflows.

Auth0 is renowned for its flexibility and ease of integration with various development frameworks and platforms. It provides extensive documentation and support for developers. The following figure shows this free asset in the Unity Asset Store:

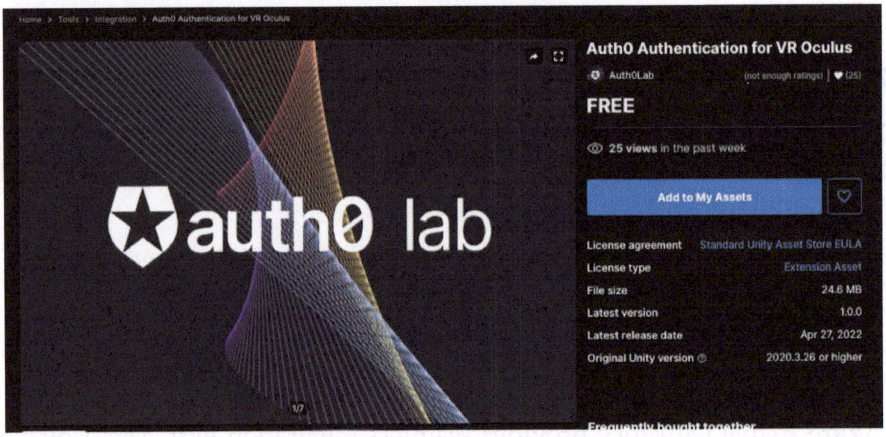

Figure 9.4: Auth0 Authentication for VR Oculus

You should note that Auth0 has SDK for multiple platforms and development languages, including Unity 3D. There is a GitHub repository with instructions on how to use the Unity SDK at this address: **https://github.com/auth0-lab/auth0-unity.**

Google Sign in

Indeed, let us compare Google Sign in with Amazon Cognito, Microsoft **Azure Active Directory** (**Azure AD**), Auth0, and Okta across various aspects. Google Sign in feature is tightly integrated with the Google ecosystem, enabling users to authenticate themselves, as shown in the following figure:

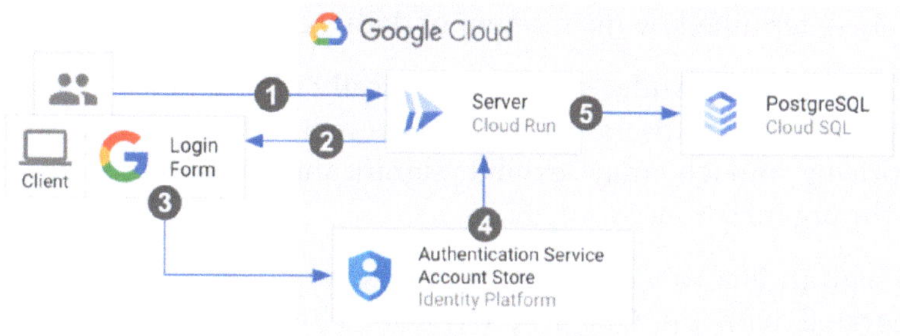

***Figure 9.5**: Integration on the Google ecosystem*

The Google Sign in feature is tightly integrated with the Google ecosystem, enabling users to authenticate themselves with their Google accounts across a diverse range of Google services and third-party applications.

Amazon Cognito, Azure AD, Auth0, and Okta provide more agnostic solutions that can be seamlessly integrated with a variety of platforms and services beyond Google, including other identity providers and social logins.

If you are already an experienced developer, the integration process will be relatively straightforward. Google Sign in offers comprehensive documentation, SDKs, and developer resources that allow you to integrate its authentication service into web, mobile, or desktop applications.

Amazon Cognito, Azure AD, Auth0, and Okta also provide robust developer resources and documentation. However, they may necessitate additional configuration and setup in comparison to Google Sign in due to their broader feature sets and customization options.

Flexibility and customization are key. Google Sign in allows developers to customize the appearance of the sign-in button, request specific user information, and implement custom authentication flows.

Amazon Cognito, Azure AD, Auth0, and Okta provide more extensive customization options, allowing developers to tailor authentication flows, implement custom login screens, and integrate with various identity providers and protocols beyond Google Sign in.

Depending on the nature of your platform, you must carefully consider its scalability. Authenticating a few thousand users is not the same as authenticating millions. The ability to grow without losing speed or functionality, fault tolerance, and enterprise-class features should be a priority if you anticipate a massive scale of your platform.

Although Google Sign in has the capacity to handle large user bases, it may lack certain advanced enterprise features offered by specialized identity management platforms such as Amazon Cognito, Azure AD, Auth0, and Okta. These platforms provide features such as user provisioning, role-based access control, audit logs, and compliance certification, making them popular choices for enterprise applications.

Google Sign in is typically available for developers to utilize for free, subject to usage limitations and quotas that are determined by the number of daily active users and API requests.

Amazon Cognito, Azure AD, Auth0, and Okta typically offer a tiered pricing plan based on factors such as the number of users, authentication methods used, and additional features required. The pricing models may exhibit significant variation based on the specific requirements of the organization.

Overall, Google Sign in is a robust authentication solution, especially for applications that are heavily integrated with the Google ecosystem. However, organizations with broader integration requirements, advanced customization needs, or specific enterprise features may prefer using platforms, such as Amazon Cognito, Azure AD, Auth0, or Okta.

The simplest authentication

Let us make an authentication example as simple as possible to understand how it works. Anonymous authentication is used to allow users to access resources without the need to provide specific user credentials, such as a username and password.

The first step is to install the Unity Package **Authentication**:

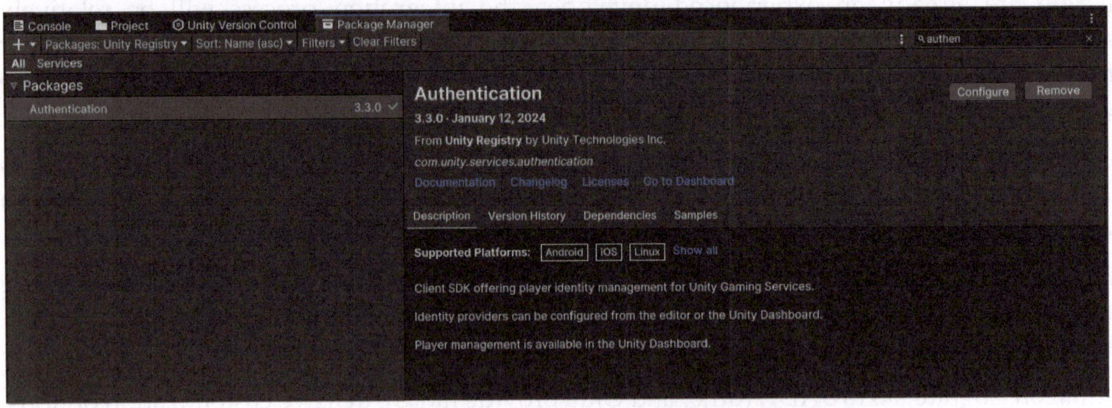

Figure 9.6: Import the Authentication Package from Unity

Once the package is installed, we are going to create an empty object and add a new C# script to it.

This chapter has a bit more code than usual, but to simplify it as much as possible and optimize compilation times, all the authentication methods have been grouped into a namespace, and a component for each of them has been created, where the call has been simplified. The code for that namespace with all the functions can be found in the project provided by the book at the path: **`Assets/Scripts/Chapter9/AuthNamespace.cs`**

The following is the simplest possible code to do an anonymous authentication (for it to work, you will need to import the **`AuthNamespace`** that comes with the sample code in this chapter):

```
using UnityEngine;
using AuthNamespace;

public class UnityAuthManager : MonoBehaviour
{
    private async void Start()
    {
        Debug.Log("Authenticating anonymously...");
        AuthService.AuthenticateUser();
    }
}
```

This method works, and we have already received a user ID and token from the system. It may be helpful to control so that users enter the system only when they want. However, it has many shortcomings, the most notable being that users cannot access their data from other devices. We will not be able to know the progress of the users either because we will not save any specific data about any of them.

Let us now consider a slightly more intricate example involving the collection of the user's email address and password. The following code enables us to effectively manage all data and progress pertaining to each individual user. To use this authentication method, you must activate it from the UGS panel:

```
using UnityEngine;
using AuthNamespace;

public class UnityEmailAuthManagerMonoBehaviour : MonoBehaviour
{
    [Header("Authentication Fields")]
    [SerializeField] private string email = "example@example.com"; // Set your test email here
    [SerializeField] private string password = "password123"; // Set your test password here
```

```

    private async void Start()
    {
        // Ensure Unity services are initialized before calling the authentication
        await Unity.Services.Core.UnityServices.InitializeAsync();

        // Authenticate with Unity using the provided email and password
        await AuthService.AuthenticateWithEmailPassword(email, password);
    }
}
```

Working of authentication

To understand how it works, first, it is necessary to learn some basic concepts.

Concept of a token

A token is a string of numbers and letters that is quite long and has no meaning or use by itself. The following is what a token looks like:

eyJ0eXAiOiJKV1QiLCJhbGciOiJIUzI1NiJ9.eyJAFXNzYWdlIjoiSldUIFJ1bGVzISIsImlhdCI6MTQ 1OTQ0ODExOSwiZXhwIjoxNDU5NDU0NTE5fQ.-yIVBD5b73C75osbmwwshQNRC7frWUYrqaT jTpza2y4

Although it seems that it has no meaning, it does have meaning for the server where we want to connect. This complex code is like the password that allows us to enter; it is the result of applying an electronic signature to ensure that only authorized users can gain access.

Tokens are signed to protect them from tampering; they are not encrypted. This means that a token can be easily decoded and reveal its contents.

Token-based authentication ensures that each request to a server is accompanied by a signed token, whose authenticity is verified by the server. Upon verification, the server responds accordingly.

The token is like having the key that opens the lock and allows us to enter the server. If you do not have the right key, you cannot access it.

If the token is correct, you can enter the server, and a session is created.

Understanding session

A session is the period of time during which a user is authorized to access resources or services after successfully authenticating. A session begins when a user successfully authenticates to the system by entering credentials, such as a username and password. It ends when the user logs out or ends their interaction with the system.

During a session, the system may establish and maintain certain information about the user, such as session identifiers, access privileges, and user preferences, among other relevant data. This information is used to manage user interaction with the system and to ensure access to resources remains within authorized limits.

It is imperative for system security to effectively manage sessions, which entails implementing measures, such as automatically terminating sessions after periods of inactivity, safeguarding against session attacks, and effectively managing user credentials for the duration. This prevents unauthorized access and protects the privacy and security of users and system data. The process can be seen in the following figure:

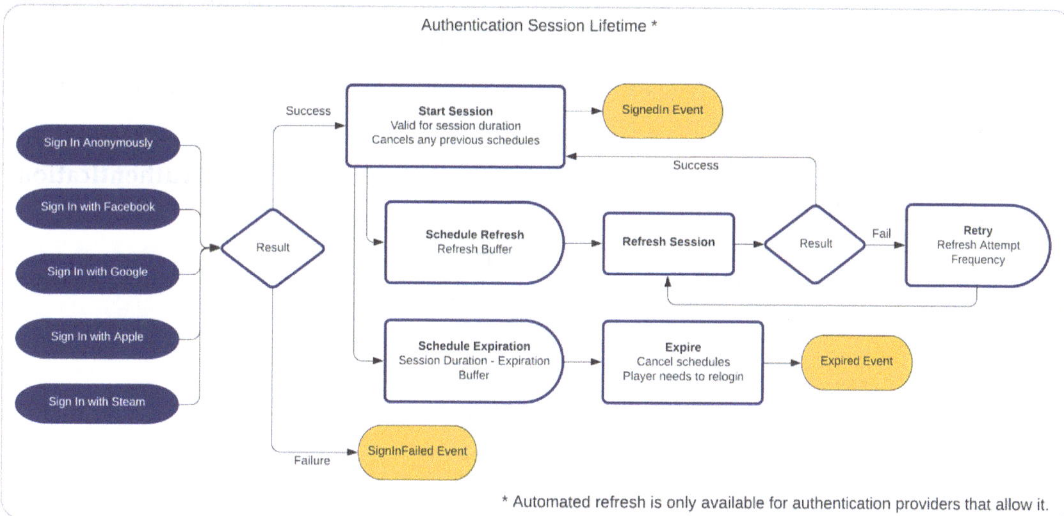

***Figure 9.7**: Workflow of how authentication works*

Unity Authentication enables users to select their preferred authentication provider, such as Apple, Facebook, or Google. Upon a player's login to your application, Unity Authentication generates the following tokens and IDs:

- **A PlayerID (a random 28-character alphanumeric string)**: Used to identify new and returning players across different devices and third-party providers.
- **A session token**: Used to re-authenticate the user after the session expires.

- **An authentication token**: Contains the PlayerID and is used to verify the user's identity, preventing unauthorized impersonation.

Tokens and PlayerID are like magic keys that unlock player information during authentication in Unity products and games. They allow the following:

- A player identification mechanism and data storage system (e.g., saving game state and recording in-app purchases).
- Ensuring consistent game experiences for the player, including leaderboard rankings and suggested in-app purchases.
- Tracking the player's game behavior across multiple devices.
- Support for multiplayer features on various platforms.

Unity Gaming Services authentication setup

We are going to see how to activate the authentication service and then how some of the main providers can be configured through the following steps:

1. First, go to your Unity Cloud console and select the project you want to add the authentication service to.
2. To add it, you must press the plus button and search for **Player Authentication**, as seen in the following figure:

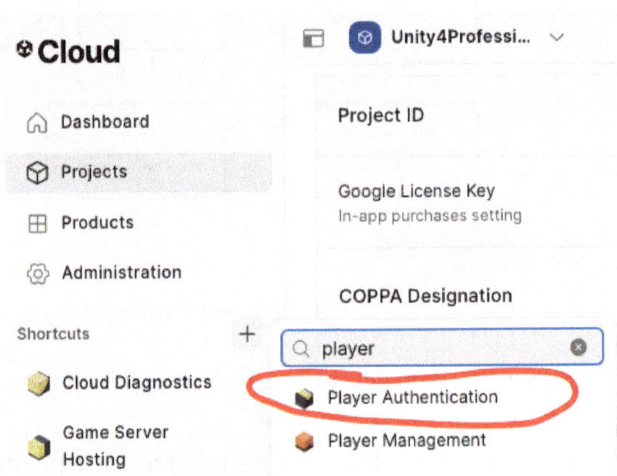

***Figure 9.8**: Add the Player Authentication to your app*

Once the service has been added and launched, we will proceed to add the service providers that we want to use for users to enter our app or game, like:

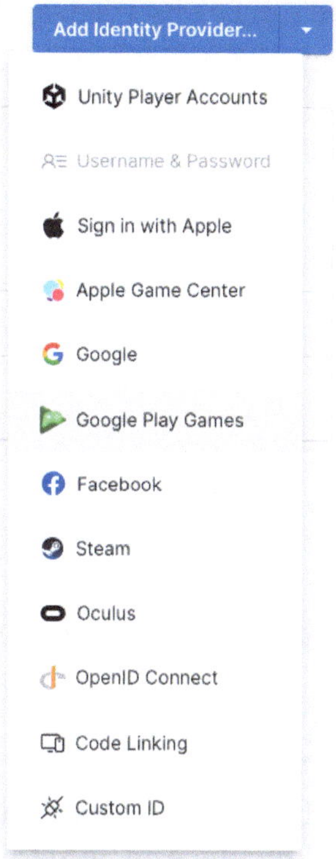

***Figure 9.9:** Some Auth providers*

For each type of service, we will need to create specific code and possibly install a package or SDK in our project. However, this integrated system makes the entire process much easier and allows us to add or remove providers if we are interested.

When we activate a provider, they will ask us for a series of keys (such as the App ID, App Secret, and Client ID) that vary depending on the provider. We also see a link to the provider's documentation for all the necessary configurations.

Once we have completed the steps indicated in the documentation, we will have the keys requested and will be able to fill out the form to activate the service.

The services that have been activated can be observed, as depicted in the following figure:

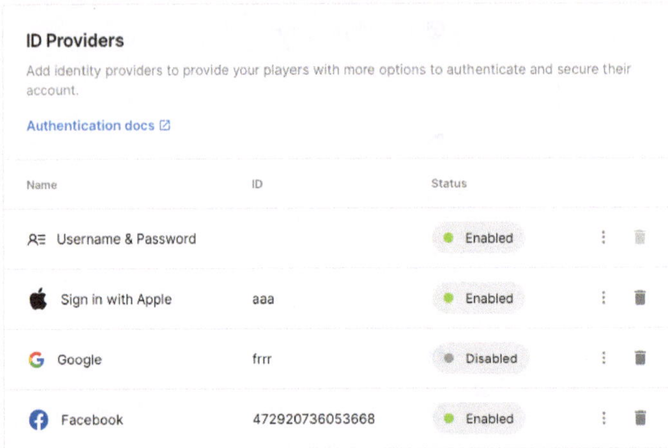

Figure 9.10: *Providers that are enabled/disabled on your app*

Facebook authentication

If you want to activate authentication through Facebook (remember that you have a large number of users), it will ask you for the **App ID** and the **App Secret,** as you can see in the following figure:

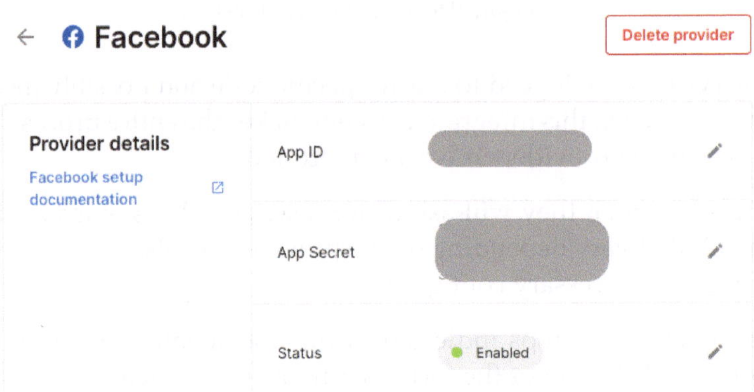

Figure 9.11: *These parameters are necessary to configure the service*

We will now see steps to obtain these IDs and be able to activate the service.

Register as a Meta developer

To perform these steps, you must be a Meta developer first. If you are already a Meta developer, you can go to the next section.

Once you have registered, you will have access to the App Dashboard and all Meta products, SDKs, APIs, development tools, and developer documentation.

Now, refer to the following steps:

1. Log-in into your Facebook account, and proceed to the following URL: **https://developers.facebook.com/async/registration.**
   a. Alternatively, one may access the Meta for Developers website by clicking on the **Get Started** button.
2. Agree to the **Terms and Policies** of Meta.
3. Verify your account. An email with a verification code is sent to the account given in the registration process.
4. Indicates your occupation. Meta also asks to know what you do before completing the registration process.

Creating an app

If you already have an app created in Meta, you can go to the next step.

Before starting, you should know the requirements that Meta has to publish an app (although you may not need all of them if it is still in development):

- Verify your company.
- A unique icon image for your app:
  - The size in pixels must be 512 x 512 or 1024 x 1024.
  - The admitted formats are JPG, GIF or PNG.
  - The size limit is 5 MB.
- Contact information for a data protection officer if you are doing business in the European Union.
- A URL to your privacy policy for your app.
- A URL to instructions or a callback that allows a user to delete their data from your app.

If you have the requirements, follow the steps to create a new app in Meta: **https://developers.facebook.com/apps/creation/**. Once you have filled out the forms, you can find the IDs that interest us in the **App settings | Basic** menu, as shown in the following figure:

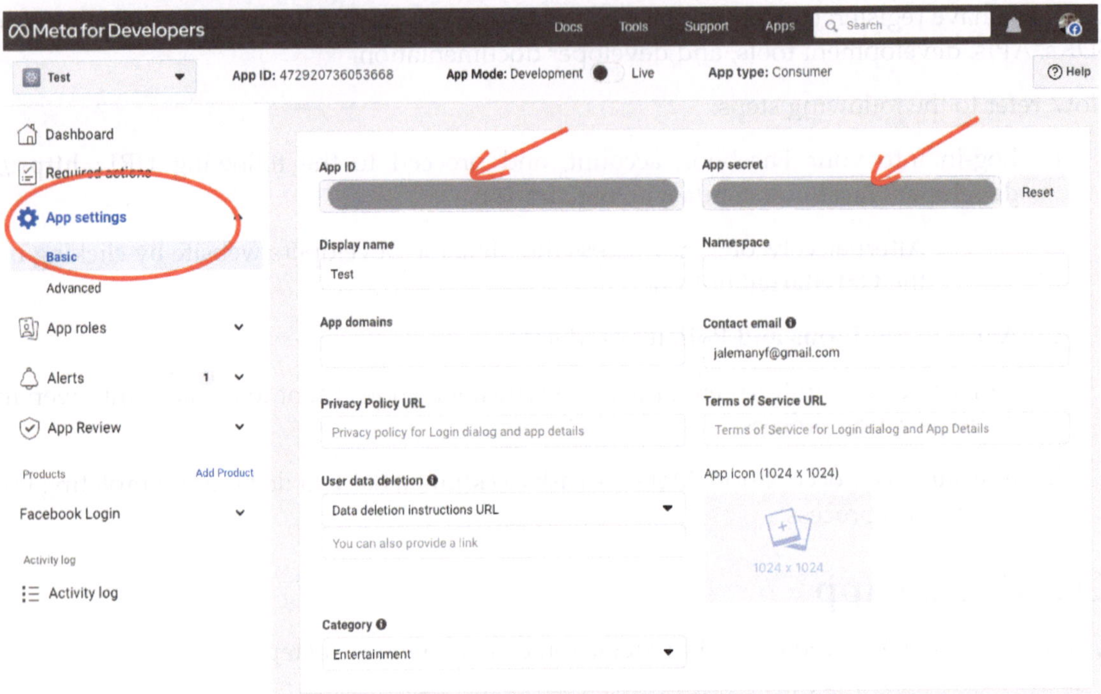

Figure 9.12: Necessary parameters

Note: These two IDs (App ID and App Secret) are the ones that Unity Gaming Services asked us to activate the service.

Once we have finished configuring the two platforms, it is necessary to add the code so that we can use authentication in our project.

Installing the Facebook Unity SDK

Perform the following steps to install the Facebook SDK:

1. Create a new project or open an existing one in the Unity Editor.
2. Download the Facebook Unity SDK. After the download, decompress the ZIP file.

    Note: You can find more code to connect Unity and Facebook at this website: https://docs.unity.com/ugs/manual/authentication/manual/platform-signin-facebook

1. In the Unity editor, click on **Assets | Import Package | Custom Package**. Next, navigate to the folder where you extracted the Facebook for Unity SDK and select **FacebookSDK.Unitypackage**.

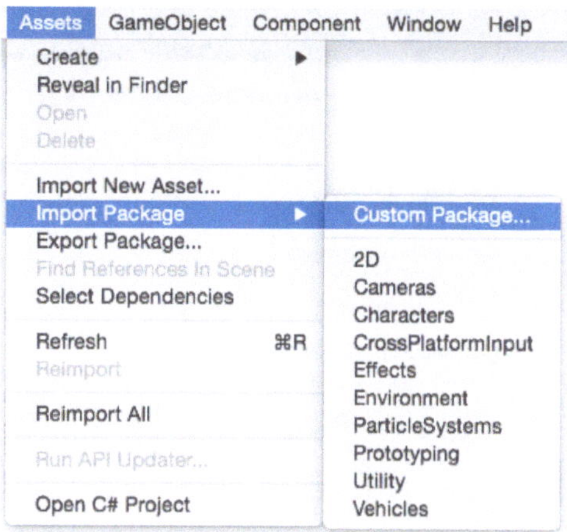

***Figure 9.13**: Import the package for Meta SDK*

2. Import all the assets included in the package, This will create the entire structure within your project. It may take a while depending on your computer's speed.
3. A new menu item called Facebook will appear on your Unity Editor after the scripts are processed. Open **Facebook | Edit Settings**.
4. Fill out the form with the data of the app in the Meta account for developers:

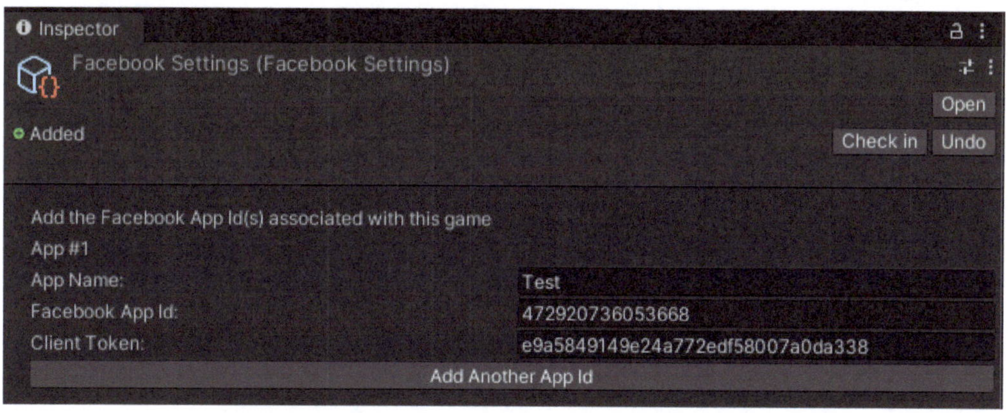

***Figure 9.14**: A new parameter is needed: Client Token*

Here, you will be asked for the **App Name**, the **Facebook App ID** and the **Client Token**. We have not mentioned this last field (**Client Token**) yet, and it is a little more difficult to find. It is found in **App settings/ Advanced** in the **Security** box:

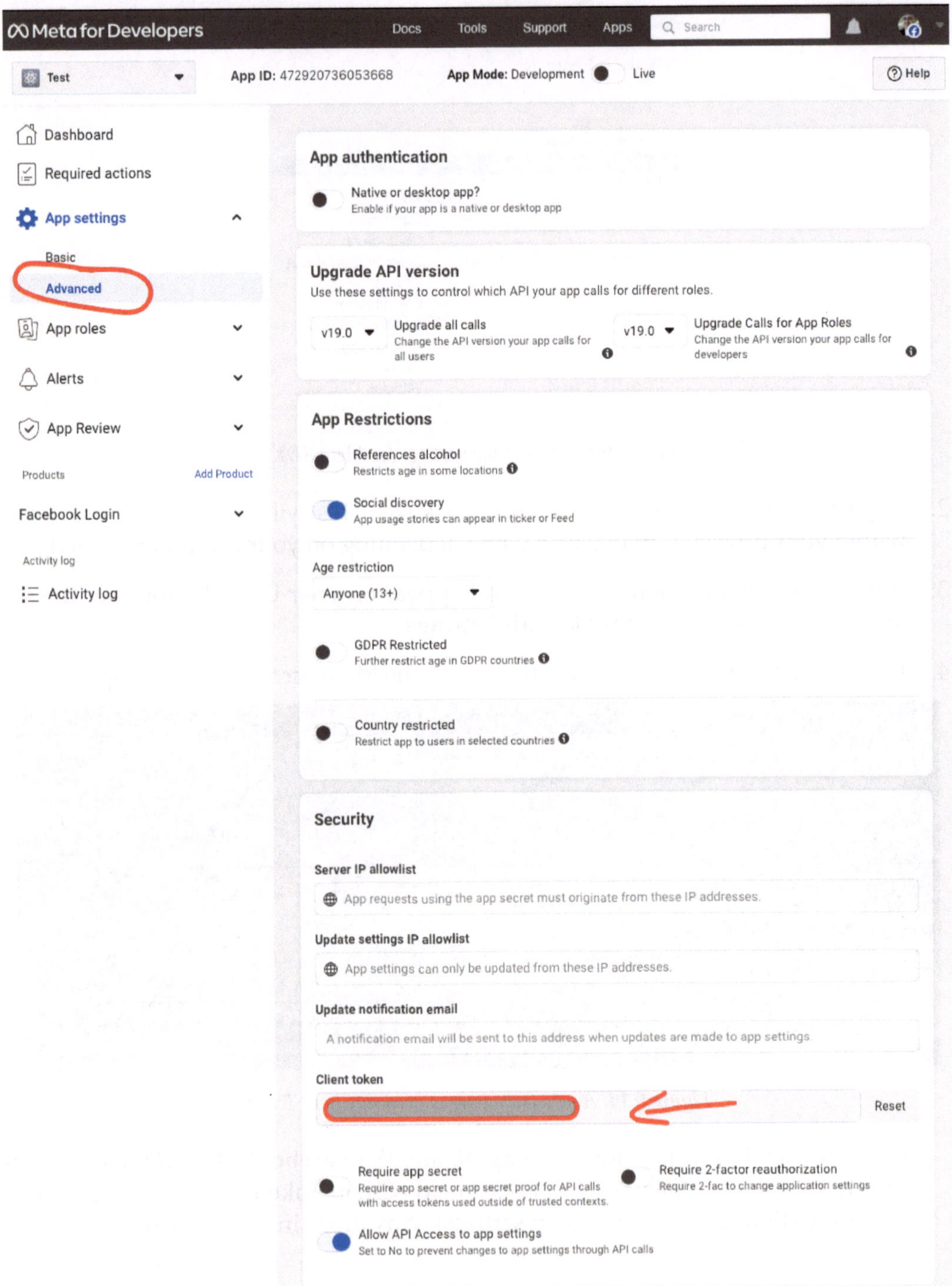

Figure 9.15: Here is the client token parameter

With everything now configured in the Unity Editor, we can proceed to implement the code required to enable Facebook authentication in our project. The following is the code containing the methods we use to authenticate with the various services we'll cover in this chapter. For ease of reading, this code has been divided into three parts.

This first part includes the necessary **using** statements, defines the **AuthNamespace** where our authentication logic resides, and starts the **AuthService** static class. It also includes the methods for handling anonymous authentication, the simplest form of authentication, and the methods required to initiate and handle the Facebook authentication flow.

Anonymous authentication provides a user ID and token, allowing temporary access, but does not preserve user data across devices. Facebook authentication, on the other hand, allows players to sign in using their Facebook credentials, enabling identity and potentially linking progress across devices:

```
// Necessary namespaces for Unity functionalities, UGS Authentication,
// Task management for async operations, and Facebook SDK.
using UnityEngine;
using Unity.Services.Authentication; // Core UGS Authentication service
using Unity.Services.Core;          // Core UGS initialization
using UnityEngine.UI;               // For UI elements like Text
using System.Threading.Tasks;       // For async operations
using Facebook.Unity;               // Facebook SDK namespace

namespace AuthNamespace
{
    public static class AuthService
    {
        /// <summary>
        /// Authenticates the user anonymously with Unity Authentication.
        /// This method provides a temporary user ID and token but
        /// does not allow data persistence across devices.
        /// </summary>
        public static async void AuthenticateUser()
        {
            // Check if the user is already signed in to avoid re-authenticating.
            if (!AuthenticationService.Instance.IsSignedIn) //
            {
                try
                {
```

```
                    // Attempt to sign in anonymously.
                    await AuthenticationService.Instance.
SignInAnonymouslyAsync(); //
                    // Log success and the assigned Player ID.
                    Debug.
Log($"User authenticated successfully. Player ID: {AuthenticationService.
Instance.PlayerId}"); //
                }
                catch (RequestFailedException ex)
                {
                    // Log any errors that occur during the authentication
process.
                    Debug.
LogError($"Error during anonymous authentication: {ex.Message}"); //
                }
            }
            else
            {
                // Log if the user is already authenticated.
                Debug.Log("The user is already authenticated.");
            }
        }
        /// <summary>
        /// Authenticates the user using a Facebook access token with Unity
Authentication.
        /// This method links the Facebook account to a UGS player identity.
        /// </summary>
        /// <param name="accessToken">The access token obtained from Facebook.
</param>
        public static async void AuthenticateWithFace-
book(string accessToken) //
        {
            // Check if the user is already signed in.
            if (!AuthenticationService.Instance.IsSignedIn) //
            {
                try
                {
                    // Attempt to sign in or link with Facebook using the
```

```
provided token.
                    await AuthenticationService.Instance.
SignInWithFacebookAsync(accessToken);
                    // Log success and the assigned Player ID.
                    Debug.
Log($"User authenticated via Facebook. Player ID: {AuthenticationService.
Instance.PlayerId}");
                }
                catch (RequestFailedException ex)
                {
                    // Log any errors during Facebook authentication.
                    Debug.LogError($"Error during Facebook authentication: {ex.
Message}");
                }
            }
            else
            {
                // Log if the user is already authenticated.
                Debug.Log("The user is already authenticated.");
            }
        }
        /// <summary>
        /// Initiates the Facebook login process using the Facebook SDK.
        /// This method handles SDK initialization and prompts the user for
permissions.
        /// Once successful, it calls AuthenticateWithFacebook to link with UGS.
        /// </summary>
        public static void LoginWithFacebook() //
        {
            // Check if the Facebook SDK is initialized.
            if (!FB.IsInitialized) //
            {
                // Initialize the Facebook SDK if not already done.
                FB.Init(() => // Callback after initialization
                {
                    Debug.Log("Facebook SDK initialised."); //
                    PerformFacebookLogin(); // Proceed with the login flow
                });
```

```
            }
            else
            {
                // If already initialized, proceed directly to login.
                PerformFacebookLogin();
            }
        }
        /// <summary>
        /// Performs the actual Facebook login request using the Facebook SDK.
        /// Requests public profile and email permissions.
        /// </summary>
        private static void PerformFacebookLogin() //
        {
            // Call the Facebook SDK login method with requested permissions.
            FB.LogInWithReadPermissions(new[] { "public_
profile", "email" }, result => // Callback with login result
            {
                // Check if the user successfully logged into Facebook.
                if (FB.IsLoggedIn)
                {
                    // Get the Facebook access token.
                    string accessToken = AccessToken.CurrentAccessToken.
TokenString;
                    Debug.Log($"Facebook Access Token: {accessToken}"); //
                  // Use the obtained token to authenticate with Unity Services.
                    AuthenticateWithFacebook(accessToken);
                }
                else
                {
                    // Log an error if Facebook login failed.
                    Debug.LogError("Failed to log in to Facebook.");
                }
            });
        }
    } // End of AuthService class (Part 1)
} // End of AuthNamespace (Part 1)
```

Explanation for part 1: This first section sets up the foundation for our Authentication code by creating a C# namespace (**`AuthNamespace`**) and a static class (**`AuthService`**) within it. Static classes are useful here because we do not need multiple instances; we just need a collection of helper functions accessible from anywhere in the code.

We include **`using`** directives for the necessary Unity and UGS components, as well as the **`Facebook.Unity`** namespace to integrate with the Facebook SDK.

The **`AuthenticateUser()`** method demonstrates the simplest form of UGS Authentication: anonymous sign-in. This is useful for basic access control or analytics without requiring user accounts. It checks if the user is already signed in via **`AuthenticationService.Instance.IsSignedIn`** before attempting **`SignInAnonymouslyAsync()`**.

The **`LoginWithFacebook()`** and **`PerformFacebookLogin()`** methods handle the interaction with the Facebook SDK. **`LoginWithFacebook()`** ensures the Facebook SDK is initialized before calling **`PerformFacebookLogin()`**, which initiates the Facebook login request and asks for specific permissions (**`public_profile`**, **`email`**). The **`AuthenticateWithFacebook(string accessToken)`** method is designed to receive the token obtained from a successful Facebook login and use it to authenticate with the UGS Authentication service. This links the user's Facebook identity to their UGS Player ID.

Part 2: Google and email/password authentication methods in **`AuthService`**

This part continues the **`AuthService`** static class, adding methods to handle authentication using Google Sign in and the Unity Email and Password service.

These methods rely on the underlying UGS authentication service (**`authenticationService.Instance`**) to perform the actual authentication calls with the provided credentials or tokens.

```
// ... (Continuing the AuthService class from Part 1)
namespace AuthNamespace
{
    public static class AuthService
    {
        // ... (AuthenticateUser, AuthenticateWithFacebook,
LoginWithFacebook, PerformFacebookLogin from Part 1)
        /// <summary>
        /// Authenticates the user using a Google ID token with Unity
Authentication.
        /// This links the Google account to a UGS player identity.
        /// </summary>
        /// <param name="idToken">The ID token obtained from Google Sign in.</
param>
        public static async void AuthenticateWithGoogle(string idToken) //
```

```
    {
        // Check if the user is already signed in.
        if (!AuthenticationService.Instance.IsSignedIn) //
        {
            try
            {
                // Attempt to sign in or link with Google
using the provided ID token.
                await AuthenticationService.Instance.
SignInWithGoogleAsync(idToken); // Note: Code spread across pages
                // Log success and the assigned Player ID.
                Debug.
Log($"User authenticated via Google. Player ID: {AuthenticationService.
Instance.PlayerId}"); //
            }
            catch (RequestFailedException ex)
            {
                // Log any errors during Google authentication.
                Debug.LogError($"Error during Google authentication: {ex.
Message}"); //
            }
        }
        else
        {
            // Log if the user is already authenticated.
            Debug.Log("The user is already authenticated.");
        }
    }
    /// <summary>
    /// Authenticates the user using Unity Email and Password service.
    /// This method is used to create or sign in a user with email/
password credentials.
    /// </summary>
    /// <param name="email">The user's email address.</param>
    /// <param name="password">The user's password.</param>
    // Note: This method in AuthService appears to primarily
handle adding/registering the user.
    // The example usage below might be slightly
```

```
different or call a similar method.
        public static async Task
AuthenticateWithEmailPassword(string email, string password) //
        {
            try
            {
                // Attempt to add a username/password to the current player.
                // If no anonymous player exists, it might
create one implicitly or handle registration.
                // The specific behavior depends on UGS Authentication
setup and context.
                await AuthenticationService.Instance.
AddUsernamePasswordAsync(email, password); //
                // Log success.
                Debug.Log($"User authenticated successfully with email. Play-
er ID: {AuthenticationService.Instance.PlayerId}"); //
            }
            catch (RequestFailedException ex)
            {
                // Log any errors during email/password authentication.
                Debug.LogError($"Error during email/
password authentication: {ex.Message}"); //
            }
        }
    } // End of AuthService class (Part 2)
    // ... (Start of UnityEmailAuthManager class in Part 3)
} // End of AuthNamespace (Part 2)
```

Explanation for part 2: Building on the static **`AuthService`** class, this section includes methods for other popular authentication providers.

The **`AuthenticateWithGoogle(string idToken)`** method handles authentication using a Google ID token. Similar to Facebook authentication, this token is typically obtained from a client-side Google Sign in SDK integration (not shown in full here) and then passed to this method to authenticate the user with UGS and link their Google account to a UGS Player ID.

The **`AuthenticateWithEmailPassword(string email, string password)`** method within the **`AuthService`** class provides functionality for the built-in Unity Email and Password authentication service. This allows developers to manage user accounts directly within UGS without relying on external social providers. The code calls **`AuthenticationService.Instance.`**

AddUsernamePasswordAsync (email, password) which seems to be used for adding email/password credentials to an existing (possibly anonymous) player, effectively registering them.

Note: **Signing in with existing email/password credentials might use a slightly different method depending on the UGS Authentication API version and pattern used.**

Part 3: MonoBehaviour manager for email/password authentication

This final part presents a separate class, **UnityEmailAuthManager**, which is a MonoBehaviour script. MonoBehaviour scripts are designed to be attached to GameObjects in the Unity Editor and provide functionality that runs within the game loop.

This script serves as a practical example of how to trigger the email and password authentication process, potentially holding the email and password values directly in the Unity Editor via **SerializeField** attributes and updating a UI element (**statusText**) based on the result. It demonstrates calling the authentication logic, likely interacting with the **AuthService** or the **AuthenticationService.Instance** directly and provide user feedback:

```
// ... (Continuing from the AuthNamespace definition in Part 2)
using TMPro;
namespace AuthNamespace
{
    // ... (AuthService class from Part 1 and Part 2)
    // This class is a MonoBehaviour, designed to be attached to a 
GameObject in Unity.
    // It demonstrates how to trigger email/
password authentication from a game object.
    public class UnityEmailAuthManager : MonoBehaviour //
    {
        // [SerializeField] attributes expose these private fields in the 
Unity Editor.
        // This allows setting the email and pass-
word directly in the Inspector for testing or configuration.
        [Header("Authentication Fields")] // Adds a header in the 
Inspector for these fields.
        [SerializeField] private string email; //
        [SerializeField] private string password; //
        [SerializeField] private TextMeshProUGUI statusText; // A 
reference to a UI TextMeshPro UI element to display status.
        /// <summary>
       /// Unity›s Start method, called automatically when the script instance 
is loaded.
```

```
        /// Here, it initiates the authentication process asynchronously.
        /// </summary>
        private async void Start() //
        {
            // You might want to add UnityServices.
InitializeAsync() here if not done elsewhere,
            // though the code examples suggest it might be called
before this script runs.
            // Call the authentication method within this MonoBehaviour.
            // Note: The original source code has a potential duplicate
method name here
            // compared to AuthService, but this one clearly interacts with UI.
             await AuthenticateWithEmailPassword(email, password); //
        }
        /// <summary>
        /// Authenticates the user with Unity Authentication using
email and password.
        /// This version updates a UI Text element with the result.
        /// </summary>
        /// <param name="email">The user's email address.</param>
        /// <param name="password">The user's password.</param>
        private async Task AuthenticateWithEmailPass-
word(string email, string password) //
        {
            try
            {
                // Attempt to authenticate (add/
register) the user with email and password.
                // This calls the core UGS Authentication service method.
                await AuthenticationService.Instance.
AddUsernamePasswordAsync(email, password); //
                // If successful, update the status text and log.
                statusText.text = "Authentication successful!"; //
                Debug.
Log($"User authenticated successfully. Player ID: {AuthenticationService.
Instance.PlayerId}"); //
            }
            catch (RequestFailedException ex)
```

```
            {
                // If authentication fails, update the
status text and log the error.
                statusText.text = $"Authentication failed: {ex.Message}"; //
                Debug.LogError($"Authentication failed: {ex.Message}"); //
            }
        }
    } // End of UnityEmailAuthManager class
}
```

One can utilize the **SignInWithFacebookAsync** method to either:

- Create a new Unity Authentication player by utilizing the Facebook credentials.
- You can log in to an existing player using Facebook credentials. One can utilize the **SignInWithFacebookAsync** method to either:
    - Create a new Unity Authentication player by utilizing the Facebook credentials.
    - You can log in to an existing player using Facebook credentials.

The simplest possible example of code for authentication on the Facebook platform is as follows:

```
using UnityEngine;
using AuthNamespace;

public class FacebookAuthManager : MonoBehaviour
{
    private async void Start()
    {
        Debug.Log("Authenticating with Facebook...");
        AuthService.LoginWithFacebook();
    }
}
```

These codes are just two examples of basic authentication, but it is highly recommended that you study the rest of the scenes and examples that come with the SDK, as you will find many more functionalities that may be useful to you.

The interface is very simple, but you will find numerous useful examples of how to use the system:

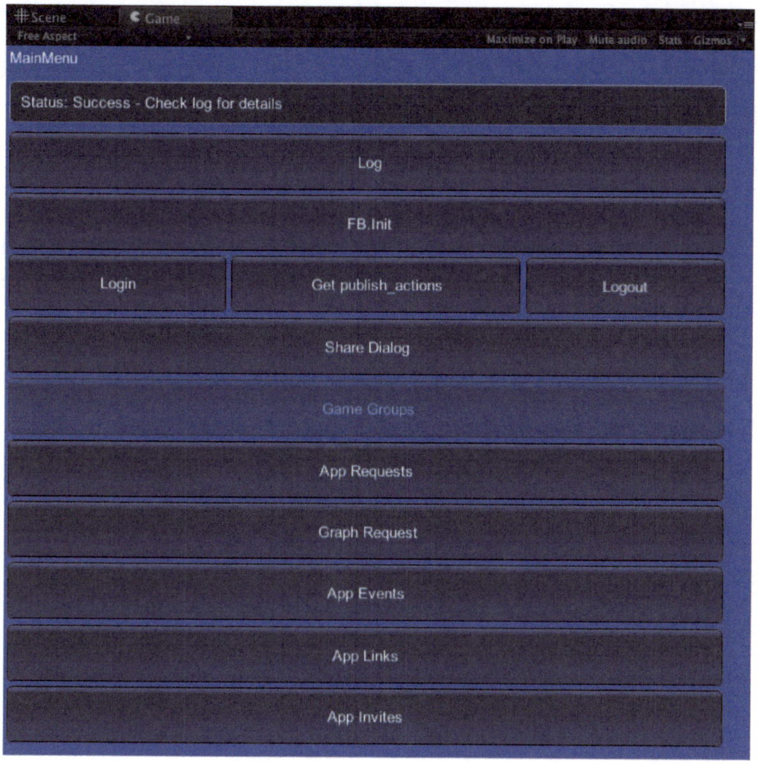

***Figure 9.16**: The SDK has a lot of samples. Explore and learn*

Sign in with Apple

The same method used to set up authentication with Meta can be applied to other providers. For each one, you will need to check which parameters are required and refer to the official documentation for configuration details. For example, to set up the app sign-in, you will need the Bundle ID, as shown in the following figure:

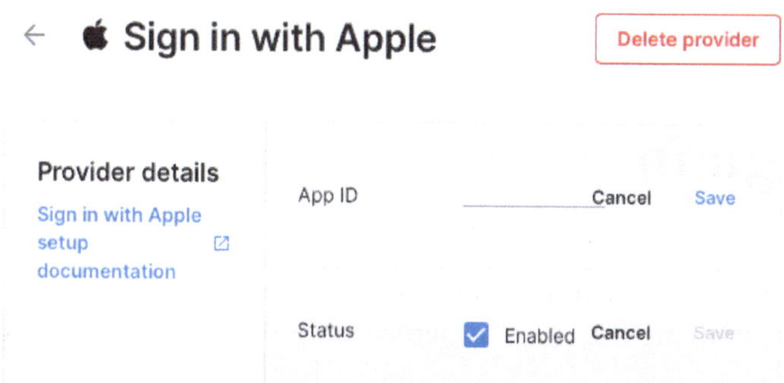

***Figure 9.17**: Apple Sign in configuration in Unity Gaming Services*

The Bundle ID should look like this: **com.something.somethingelse**.

The code to sign in to Apple is a little bit different. You can find all the Apple documentation at this URL: **https://developer.apple.com/help/account/**

The other part of the code is practically identical to the Facebook, changing the name of the provider, and it is very easy to implement in the same way.

It is important to note that Apple has two authentication systems: one for the Apple Game Center (which is only for games) and the Apple one (used throughout the Apple ecosystem).

The following code is a simple example of authentication using Apple ID:

```
using UnityEngine;
using AuthNamespace;

public class AppleAuthManager : MonoBehaviour
{
    [SerializeField]
    private string appleIdToken; // Input your Apple ID Token here

    private async void Start()
    {
        if (string.IsNullOrEmpty(appleIdToken))
        {
            Debug.LogError("Apple ID Token is not set!");
            return;
        }

        Debug.Log("Authenticating with Apple...");
        AuthService.AuthenticateWithApple(appleIdToken);
    }
}
```

Google Sign in

Google also has two authentication solutions: Google Sign in and Google Play Games.

In this chapter, we have primarily focused on the authentication service. The steps to access the authentication system are the same as before; only the final code changes slightly:

```
using UnityEngine;
using AuthNamespace;
```

```

public class GoogleAuthManager : MonoBehaviour
{
    [SerializeField]
    private string googleIdToken; // Input your Google ID Token here

    private async void Start()
    {
        if (string.IsNullOrEmpty(googleIdToken))
        {
            Debug.LogError("Google ID Token is not set!");
            return;
        }

        Debug.Log("Authenticating with Google...");
        AuthService.AuthenticateWithGoogle(googleIdToken);
    }
}
```

Firebase

Google also has another way to authenticate users that is not included in Unity Gaming Services, but is quite common, that is, through using Firebase.

Google Firebase is a real-time database and set of cloud-based development tools that help mobile app developers build, deploy, and scale their apps.

Firebase Authentication offers a range of backend services, user-friendly SDKs, and pre-designed user interface libraries to authenticate users to your application. The system provides authentication via passwords, phone numbers, and popular federated identity providers such as Google, Facebook, and Twitter, among other options.

There is a sample App with some interesting examples at this GitHub repository: **https://github.com/google/mechahamster**

Oculus

Oculus is the authentication system created for the virtual reality headset. Meta has many apps (WhatsApp, Instagram, Facebook, Oculus), and each has its own system initially. These are the steps you will need to follow to authenticate through Oculus:

- Sign up and configure an application with Oculus and find your App ID and App Secret (has the link in the footer).
- Go to the Unity Dashboard and select the project you want to authenticate.
- Under Suites, go to **LiveOps** | **Authentication** | **Identity Providers**.
- Select the option **Add Identity Provider** / **Oculus**.
- Write exactly the provided App ID and Secret ID. After that, enable the **Enable Identity Provider** checkbox.
- Choose **Add provider**.

On the Meta developer website, you should access the **Development/ API Menu,** and there you will find all the necessary IDS to work with the app:

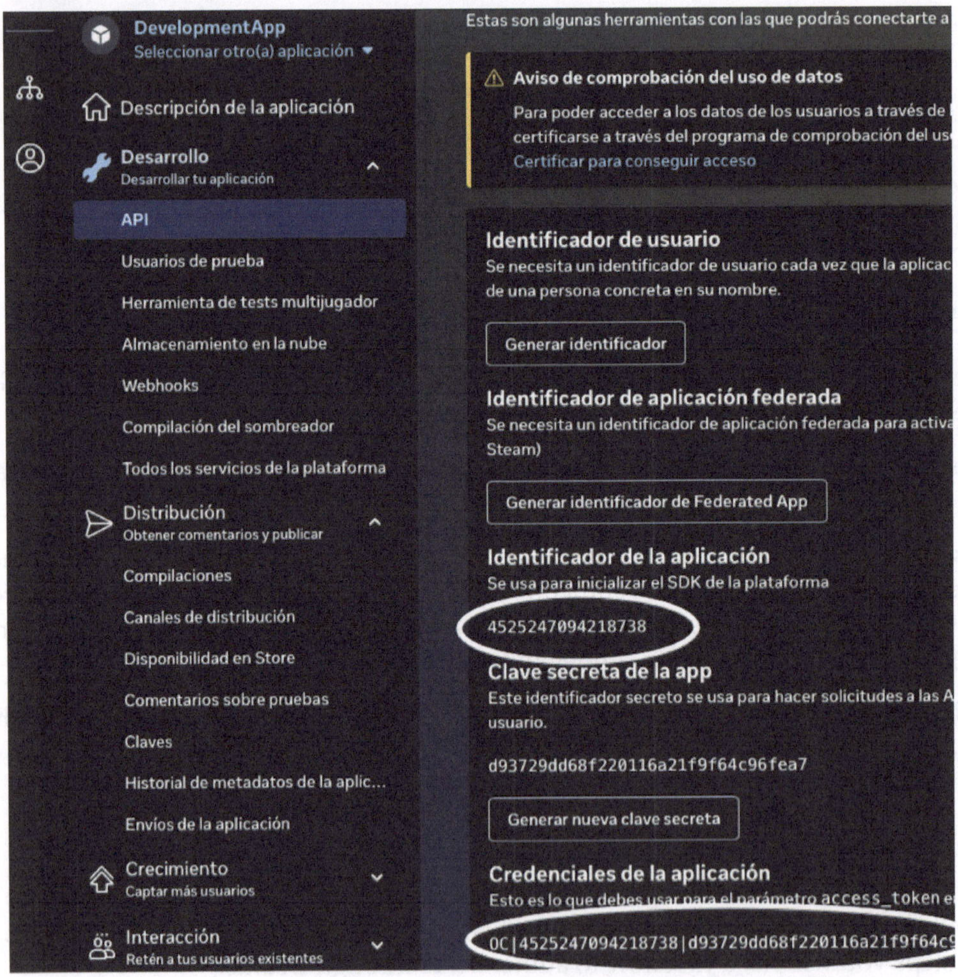

Figure 9.18: *Your app's IDs on the Meta platform*

For further information on developing for Meta, please refer to the following page: **https://developers.meta.com/horizon/develop/unity/**

Steam

The process with Steam is exactly the same as with Oculus. The only difference is that when we select the vendor ID, it should be Steam instead of Oculus. These are the steps to follow:

- Sign up and configure an application with Oculus and find your App ID and App Secret (has the link in the footer).
- Go to the Unity Dashboard and select the project you want to authenticate.
- Under Suites, go to **LiveOps** | **Authentication** | **Identity Providers**.
- Select the option **Add Identity Provider** | **Steam**.
- Write exactly the provided App ID and Secret ID. After that, enable the **Enable Identity Provider** checkbox.
- Choose **Add provider**.

In this link, you can register your Steam App:

https://store.steampowered.com/app/353380/Steam_Link/

OpenID

Finally, if none of the above providers convince you and you prefer to use a system that is not tied to any large corporation, you can use **Custom OpenID Connect** (**OIDC**). The steps are as follows:

- Sign up and configure an application with OIDC and find your App ID and Issuer URL (has the link in the footer).
- Go to the Unity Dashboard and select the project you want to authenticate.
- Under Suites, go to **LiveOps** | **Authentication** | **Identity Providers**.
- Select the option **Add Identity Provider** / **OpenID Connect**.
- Write exactly the name of the OIDC provider, the client ID, and the issuer URL.
- **Enable Identity Provider** checkbox.
- Choose **Add provider**.

Considerations to take into account for the OIDC provider's name:

- It is mandatory to start with the prefix **`oidc-`**.
- The maximum length must be 20 characters (this includes the **`oidc-`** prefix).
- Cannot contain any **`strange`** character: only numbers from 0 to 9, letters from a to z, and the symbols [.][-][@][_].

Considerations to take in mind for the issuer URL:

- It must be in the https protocol scheme.
- The length must not exceed 100 characters.
- The OpenID configuration response cannot be larger than 20,000 bytes.
- The JWKS response cannot exceed 20,000 bytes.

Conclusion

In this chapter, we have primarily focused on the authentication service. It has been seen from a more global point of view, taking into account that the legal considerations involved and the different cloud providers that have developed specific and unified solutions must be taken into account. These providers include tech giants like Google, Facebook (Meta), Apple, Amazon, and Microsoft, as well as specialized platforms like Auth0.

We have also seen how we can implement some authentication systems from the most basic, where we do not need a username/password, to the Meta, learning along the way what Tokens or Sessions are and how all of this can be integrated into the Unity platform.

You now understand how to integrate an authentication system into Unity Gaming Services and connect it with major providers to enhance your app's user experience and reliability. Building upon the foundational concepts of authentication and identity management, the next chapter delves into another critical aspect of modern game development: scaling multiplayer games with game server hosting. You will learn about the complexities of multiplayer development, key concepts such as bandwidth, latency, **concurrent users** (**CCU**), precision, and scalability. The chapter will introduce techniques like game server hosting, different network topologies (peer-to-peer and relay servers), and various networking frameworks, including Unity's new Netcode solutions.

Multiple choice questions

1. **Which stages are explicitly recognized components of the Player Lifecycle in game development optimization using analytics?**
   a. Beta testing
   b. Onboarding or installation
   c. Churn or attrition
   d. Performance optimization
2. **In game performance analytics, what does the daily active users (DAU) metric specifically measure?**
   a. The percentage of monthly active users (MAU) who played on a specific day.
   b. The number of players in your game who initiate a session on a given calendar day.
   c. The total duration of gameplay sessions recorded within a 24-hour period.
   d. The number of new players who transmitted data from the game for the first time.
3. **The strategic phase of the player lifecycle that focuses on maintaining players' interest and ensuring their continued engagement with the game over time, contrasted with attrition, is known as which of the following?**
   a. Reactivation
   b. Monetization
   c. Retention
   d. Onboarding
4. **According to Unity's predefined audiences, which criteria define an 'Engaged Player':**
   a. Players who have played every day in the last week.
   b. Players who have made a purchase in the past seven days.
   c. Players with a Days Played Last 7 Days metric greater than or equal to 7.
   d. Players who have played more than 100 sessions lifetime.

5. **Which monetization strategy involves players voluntarily viewing an advertisement in exchange for in-game rewards, positioning it as a non-intrusive method?**
   a. Subscription-based models
   b. Interstitial ads
   c. Rewarded advertisements
   d. In-game virtual currency purchase
6. **In the context of game analytics, what is the primary role of a Funnel?**
   a. To provide a visual representation of how players navigate through a series of key stages.
   b. To monitor real-time network latency across different platforms.
   c. To identify potential impediments or specific drop-off points in the player's journey.
   d. To facilitate the direct integration of third-party advertising SDKs.
7. **The initial step in using engagement data for data-driven decision-making, according to the recommended methodological guide, is to:**
   a. Optimize the monetization strategy based on A/B test results.
   b. Identify pain points by analyzing areas where engagement is low.
   c. Establish Key Performance Indicators (KPIs) aligned with game objectives.
   d. Collect and analyze data on player behavior and interactions.
8. **A Unity developer observes that a player, identified by PlayerID: 5X3RT9, last logged a session event 17 days ago. Which predefined audience should this player be segmented into for reactivation efforts?**
   a. Dormant Players
   b. Unengaged Players
   c. New Players
   d. Churned Players
9. **Analytic dashboards, such as the Game Performance reports, allow developers to view segmented data related to which of the following metrics?**
   a. Daily new users
   b. Segmentation by acquisition channel

c. Average session length

d. Backend database schema modifications

10. When addressing optimization during the Onboarding phase, analytics funnels are critically utilized to primarily assess:

a. The average session length required to achieve monetization.

b. Conversion rates and drop-off points within the tutorial steps.

c. The total number of unique monthly active users (MAU).

d. Player feedback and satisfaction scores regarding graphics quality.

Answers

1	b, c
2	b
3	c
4	a, c
5	c
6	a, c
7	c
8	d
9	a, b, c
10	b

References

1. Unity Documentation of Firebase: **https://firebase.google.com/docs/auth/unity/start**

2. **https://partner.steamgames.com/doc/store/application#:~:text=New%20Applications%20can%20be%20created,on%20the%20Steamworks%20landing%20page.**

3. **https://developers.meta.com/horizon/resources/publish-create-app/**

CHAPTER 10

Scaling Multiplayer Games with Game Server Hosting

Introduction

Unity's **Netcode for GameObjects** (**NGO**) equips developers with a high-level, component-based framework for building reliable, low-latency multiplayer games. In this chapter, you will learn how to harness NGO from the ground up: setting up and controlling the Network Manager, creating simple host/client/server interfaces, and integrating networked behaviours into your scenes.

You will start with a Hello World tutorial that walks through the basic API calls and UI logic needed to launch a local multiplayer session. From there, we dive into richer sample projects such as Galactic Kittens, which demonstrates full gameplay loops, player movement, object spawning, and **remote procedure calls** (**RPCs**). We then examine Enter the Boss Room, an advanced example that tackles common challenges—latency concealment, replicated objects, RPC handling, and integration with Unity's Relay, Lobby, and Authentication services.

Recognizing that many games require handling large numbers of dynamic entities, we cover Netcode for Entities and Unity's **Data-Oriented Technology Stack** (**DOTS**). The Megacity Metro demo illustrates how ECS can deliver high-performance networking for complex, data-heavy scenarios.

Finally, we will look at some features that were incorporated into Unity6 to streamline multiplayer development: a multi-instance editor mode for simultaneous client testing, a replay system for debugging and analytics, automated server build pipelines, and distributed authority to offload simulation workload. Throughout the chapter, you will also find pointers to community resources—forums, Discord channels, GitHub repositories—to help troubleshoot issues and stay connected with other developers.

Structure

The chapter covers the following topics:

- Bandwidth
- Latency tolerance

- Called concurrent users
- Precision
- Scalability
    - Game server hosting
    - Peer-to-peer
    - Relay server
- Network frameworks
    - UNet
    - Mirror
    - Photon fusion
    - FishNet
    - DarkRift networking 2
- New Unity solution
    - Unity Transport
    - Unity Netcode for GameObjects
    - Unity Netcode for Entities
    - Unity 6 new features

Objectives

By the end of this chapter, you will have a solid foundation in NGO's core concepts, practical experience from proven examples, and an understanding of how Unity's newer tools can further scale your multiplayer projects.

Bandwidth

According to the *Cambridge Dictionary*, bandwidth is a measurement of the amount of information that can be sent between computers, through a phone line, etc.

Bandwidth is usually more or less stable and is the amount of megabytes that telephone operators sell when they want us to buy their services (600Mb of fiber, for example). Since we are going to need to send a lot of data constantly (such as our position, rotation, and actions), it is important that the bandwidth is able to absorb all that amount of data without delay. Bandwidth could be explained as the number of lanes that a highway has to absorb traffic. If we do not have enough information, it will start to create a bottleneck and flow more slowly.

When that happens, when traffic begins to slow down and does not move at the expected speed, a phenomenon called latency occurs.

Latency tolerance

When communications fail, and there is always a time when that happens, we must establish how long we are willing to wait; what level of tolerance we can afford before the game begins to lose playability. Of course, a **first person shooter** (**FPS**) game where a small delay can mean that the player dies is not the same as a chess game or a collaborative environment in the metaverse. We will have to know our development very well and adjust it appropriately so that it remains playable. Various techniques have been developed to minimize the impact of latency, such as prediction and reconciliation.

Called concurrent users

The number of users who play the same game or session is **called concurrent users** (**CCU**). Since there are more players, more data must be exchanged and synchronized over the connection.

If the number of users is extremely large, it may cause delays (lag), prompting a decision to reduce the level of detail of the resources to maintain the frame rate. Alternatively, you can adjust the amount of information transmitted between peers to accommodate more players. It is imperative to consider the nature of the game or application in question in order to comprehend the network and calculation prerequisites that will be required. A chess game is not the same as a shooter, where the slightest deviation can mean the difference between a player dying or remaining standing. Another important factor in making a multiplayer game is precision.

Precision

The precision requirements of your game will impact all systems involved in calculating the world state and its actors. For more accurate results, you will need additional resources and a larger memory footprint.

In multiplayer, the level of accuracy significantly affects the network footprint and server performance.

Not all aspects require precision; therefore, it is crucial to distinguish between elements essential to the ruleset and the game's outcome. By doing so, you can utilize lower-degree approximations to enhance overall performance.

Scalability

Scalability is the measure of a system's ability to increase or decrease performance and cost in response to changes in system and application processing demands in response to changes in system and application processing demands.

In the development of Unity multiplayer, this signifies the capability to accommodate user growth in a brief period of time without compromising the playability or response time.

How can one achieve a conversion rate of 10,000 CCU to 1000,000 CCU in a matter of minutes? There exists a multitude of techniques and architectures that possess considerable utility.

Game server hosting

One of the techniques employed to ensure the scalability of multiplayer is the provisioning of game servers.

Game hosting involves deploying and managing servers specifically designed to meet the computational and networking demands of multiplayer games. These servers serve as central hubs where game state information is stored and updated, thereby guaranteeing consistency among all connected clients. Moreover, they facilitate player interaction by overseeing tasks such as player authentication, matchmaking, creating game sessions, and transmitting data among clients.

The hosting of game servers alleviates the complexity of managing and managing infrastructure on a large scale, thereby enabling your development team to concentrate on creating engaging experiences for players. To achieve this, we recommend using a grouping of servers that perform a similar function and need to be managed in a similar way. Game server hosting groups these servers together in order to help you manage them. This group of servers is called the fleets.

The following figure represents the typical two-tier client/server structure. With a central server (which today is often a container orchestration with Kubernetes) and the users as clients:

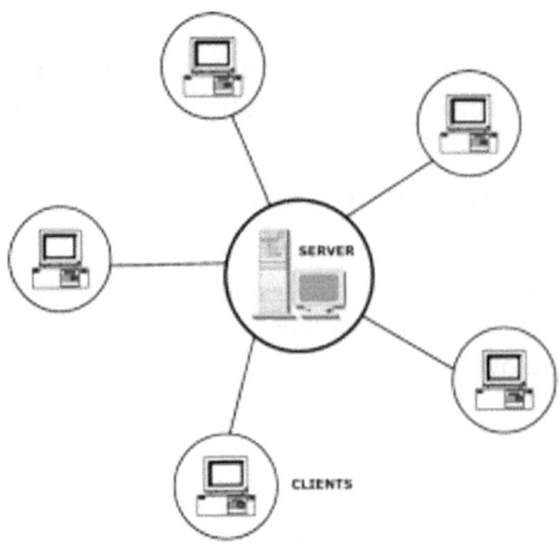

***Figure 10.1**: Centralized network for Game Hosting*

Source: *https://www.researchgate.net/figure/Simplified-configuration-of-P2P-and-client-server-network_fig2_264931412*

Peer-to-peer

Peer-to-peer (**P2P**) is a network architecture in which participants communicate directly with one another, eliminating the necessity of a central authority or server. In a P2P network, each participant assumes the roles of both a client and a server, facilitating the exchange of resources and services directly with their peers.

In order to enhance comprehension, we shall provide a concrete illustration. As the popularity of internet downloads grew and a significant number of individuals downloaded MP3s and movies from pirated websites, authorities-initiated measures to shut down the central servers from which all this pirated content was distributed.

It was then that a protocol called *BitTorrent* appeared, which, in reality, was a P2P system in which each and every computer connected was both a client and a server. That way, the authorities could not close any central servers (because there were none), and they could not imprison all the people who were connected.

Simple example of a P2P network where all nodes are both client and server at the same time:

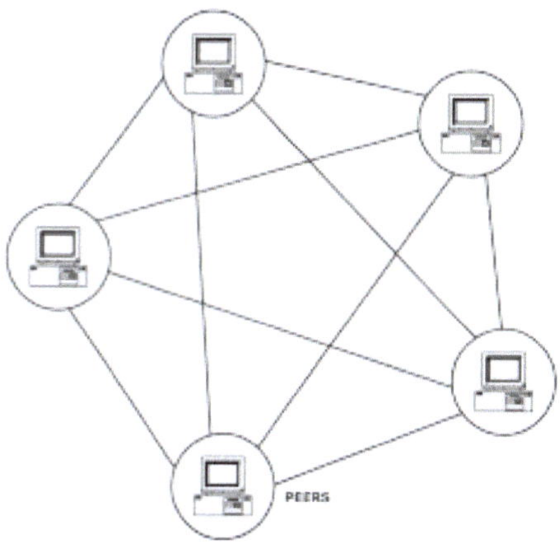

Figure 10.2*: Peer-to-peer diagram*

Relay server

Having a dedicated server can be costly, and establishing direct connections between users through peer-to-peer is often challenging due to the presence of firewalls and other security measures that can complicate these connections.

Due to all of these factors, there exists a particular type of intermediate network known as a relay server.

The relay service makes it possible to support multiplayer without dedicated game servers by allowing players to communicate with each other through relay servers. Relay servers deliver messages between connected players by exchanging low-latency datagrams between game clients so that no two players ever connect directly to each other. Relay servers are ideal for games that use a listening server pattern in which one player (the host player) acts as a server while the other players (the joining players) act as clients. Refer to the following figure:

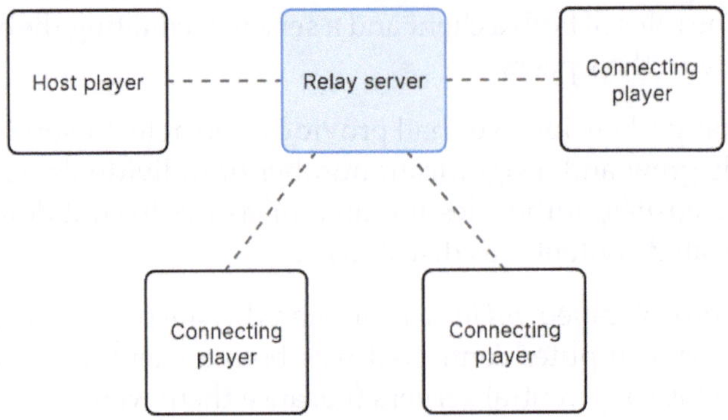

***Figure 10.3**: Relay server structure*

Relay servers are public endpoints accessible to all players. This design addresses common issues related to changing network and IP addresses, network address translation, and firewalls between players. Each player can use the same IP address and port, and game clients can trust that the connection information will remain the same throughout the game session. Through this indirect addressing, players in a game session do not need to know each other's IP addresses, thereby increasing security and privacy.

Network frameworks

We have seen some of the network typologies, and now we will see different frameworks that will help us develop multiplayer.

You may be confused about which networking stack to use and what options you have. Let us review the different options available and their advantages and disadvantages.

UNet

The first network option is now completely deprecated (It is not recommended that anyone use it currently).

UNet was long the official solution for developing multiplayer games, but was removed from the editor in version 2022.2.0a5 in February 2022.

You can still continue using UNet LLAPI if you use Unity 2021.3 **long-term support** (**LTS**) since it has 2 years of support, but you must think about how to migrate the code to something more updated.

It is possible that you will find it in an old project or in an asset, so it is always good to know about its existence.

Mirror

Mirror was born as a substitute for UNet. It has some performance benefits over the previous platform but maintains a very similar workflow, so it was easily adopted by developers. Allows you to send messages back and, together with **remote procedure calls** (**RPCs**), synchronize variables.

They are not what would be considered optimal for a game where transfer speed is important, such as e-sports or something very competitive like a shooter.

Mirror is designed for games/apps where speed is not so important. A very popular developer example with Mirror is MMORPG Engine:

***Figure 10.4**: MMORPG Engine is a very popular asset that uses Mirror*

You can learn more about it on the following link: **https://assetstore.unity.com/packages/templates/systems/ummorpg-2d-remastered-mmorpg-engine-102632**

Photon Fusion

Photon is a company that has built multiple network systems. The first system was called PUN, and although it worked well and was easy to use, it did not have much speed or performance. Several updates have been made with improvements (the latest is PUN 2+). It allows the use of up to 100 CCU, although it has a purchase cost per seat.

The next iteration was Bolt, which improved speed, but the version that really represented a substantial change in speed increase was Fusion.

Fusion is one of the fastest networking options with low latency and good messaging plus motion prediction (server-side). It is not free, but you can download the **system development kit** (**SDK**) completely free and start developing with it (they have a fee that allows you to do the development at no cost).

If you need a platform where speed is important, Fusion may be a good option.

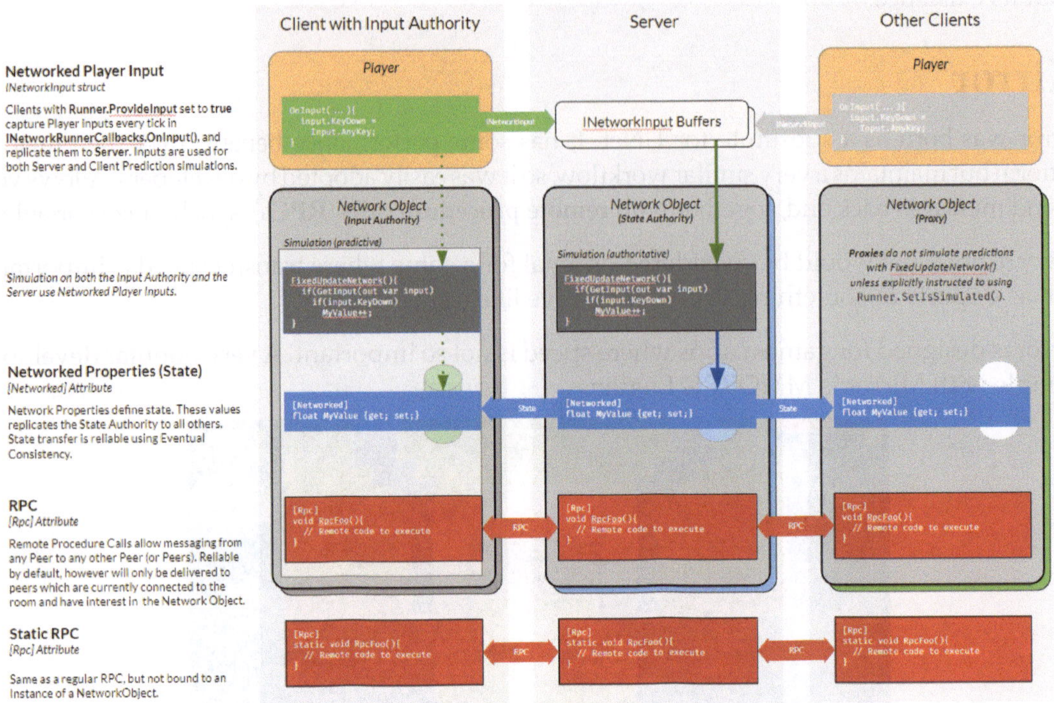

Figure 10.5: Photon Fusion is a high-performance networking library for Unity

FishNet

FishNet is server-authoritative by design, enabling the utilization of dedicated servers. However, it also facilitates users acting as both servers and clients, expediting development and testing processes.

The transport system provides comprehensive support for various network topologies. Communication between servers, clients, and even third parties can be achieved through a diverse range of technologies.

This high-level API empowers users to swiftly access the capability of synchronizing states, logic, objects, and more without the necessity of manual intervention. Additionally, we prioritize providing an optimal user experience, allowing users to also access low-level functionality through included events or inheritance.

Fish Networks promises that it will not release any breaking API or behavior changes between major versions. Major releases will not occur more frequently than every six months unless absolutely necessary.

FishNetworking (refer to *Figure 10.6)* is the only solution offering free long-term support. It emerges as a free and versatile networking solution for Unity, offering high performance and flexibility in development.

Figure 10.6*: FishNet is an free versatile networking solution*

In the following table, you can see a comparison between Mirror and FishNetworking[1]:

Objects	FishNetworking	Mirror
0	1.5ms	1.5ms
500	1.5ms	1.9ms
1000	1.5ms	2.2ms
2000	1.5ms	2.9ms
4000	1.5ms	4.2ms

Table 10.1*: Mirror becomes slower with the use of many objects simultaneously, while FishNetworking is constant*

The results are:

- **Client FPS:** FishNet clients exhibited a significant performance advantage, achieving 70% higher frame rates compared to Mirror.
- **Bandwidth**: FishNet demonstrated a substantial reduction in bandwidth usage, consuming 67-78% less compared to Mirror.
- **Server performance (200 CCU):** FishNet maintained an impressive 92.6% server performance, while Mirror's performance was severely compromised, retaining only 16.8%.
- **Server performance (4000 idle objects):** FishNet consistently demonstrated optimal server performance, maintaining 100%, while Mirror's performance degraded to a mere 36%.

DarkRift Networking 2

Another open-source alternative is the DarkRift Network library 2.

This library is quite powerful and has some important advantages: it allows unlimited use of CCUs, the code is highly optimized and written at a low level (internally everything is programmed in multithreaded for maximum throughput).

1 You can consult all the data at the address: https://fish-networking.gitbook.io/docs/manual/general/performance/fish-networking-vs-mirror

If you buy the PRO version, you can get all the source code.

It also has some drawbacks. Although it is really a great project, it seems that it has been developed by one person, and that can be a drawback in the long term.

The code is so optimized that advanced knowledge of C# is required to understand it well.

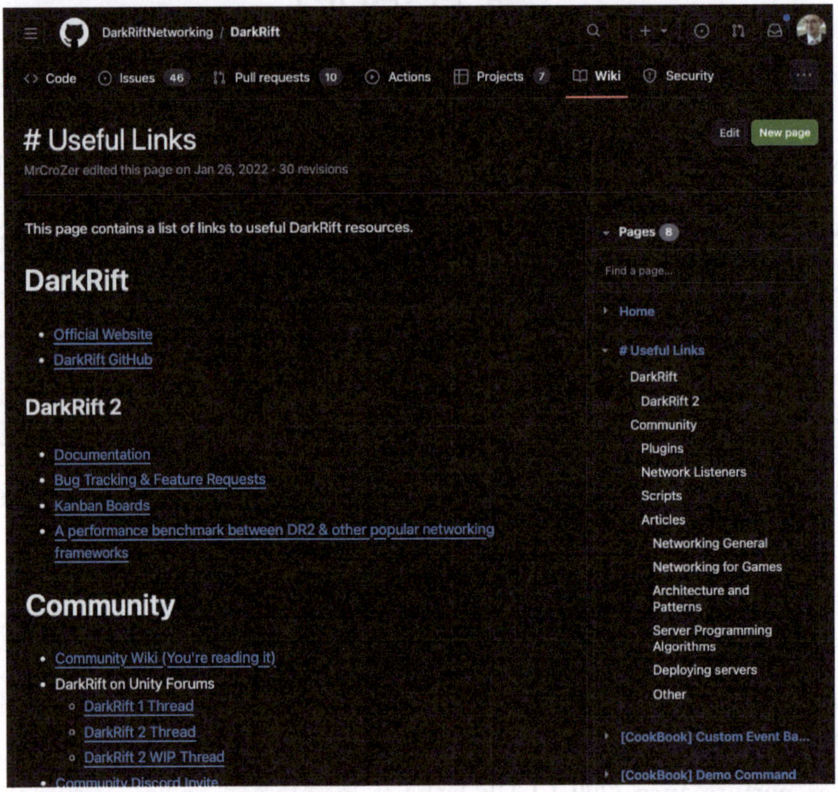

Figure 10.7: DarkRift has good documentation on GitHub and an active community that uses it for its developments

New Unity solution

Unity Technologies is very aware that it must offer a professional alternative at the level of its magnificent development environment. That is why they have been developing a new solution that allows us to deal with current development challenges.

Unity Transport

The Unity Transport package is a low-level networking library aimed at multiplayer game development. It provides a connection-based abstraction layer over **User Datagram Protocol** (**UDP**) sockets with optional functions like reliability, ordering, and fragmentation.

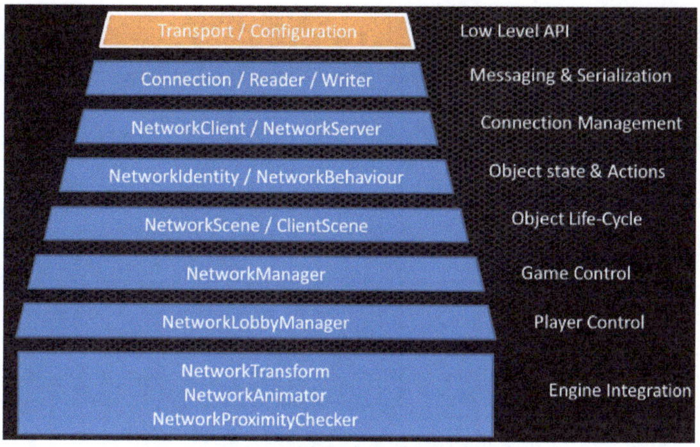

Figure 10.8: *The new network's layers structure*

The transport layer is a thin layer working on top of the operating system's sockets-based networking system. It is capable of sending and receiving messages represented as arrays of bytes and offers a number of different quality of service options to suit different scenarios. It is focused on flexibility and performance and exposes an API within UnityEngine. Networking is the art of networking. The NetworkTransport class is used to transport network traffic.

This new system is based on a highly optimized low-level transport layer on which the system has been built.

Version 2.X works starting with Unity 2022.2 and LTS. It is required to install the **`com.unity.transport`** package to use it.

From this basic library, Unity has developed Netcode for GameObjects and Netcode for Entities. Unity Technologies is working on a series of templates to get developers to start.

Unity Netcode for GameObjects

Unity **Netcode for GameObjects** (**NGO**) is a mid-level networking library created for the Unity game engine that is perfect for when we do not have to use hundreds or thousands of objects moving simultaneously (that is what Netcode for Entities, together with DOTS, is ideal for). As always, it is installed using a package that we can download from Unity.

The following figure shows how the **Netcode for GameObjects** package was installed using the **Package Manager** window:

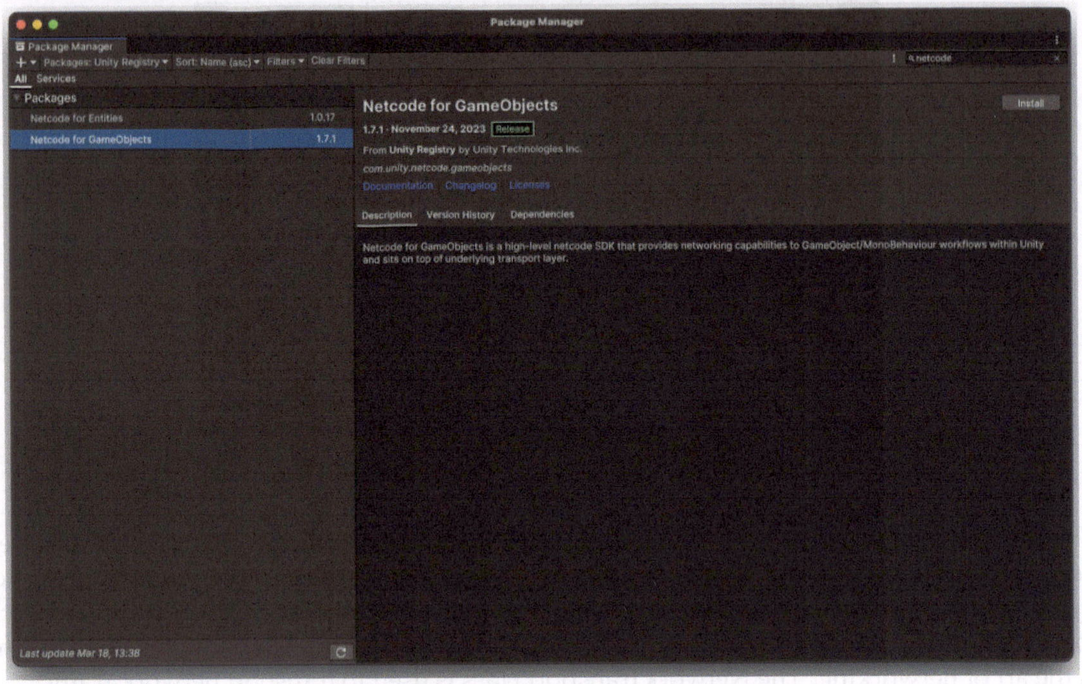

Figure 10.9: *Install Netcode for GameObjects*

The essential components of using NGO are:

- A player object
- A manager for the net component
- An Unity scene

When we implement the NGO solution, we will need to add a component to control the network.

It will appear as the following figure:

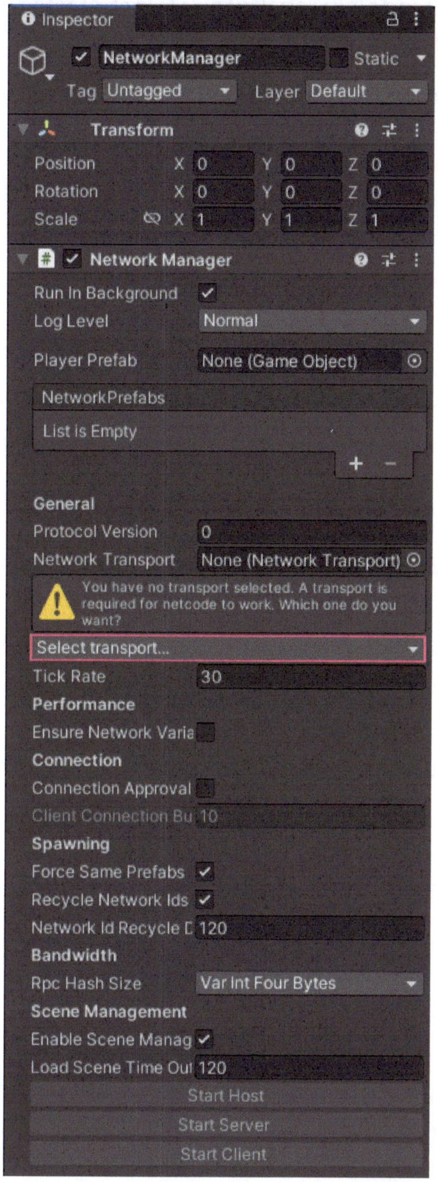

***Figure 10.10**: The Network Manager from the inspector*

Once you add the component, you will see a warning until you select the network transport.One of the advantages of using an NGO is that Unity is trying hard to get us developers to use their tools, and they have published several step-by-step example projects to make it easy to adopt.

Similarly, in the editor, you must also add the **`<PlayerNetwork>`** component to the player object.

The simplest example of all is always a Hello World. This is the address: **https://docs-multiplayer.unity3d.com/netcode/current/tutorials/get-started-ngo/**, so you can try how to implement it in a multiplayer environment:

```
using Unity.Netcode;
using UnityEngine;
namespace NetCodeNameSpace
 {
     public class NetCodedManager : MonoBehaviour
     {
         void OnGUI()
         {
             GUILayout.BeginArea(new Rect(10, 10, 300, 300));
             if (!NetworkManager.Singleton.IsClient && !NetworkManager.Singleton.IsServer)
             {
                 InitUI();
             }
             else
             {
                 UpdateUI();
     SendLocation();
             }
             GUILayout.EndArea();
         }
         static void InitUI()
         {
     if (GUILayout.Button("Host")) NetworkManager.Singleton.StartHost();
             if (GUILayout.Button("Client")) NetworkManager.Singleton.StartClient();
             if (GUILayout.Button("Server")) NetworkManager.Singleton.StartServer();
         }
         static void UpdateUI()
         {
```

```
            var type = NetworkManager.Singleton.IsHost ?
                "Host" : NetworkManager.Singleton.IsServer ? "Server" : "Client";

            GUILayout.Label("Unity Transport: " +
                NetworkManager.Singleton.NetworkConfig.NetworkTransport.GetType().Name);
            GUILayout.Label("Type: " + type);
        }

        static void SendLocation()
        {
            if (GUILayout.Button(NetworkManager.Singleton.IsServer ? "Move" : "Request Location"))
            {
                if (NetworkManager.Singleton.IsServer && !NetworkManager.Singleton.IsClient )
                {
                    foreach (ulong uid in NetworkManager.Singleton.ConnectedClientsIds)
                        NetworkManager.Singleton.SpawnManager.GetPlayerNetworkObject(uid).GetComponent<PlayerNetwork>().Move();
                }
                else
                {
                    var playerObject = NetworkManager.Singleton.SpawnManager.GetLocalPlayerObject();
                    var player = playerObject.GetComponent<PlayerNetwork>();
                    player.Move();
                }
            }
        }
    }
}
```

Note: For the following code to work correctly, in addition to having a Network Manager, the player must have the `<PlayerNetwork>` component.

Another very interesting example of how to use an NGO is *Galactic Kittens*, a multiplayer game developed by *Esteban Maldonado*, which can be downloaded from the following Github repository:**https://github.com/UnityTechnologies/GalacticKittens**

If you want to go deeper into the entire development process of this example, it is recommended that you read the following blog post, where it is explained step by step: **https://blog.unity.com/games/building-a-multiplayer-game-first-time-netcode-for-gameobjects**

Unity Technologies is very aware that it must provide examples of the correct use of its system. Galactic Kittens is an excellent example of how to implement multiplayer functionality using Unity Netcode for GameObjects:

Figure 10.11*: Galactic Kittens is a very useful sample for developers*

Finally, the example project **Enter the Boss Room** demonstrates how some of the primary multiplayer challenges have been addressed: latency concealment, replicated objects, **remote procedure calls** (**RPCs**), and integration with the Relay, Lobby, and Authentication services.

Enter the Boss Room, as shown in the following figure, is an example project that demonstrates how to address primary multiplayer challenges such as latency concealment, replicated objects, and RPCs:

Figure 10.12: *Enter the Boss Room is a piece of art to learn*

One of the most active and participatory communities in the world of development is, without a doubt, the Unity community, and in this case, it is even more so. You can find other developers who have had or are having problems similar to the ones you will encounter at these addresses:

- **The Unity Forum**: **https://forum.unity.com/forums/multiplayer.26/**
- **The Discord server**: Discord has a large community of servers and developers who can help you. The official server is: Unity 3D Development Community.
- **The GitHub repository**:

  https://github.com/Unity-Technologies/com.unity.netcode.gameobjects

Unity Netcode for Entities

In much more complex environments and with a much larger number of mobile objects interacting with each other, a tool specially optimized for this is useful.

Netcode for Entities is part of Unity's DOTS for large amounts of data.

Entity Component System (**ECS**) and DOTS are a new technology stack, a data-oriented design applied to the game architecture to empower game creators to build more ambitious games.

Figure 10.13 illustrates the Megacity Metro demo, which showcases the functionality of Netcode for Entities in a complex multiplayer environment:

***Figure 10.13**: Megacity Metro: End-to-end multiplayer demo to see Netcode for Entities working*

One of the best samples to learn using Netcode for entities is Megacity Metro: **https://unity.com/demos/megacity-competitive-action-sample**

Unity 6 new features

Unity version 6 introduced a multiplayer game mode that allows multiple instances of the editor/client to run simultaneously on the same server. Devices using the same source code and disk resources provide a more efficient and faster development cycle for multiplayer games, something you can see in action as a developer.

Replay mode will support local mode and remote deployment of a dedicated server, which will keep its iteration cycle as short as possible, even when you have a complex network topology. The objective of the new system is to establish a dedicated server that enables developers to create both the client and the server. A single project server greatly reduces development complexity and iteration time, and content selection functions help to make the server as efficient as possible.

We have taken steps to automate the build load on the final game server hosting solutions.

Unity game services allow you to mix and match automated client and server creation to run deployment scenarios faster, saving integration steps.

Also, the distributed authority aims to achieve leveraging the familiar Unity's Netcode distribute the simulation workflow between customers in a way that is scalable and resilient, reducing the load on the server and opening new possibilities for multiplayer.

Conclusion

A critical factor for success is driving deep player engagement, which includes making sure your game delivers. Today's gamers expect a complete multiplayer experience. Getting the multiplayer system working well is one of the best ways to add gameplay to your game. Among friends, rivalry and competition naturally arise.

In this chapter, we saw some concepts, techniques, and architectures used to achieve a better multiplayer experience. However, there is no perfect solution that works in all environments, and we must know very well what the needs of our project are to use the best possible solution. At first, it can be a little discouraging to see that there are so many options, and it is somewhat complicated to choose one of them, but it is much better to have so many alternatives, and it is once again shown that Unity is a system capable of adapting and incorporating all types of technologies.

To help us achieve a better multiplayer experience, Unity Technologies has developed several chat systems, both text and voice, that greatly facilitate player communication in a game. In the next chapter, we will look at the Vivox platform, what it offers, and implement some examples.

The next chapter focuses on integrating Vivox to implement robust voice and text chat systems that enhance the multiplayer experience established in the previous chapter. You will learn to configure channels for 3D positional audio, utilize accessibility features like text-to-speech, and manage community safety using moderation tools like Safe Voice.

Chapter 11
Enhance Your Game with Vivox

Introduction

Effective communication between players is the backbone of any successful multiplayer game, allowing participants to strategize, socialize, and fully immerse themselves in the experience. Building a robust chat system for voice and text can be daunting as it requires fast, stable, scalable, and cross-platform solutions. Instead of building this system from scratch, developers can rely on tools like Vivox to integrate high-quality communication features into their games effortlessly.

Vivox is a powerful voice and text chat platform designed for seamless integration with game engines such as Unity, Unreal, or even custom-designed ones. By using Vivox, developers can offer players features such as low-latency voice communication, 2D/3D positional audio, and a scalable infrastructure that supports thousands of users on different platforms. Unity, which acquired Vivox in 2019, has facilitated the integration of this tool into the Unity ecosystem as part of Unity Game Services.

In this chapter, you will learn the advantages and key characteristics of Vivox and how to configure Vivox for your Unity project. You will explore its core functionalities such as channel types, voice-to-text and text-to-speech capabilities, and discover best practices for managing voice data transmission and improving accessibility. You will also learn about moderation tools like Safe Voice to foster a safe and inclusive player environment.

Structure

The chapter covers the following topics:

- Learning about Vivox
    - Vivox, a brief history
- Vivox SDK installation
- Connect your Unity project to Vivox
- Channels

  - o Channel types
- Automatic connection recovery
- Speech-to-text transcription
- Text-to-speech
- Transmission
- Safe Voice

Objectives

By the end of this chapter, you will have the knowledge to integrate Vivox into your game, enhancing your players' experience through intuitive, immersive, and reliable communication systems. However, it is important to mention that there are other platforms that work with Unity and offer us some similar functionalities. Surely, the best known is Photon (which we also saw in the multiplayer game).

Learning about Vivox

Vivox Core SDK is an engine-agnostic voice and text chat system, also used in other engines like Unreal, that facilitates in-app communications within your project.

The Vivox SDK provides the following core capabilities:

- The ability to operate on multiple platforms.
- Provide direct voice and text communication services.
- Vivox also offers friendship and presence services to manage user relationships and online status.

Game developers have the ability to directly incorporate these capabilities into game clients and companion applications using the Vivox SDK. If you use Photon to implement multiplayer, you may also find it very interesting to see how the chat and voice service works. The following links can be interesting for developers:

- **Photon Chat: https://doc.photonengine.com/chat/current/getting-started/chat-intro**
- **Photon Voice: https://doc.photonengine.com/voice/current/getting-started/voice-intro**

Vivox offers additional features for speech-to-text and text-to-speech transcriptions to improve accessibility for users. Additionally, server-side recording can help reduce in-game toxicity.

For expanded functionality, game developers have the option to add web services enhancements through the Vivox server-to-server web API, which is a simple XML over HTTP protocol that can be accessed through a variety of server technologies.

The platforms supported by Vivox are:

- Android API 14 and later (armv7, arm64, x86, x86_64)
- iOS 10.3 and later (arm64, armv7, armv7s)
- Nintendo Switch
- PlayStation 4
- PlayStation 5
- Windows 10 (32-bit, 64-bit)
- Windows 11 (32-bit, 64-bit)
- Xbox One
- Xbox Series X | S

That means that we can have players, each on a different platform, but who may be communicating with each other through Vivox.

In a development environment like Unity (especially designed to reach the maximum number of platforms possible with the same code), this is especially useful.

The versions for *Apple* are not yet compatible with the Silicon architecture. For it to work correctly, it must be compiled for Mac with Intel-64-bit architecture, and the Rosetta system allows it to work perfectly (although we will lose some execution speed):

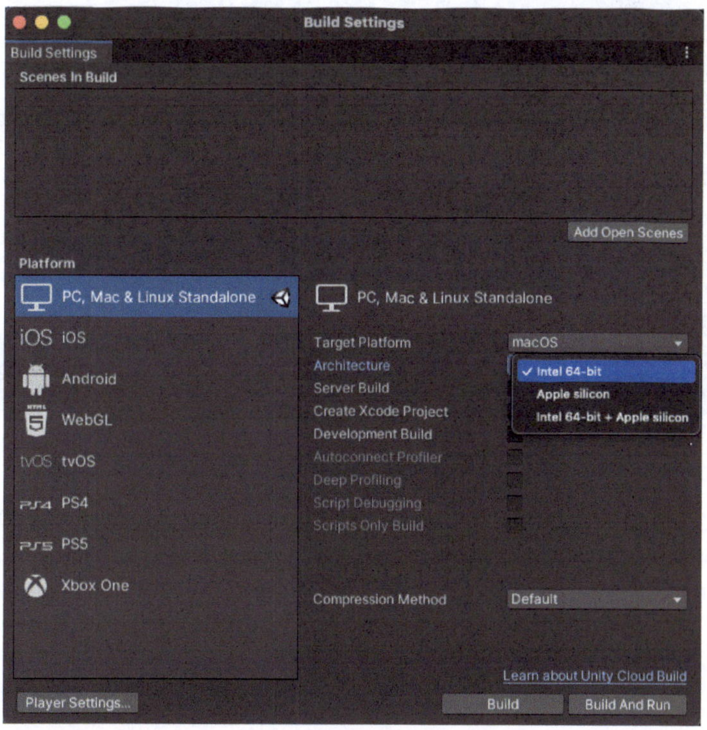

***Figure 11.1**: The Apple version does not yet work for the Silicon architecture, only for Intel-64 bits*

Vivox, a brief history

Vivox is a text and voice chat service that has been used by many top-tier games in the past. In this brief introduction, we will see some of the most important milestones in its history, shown in the following figure:

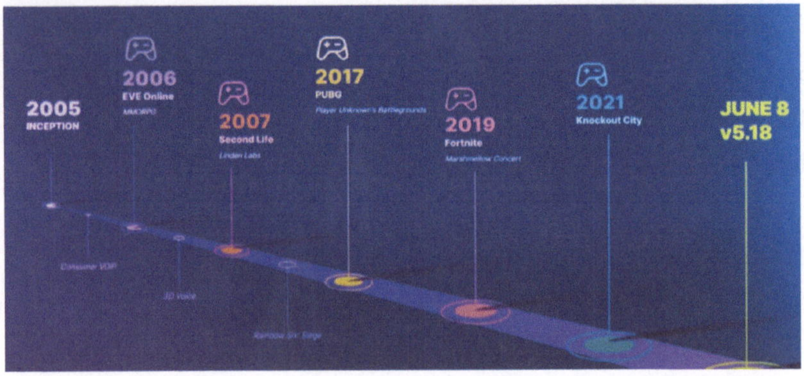

Figure 11.2: Some of the most important milestones in Vivox's history

A year later, in 2006, EVE online was one of the biggest successes, and they demonstrated their ability to scale the system with many concurrent users:

Figure 11.3: EVE online was the first Big Title

In 2007, Vivox became the communications platform for the popular MMO Second Life (See *Figure 11.4*), considered by some to be the first metaverse. This marked a major milestone for the company, consolidating its reputation. One of the most notable innovations introduced at the time was 3D positional voice chat, which added spatial audio realism to in-game conversations.

***Figure 11.4**: Second Life incorporate the 3D voice*

With this functionality, when participants move away, moving in the virtual world, the sound is attenuated. As users get closer, the sound becomes louder, creating the intended immersive feeling.

2018 saw one of the greatest milestones, Fortnite. This unreal engine game has captivated thousands of players around the world:

***Figure 11.5**: Fortnite is one of the most important titles that uses Vivox*

Epic wanted the game to be as cross-platform as possible, so they had to develop the versions for Android and iOS and, a little later, the Nintendo Switch.

In 2019, *Unity Technologies* acquired the company and simultaneously held a significant online concert with over 8 million simultaneous speakers during the Marshmallow Fortnite in-game concert.

In 2021, significant improvements were made to enhance voice quality on mobile devices, as the platform was originally designed for use on computers and consoles.

Vivox is a strong and scalable platform. Some impressive data to corroborate this is that they have had more than 120 million active users in one year, they have transmitted more than 50 billion minutes per month, and are present in more than 190 countries around the world with guaranteed stability of 99.9% of the time.

Vivox SDK installation

As usual, in order to use a service in Unity Gaming Services, we will need to perform the following two steps:

1. Access the Dashboard, search among the available services, and launch Vivox. When you select the service and it is activated, you must select the engine with which it is going to be used (Unity, Unreal, or custom), link the project, and then download the package.

   Note: The packages to be installed and the versions of Unity differ depending on the platform to be utilized (for instance, the version of Unity for Windows is distinct from that for macOS).

   Additionally, it is imperative to consider that for certain platforms, explicit access requests (as depicted in the following figure with red locks) are required:

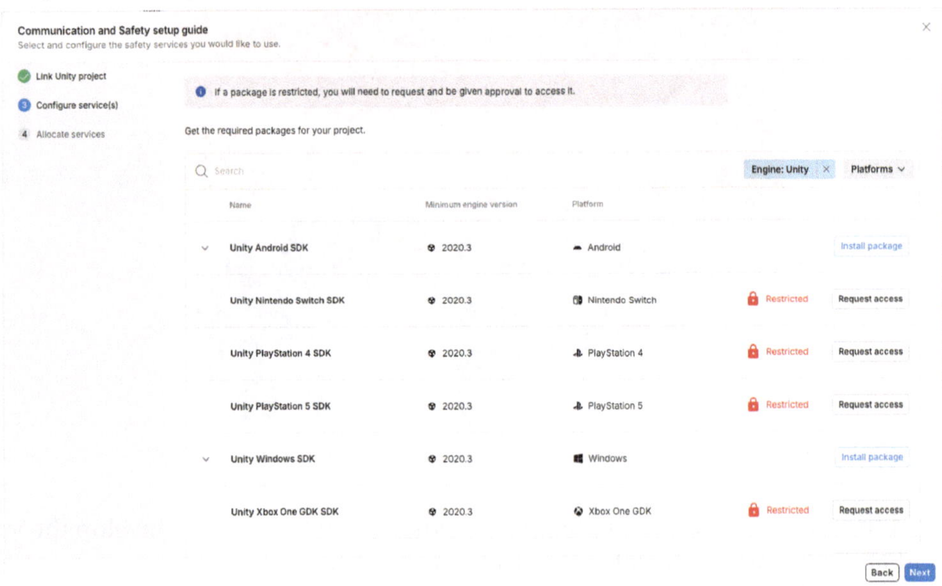

Figure 11.6: Activate Vivox Service on the Unity Dashboard

There are two types of downloads available: those that are Core SDK and those that are Unity SDK. The difference is that those that are core are coded in C++ to be able to do the implementation directly at a low level, while those that are Unity are for our preferred engine and with calls in C#.

2. Install and activate the service within our Unity project. In order to install the package, you must have enabled the pre-release packages option:

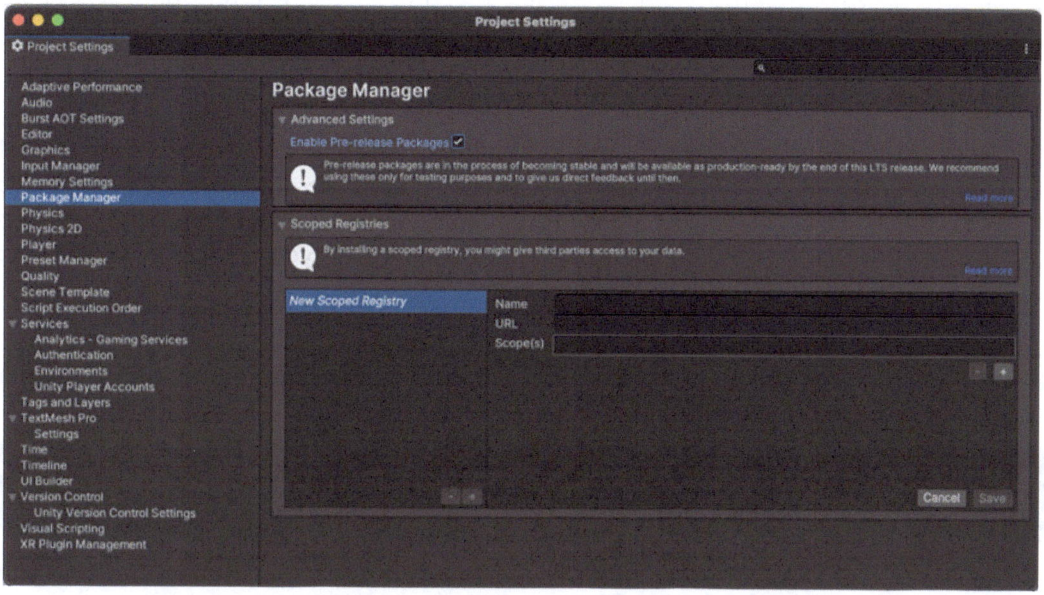

Figure 11.7: The pre-release packages option must be enabled to install Vivox

3. To accomplish this, go to **Edit | Project Settings | Package Manager** and click the option available within the **Advanced Settings** section.

4. Open the **Package Manager** window, select the packages from Unity Registry, and search for Vivox:

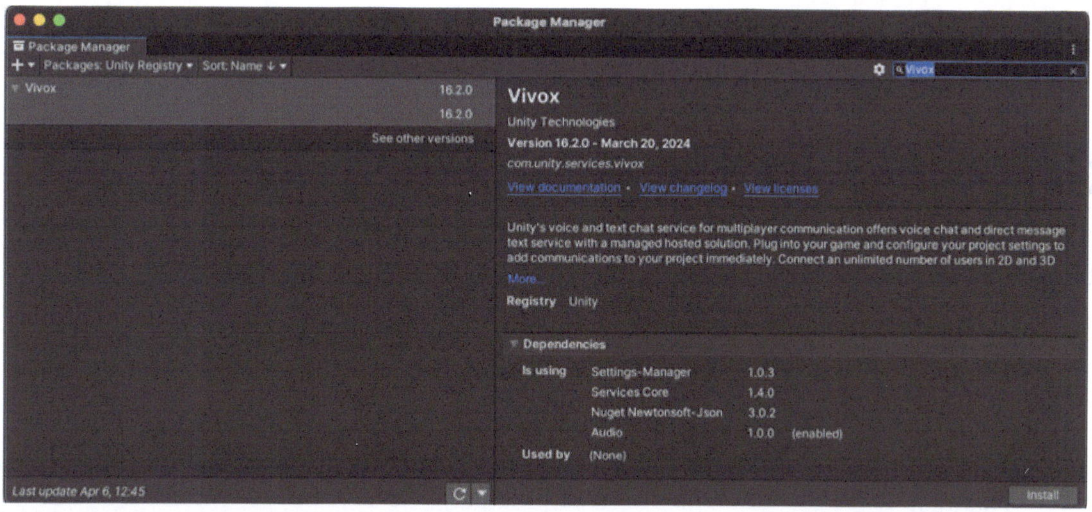

Figure 11.8: Install the Vivox package from the Package Manager window

5. If you encounter an error like the following, it is because you must also have the authentication package installed in the Unity project. To engage in a conversation, it is imperative that the user is recognized, and to accomplish this, they must first be authenticated.

   The error looks like the following:

   ```
   Assets/Samples/Vivox/16.2.0/Chat Channel Sample/Assets/ChatChannelSample/Scripts/UI/LobbyScreenUI.cs(2,22): error CS0234: The type or el.phncdn.com/pics/gifs/024/614/511/24614511a.webm name 'Authentication' does not exist in the namespace 'Unity.Services' (are you missing an assembly reference?)
   ```

Upon installing the Vivox package, an optional feature is available to install some examples. It is strongly recommended that you install these examples to thoroughly understand the demo scenes and gain a comprehensive understanding of how to utilize the software effectively:

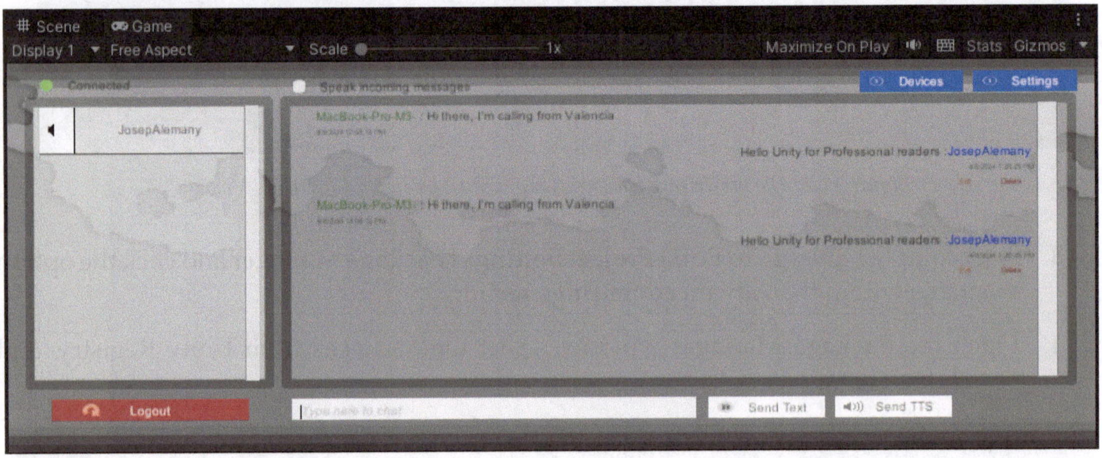

Figure 11.9: Complete chat example on the Vivox package samples

Connect your Unity project to Vivox

The following example explains the first steps to implement Vivox into our projects. To make it easier to understand, the following steps have been done sequentially:

1. We establish the Vivox service.
2. We log in with the username (Josep in this case).
3. We joined a channel called Unify4Prof.
4. We dispatch a text message to engage in conversation with the other members of the channel:

```
using UnityEngine;
using ViVoxNameSpace;
public class VivoxController : MonoBehaviour
{
    // The name of the the user who send the messages.
    private string _user;

    // The name of the Vivox channel the user will join.
    private string _channel;
    // Instance of the Chat class to handle Vivox functionality.
    private Chat _chatInstance;
    private void Start()
    {
        // Create a new instance of the Chat class.
        _chatInstance = new Chat();
        // Define the user name
        _user = "Josep Alemany";

        // Define the channel name to join.
        _channel = "Unity4Prof";
        // Initialize the chat service with a username and channel name.
        _chatInstance.Init(_user, _channel);
    }
    // Method triggered by a UI button to send a text message to the channel.
    public void ButtonSendTextMessage(string text)
    {
        Debug.Log("CLICK BUTTON to send Message"); // Log when the button is clicked.
        _chatInstance.SendTextMessage(text); // Send the message via the chat instance.
    }
}
```

Once the Vivox Unity package is installed, you will be able to add a new audio component called **Vivox Channel Audio Tap**. They are readily available through both the GameObject and component addition menus under **Audio**:

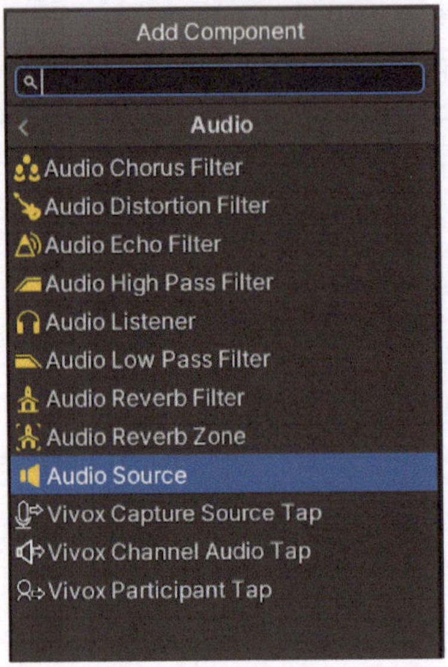

***Figure 11.10**: Add Vivox components*

By incorporating a tap, an **Audio Source** component is added to the corresponding GameObject. It is possible to modify the audio provided by the taps directly through GameObject components, such as those provided by Unity under Audio, or by routing it through an Audio Mixer.

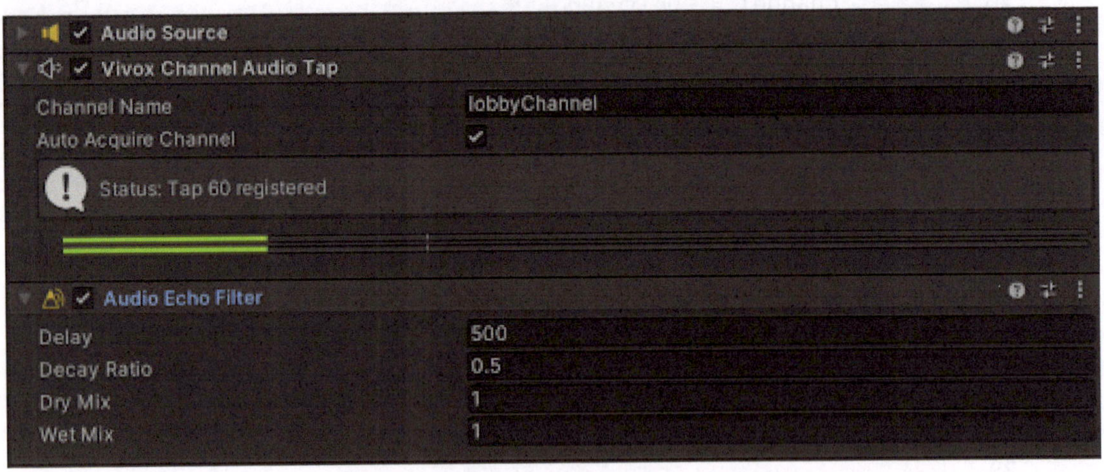

***Figure 11.11**: Detail of how the component looks in the Inspector tab in the Unity editor*

You can add the capture source and channel audio taps to a scene using a C# script. An example of how to add an echo effect to **Vivox Channel Audio Tap** audio through a script is as follows:

```
private GameObject _channelAudioGameObject;

```

```
public void AddChannelAudioEffect()
{
    // Create the GameObject
    _channelAudioGameObject = new GameObject("ChannelAudioGameObject");
    // Add the Tap as a Component to the GameObject
    _channelAudioGameObject.AddComponent<VivoxChannelAudioTap>();
    // You can add filter effect: echo in this case
    _channelAudioGameObject.AddComponent<AudioEchoFilter>();
}
```

Channels

Vivox provides group text and voice communication channels. Users have the capability to communicate with one another by joining the same channel.

Channels have the following characteristics:

- Channels are identified through the use of channel IDs.
- The game assigns channel IDs.
- Channels are platform-agnostic, allowing game clients on different platforms to seamlessly communicate with one another.
- Channels are created automatically, and inactive channels do not consume any Vivox resources. To avoid problems, when naming a channel, keep in mind that the maximum length is 200 characters and always use alphanumeric characters (some symbols are allowed, but it is better not to risk it).

By default, the maximum number of users in text channels is limited to 200 users, but it can be changed to support more than 2000 simultaneous users.

To achieve this, it is necessary to modify the channel settings, and for the changes in the configuration to take effect on an existing channel, all the occupants of the channel must first leave, and it must be destroyed.

Channels type

Depending on their functionality, there are several types of channels that are more or less suitable. They are as follows:

- **Echo channels**: They are test or development channels. They are used to test the correct operation of the connectivity or the microphones. To join an echo channel, the call is made with the following syntax:

  ```
  JoinEchoChannelAsync("NameofEchoChannel", ChatCapability.AudioOnly)
  ```

- **Group channels**: Group channels allow you to send audio and text, but spatial information is not shared within the game, nor are coordinates or rotation angles sent. These types of channels are the most commonly used. Users can use them to coordinate in a squad attack or socialize in an MMO.

  The syntax to join a group channel is as follows:

```
JoinGroupChannelAsync("GroupChannel", ChatCapability.TextAndAudio)
```

- **Positional channels**: This particular channel, in addition to text and voice chat, takes into account the user's location within the game world and the distance between users, resulting in an attenuated voice creating a greater immersive sensation. This implies that it is imperative to provide the coordinates of each player at all times, which significantly increases network traffic and computations, thereby facilitating the processing of audio in real-time.

  To enhance code management and reusability across various projects, all Vivox functionalities have been organized into a namespace named **ViVoxNameSpace**. This approach facilitates centralized modifications, simplifying the code within the components. The following is the code for the namespace:

```
// Create a new instance of 3D audio properties for a Vivox positional (spatial) voice channel.
Channel3DProperties props = new Channel3DProperties()
JoinPositionalChannelAsync(
    "PositionalChannel",          // The unique channel name to join
    ChatCapability.TextAndAudio,  // Enable both text and voice chat
    Channel3DProperties     // The 3D audio configuration defined above
    );
```

The preceding code focuses on showing the creation of the instance, but the complete code needed for everything to work is as follows:

```
using UnityEngine;
using Unity.Services.Authentication;
using Unity.Services.Core;
using Unity.Services.Vivox;
namespace ViVoxNameSpace
{
    // This class handles chat functionality using Unity's Vivox service.
    public class Chat
    {
        // Private variables to store the username and channel name.
```

```
    private static bool Joined;
    private static string _userName;
    private static string _channelName;
    // Initializes the chat service with the given username and channel name.
    // Calls the Initialization method to start the service.
    public void Init(string user, string channel)
    {
        Joined = false;   // Control si the user is joined to the channel before sending a message
        _userName = user; // Set the username for the session.
        _channelName = channel; // Set the channel name to join.
        Initialization(); // Start the Vivox service initialization process.
    }

    // Handles the asynchronous initialization of Unity Services, Authentication, and Vivox.
    private async void Initialization()
    {
        await UnityServices.InitializeAsync(); // Initialize Unity Services.
        await AuthenticationService.Instance.SignInAnonymouslyAsync(); // Authenticate anonymously.
        await VivoxService.Instance.InitializeAsync(); // Initialize the Vivox service.
        Login(); // Proceed to login after initialization.
    }

    // Logs the user into Vivox and joins a channel.
    private async void Login()
    {
        // Configure Vivox login options.
        LoginOptions myOptions = new LoginOptions
        {
            DisplayName = _userName, // Set the display name.
            EnableTTS = true // Enable Text-to-Speech functionality.
```

```
            };
            await VivoxService.Instance.LoginAsync(myOptions); // Perform the login.
            JoinToChannel(); // Join the specified channel after logging in.
            Debug.Log("You are logged to Vivox, " + _userName); // Confirm successful login in the console.
        }

        // Joins a specified Vivox channel with chat capabilities (text and audio).
        private async void JoinToChannel()
        {
            ChatCapability _chatCapability = ChatCapability.TextAndAudio; // Define chat capabilities.
            await VivoxService.Instance.JoinEchoChannelAsync(_channelName, _chatCapability); // Join the channel.
            Joined = true;
            Debug.Log("You are chatting on channel: " + _channelName); // Confirm channel join in the console.
            SendTextMessage("Hi there! You are doing well!"); // Send an initial greeting message to the channel.
        }
        // Sends a text message to the current channel.
        public void SendTextMessage(string text)
        {
            if (Joined)          // Check if the user is already joined to the channel before sending the message.
            {
                VivoxService.Instance.SendChannelTextMessageAsync(_channelName, text); // Send the message to the channel.
                Debug.Log("Message sent: " + text + " to channel " + _channelName); // Log the message for debugging.
            }
        }
    }
}
```

Automatic connection recovery

In complex systems, where many external factors are involved, connection issues are inevitable (imagine a user who connects from a train and goes through a tunnel, for example, or when a device changes between a mobile data connection and a home wireless network connection). For this reason, a feature of the Vivox SDK that automatically recovers if the connection drops in short periods of interruption is especially important. This connection recovery occurs without intervention from the application.

When network connectivity is lost, Vivox SDK attempts to restore connectivity for a duration of up to 30 seconds.

To keep track of when the connection is recognized as lost and recovery begins, you can subscribe to the following two events:

- `VivoxService.Instance.ConnectionRecovering`
- `VivoxService.Instance.ConnectionRecovered`

By monitoring the status of these preceding events, the connection with Vivox can be tracked, and the user can be properly informed.

Speech-to-text transcription

This is a service that, as the name suggests, converts voice audio into textual form. It is widely used by developers to comply with the **Communications and Video Accessibility Act** (**CVAA**) to make it easier for people with reduced hearing to use their games or applications.

Apps with speech-to-text transcription enabled can provide transcribed audio to any user who has opted in to receive it. The audio is returned in text message format with an indication that it was transcribed from voice. These messages can also indicate if the transcribed text came from the user who requested the transcription.

This is an optionally billed service that enables voice transcription on one or more connected positional or non-positional voice channels for each user. If you are interested, you should check the price according to your needs since it depends on many factors, such as the location of the server, the language, or the number of users.

The transcription of speech-to-text typically does not consider the audio volume of speech, but rather the clarity of the spoken words. The accuracy of the transcribed speech is not affected by hardware or software volume adjustments. Nonetheless, a person's silence or mumbling can have a detrimental effect on transcription, although this is beyond the developer's control.

A sample code to subscribe to the **`SpeechToText`** looks like the following:

```
await VivoxService.Instance.SpeechToTextEnableTranscription( _
nameOfChannel);
```

To change the transcription language, you can specify a list of three spoken languages with the following code:

```
1. loginOptions = loginOptions ?? new LoginOptions();
2. loginOptions.
   SpeechToTextLanguages = new List<string>{"en", "es", "fr"};
```

The format in which the language is specified is a two-letter string, which complies with the regulation found at the following link: **https://www.rfc-editor.org/info/bcp47**.

Since the audio is sent over the network, its quality is essential for the transcription to be accurate. On the other hand, the higher the quality, the more bandwidth and computing resources we consume. So, a balance point must be found between what we can consume and the quality that is necessary.

The following comparison table, showcasing four different codecs, will help you choose the codec that best suits your needs:

Codec name	Opus	Siren 14	Siren 7	PCMU
Network Bitrate	40 kbit/s	32 kbit/s	32 kbit/s	64 kbit/s
CPU usage (Encoding)	Moderate	Low	Lower	Lowest
CPU usage (Decoding)	Low	Low	Lower	Lowest
Supports configurable bitrate?	Yes (6 to 128 kbit/s)	No	No	No
Audio sample rate	48 kHz	32 kHz	16 kHz	8 kHz
Audio quality	Best (20+ kbit/s)	Good	Fair	Poor

Table 11.1: Comparison of the four codecs used by the Vivox SDK

Note: The preceding numbers exclude 14.4 kbit/s overhead from Vivox packet headers while voice is active.

They are the default bitrate for each codec for a speech stream at the theoretical maximum.

The codec bitrate is only in effect while voice is active (either transmitted or received).

Text-to-speech

Text-to-speech (**TTS** from now on) is a service that converts text to synthesized speech. This service is widely used by developers to help people who cannot speak, or not clearly enough, to make games more inclusive and comply with CVAA.

When a voice channel participant uses TTS, this service converts their text messages to synthesized speech, which is then transmitted to the voice channel. When TTS generates the voice audio, you can choose three options:

- Play a locally synthesized phrase through the user's output audio device.
- Broadcast and play it for remote participants.
- Play it locally and broadcast it to remote participants simultaneously.

Transmission

In order for the entire system to work smoothly, it is very important to control how data transmission will be carried out (especially for users who connect to multiple channels simultaneously)

Through **`Vivox.Service.Instance`** and the **`TransmissionMode`**, we can control which channel the microphone audio and the injected audio are transmitted to.

Even if you choose to allow other participants to hear the voice of a specific user, you should keep in mind that there are other factors that can affect this option. That user may have been muted by the channel moderator (if he or she deems it appropriate) and may also have been muted locally.

With the Vivox package, you can install some examples of voice chat to see all its features and how to program to access its services. In the following figure, you can see one of the perfectly functional examples:

***Figure 11.12**: This is one of the samples that Unity has to show the functionalities of Vivox*

Safe Voice

In any environment with a large number of users, incidents are bound to occur. That is why these types of platforms must have a mechanism for controlling abusive users.

The Safe Voice is an API that enables game developers to request monitoring of an ongoing Vivox voice channel to provide analysis based on specific events within the game.

The backend service of the game initiates the request. After successful recording and analysis of the monitored voice channel, Safe Voice stores the audio data and analysis results in customer-provided storage. The moderation team can utilize the recordings and analysis outcomes to conduct an investigation into incidents within the community.

Moderators can explore sessions in which incidents occur, analyze what happened, and take action. The sessions page lists all the results of processed sessions and contains two tabs, one for active sessions and one for resolved sessions. The active tab displays all live results, while the solved tab displays all analyzed and solved sessions.

The following figure shows an example of the architecture used to enable Vivox to operate with the highest number of simultaneous users. It is important to highlight how the load is distributed between the client and the server to maximize efficiency:

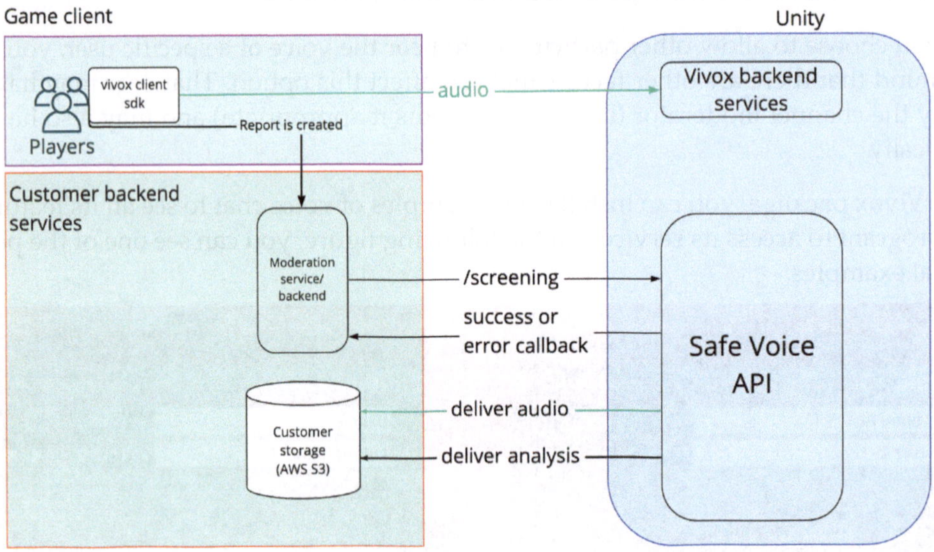

Figure 11.13: *Vivox Client/Server sample architecture*

To help moderator teams identify sessions with problematic content, Safe Voice allows administrators with the Security Administrator role to configure certain features. These features can be customized to help optimize processes, relative to the needs of the respective gaming communities and moderating teams. In the following figure, we can see the menu from where we access the configuration to be able to moderate Vivox conversations:

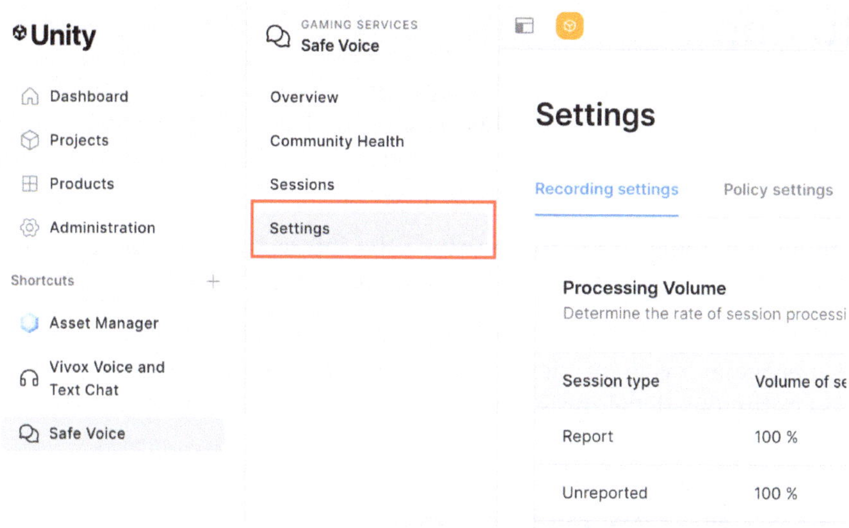

Figure 11.14: Configuring the settings of the Safe Voice

Player segments are used to determine who is most at risk of toxicity or being a toxic player. Safe Voice detects and highlights the presence of these players. In *Figure 11.15*, we can clearly see how a column appears that is used to make a selection of those players who can be potentially toxic or cause more problems.

This selection greatly helps moderators to focus on the most controversial users. If a player is identified as belonging to a player segment within a session, it is marked in the player segment column on a session results page:

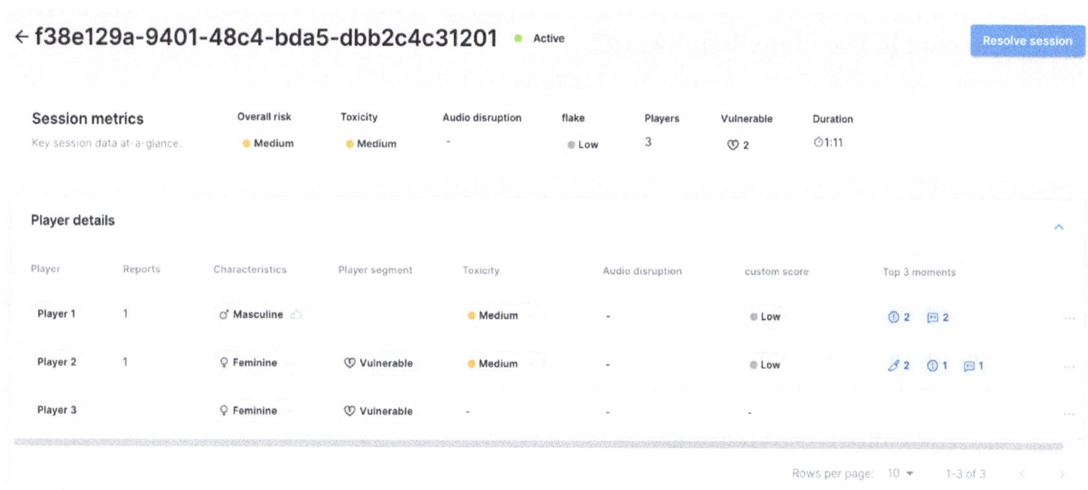

Figure 11.15: Segment the users on the sessions to find toxic behaviors

Conclusion

In this chapter, we have seen how Unity Gaming Services offers us a platform so that our players can communicate with each other, freeing us from the technical complexity that it entails. That gives us many more possibilities (surely, we could never develop ourselves) and allows us to focus on the development of our project.

Communications are going to greatly improve the interactive and social experience of our players and are a fundamental part of generating the engagement that we all want.

In the next chapter, we will delve into the functions performed by the term DevOps and explore the perpetual cycle of development, testing, installation, and monitoring that encompasses continuous development and continuous integration within the realm of Unity 3D development.

Multiple choice questions

1. **Vivox is characterized as a powerful voice and text chat platform designed for seamless integration with game engines. Which major technology company acquired Vivox in 2019, integrating it into Unity Game Services?**
   a. Epic Games
   b. Amazon Web Services (AWS)
   c. Unity Technologies
   d. Microsoft
2. **Which two primary functionalities distinguish a Positional Channel from a Group Channel in the Vivox framework?**
   a. Positional Channels enforce mandatory text transcription.
   b. Positional Channels transmit spatial information (location and distance) between users.
   c. Positional Channels result in increased network traffic and computational processing for real-time audio.
   d. Positional Channels are exclusively used for testing connectivity and microphones.
3. **What is a mandatory software dependency required in a Unity project to enable user recognition before the conversation services can be engaged using Vivox?**
   a. The Unity DOTS package
   b. The Unity Authentication package
   c. The Unity Transport package
   d. The Unity Ads SDK

4. **To support accessibility and comply with mandates like the CVAA, Vivox offers which two specific transcription services?**

   a. Text-to-display transcription

   b. Server-side recording analysis

   c. Text-to-speech synthesis

   d. Speech-to-text conversion

5. **What is the core function of the Safe Voice API in channel management and moderation?**

   a. It automatically blocks users identified as Dormant Players by analytics.

   b. It enables game developers to request monitoring of ongoing voice channels for analysis and subsequent storage of audio data.

   c. It performs real-time audio compression to minimize bandwidth usage during toxic exchanges.

   d. It prevents players who have not authenticated with email and password from joining any channels.

6. **A developer has changed the maximum number of users allowed in a specific Vivox Group Channel from the default limit. Which action must occur for this new capacity configuration to take effect?**

   a. The entire Unity project must be rebuilt and redeployed to the cloud.

   b. All current occupants must leave the channel, and the channel must be restarted (destroyed and recreated).

   c. The user must manually flush the analytic events buffer using the Flush command.

   d. The developer must recompile the Vivox Core SDK manually using C++.

7. **If a player suddenly experiences a short loss of network connectivity (e.g., traveling through a tunnel), how does the Vivox SDK respond to maintain the session?**

   a. It relies entirely on client-side prediction until the network is manually restored.

   b. It attempts to automatically restore connectivity for a duration of up to 30 seconds.

   c. It immediately forces a full restart of the authentication session and token generation.

   d. It alerts the server, which then attempts to synchronize the state via reconciliation.

8. **Historically, which innovation, used prominently in games like Second Life, marked a consolidation milestone for the Vivox team by allowing sound attenuation based on movement in the virtual world?**
   a. Rewarded advertising models
   b. Cross-platform functionality across all major consoles
   c. 3D voice chat
   d. Automatic connection recovery
9. **In the context of installation, what is the key distinction between the Vivox Core SDK and the Vivox Unity SDK?**
   a. The Core SDK supports only Android and iOS, while the Unity SDK supports consoles.
   b. The Core SDK is engine-agnostic and coded in C++, while the Unity SDK is tailored for Unity (C#) integration.
   c. The Core SDK manages friend lists, while the Unity SDK manages group channels.
   d. The Core SDK is free, while the Unity SDK requires a paid subscription.
10. **When utilizing the speech-to-text transcription feature, which factor is explicitly noted as contributing to the accuracy of the transcribed speech?**
    a. The audio volume adjustments made via hardware or software.
    b. The player's current geographic location relative to the transcription server.
    c. The clarity of the spoken words.
    d. The total number of unique players currently connected to the server fleet.

Answers

1	c
2	b, c
3	b
4	c, d
5	b
6	b
7	b
8	c
9	b
10	c

CHAPTER 12
Unity DevOps for Streamline Game Development

Introduction

The chapter will cover a variety of topics related to Unity DevOps, including its definition and fundamental concepts. It will also explore the Unity Version Control system, repositories, and the management of users and groups. Furthermore, the chapter will delve into Cloud Build, specifically continuous integration and automatic build processes, as well as deployment. The chapter will also discuss the Cloud Content Delivery service, the command line interface, and how to upload a build.

DevOps is defined as the union of people, processes, and technology to deliver value to customers, with development encompassing planning, programming, and testing, and operations including the services to deploy and manage a game. **Continuous integration** (**CI**) involves making small, incremental modifications and using automated testing to enhance team efficiency and reduce risks by adding changes to a repository multiple times a day. **continuous deployment** (**CD**) facilitates the process of releasing game versions. The chapter will also discuss how to use the Unity Version Control system, including Plastic SCM, as well as how to activate DevOps and connect to a source control provider. Finally, the chapter will cover topics such as artifact management, Cloud Build automation, and Cloud Content Delivery.

Structure

The chapter covers the following topics:

- DevOps definition and fundamental concepts
    - Continuous integration
    - Continuous deployment
    - Continuous delivery
    - Challenges and considerations

  - Best practices for CI/CD in Unity
- Unity Version Control system
  - Activating DevOps on Unity Cloud
  - Using Plastic SCM
- Repositories
  - Check in
  - Ignore file
- Users, groups and usage
- Cloud Build
  - Automatic Build
  - Artifact management
- Deployment
- Cloud Content Delivery service
- Command line interface

Objectives

The chapter aims to clarify the meaning of DevOps and its fundamental concepts and to understand the Unity Version Control system. You will explore how repositories are a secure storage space where all game files, including previous versions, are stored. The repository is considered the center of the project, enabling the tracking and management of code changes.

You will also learn the complexities of user and group management, a critical aspect when coordinating multiple contributors on a project. The chapter will cover Cloud Build, specifically CI and automatic build processes, and the process of deploying game versions to specific environments, often for testing. CD facilitates the release of game versions and helps to reduce errors. You will learn about **Cloud Content Delivery** (**CCD**) service, a managed cloud service that hosts and delivers content to application users without requiring a new installation of the application and **command line interface** (**CLI**).

DevOps definition and fundamental concepts

DevOps is a fusion of the terms, development and operations. It encapsulates the integration of individuals, processes, and technology to consistently deliver value to customers.

Development encompasses all aspects of planning, programming, collaboration, construction, and testing for a game. Operations encompass the services utilized for deploying, configuring, and managing the game.

DevOps can be succinctly described as a perpetual cycle of software progression through various stages, wherein all teams involved contribute to continuous improvement through automation, collaboration, and iterative refinement. Even a solitary developer can enhance their productivity by comprehending and effectively employing fundamental DevOps practices.

Following is a visual representation of the CI/CD process, illustrating the continuous, iterative process of developing, testing, delivering, and maintaining software efficiently through automation:

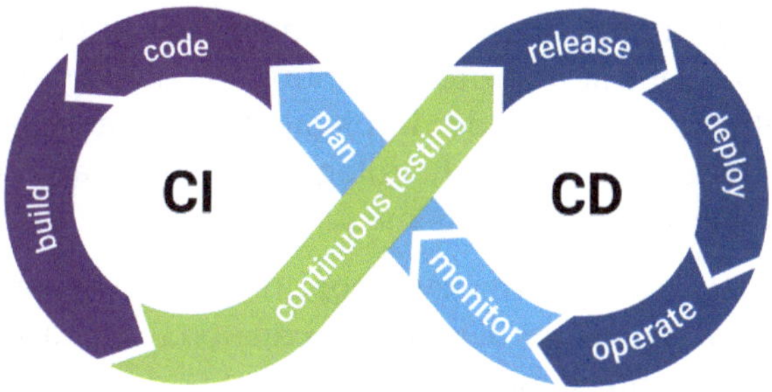

***Figure 12.1**: This is the infinite loop of CI/CD*

Continuous integration

CI is a software development approach that places emphasis on small, incremental modifications as you work on your game (or other software), utilizing automated testing to enhance the efficiency of your team and mitigate risk.

Ideally, changes will be pushed multiple times a day. This approach keeps changes minimal, making rollbacks simpler and less error-prone when needed.

Every time some small advances are made in the development, a backup copy is made in the cloud (in a repository) where it records what changes have been made and allows returning to a previous version if it is estimated that the changes have not worked.

A repository is a dedicated, secure storage space where all your game files (including previous versions) are stored as if they were an incremental copy to which variations from the previous copy are added.

Permissions can be granted so that other developers (members of your team or not) can access the repositories.

Continuous deployment

CD facilitates the process of releasing game versions. Using continuous delivery and deployment (also known as CI/CD) reduces the possibility of errors and defects in the game development process.

Secure and traceable version control: Implementing complex projects requires the implementation of robust and traceable version control, which involves managing and tracking a wide range of assets (not just source code).

Sometimes, many files are large (especially those created by designers and artists). This requires a complete version control system with a powerful set of features that allows you to control all changes and revert them if necessary.

Build automation (CI/CD): Continuous integration means the automatic merging of work from one or more sources into a central repository. Continuous delivery is the process of creating new builds automatically as you develop. Implementing an automated CI/CD pipeline is an established best practice in agile methodology, providing a consistent and automated approach to build, package, and test your game.

The following figure presents a detailed overview of Unity's DevOps pipeline, a comprehensive, engine-agnostic solution designed for 3D content creation, emphasizing asset management, validation, and deployment while avoiding the hassles:

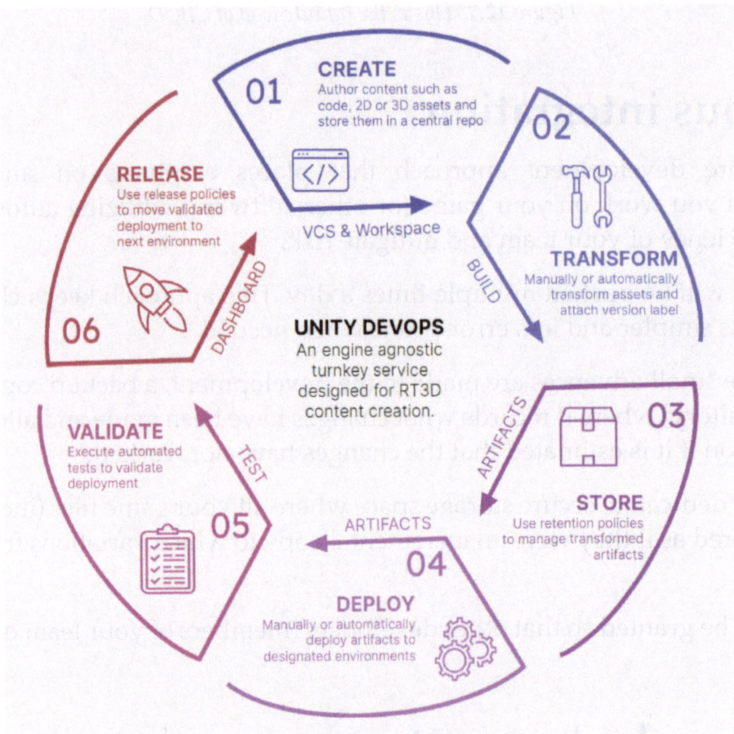

Figure 12.2: A six-step process for real-time 3D (RT3D) content creation with an emphasis on automation and efficient asset management

There are many systems for version control in source code. Surely one of the best known is git (developed by *Linus Torvalds* for the development of the fantastic Linux operating system). Git has multiple platforms and tools such as GitHub, GitLab, and SourceTree.

Continuous delivery

CD involves the automatic deployment of code changes to a staging or testing environment. This ensures that the code is always in a deployable state, allowing teams to release updates to production quickly and reliably:

- **Reliable releases**: With automated deployments, code can be pushed to production with confidence, knowing that it has undergone rigorous testing.
- **Reduced manual effort**: Automation minimizes the chances of human error during deployment processes, resulting in a more efficient workflow.

Challenges and considerations

Establishing an efficient **CI/CD** pipeline in Unity presents several challenges, primarily due to the complexities inherent in managing multi-platform projects. Unity's capability to support various platforms comes with the caveat that developers must ensure compatibility and avoid unsupported solutions, particularly when dealing with native plugins. This complexity necessitates that Unity developers possess a foundational understanding of the operating systems they target, even if they are not required to be experts in those environments.

Another challenge lies in the automation of the build process. Despite Unity being a well-established solution, its ability to streamline CI/CD is sometimes hindered by the lack of comprehensive Linux support and reliance on macOS for build targets in Unity's Cloud Build service. Furthermore, the integration of effective monitoring and rollback mechanisms is essential for maintaining pipeline stability, allowing for rapid recovery from deployment failures.

Best practices for CI/CD in Unity

To maximize the effectiveness of a CI/CD pipeline in Unity, several best practices should be implemented. These include building only once to streamline the build process, conducting thorough automated testing to catch bugs early, and establishing robust deployment strategies that include rollback mechanisms like blue-green deployments or canary releases. By adhering to these best practices, development teams can enhance their efficiency in delivering stable software, fostering improved customer satisfaction, and faster bug resolution.

Some key CI/CD tools for Unity 3D are:

- **Jenkins**: Jenkins is an open-source automation server widely utilized for **continuous integration and continuous deployment** (**CI/CD**) purposes. It enables developers to automate the building and testing of applications, integrating seamlessly with a diverse range of plugins to support various development workflows. Jenkins stands out as an exceptional choice for Unity projects, owing to its adaptability and extensive community support.

- **GitLab CI/CD**: GitLab CI/CD provides a comprehensive and integrated platform for managing software development processes. It offers features for collaborative project management, continuous integration, and deployment processes, making it a valuable tool for Unity developers. Additionally, it includes built-in issue tracking and version control capabilities, further enhancing its usefulness in team projects.

Unity Version Control system

First of all, you should know a couple of fundamental characteristics of the version control system that Unity offers us.

Unity version control is engine-agnostic, meaning it can be used seamlessly with other game engines such as Unreal Engine or Godot. It can also be used with applications other than the editor, such as an **integrated development environment** (**IDE**), such as Visual Studio, Visual Studio Code, Jetbrains Rider, and with different CI/CD systems, such as Jenkins, TeamCity, Bamboo.

Although we can use third-party tools, the system provided by Unity is the one that best integrates with the Unity Workflow and is free under certain conditions, such as:

- Have less than three users.
- Use less than 5 GB of cloud storage space.

This last condition makes it viable for Indie developers and small studios, but in practice, if one works seriously with this tool, one must end up paying. This is why many developers opt for other, better-known, and cheaper alternatives, but they miss out on some of the benefits that this interesting tool can bring them. Unity Version Control can be used in the following three ways:

- **On the Unity Editor**: With the Unity Editor open with your project, select **Window** | **Unity Version Control** from the main menu. The Unity Version Control window will be located at the bottom of the Editor window.
- **Directly on the Unity Gaming Services Dashboard**: It is necessary to sign in with your Unity ID and possess an active DevOps subscription. With this method, there is no need to install anything.
- The third way is installing and using an external application specially designed for this: **Plastic SCM.**

Activating DevOps on Unity Cloud

To activate DevOps for your projects, you must perform the following steps:

1. In the Unity Gaming Services dashboard, navigate to the project where you want to enable DevOps and select it:

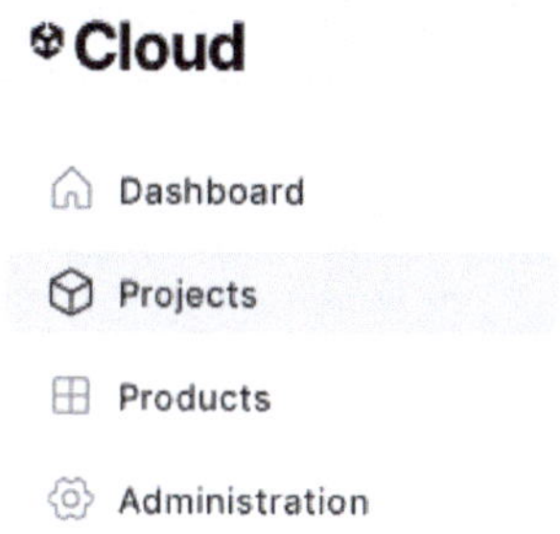

Figure 12.3: *Select the project where to implement the CI/CD system*

2. At the bottom, where it says **Services,** look specifically for **DevOps** and click the **Launch** button:

Figure 12.4: *From the available options, select DevOps and the Launch button*

The following options will appear that you can configure or activate depending on your needs:

Connect your Build Automation service to your preferred source control provider. You can do it from the **Build Automation Settings** page.

Set up integrations to be notified of the important parts of your team's workflow.

Set up build configurations to trigger builds and automate across platforms. You can do it from the Build Automation Configurations page.

Once you have DevOps enabled in Unity Cloud, you can invite team members to the project to help manage it.

Connecting to your source control provider

The Unity connection is capable of connecting to today's major version control providers. In order to connect, the security system that each of them requires will have to be installed. For example, GitHub requires a Persona Access Token, but Azure will also require the name of the Azure Organization. In some cases, encryption and the encryption method may be activated.

There are many version control systems (each has its advantages and disadvantages). Unity allows connection to a large number of them. The list can be seen in the drop-down menu, shown in the following figure:

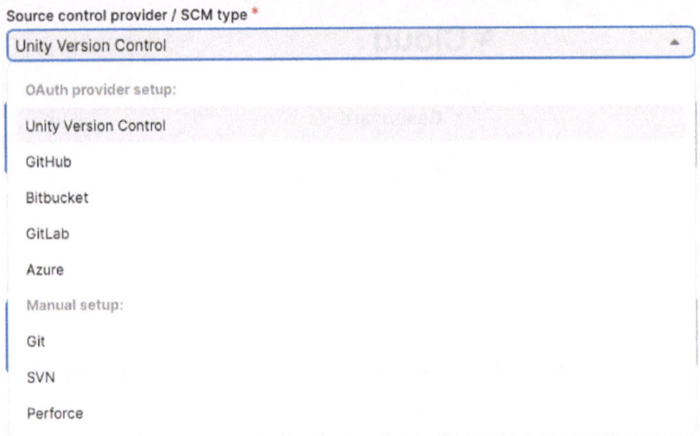

Figure 12.5: You can connect to a lot of source control providers

Using Plastic SCM

Unity has its own version control system: Plastic **source control management** (**SCM**). It is true that Unity can be used with almost any version control system, and, on many occasions, developers prefer others (because they already know them), but Plastic behaves exceptionally well with all assets that are large in size.

Plastic SCM has been acquired by Unity to become part of its developer tools. The new name is Unity Version Control, but many documents and tutorials are still known as Plastic SCM.

The following figure shows what the main screen of Plastic SCM looks like:

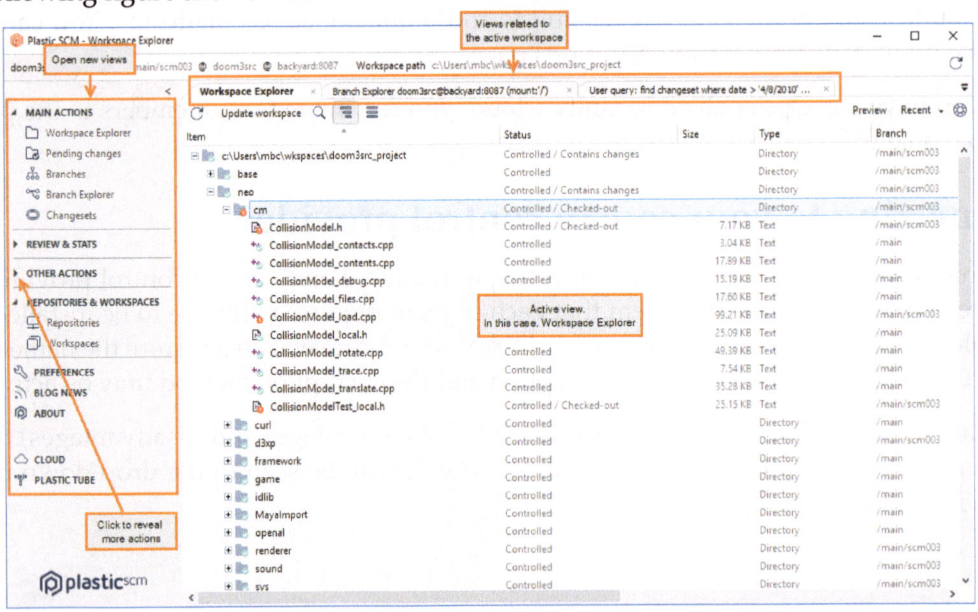

Figure 12.6: The interface of Plastic helps a lot to understand the status of every file on the repository

In the development of games, VR, or multimedia, there are usually files that are very large (high-resolution videos, textures, 3D objects with millions of polygons, etc.). This is where Plastic works much better than other general platforms.

Plastic SCM offers seamless integration with Unity, offering specific features tailored to Unity developers, such as locking binary files (to avoid conflicts), automatic scene merging, and support for Unity-specific metadata.

It is imperative to emphasize the importance of the permission system, which, in Plastic SCM, enables access to the file or folder level. This capability to define security is referred to as granular access control and is of utmost significance when working on intricate projects involving numerous users.

The graphical interface for branch control is very intuitive and makes it much easier when things get complicated. Plastic SCM offers flexible branching and merging capabilities, allowing teams to adopt different branching strategies depending on their workflow requirements.

The Plastic SCM interface makes it very easy to track versions and branches:

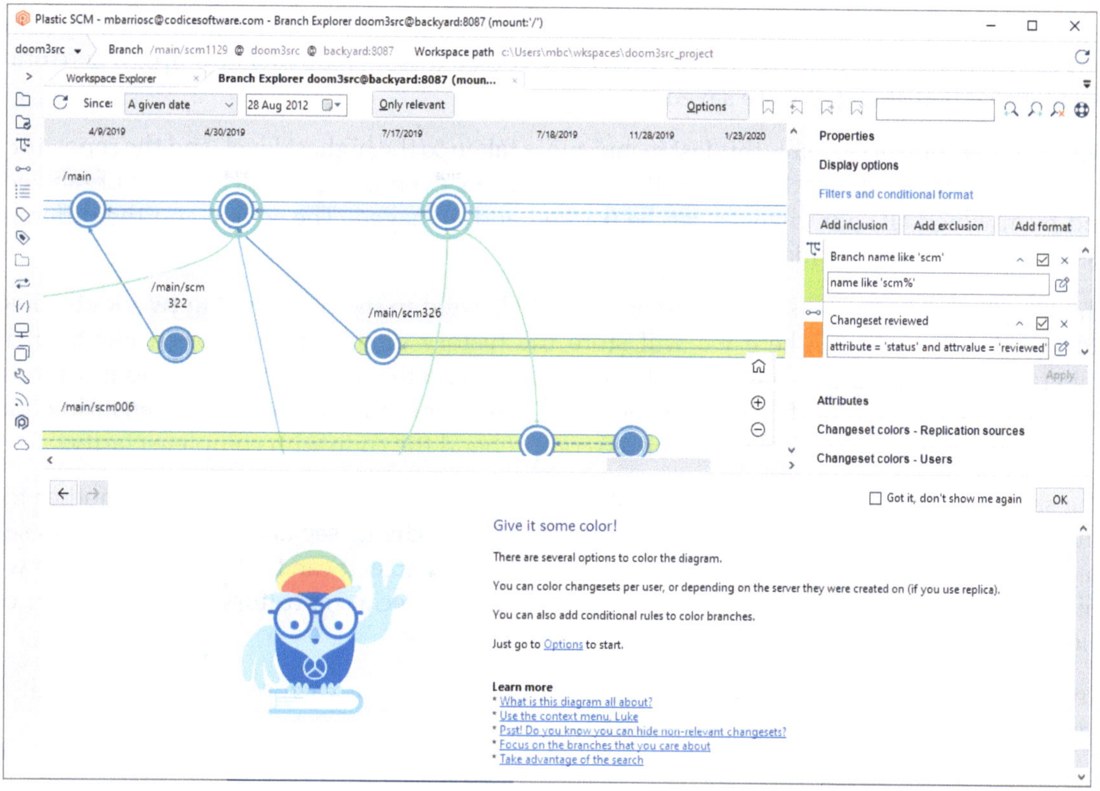

Figure 12.7: *One of the best features is the branch management*

One of the main advantages of Plastic, which greatly speeds up the code review process, is that changes can be reviewed directly within the version control system without having to go to the development environment. When it is a minor change, this functionality makes changes much easier for team members.

In the following figure, you can see all the elements of the workflow:

Figure 12.8: Plastic SCM interface to manage each of the stages

Plastic is well-documented and has a REST API that allows it to be connected to third-party tools. On the following website: **https://docs.plasticscm.com**, you can find the documentation and even some eBooks to get the most out of this fantastic tool.

Repositories

In the past, full backups were used to ensure the security of software projects — everything was copied to prevent data loss. Over time, this evolved into incremental backups, where only the files that had changed were saved.

With version control systems, this last technique is taken to the highest level, and the repository is considered the center of the project. It is a copy where everything is kept safe and organized, and from which all code changes can be tracked and managed. The source and the different assets over time are considered.

The repository is a digital storage system, usually located in the cloud or a **network attached storage** (**NAS**) system, where we will store the history of our entire project. Hence, it is imperative that each step is meticulously documented and that upon uploading modifications, it is evident what modifications have been made and their ramifications, thereby ensuring that the remainder of the team members (or us) comprehend the code with complete clarity.

The simplest repository structure is usually one repository for development and another for final or published versions. This allows us to keep what clients see and what developers see in watertight compartments and differentiated, but, of course, it can be as complicated as we think necessary: you can have a sandbox for testing, a special repository for beta testers or clients, specials with access to the betas.

Another advisable practice is to have a different repository for each platform on which it is developed, as shown in the following figure:

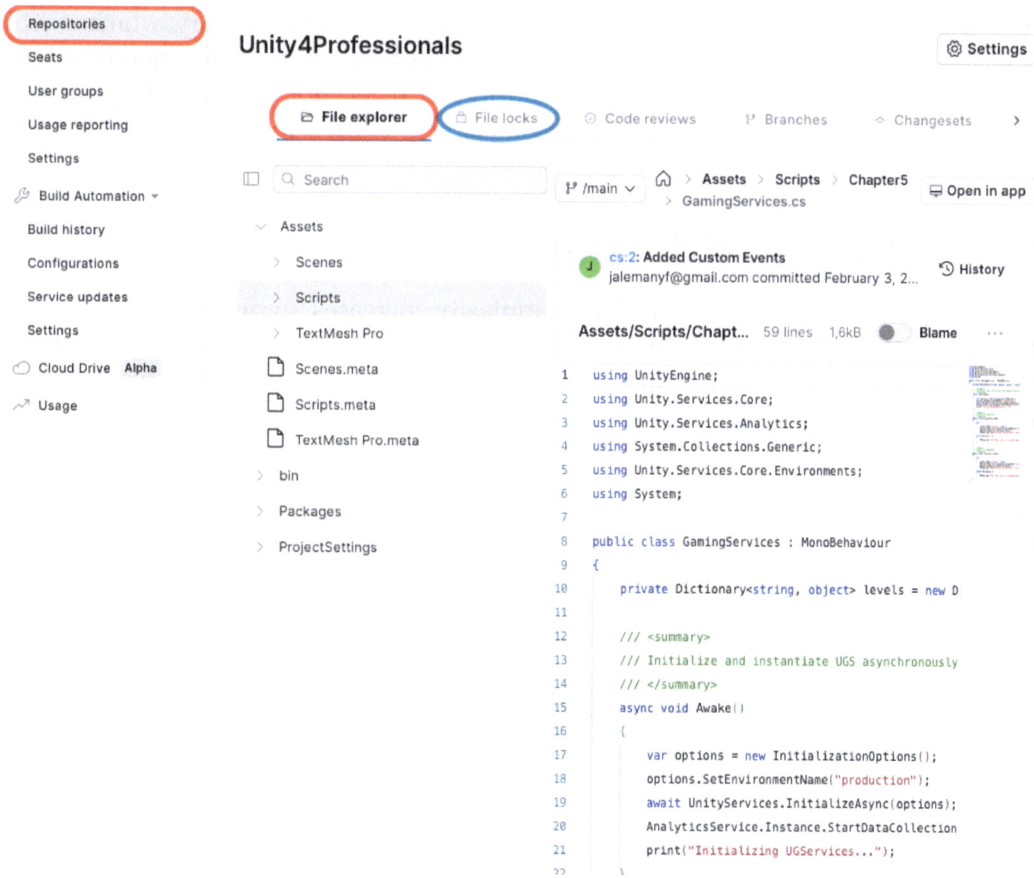

***Figure 12.9**: You can access the files, edit them, or lock them directly from the Repositories management*

Check in

Checking in is the process of submitting changes to the repository. It is imperative that you enter a comment in the text box prior to submitting your modifications. This makes it easy to keep track of what changes have been made at each step.

Ignore file

Many development systems create local files that are then used by the next tool to improve its operation. These files are not essential for the preservation of the project code, and in the event of their loss, they are typically generated automatically.

In Unity, a clear example is the **`.meta`** files or the Library folder. These files are used by the Editor to have a cache of where all the assets are located. If they are deleted, nothing important happens. They are simply regenerated (sometimes it is even beneficial for the project).

For this reason, they should not be stored in the version control repository, which is why all tools have a configuration file where it is indicated which folders and files should be ignored by version control. These files shall not be considered when uploading to the repository. It does not matter whether they are created, deleted, or modified for the project; they are not present and will be completely ignored.

User, groups, and usage

As discussed in the repositories section, complexity increases significantly when multiple users are involved. To simplify management and ensure that each user has appropriate access — without risking accidental deletion of critical files — Unity provides group-based permission management. This works in a similar way to how a network is managed, but has the peculiarity that there are already many defined profiles.

The following figure shows the large number of permissions that can be used for users and groups. This way, we can be very precise about what each of them can do:

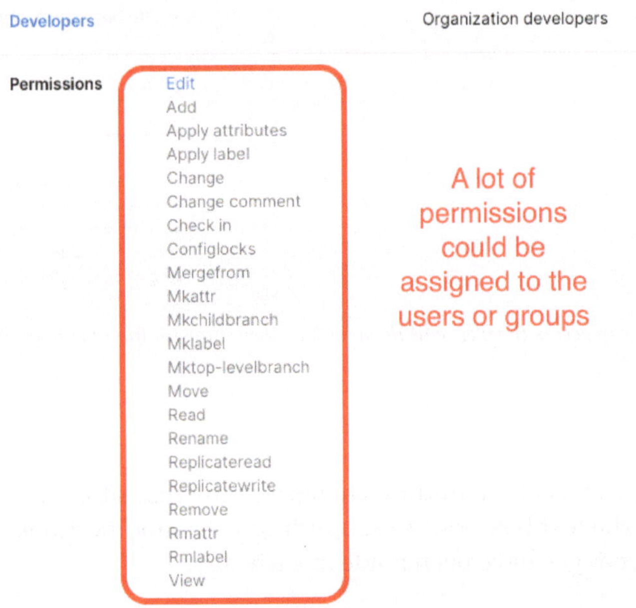

***Figure 12.10**: Permissions we can assign to users or groups*

Usage: Since the storage service has a cost, if you start generating versions automatically without control, the bill will skyrocket. We have an integrated tool that allows us to control the space used in the repositories and the cost.

This tool can be found in the **Administration** menu under **Cost and usage reporting**. We can view the costs we have daily and by project or product. We can also check when the next invoice will arrive in order to make financial forecasts.

Cloud Build

To make the task easier, Unity automates the entire build process, ensuring CI by automatically creating and publishing your project whenever changes are detected in the version control system you have set up.

The automatic system provides the following two advantages:

- It ensures that you always have a build of your game / app based on the latest confirmed working version.
- Since the entire process is done automatically, it gives you precise clues as to when and where errors occur (from when it stopped compiling, for example).

If you want to enable automated build generation, set the **Automatic Build** switch to **Yes** in **Build Automation | Settings | Basic Information Settings**.

Automatic Build

Build Automation establishes a connection with your version control system, whether it be Unity **Version Control System (VCS)** or another system, and continuously monitors that system for any modifications made to your project. When it detects any changes to your project files, Build Automation downloads and builds your project for its target platforms. When builds are complete, Build Automation will notify you with a link to download, share, and install the builds. If there are any errors, the build automation will notify you immediately, so you can fix them quickly, commit changes, and trigger new builds.

You have to select the target platform to build in:

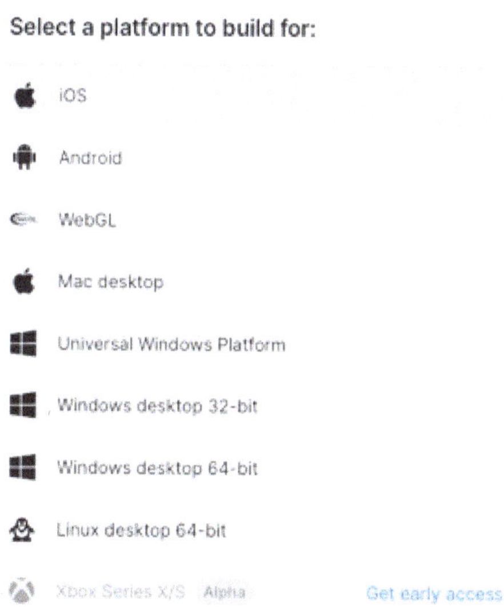

Figure 12.11: *Available platforms for CI*

This user interface facilitates the configuration of a new integration within Unity Build Automation. Users can select specific events, including build successes, failures, and uploads. Additionally, they have access to options for failure diagnostics and user reporting:

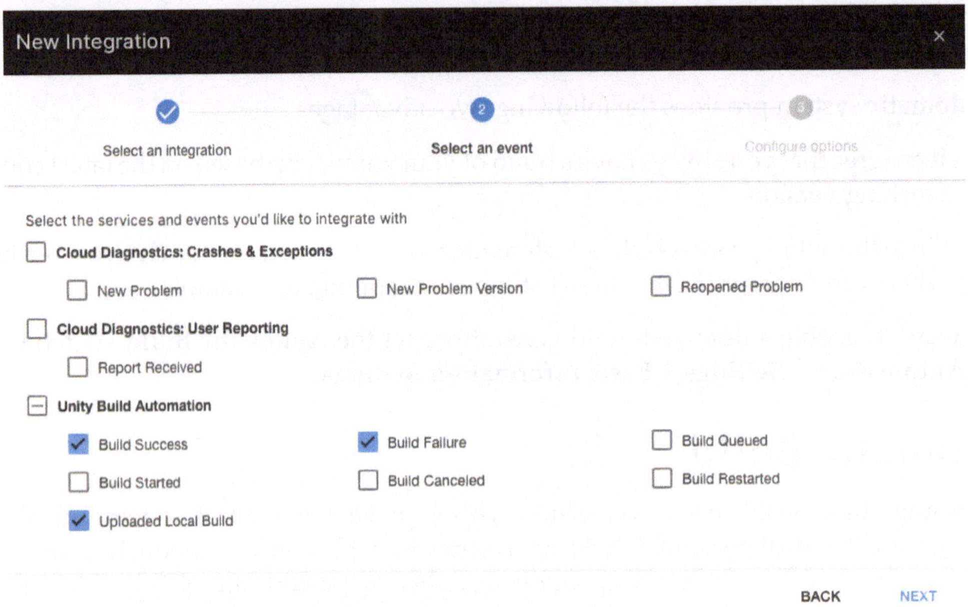

***Figure 12.12**: Define when the CI is going to notify you*

It is important to note that the system can be connected and integrated with some of the main development and management systems to facilitate implementation in all types of business environments. The following is the window that appears when connecting to various third-party management systems:

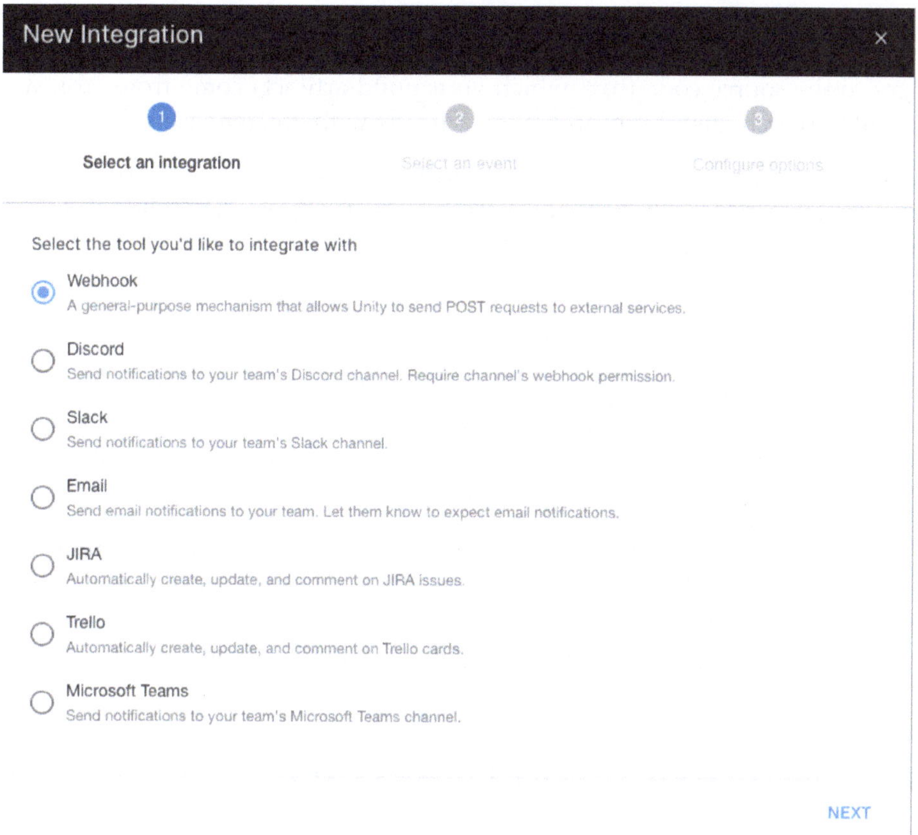

***Figure 12.13:** The system can be connected with management systems like JIRA or Trello*

Over time, as you generate more builds, such as packages or executables, it can become difficult to remember which artifact corresponds to which build and code change. So, you need a good system to manage artifacts and keep track of all these different versions.

Artifact management

Since Unity uses many binary files (apart from the source code), it is important to define what an Artifact is. Artifacts include a wide variety of dependencies, including base images, software packages, Helm charts, metadata, and other tangential but critical resources. An artifact manager provides a central repository for everything needed to build or deploy apps or games, complementing the version control of the source code.

As you build more and more builds, such as packages or executables, it can become difficult to remember which artifact corresponds to which build and code change. You need a good system for managing artifacts and keeping track of all the different versions.

The next tool for DevOps, Artifact Center, addresses this issue. The Artifact Center serves as a repository for all prior project builds. With Artifact Center, you can view your build attempts and changes to the source code from which your build artifacts come from. You will also be able to tag, filter, search, distribute, and share artifacts with greater ease.

Artifact Center integration with Build Automation allows you to track your favorite builds and tag your artifacts in ways that support your team's workflows. This allows you to evaluate builds and automate their eventual deployment.

Deployment

After successfully creating your game's executable files, it is possible to deploy your game version to a specific environment. This is usually a closed environment so that beta testers can check and evaluate whether everything works correctly and is well implemented. These environments are often called **user acceptance testing** (**UAT**) or sandboxes.

It is essential to have multiple test environments in order to ensure that every released product has been properly reviewed. This initial version of the build is typically utilized for internal playtesting or when your quality assurance team is required to evaluate the most recent version of your game prior to its release to the general public. The final environment is known as the production environment.

Cloud Content Delivery service

As we saw in *Chapter 7, Engagement, Gamification and Retention*, one of the most popular features, the **Cloud Content Delivery** (**CCD**), is Unity's managed cloud service that hosts and delivers content to your application users around the world without having to reinstall a new version of the application.

With this system, you can update assets for applications that have already been published.

This system is widely used to send, for example, special graphics for *Halloween* or *Christmas* in an app that users are already using.

Some developers also make their initial app contain almost no graphics (so that its weight is very little and it can be among the first in the app stores). When the app is started for the first time, it downloads all the largest files using the method shown in the following figure:

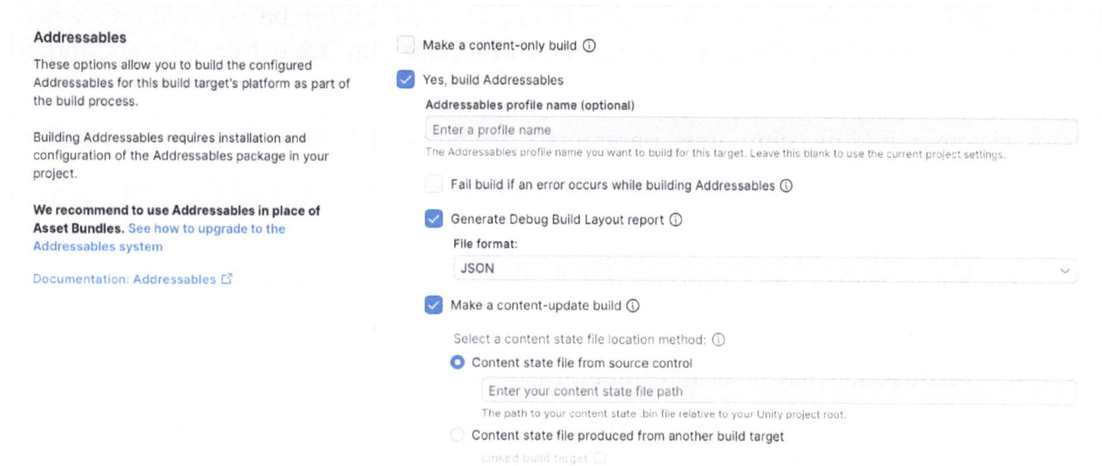

Figure 12.4: Configuration of the CCD in Unity Cloud

To activate the addressable upload system to the CCD service from Build Automation, you must do the following steps:

1. Within **Unity Gaming Services / DevOps from the Configurations** menu, select the configuration on which you want to activate CCD (if they do not have any, you must create it by filling out the form with the necessary data).
2. Within the settings, select **Advanced settings** and, in the form that appears below.
3. Select the **Upload addresses to the Cloud Content Delivery service**.
4. Select the required CCD repository from the **Content Delivery Repository** drop-down menu.
5. Your content delivery API key should already be populated in your field. If not, add it.
6. To automatically create a CCD version from the selected repository, select **Automatically create a Cloud Content Delivery version from repository**.
7. Select **Save and Build**.

Note: This service has an associated cost, and you must control the changes that will occur on your invoice.

Command line interface

The tool that is most used is the command line. Despite the many advances that have been made in graphical interfaces, sometimes nothing beats a command with many parameters if you know it well.

That is why we can install a tool called CLI that will allow us to use commands to perfectly manage our Unity services in the cloud.

There are versions for Windows, macOS, and Linux. On Linux, it can be installed on the most popular distros, but Ubuntu and Alpine stand out because they are extremely light and are often used for Docker containers.[1]

As with all command line commands, parameters can be passed. Some of the simplest are:

- **-version:** To see the version of the CLI you are currently using, add the `--version` flag

  ```
  $ ucd -version
  ```

- **-h, --help**: Display any additional parameters or flags for a given command.
- **-q, --quiet**: Disable the display of operations performed by the specified command.
- **-v, --verbose**: Display error information.

For CLI versions greater than 0.11.0, you need to add the `--environment` flag to most commands. See CLI examples and using CCD via the CLI.

Let us look at some examples:

- To create a bucket:

  ```
  $ ucd buckets create [project_id] [bucket_name]
  ```

- To delete a bucket:

  ```
  $ ucd buckets delete [bucket_id]
  ```

- To list all `buckets` for a project, including their `bucket_id`:

  ```
  $ ucd buckets list [project_id]
  ```

- To set the current bucket as the active bucket:

  ```
  $ ucd config set bucket [bucket_id]
  ```

- To synchronize a local folder with the current bucket:

  ```
  $ ucd entries sync [local_dir_path]
  ```

- To view a list of all entries in the current bucket:

  ```
  $ ucd entries list
  ```

Conclusion

In this chapter, we have explored how agile development techniques enable continuous code maintenance and incremental improvements without compromising security. This fosters a more comfortable and efficient work environment for developers.

Furthermore, Unity Technologies' integration tools facilitate seamless connectivity with our work systems, automating repetitive and time-consuming tasks.

---

1 You may not know Docker, it is a very powerful tool and popular among DevOps. Although it is beyond what this book covers, it is highly recommended that you know it: https://www.docker.com/products/docker-desktop/

While developers typically concentrate on their specific tasks, this system significantly enhances control throughout the development lifecycle. It encompasses source code management, platform compilation, and version distribution for testing and final releases.

In the forthcoming chapter, the reader will delve into the realm of crash and error reporting with Cloud Diagnostics Advanced, a comprehensive solution powered by Backtrace. This solution empowers game developers to effectively identify and resolve issues that compromise game performance and player experience.

The next chapter will encompass a wide range of topics, including error management, traditional code analysis tools, and additional utilities such as the **Android Debug Bridge** (**ADB**) and Unity Profiler. It will also provide insights into utilizing Unity Adaptive Performance for runtime optimization and remote crash detection capabilities through Backtrace and Unity Cloud Diagnostics.

Furthermore, the chapter will elucidate the process of integrating these tools into a workflow through third-party applications.

Multiple choice questions

1. **The strategic methodological guide for data-driven decision making suggests that the initial step is to?**
   a. Identify pain points by analyzing areas where engagement is low.
   b. Optimize the monetization strategy based on A/B test results.
   c. Establish KPIs aligned with game objectives.
   d. Collect and analyze data on player behavior and interactions.
2. **What crucial components does the definition of DevOps combine to achieve the continuous delivery of value to customers?**
   a. Planning, collaboration, and monetization.
   b. Continuous integration, continuous delivery, and monitoring.
   c. People, processes, and technology.
   d. Artifact management, deployment, and command line interface.
3. **Which term defines the process of deploying game versions to specific environments, often utilized for testing prior to final release?**
   a. Continuous integration (CI).
   b. Source control management (SCM).
   c. Deployment.
   d. Artifact management.

4. **In Unity DevOps, what event triggers the automated build generation process within Cloud Build?**
   a. Manually setting the Automatic Build switch to Yes.
   b. Detecting changes or modifications in the version control system.
   c. The successful compilation of the client-side code on a local machine.
   d. A command executed via the Cloud Content Delivery (CCD) interface.
5. **What does CI primarily involve in the context of agile software development methodologies?**
   a. The process of deploying code changes automatically to a staging or testing environment (continuous delivery).
   b. Securing and tracking large binary assets using granular access controls.
   c. Making small, incremental modifications and utilizing automated testing to enhance team efficiency and reduce risks.
   d. Releasing game versions reliably to reduce the possibility of errors (continuous deployment).
6. **Why are certain locally generated files, such as Unity's .meta files and the Library folder, typically directed to be excluded using an Ignore File during version control check-ins?**
   a. They contain sensitive configuration data specific to production servers.
   b. They are always necessary for rollback mechanisms, requiring exclusion via special permission.
   c. They are considered transient and non-essential for project preservation, often automatically regenerated by the Unity Editor.
   d. They exceed the size limits imposed by most version control providers.
7. **What is the primary function of a Repository within the Unity Version Control system?**
   a. To define customized user and group permissions (granular access control).
   b. To automate the compilation and packaging of project files for different platforms (Cloud Build).
   c. To serve as a secure storage space for all game files, allowing the tracking and management of code changes and previous versions.
   d. To host and deliver content updates to application users without requiring a new installation (CCD).

8. **Which of the following statements accurately describes a fundamental characteristic of the Unity Version Control system?**
   a. It requires mandatory payment for use regardless of the team size or storage consumption.
   b. It is dependent exclusively on the Unity Editor for all operations and management.
   c. It is designed to be engine-agnostic, enabling its use with other game engines and development environments.
   d. It uses a low-level API tailored solely for source code file synchronization.
9. **A developer is using the CLI tool. Which task is the CLI most appropriately used for within the Unity Gaming Services ecosystem?**
   a. Designing custom asset pipelines using the graphical node-based editor.
   b. Managing Unity services in the cloud, such as listing buckets or synchronizing local folders.
   c. Generating 3D character animations based on text prompts.
   d. Providing a graphical visualization of the continuous integration status (CI/CD loop).
10. **Scenario: A game studio wants to deploy new holiday graphics and content updates to players immediately without forcing them to download a full new version of the app from the store. Which Unity DevOps service should they utilize?**
    a. Unity Version Control system (VCS).
    b. Artifact Center Management.
    c. Cloud Content Delivery service (CCD).
    d. Cloud Build Automation (CI).

Answers

1	c
2	c
3	c
4	b
5	c
6	c
7	c
8	c
9	b
10	c

Join our Discord space

Join our Discord workspace for latest updates, offers, tech happenings around the world, new releases, and sessions with the authors:

https://discord.bpbonline.com

CHAPTER 13
Crash and Error Reporting with Cloud Diagnostics Advanced

Introduction

This chapter focuses on crash and error reporting for game developers, using tools to identify and resolve issues impacting game performance, player experience, and revenue. The chapter covers topics such as crashes, which examine the nature of crashes, which are sudden and unexpected application failures, and error management, which explores techniques to solve errors, especially when the conditions of the crash can be reproduced. It includes strategies for isolating and locating the error, reproducing it, and determining the moment in the code where it occurs. We will also learn about traditional code tools. The chapter also covers using logging statements to track program flow and variable values to help find the source of errors. Unity offers tools like ADB, Unity Profiler, and Unity Adaptive Performance. This chapter introduces Backtrace and Unity Cloud Diagnostics for application performance and stability monitoring.

The chapter provides developers with insights and tools to improve game performance and user experience by effectively managing errors and crashes.

Structure

The chapter covers the following topics:

- Crashes
    - Error management
- Traditional code tools
- Other tools
    - Android Debug Bridge
    - Unity profiler

- Control the performance with Unity adaptive performance
- Detecting remote crashes
    - Backtrace
    - Unity Cloud Diagnostics

Crashes

When you develop projects of a certain size, it is very likely that a bug will appear that causes your app to crash. Suddenly and without warning, the app freezes, gives an error message (often difficult to decipher), and exits the operating system or directly restarts the computer, as shown in the following figure:

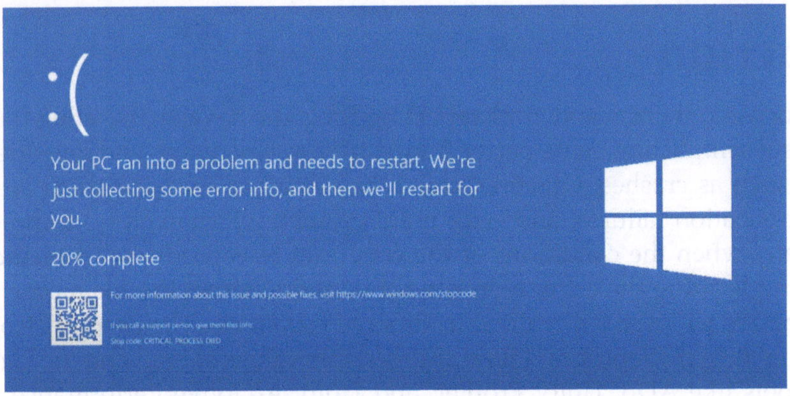

***Figure 13.1:** The infamous blue screen of death*

This should not happen, but it happens more often than developers like to admit. Fortunately, there are various techniques that we can apply to investigate what has escaped our control and has produced such an unpleasant outcome:

***Figure 13.2:** This is the Nintendo GameCube's crash message*

Error management

If you are one of the developers, there are several techniques that can be applied to solve the problem.

When we can reproduce the conditions in which the program has crashed, and we have the source code (these circumstances usually occur in the development process or because a client has reported an incident to us) we can investigate and reproduce the conditions under which it occurs.

To resolve an error of this type, it is best to put yourself in *Sherlock Holmes* mode and try to find out step by step what the cause may be (no matter how unlikely it may seem). Some of the techniques that may be useful to you are:

- **Isolate and locate the error**: This will be useful for us to reproduce the error in laboratory conditions and to know the magnitude of the problem (it is not the same, as it only affects a few users, as it does all the platforms and in all the versions that we have already distributed!).
- **Isolate the problem**: Determine which part of your application is causing the crash. It could be a specific feature, function, or module.
- **Reproduce the error**: Try to reproduce the error consistently. Understanding the conditions that lead to the accident is essential to diagnosing and solving it.
- **Determine the moment in the code where it occurs**: Carefully review the code related to the moment where the accident occurs (pressing a specific button, loading a scene, sending a network request). Once you have defined the area of the code where the problem occurs, the ideal thing is to set a breakpoint just before it occurs and debug, step by step, from that point in the execution. Most development environments have debugging tools. These tools allow you to stop execution at a breakpoint and then step through the code, inspect variables, and identify when it crashes.

Traditional code tools

In Unity, the Visual Studio and Jetbrains Rider development environments have built-in debugging tools. Visual Studio Code can also debug Unity C# code, although an extension will need to be installed for this.

Visual Studio, the development environment that is installed by default with Unity, has very well-integrated step-by-step debugging tools, as shown in the following figure:

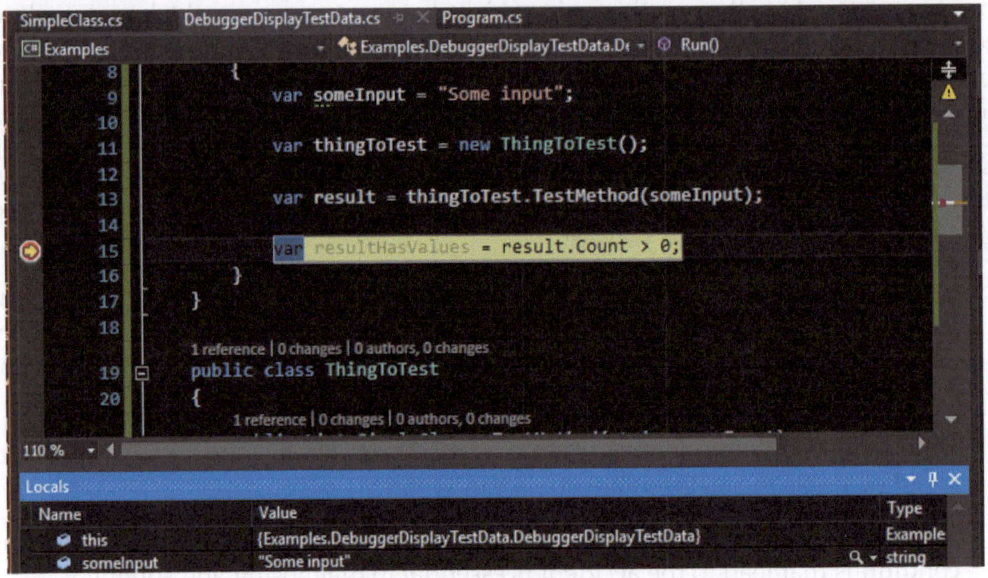

Figure 13.3: Detail of Visual Studio debugging tools

The most common errors are usually logic, uninitialized variables, memory leaks, pointing to inaccessible or non-existent memory areas, or other common sources of errors. When it cannot be executed step by step, because the execution occurs on another computer (for example, on a mobile device), one of the techniques that has always been used is the generation of a log:

Logging: Introduce logging statements in your code to track the program flow and variable values that lead to the crash. This can provide valuable information about what is happening and when the accident occurs.

Once you have found a solution, make sure that the change does not affect other parts of the code. Do regression testing to be sure the change does not introduce new bugs. If you still cannot find the reason for the error, you are advised to review the code with a colleague. Sometimes we get confused, and a new approach helps us a lot to detect the problem.

Another possible source of problems sometimes comes not from our code, but from an external dependency. When we use third-party code, it may change, and updates may cause our code to stop working. Be sure to review dependencies and third-party frameworks in the following ways:

- **Consult documentation and community**: Consult the documentation for the programming language, framework, or library you are using. Look for known issues or common errors that may be related to your problem. Additionally, forums, discussion groups, or *Stack Overflow* can be valuable resources for community help.
- **Thorough review**: Once you have identified and fixed the error, check that the same error does not exist elsewhere in the code.

- **Take precautionary measures**: After the crisis, remember to write additional unit tests that account for the error so that it does not happen again.

Having debugging tools is essential for troubleshooting code. The following figure shows the debugging environment of the popular **integrated development environment** (**IDE**) JetBrains:

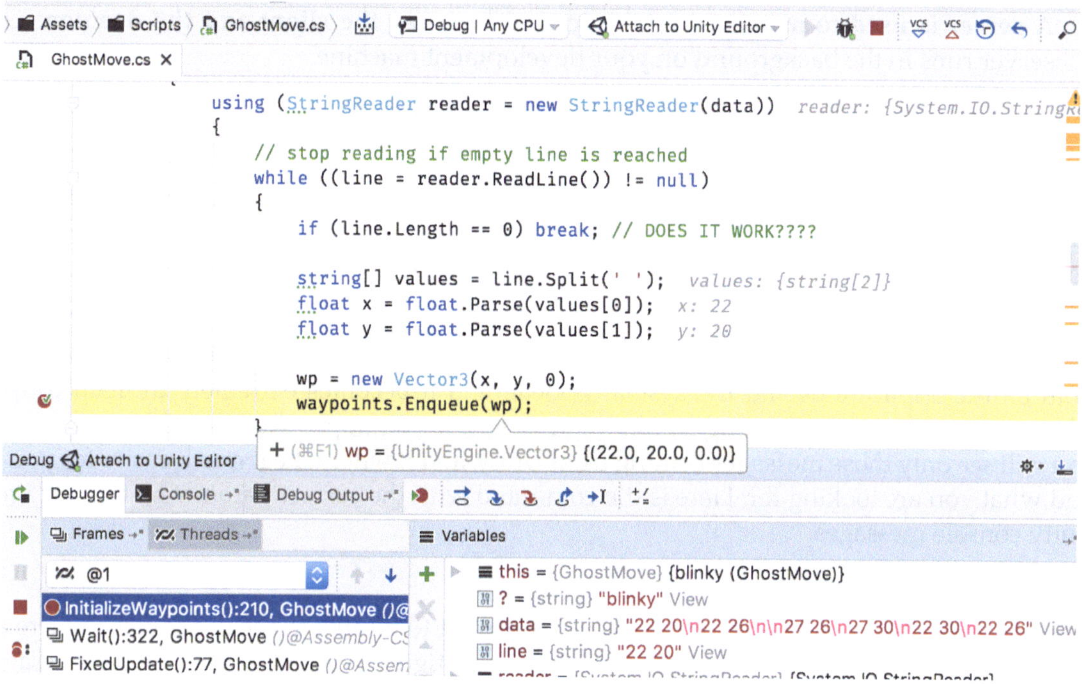

***Figure 13.4**: Detail of JetBrains Rider debugging tools*

Other tools

Apart from the tools of the development environments, there are some other tools specific to the devices or even optimization that can help us. Some of these specific tools can be seen in the following sections.

Android Debug Bridge

According to the official documentation for Android developers, the **Android Debug Bridge** (**ADB**) is a command-line tool that lets you communicate with a device (It is normally done through the data cable connected through the USB port, although it can also be done via a wireless network). The adb command facilitates various device actions, such as installing and debugging apps. The adb provides access to a Unix shell that can be utilized to execute various commands on a device. It is a client-server program with the following three components:

- **A client that receives commands**: The client is installed on your development machine. One may initiate a client from a command-line terminal by issuing an **adb** command.
- **A daemon (adbd), which executes commands on a device**: The daemon operates as a background process on every device.
- **A server is used to manage communication between the client and the daemon**: The server runs in the background on your development machine.

The Android SDK platform tools package includes adb. **You can find more information about adb at this website: https://developer.android.com/tools/adb**

These types of tools are particularly interesting in devices like **virtual reality** (**VR**) glasses (in which we cannot see anything that is happening). Many of them use Android-based operating systems and, therefore, ADB works perfectly (for example, the PICO or Meta headsets).

If you are going to use ADB from your computer's console, keep in mind that when the command is launched, not only do the logs of your application appear. When you call it, those from all the applications and the system appear, and it becomes extremely difficult to find what you are looking for among so many messages. If you apply the following parameters, you will see only those messages coming from Unity, and it will make it much easier for you to find what you are looking for. Here is the command with the correct parameters to view only Unity console messages:

```
1. adb logcat Unity:V *:S
```

When working with an Android device, it is important to be able to see the console where all the warning or error messages appear. In the following figure, we can see the console messages within a development environment:

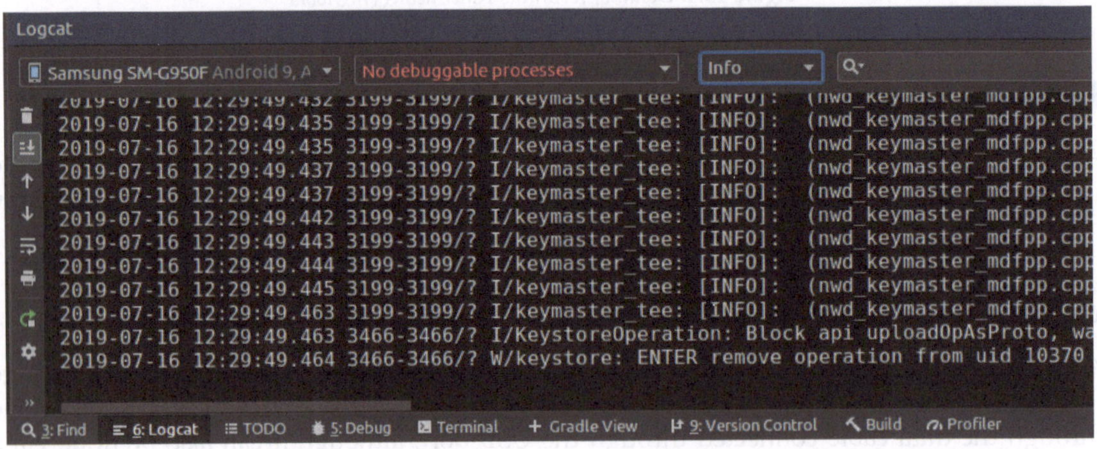

Figure 13.5: Android logcat let us see the error and warning messages on the Android device

Unity Profiler

For example, the Profiler is a tool in the Unity editor that is normally used to measure performance and help in its optimization, but it can also be very useful to see the excessive consumption of resources, such as memory or overload.

When we are developers, we tend to test only the part we are working on, and we do it quickly. Many times, we do not spend much time with intensive use of the application (that is what ends up happening when it is in production). Every time we test, we restart the app and the variable buffers. Everything works well, but it does not have to do so for long periods.

When running an app that we have developed in Unity, it must be loaded into memory. It is very important to be able to know and understand how our app consumes resources on different devices in order to optimize its operation and solve possible problems due to running out of memory. The Unity Profile tool does a magnificent job by graphically showing us the memory consumption on the hardware by our app, as can be seen in the following figure:

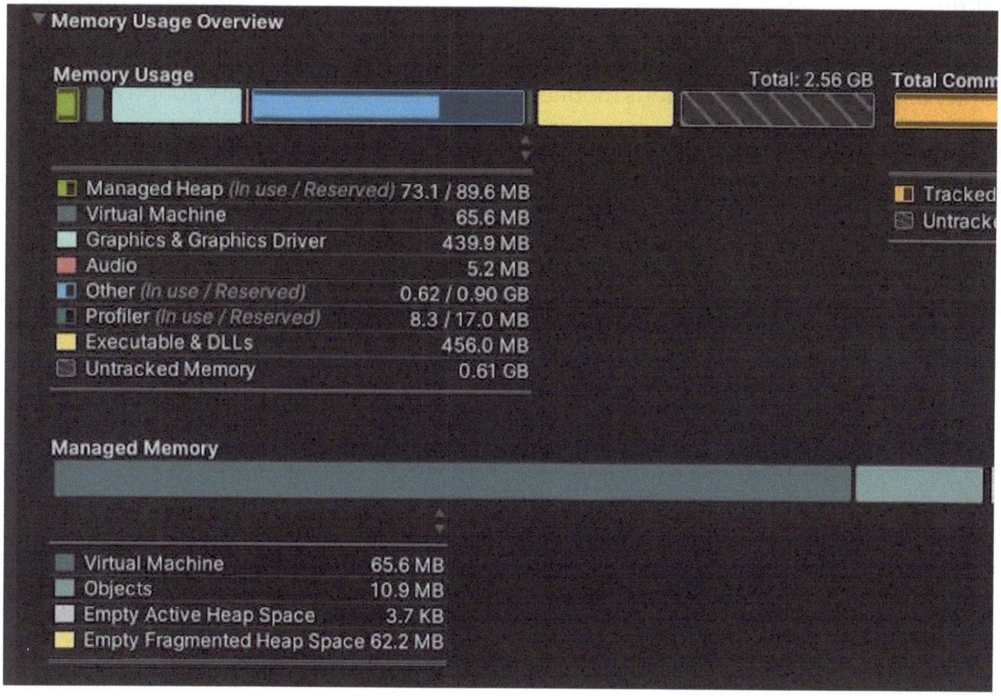

Figure 13.6: Unity Profile let us control how much memory is using our application

Control the performance with Unity adaptive performance

In the development of mobile devices, two additional factors must be considered in addition to those considered in conventional software development[1]:

- The battery consumption.
- The temperature of the device.

If we excessively utilize the performance of the CPU and graphics card, as if we were producing a game of exceptional quality for a well-equipped computer or the latest generation console, the device will start to heat up dangerously, and battery consumption will skyrocket. Both scenarios can have disastrous consequences. If the battery runs out rapidly, our users will stop playing, and that is the last thing we want.

If the device experiences excessive heating, it can cause crashes. Some operating systems control this.

Unity has developed a set of features and tools to help developers optimize the performance of their Unity applications across various mobile devices and platforms: Unity adaptive performance.

It aims to maintain a constant frame rate and enhance the overall user experience by dynamically adjusting graphical settings based on the device's capabilities and workload, as shown in the following figure:

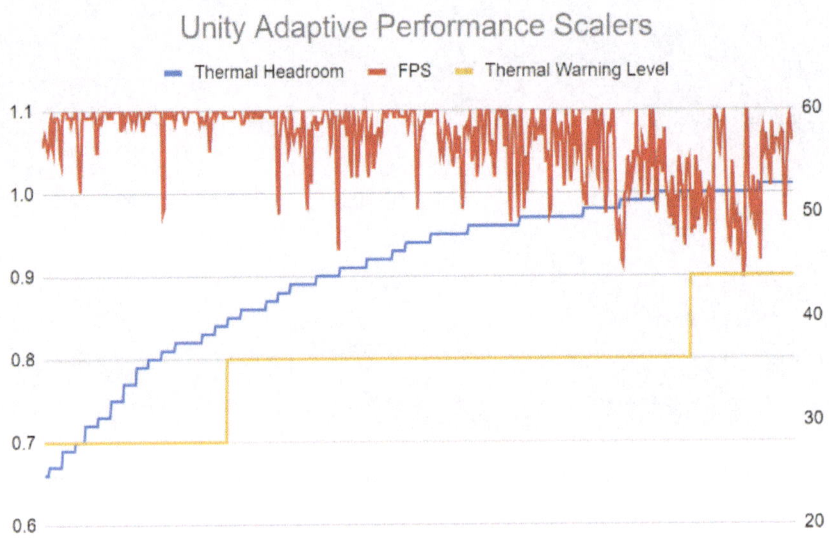

Figure 13.7: Unity adaptive performance

1 You can find all the information here: https://docs.unity3d.com/Packages/com.unity.adaptiveperformance@4.0/manual/user-guide.html

Unity adaptive performance can help you detect if your game or application hangs due to excess heat on the device.

Detecting remote crashes

So far, we have seen tools to detect and solve crashes in equipment when we are in the development process, but what happens when we already have an application that clients have, and we have it in production? Now, we are going to analyze how to record and control failures in client equipment to analyze them thoroughly and try to solve them as soon as possible.

We are going to see two platforms (Backtrace and Unity Cloud Diagnostics) that will allow us to monitor and analyze the performance and stability of their Unity-powered applications.

Backtrace

Backtrace is a platform specialized in error detection for applications in production. Some of its main features are:

- **Backtrace is cross-platform**: You can use Backtrace on all the following platforms and development platforms:
  - Windows
  - Linux
  - Mac OS
  - Android
  - iOS
  - Xbox
  - C/C++
  - Electron
  - C#
  - Unity
  - Unreal Engine
- **Flexible pricing**: The other great feature is that you only pay for a certain amount (manage up to 25,000 monthly errors, with one-month retention and ten GB of storage). So, if you are an Indie developer or you are learning, you can possibly use it for free.
- **Integrates easily with third-party tools**: These third-party tools are commonly used for the internal management of companies. It can be very easily connected so that

when an incident occurs and is detected, a ticket is sent to control it from Slack or Jira, for example:

Figure 13.8: Backtrace integrares with third-party tools

Install and configure Backtrace

The installation and configuration is easy. You can install the package in a few minutes. The step-by-step guide is as follows:

1. First of all, you must register yourself on the platform: **https://backtrace.io/sign-up**
2. After logging in, download the backtrace-unity library. You have the following two places to download it: **https://github.com/backtrace-labs/backtrace-unity/releases** or **https://openupm.com/packages/io.backtrace.unity/#google_vignette.**
3. One of the requirements to proceed is having the Node.js package installer (`npm`). To install Node.js, you can go to this website: **https://nodejs.org/en/download**

   If you have never installed an open Unity package, you will need to install it on your command line with the following instructions:

```
# Install openupm-cli
npm install -g openupm-cli

# Go to your Unity project directory
cd YOUR_UNITY_PROJECT_DIR

# Install the latest io.backtrace.unity package
openupm add io.backtrace.unity
```

4. The process will take a while, because it is downloading all the necessary files. Once finished, a window like the following will appear:

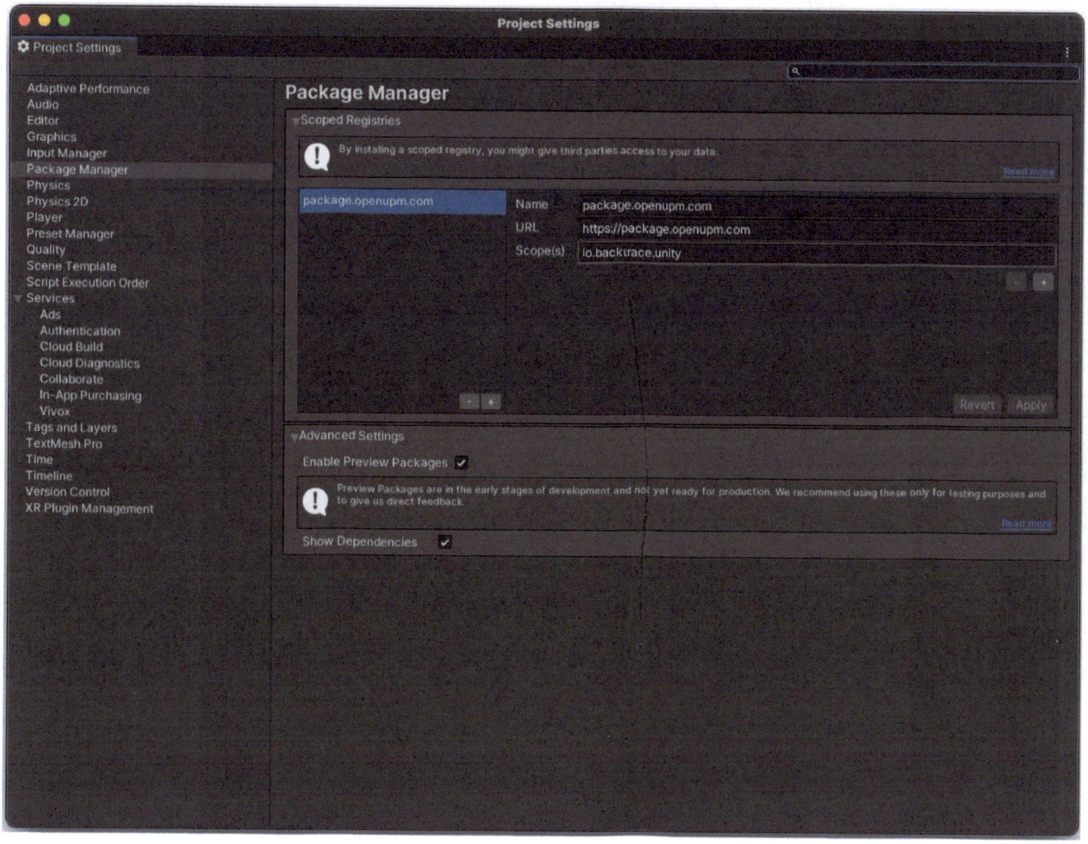

***Figure 13.9:** Installation of Backtrace from Package Manager*

5. This window informs us that a new scope has been created. Close the window, and you can open the Package Manager. If everything went well, you should have the new package already installed and active:

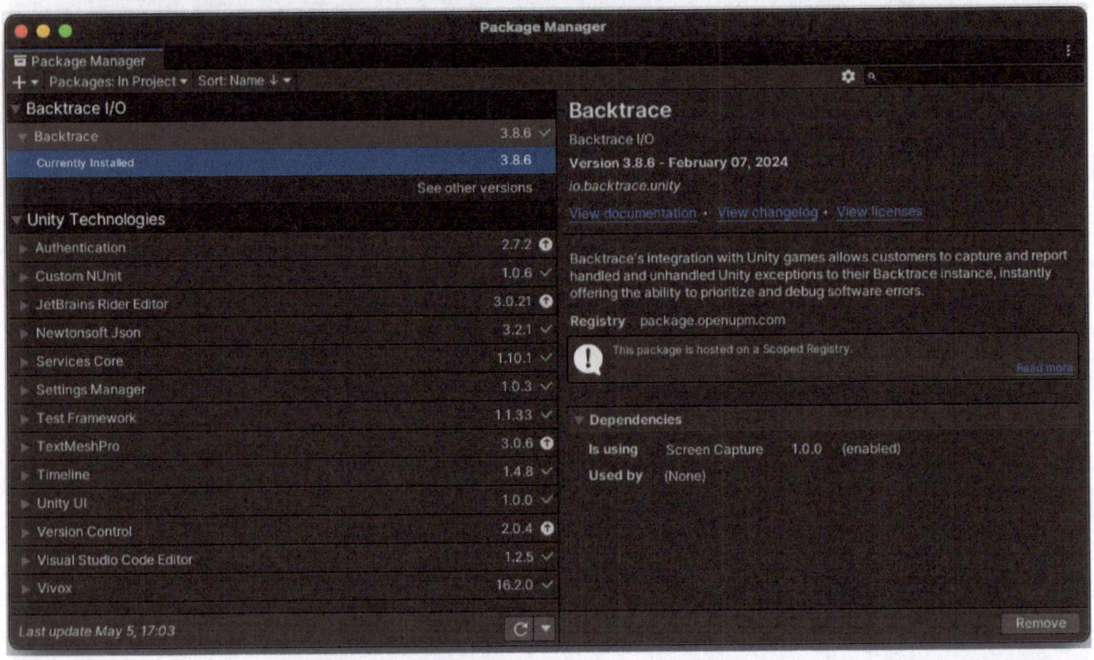

Figure 13.10*: Detail of the Backtrace recent installed*

6. Now we are going to do the necessary steps to call Backtrace within our project. In the hierarchy window, create an empty GameObject and add the component **Backtrace Client** to it. You will see the next menu.

7. In the **Assets** folder of your project, click the right-click buttons and create a **Backtrace Configuration** file, as shown in the following figure:

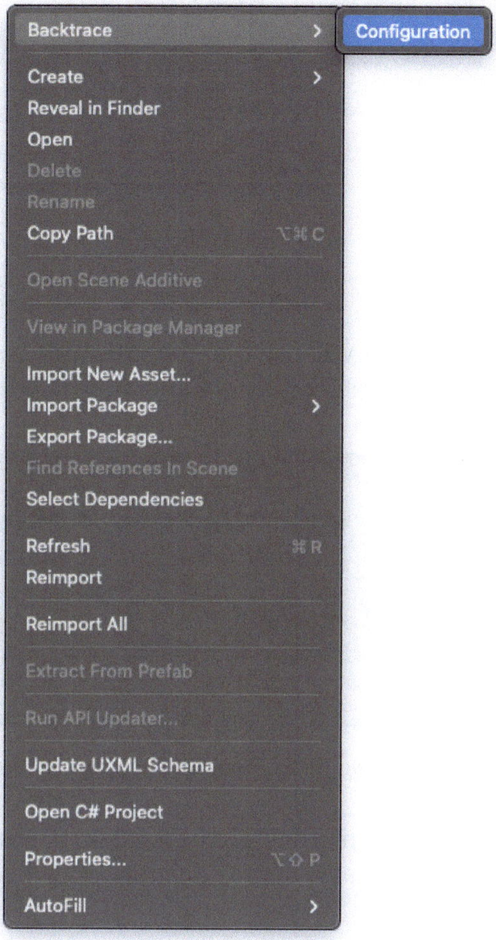

***Figure 13.11**: You must select Backtrace/Configuration on the menu*

Return to the Backtrace website, create a new project (if you have not already done so), and on the main page, when all the platforms to configure appear, select **Unity Integration Guide**, shown in the following figure:

Figure 13.12: This is the aspect of the website to integrate Backtrace and Unity

In point 2 of this guide, you will see that they provide you with the server address that we need. Copy it and return to the Editor to paste it into the **Backtrace client configuration** field:

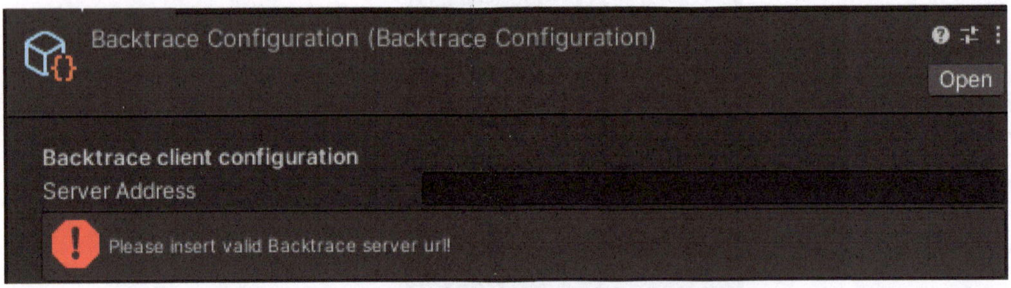

Figure 13.13: Writing the server address to start using Backtrace

8. The last step is to assign the configuration scriptable to the **Backtrace Client** component that we added to the empty GameObject Backtrace. You can do it with a drag and drop or by clicking and selecting it:

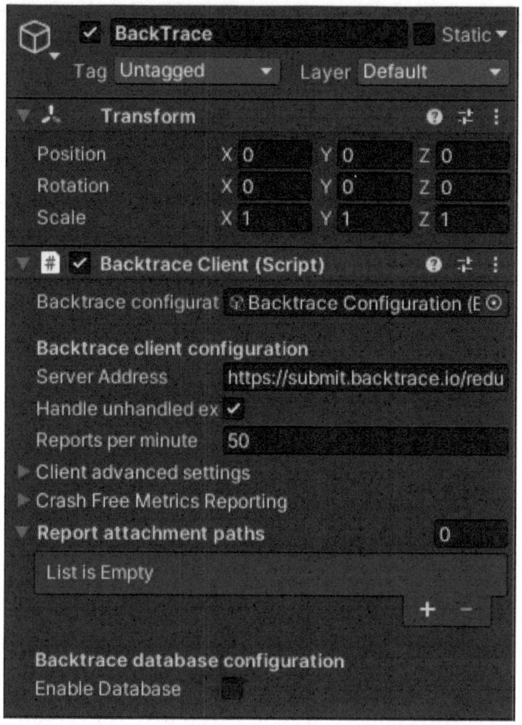

__Figure 13.14__: You must drag the Backtrace configuration on the first field under Backtrace client (script)

Over time, errors will accumulate (Hopefully, not too many), and interesting metrics will appear that can be grouped by version, type of operating system, or device. This dashboard is a true x-ray of the status of your project, and it is strongly advised to incorporate this system into your WorkFlow to improve the quality of monitoring.

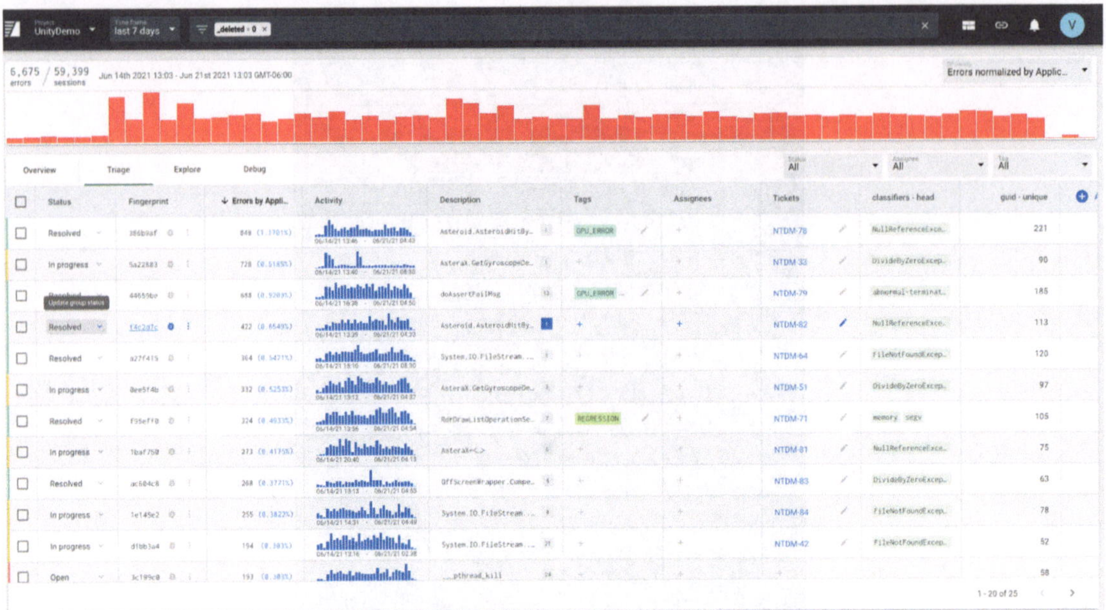

Figure 13.15: This is the aspect of Backtrace's console when you have some data registered

Furthermore, one of the advantages is that the bugs are very well documented, as shown in the following figure. Taking advantage of all the available information and exposing it in a very simple way:

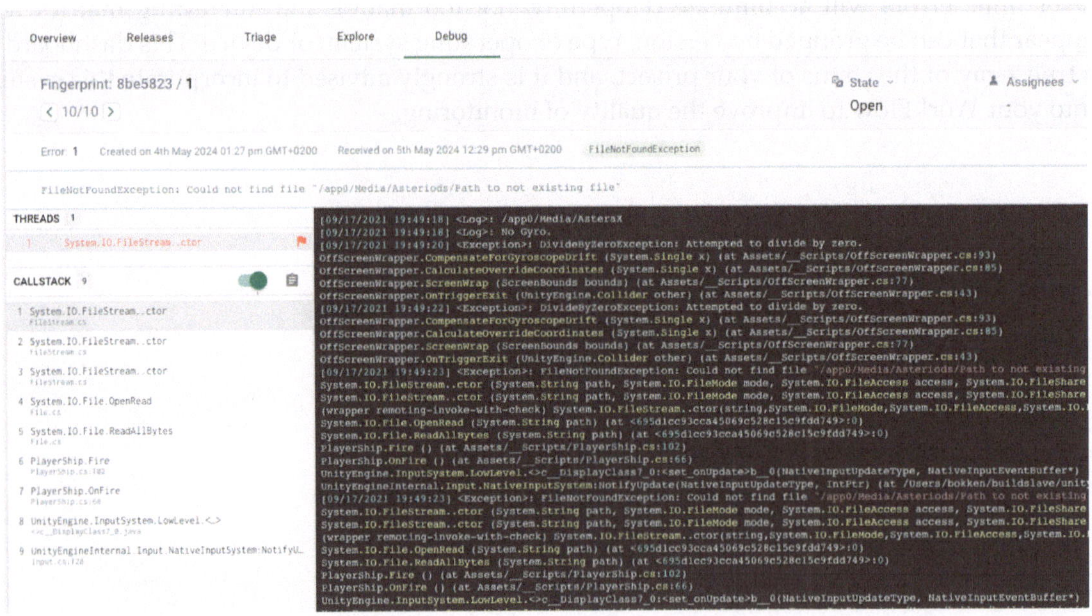

Figure 13.16: The error descriptions are very detailed and help to easily find the problem

Note: **Once an incident occurs, we can assign it to a person to take care of it and track its status.**

With the connection to third-party workflow tools (such as Slack or Jira), the integration is completed, helping in the entire CD/CI process (which we saw in the previous chapter), even for the most complex errors.

Backtrace is widely used by renowned clients. For instance, some of its most prominent clients include ROBLOX, CRYPTIC, Team17, SKYDANCE, and Respawn Entertainment.

Unity Cloud Diagnostics

Unity Cloud also has a solution that helps us log errors when our system crashes. Unity Cloud provides us with a collection of Cloud-enabled tools that assist in collecting and identifying potential issues when one of your published applications starts logging issues.

We have previously looked at Backtrace in detail because, as you will see, the solution that Unity provides us is based on this solution.

Cloud Diagnostics offers us two types of tools, which are as follows:

- **Automatic reporting**: When our application fails, an exception report will be generated and uploaded to the cloud for collection and study. These reports may contain debugging symbol files, which will allow us to investigate the causes that produced the failure.
- **User reports**: We give our customers the option to directly submit issues they have identified, although the issue does not always have to be a crash. With this system, we make users feel part of the project by including them in our improvement process, but they also often provide us with very valuable information about uses that we had not anticipated. They can provide a basis for future improvements.

Many of the concepts we have seen for Backtrace are applicable to Cloud Diagnostics:

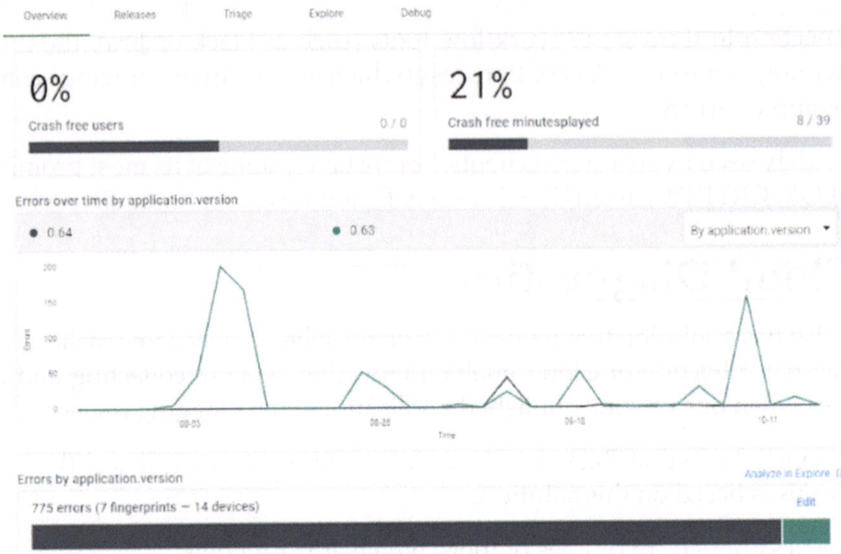

Figure 13.17: This graph shows the number of computers that have been affected by an incident

Install and configure Cloud Diagnostics through the following steps:

1. From your dashboard project, go to **LiveOps | Cloud Diagnostics Advanced | Diagnostic | Settings**:

Figure 13.18: This is the Unity Cloud's service to report crashes and exceptions

Once we have activated the cloud service, we will have to do the same in our editor. However, when you go to the technical documentation to do the installation, you find that you must install Backtrace.

Initialize the Backtrace client with GameObject#

In this step, you create the Backtrace Configuration asset, create a new GameObject, add the Backtrace Client component to the GameObject, then add the Backtrace Configuration to the Backtrace Client component.

You can add the Backtrace Client component to any GameObject in your game scene.

1. Open your project in the **Unity Editor**.
2. From the **Unity Editor** menu, select **Assets** > **Backtrace** > **Configuration**. (Note: if no Backtrace option appears under Assets then close and reopen the project, and confirm the package is installed correctly.)
3. Go to **GameObject** > **Create Empty**.
4. Enter a name for the new GameObject.
5. In the **Inspector**, select **Add Component**.
6. Search for "**Backtrace**", then select **Backtrace Client**.
7. From the **Assets** folder, drag the **Backtrace Configuration** file to the **Backtrace Configuration** field.

Figure 13.19: *This is the Unity Documentation where install Backtrace*

Source: *https://docs.saucelabs.com/error-reporting/platform-integrations/unity/setup/*

To evaluate the integration, utilize a try/catch block to generate an exception and initiate the transmission of reports. You can write a C# script like this one:

```
using Backtrace.Unity;
using Backtrace.Unity.Model;

//Read from manager BacktraceClient instance
var backtraceClient = GameObject.Find("manager name").
GetComponent<BacktraceClient>();
//Set custom client attribute
backtraceClient["attribute"] = "attribute value";
//Read from manager BacktraceClient instance
var database = GameObject.Find("manager name").
GetComponent<BacktraceDatabase>();
try {
    //throw exception here
}
catch(Exception exception) {
    var report = new BacktraceReport(exception);
    backtraceClient.Send(report);
}
```

There seem to be some important best ones if using from the cloud, for example, there are many filters focused on all the possibilities that can occur in Unity.

It also looks like a few more integration platforms have been added, as shown in the following figure:

***Figure 13.20**: The number of platforms is really large*

Integration on your workflow

Use workflow integrations to integrate with your existing workflows to notify and alert users through third-party tools, such as Jira, Slack, Circonus, and more. You can integrate with the following tools:

- Messaging tools:
  - Slack
  - Email
  - Amazon SNS
- Issue tracking:
  - GitHub
  - Jira, Phabricator
  - Asana
- Alerting and operations:
  - PagerDuty
- Monitoring:
  - Datadog
  - Circonus
- Custom:
  - Webhook

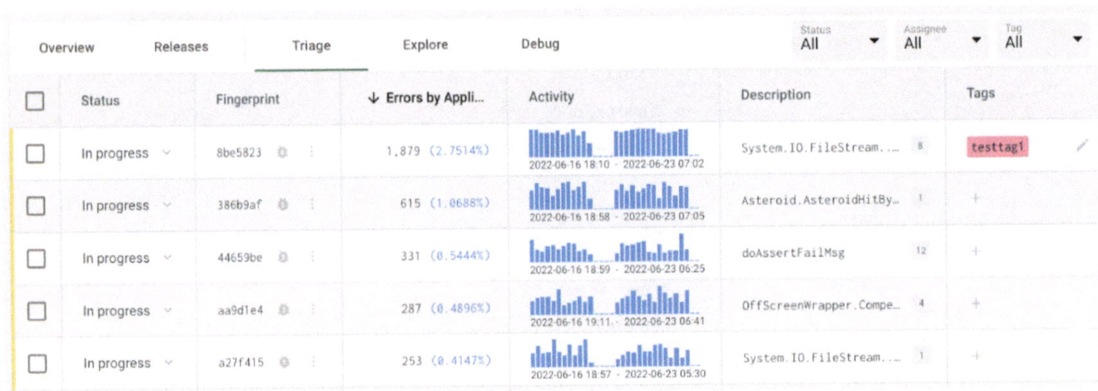

***Figure 13.21**: The statistics are similar to Backtrace, but Unity has an interesting number of filters*

Conclusion

In this chapter, the reader has learned that software development, particularly in games, often involves finding bugs that can cause crashes. However, developers can effectively identify, isolate, and resolve these issues through systematic investigation and various techniques like bug reproduction, breakpoint debugging, and program flow logging.

The importance of discussing issues with colleagues, performing thorough testing, and monitoring recurring issues to maintain application stability was also discussed.

The chapter also introduced platforms such as Backtrace and Unity Cloud Diagnostics as tools to monitor, analyze, and address crashes in both development and production environments.

Additionally, the chapter discussed other tools such as **Android Debug Bridge** (**ADB**), Unity Profiler, and Unity Adaptive Performance

In the next chapter, the reader will learn about different strategies for sustainable monetization. These include using social media, IAP, and Unity Ads to maximize user engagement and app or game revenue.

Multiple choice questions

1. **When diagnosing system failures, what type of tool allows a developer to stop the execution of code at a designated point and inspect variables immediately before the expected moment of a crash?**
   a. A continuous deployment (CD) pipeline server.
   b. A traditional code debugger utilizing a breakpoint mechanism.
   c. The Unity Adaptive Performance dynamic graphics adjuster.
   d. A logging statement generator that outputs trace information to a text file.
2. **Which steps are integral parts of the recommended systematic methodology for managing and resolving an error when the conditions leading to a program crash can be successfully reproduced?**
   a. Identifying pain points by analyzing areas where engagement is low.
   b. Determining the moment in the code execution where the problem specifically occurs.
   c. Isolating the problem to pinpoint the specific feature or module causing the crash.
   d. Consulting internal documentation and community forums for known issues or common errors.
3. **The adb utility functions as a client-server program composed of which three distinct components?**
   a. A client is installed on the development machine that sends commands.
   b. A server that runs in the background on the development machine to manage client-daemon communication.
   c. A daemon (adbd) that operates as a background process on the device to execute commands.
   d. A monitor that analyzes network latency between the client and the server.

4. **In the context of optimizing mobile game performance and stability, what specific non-conventional factors related to mobile device limits are managed by Unity Adaptive Performance?**
   a. Adjusting graphical settings dynamically based on device temperature.
   b. Ensuring that the application remains within a designated memory footprint.
   c. Preventing the excessive utilization of the CPU that leads to high battery consumption.
   d. Analyzing player progression data to enhance game balancing.
5. **For developers, which of the following tasks is the Unity Profiler most effectively utilized for?**
   a. Tracking variable values on a mobile device where step-by-step debugging is unavailable.
   b. Monitoring excessive resource usage, such as memory or system overload, particularly over long periods of intensive use.
   c. Generating a complete source code analysis to detect uninitialized variables.
   d. Providing a Unix shell interface to execute various commands on a connected device.
6. **What is the core definition of a crash in the scope of game development error reporting?**
   a. Any application shutdown event caused by the user intentionally exiting the program.
   b. The process of intentionally reproducing an unexpected behavior in laboratory conditions.
   c. A sudden, unexpected failure of the application that may result in the app freezing or exiting the operating system.
   d. An error that can be fixed immediately using cloud code modules.
7. **Backtrace and Unity Cloud Diagnostics Advanced are platforms used for detecting remote crashes in production applications. Which integration capabilities do these platforms commonly support?**
   a. Integration with third-party tools like Jira or Slack for issue tracking and notification.
   b. Automated rollback mechanisms to revert the build upon crash detection.
   c. Cross-platform support, including applications built with Unreal Engine.
   d. Automatic Reporting and the collection of debugging symbol files when a failure occurs.
8. **Scenario: A developer is working on a VR application that uses an Android-based headset. To view error messages and console output from the device directly on the development machine, which command-line filter should be applied when utilizing the adb?**
   a. `adb logcat | grep Unity`
   b. `adb logcat Unity:V *:S`.
   c. `adb logcat -v time`
   d. `adb logcat -e`

9. **In circumstances where traditional debugging methods are infeasible due to remote execution (e.g., debugging on a connected mobile device), what is the most common substitute technique used by developers?**
   a. Employing the Unity transport layer for highly optimized network communication.
   b. Introducing logging statements into the code to track the program flow and variable values.
   c. Utilizing the dedicated `adb logcat Unity:V *:S` filter to isolate relevant console output from the device.
   d. Running a performance test using Unity Profiler to simulate the crash conditions.
10. **Unity Cloud Diagnostics Advanced differentiates between two types of reports used for gathering application issues. What are these two types?**
    a. Automatic Reporting, which generates exception reports and debugging symbol files upon failure.
    b. Real-time Crash Dumps, which capture core memory information when the application exits.
    c. User Reports, which allow customers to submit issues directly, even if they are not system crashes.
    d. Automated Server Reporting, which sends detailed configuration data from the hosting fleet.

Answers

1	b, c
2	b, c
3	a, c, d
4	a, c
5	b
6	c
7	a, c, d
8	b
9	b, c
10	a, c

Join our Discord space

Join our Discord workspace for latest updates, offers, tech happenings around the world, new releases, and sessions with the authors:

https://discord.bpbonline.com

Chapter 14
Strategies for Sustainable Monetization

Introduction

In this chapter, developers will navigate the intricate landscape of monetizing mobile games, particularly in the context of evolving regulations and industry consolidation. The chapter will elucidate the collaboration between monetization and development teams to foster long-term, sustainable growth, propelled by innovative ad technology that facilitates free gaming while establishing profitable revenue models for creators.

Specifically, the chapter will delve into several pivotal areas to optimize user engagement and the monetization of mobile applications or games. Initially, it will explore the utilization of social networks as potent tools to acquire new users, promote applications, and ensure long-term revenue generation. Subsequently, the chapter will provide an exhaustive overview of **in-app purchases** (**IAPs**) as a commonly employed monetization strategy.

A substantial portion of the chapter will then focus on Unity ads and advertising, encompassing various ad formats such as banner ads, interstitial ads, playable ads, and rewarded video ads. Furthermore, the chapter will elucidate placements and **effective cost per mille** (**eCPM**) targets to optimize advertising revenue. The chapter will also demonstrate how to utilize the Unity ads report to monitor and analyze the performance of monetization strategies. Finally, the chapter will discuss techniques for maximizing profits generated from monetization efforts. By exploring these topics, this chapter equips developers with the requisite knowledge and strategies to achieve sustainable monetization for their mobile games.

Structure

The chapter covers the following topics:

- In-app purchases
    - Implementing in-app purchases in Unity
- Unity ads and advertising
    - Enabling Unity ads in the dashboard

- Playable ads
- Rewarded video ads
- Understanding finances
  - o Placements and eCPM targets
- Social networks

Objectives

In this chapter, readers will explore different techniques and strategies to maximize user engagement and monetization of your app or game.

In-app purchases

One of the most used monetization strategies is IAP. These are particularly beneficial because what is sold is not a tangible object (which is manufactured, transported, and generates expenses). What is sold are objects or virtual goods that can be replicated as many times as needed and only have the cost generated at the time of development.

This form of transaction allows users to enhance their gaming experience by acquiring additional resources or benefits without leaving the application.

In-app purchases serve as an important monetization strategy for mobile games and apps, providing both developers and businesses with a steady stream of revenue through recurring purchases. By offering in-app purchases, game designers can create a more engaging experience that encourages users to spend real money on virtual goods or services.

For example, in a gaming app where players have to pay to win, in-app purchases might include buying extra lives when the player runs out, unlocking new levels, getting extra coins, or even customizing avatars. On the other hand, an informative app may offer premium features, such as advanced analytics or access to exclusive content for users who make in-app purchases.

However, it is not advisable to abuse this formula. It is important that the purchase of IAP is not a necessary condition to play the game. Otherwise, it will draw the ire of players who are frustrated at not being able to continue if they do not buy premium items/goods. Ideally, these are just enhancements that make things easier or more interesting, but are not mandatory.

Therefore, incorporating in-app purchases into your game or mobile app can significantly increase user engagement while providing an additional revenue stream. This monetization model has become increasingly popular due to its convenience and the ease with which users can transact without leaving the app:

***Figure 14.1**: Sample of in-app purchases on Angry Birds*

Implementing in-app purchases in Unity[1]

As always, Unity Cloud offers us an interesting tool to integrate in-app purchases within our projects. These are the steps you need to take to be able to activate them:

1. Open your Unity project in the Unity Editor.
2. From the menu, select **Window** | **General** | **Services** to access the **Services** window.
3. Create a project ID and then connect it to an organization.
4. Please respond to the COPPA compliance inquiries.
5. The **Services** window displays a comprehensive listing of services. Please select the **In-App Purchasing** option, as shown in the following figure:

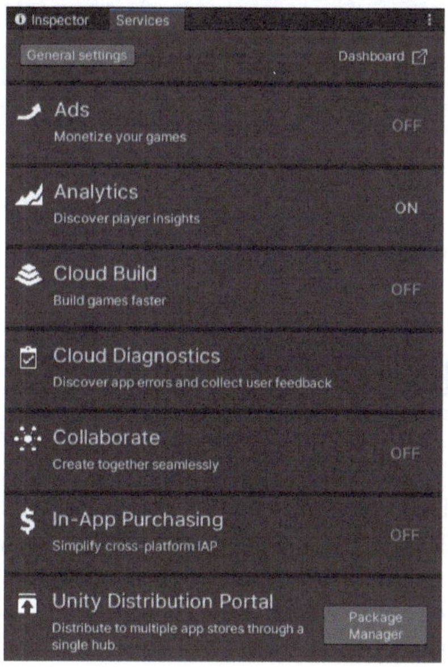

***Figure 14.2**: List of the services enabled and disabled*

1 You can find all the in-app purchases at this address: https://docs.unity3d.com/Packages/com.unity.purchasing@4.11/manual/index.html

6. On the project settings window, click the toggle next to **In-App Purchasing Settings** to **ON**:

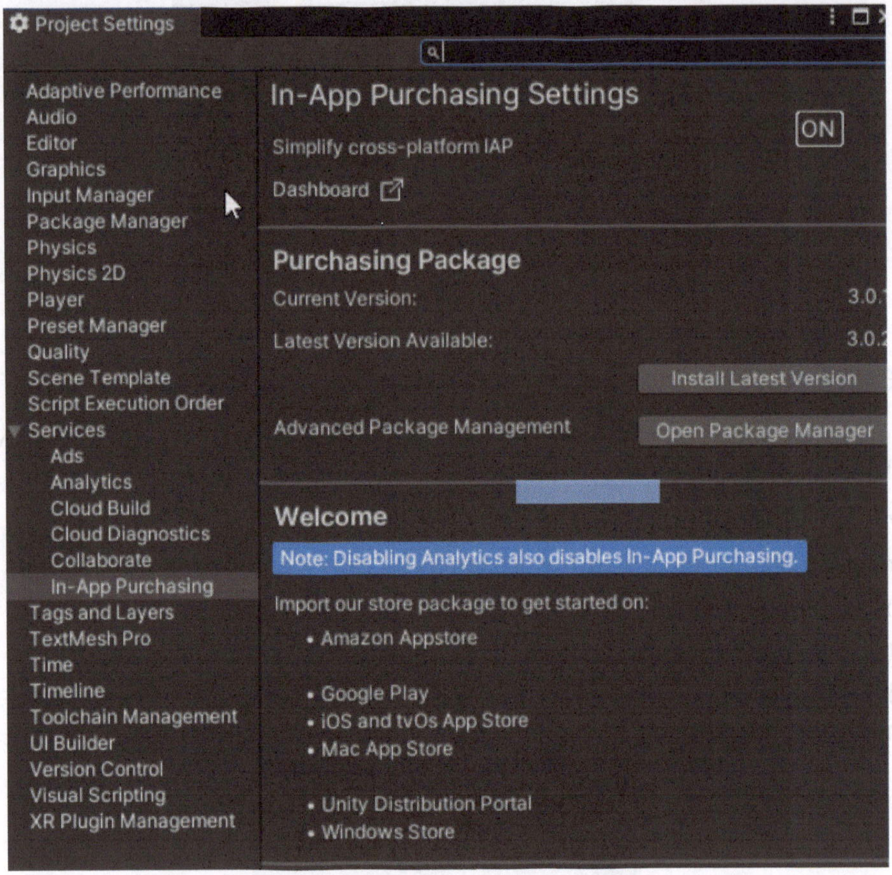

Figure 14.3: *Detail of the in-app purchases on the Unity Editor*

When it has been activated, the corresponding package will be automatically loaded. Once compiled, new options will appear from where you can define your new virtual products.

Defining your products

For each product, the data in a database table must be defined. The fields for each product are:

- **ID**: It is a unique and unrepeatable identifier for each product. It will work for all platforms and may only contain lowercase letters, numbers, underscores, or periods.
- **Type**: It is the classification of the product according to its nature and characteristics. There are three different types:

  - **Consumable**: Users have the option to purchase the product on an ongoing basis. The restoration of consumables is not possible. Examples of consumables are health potions and temporary power-ups.
  - **Non-consumable**: Users are allowed to purchase the product only once. Products that are not consumable may be restored. Samples of non-consumable items are a special sword or armor, and access to extra content.
  - **Subscription**: The product is available for a limited period of time. Subscription products can be restored. Examples of subscriptions are the monthly access to an online game and VIP status, granting daily bonuses.

The section called metadata is where we will enter all the additional information that will appear in the in-game store. This is where we will put the description so that the user finds it attractive and ends up buying your app/game. It will also be necessary to define in which virtual store the product is accessible (it must be taken into account that some products will be available only in some parts of the world, for cultural reasons, for example). The fields are:

- **Product Locale**: Determines the app stores available in your region.
- **Product Title**: This is the name under which the product will appear in the virtual store.
- **Product Description**: The descriptive text for your product, as it appears in an app store, usually includes an explanation of what the product is and what its benefits are.

Creating products by code

Products can be created by code or with a graphical interface. A simple code to create a product is as follows:

```
using UnityEngine;
using UnityEngine.Purchasing;

public class MyIAPManager {
    public MyIAPManager () {
        var builder = ConfigurationBuilder.Instance(StandardPurchasingModule.Instance());
        builder.AddProduct("magic_sword", ProductType.Consumable);
        // Initialize Unity IAP...
    }
}
```

Creating products with the graphic user interface

To open the graphical interface and create products, you must select the Unity Editor menu **Services | In-App Purchasing | IAP Catalog**.

You can also locate the IAP button's script component in the **Inspector**, then click **IAP Catalog**:

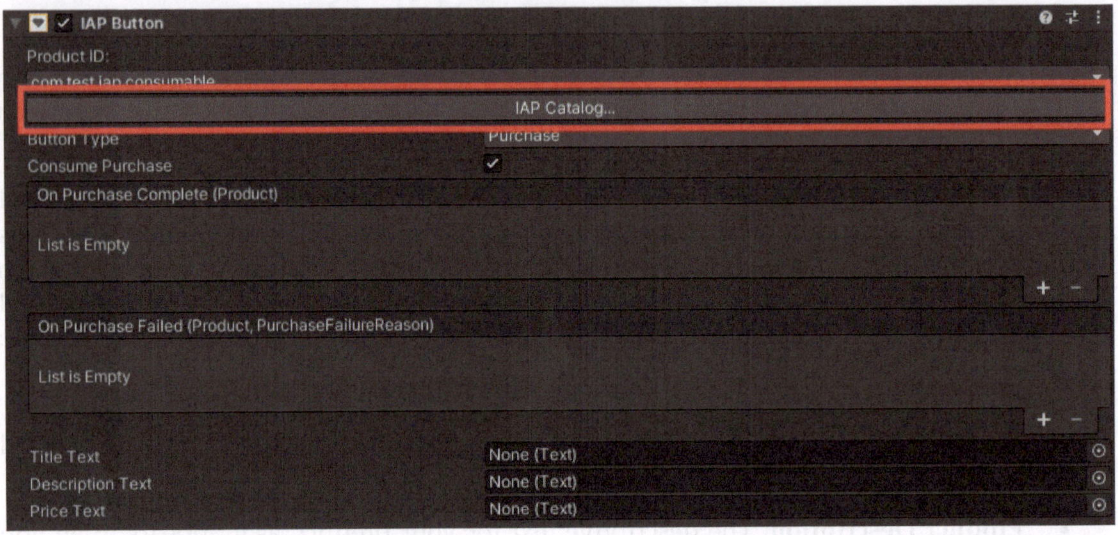

***Figure 14.4**: Adding new products to your store*

Then, use the GUI to define the fields we previously discussed for each of the products in your store.

> Note: **You can replace the identifier with store-specific unique identifiers using the Advanced option.**

Here, you must define the type of product you are going to sell and there are only three possible categories: consumable, non-consumable or subscription:

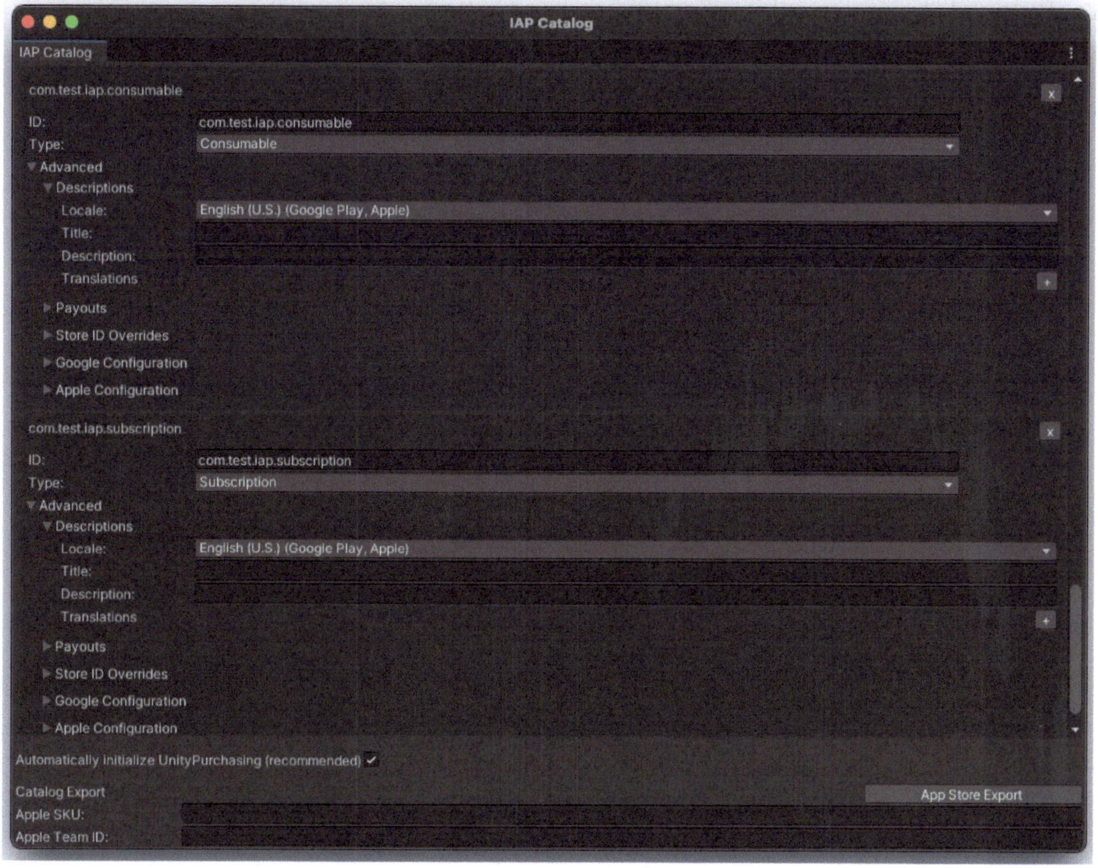

***Figure 14.5:** Detail of the fields on IAP products*

The interface that Unity IAP uses to notify your application of purchase-related events is called **IDetailedStoreListener**. So, the script will be an implementation of this interface.

To start the initialization process, you will need to call the **`UnityPurchasing.Initialize`** method which provides the listener implementation and configuration.

Note: The initialization will not fail if the network is not available. Unity IAP will continue to attempt to initialize in the background indefinitely.

This has significant repercussions if the user does not have connectivity (because they are in a remote location or on airplane mode). If you do, Unity IAP will continue indefinitely to try to establish the connection in the background. It will only fail if Unity IAP encounters an unrecoverable problem, such as a misconfiguration or disabling IAP in the device settings.

To avoid problems with this functionality, you must check that everything is correct before the user opens the store. You must prevent users from attempting to make purchases if the initialization did not complete successfully.

A sample code to implement in-app purchases in your project:

```
using UnityEngine;
using UnityEngine.Purchasing;
using UnityEngine.Purchasing.Extension;

public class MyIAPManager : IDetailedStoreListener {

    private IStoreController controller;
    private IExtensionProvider extensions;

    public MyIAPManager () {
        var builder = ConfigurationBuilder.Instance(StandardPurchasingModule.Instance());
        builder.AddProduct("magic_sword", ProductType.Consumable, new IDs
        {
            {"magic_sword_google", GooglePlay.Name},
            {"magic_sword_mac", MacAppStore.Name}
        });

        UnityPurchasing.Initialize (this, builder);
    }

    /// <summary>
    /// Called when Unity IAP is ready to make purchases.
    /// </summary>
    public void OnInitialized (IStoreController controller, IExtensionProvider extensions)
    {
        this.controller = controller;
        this.extensions = extensions;
    }

    /// <summary>
    /// Called when Unity IAP encounters an unrecoverable initialization error.
    ///
```

```
    /// Note that this will not be called if Internet is unavailable; Unity IAP
    /// will attempt initialization until it becomes available.
    /// </summary>
    public void OnInitializeFailed (InitializationFailureReason error)
    {
    }

    /// <summary>
    /// Called when a purchase completes.
    ///
    /// May be called at any time after OnInitialized().
    /// </summary>
    public PurchaseProcessingResult ProcessPurchase (PurchaseEventArgs e)
    {
        return PurchaseProcessingResult.Complete;
    }

    /// <summary>
    /// Called when a purchase fails.
    /// IStoreListener.OnPurchaseFailed is deprecated,
    /// use IDetailedStoreListener.OnPurchaseFailed instead.
    /// </summary>
    public void OnPurchaseFailed (Product i, PurchaseFailureReason p)
    {
    }

    /// <summary>
    /// Called when a purchase fails.
    /// </summary>
    public void OnPurchaseFailed (Product i, PurchaseFailureDescription p)
    {
    }
}
```

Downloading the store

One of the known issues is that if you create a lot of products, it can take too long to download. To avoid this, it is best not to download all the products the first time. What we will do is download only a considerably smaller initial set and, as needed, fetch additional products in batches using the **IStoreController**'s **FetchAdditionalProducts** method:

```
/// <summary>
/// This will be called when Unity IAP has finished initialising.
/// </summary>
public void OnInitialized(IStoreController controller, IExtensionProvider extensions)
{
    var additional = new HashSet<ProductDefinition>() {
        new ProductDefinition("coins.500", ProductType.Consumable),
        new ProductDefinition("armour", ProductType.NonConsumable)
    };

    Action onSuccess = () => {
        Debug.Log("Fetched successfully!");
        // The additional products are added to the set of
        // previously retrieved products and are browseable
        // and purchasable.
        foreach (var product in controller.products.all) {
            Debug.Log(product.definition.id);
        }
    };

    Action<InitializationFailureReason> onFailure = (InitializationFailureReason i) => {
        Debug.Log("Fetching failed for the specified reason: " + i);
    };

    controller.FetchAdditionalProducts(additional, onSuccess, onFailure);
}
```

IAP button

We have already created the articles and seen how they should be downloaded, now we need the most important thing: to buy them! You can make the purchase button from the graphical interface or from code.

To add a buy button in the Unity Editor, go to the **Window menu | Unity IAP | Create IAP Button.**

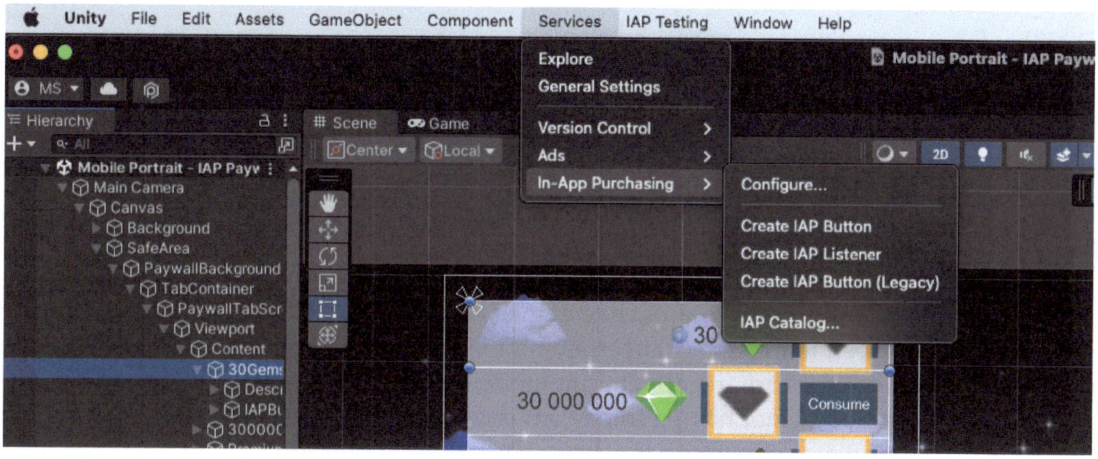

Figure 14.6: Adding an IAP button to the user interface

Once the store retrieves the product information, an event called **`OnProductFetched`** will occur. Now is the right time to update the button information (product name, description, price). Thus, the user interface will be well updated. The code to implement this button is as follows:

```
UnityEngine;
using UnityEngine.UI;
using TMPro;
using UnityEngine.Purchasing;

 public class IAPButtonView : MonoBehaviour
 {
     [SerializeField]
     Text title;
     [SerializeField]
     TMP_Text price;

     public void OnProductFetched(Product product)
     {
```

```
        if (title != null)
        {
            title.text = product.metadata.localizedTitle;
        }

        if (price != null)
        {
            price.text = product.metadata.localizedPriceString;
        }
    }
}
```

Unity ads and advertising

One of the most popular ways to monetize games or applications is to place advertising on some part of the screen (banners) or at certain moments in the game. In this way, it has been achieved that many games are free (freemium model), and this facilitates the mass download of many users attracted by not having to pay anything.

The premium model needs a significant number of downloads to be profitable. If nothing else, it can be interesting in many cases and worth considering.

Although you have to be careful, an app that does not stop making ads (especially in interesting moments of the game) can annoy (and a lot) the players. It is best to place the ads when you are in the menus so as not to disturb the user's experience.

Not so long ago, when a developer wanted to start using a freemium model, he had to arm himself with the value to fight with all the advertising agencies and the content they offered

Note: In an application intended for minors, you cannot put advertising dedicated to an adult audience.

Fortunately, this model has been consolidated, and today, we can enjoy fairly consolidated standards.

Unity technologies itself offers Unity Ads. It is an advertising platform that allows developers to monetize their games or mobile apps through interactive, video, and multimedia ads. With this platform, developers can have access to a wide range of ad formats and targeting options to ensure maximum revenue while maintaining a good user experience.

There are more platforms that offer to post ads within our apps. Unity Cloud, as always, makes an effort to integrate the different systems available. Let us see the main advantages and how we can activate and configure Unity Ads in the dashboard.

The main advantages of using Unity Ads are:

- **Multi-platform support**: Initially, it is noteworthy that Unity Ads can be utilized from various development environments, including but not limited to Xcode or Android Studio.
- **Different ads formats**: This platform makes it easy to select the best ad format for your game format. For example, you could introduce rewarded video ads to create a stronger in-game economy and generate revenue for your business. You could also introduce full-screen interstitial ads during natural game breaks without disrupting the player experience. The Unity Ads SDK facilitates the connection of your game to over 60 demand sources via a single SDK.
- **Centralized control dashboard with centralized controls**: To manage and optimize your game's spawn points, use the Unity Ads monetization dashboard. You can use powerful reporting tools to optimize your advertising strategy and maximize your income.

Enabling Unity Ads in the dashboard

From the Unity Ads monetization dashboard, select **Get Started** from the secondary navigation menu. The following figure likely shows the initial screen or button to **Get Started** with Unity Ads monetization:

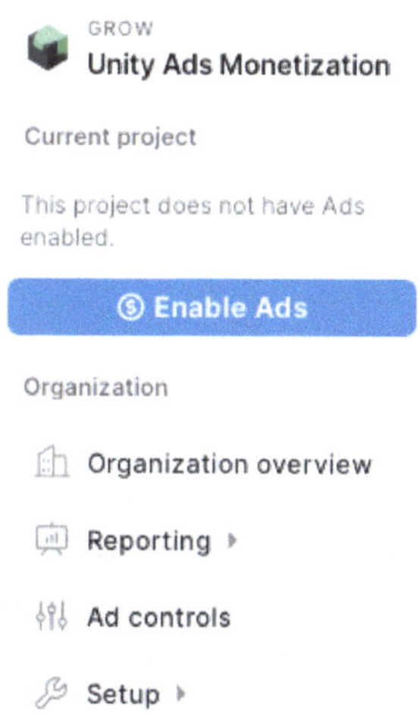

Figure 14.7: Unity Ads monetization dashboard - Get Started

Once we press **Enable Ads**, a form will appear where we are asked for the basic data of our company and the country where it is located.

In the next step, we will be asked which model we want to use. The available options are shown in the following figures. You can select to use mediation.

The following figure presents the available options for selecting the advertising model in the Unity Ads dashboard, specifically highlighting the choice between using only Unity Ads or incorporating mediation to include other ad sources:

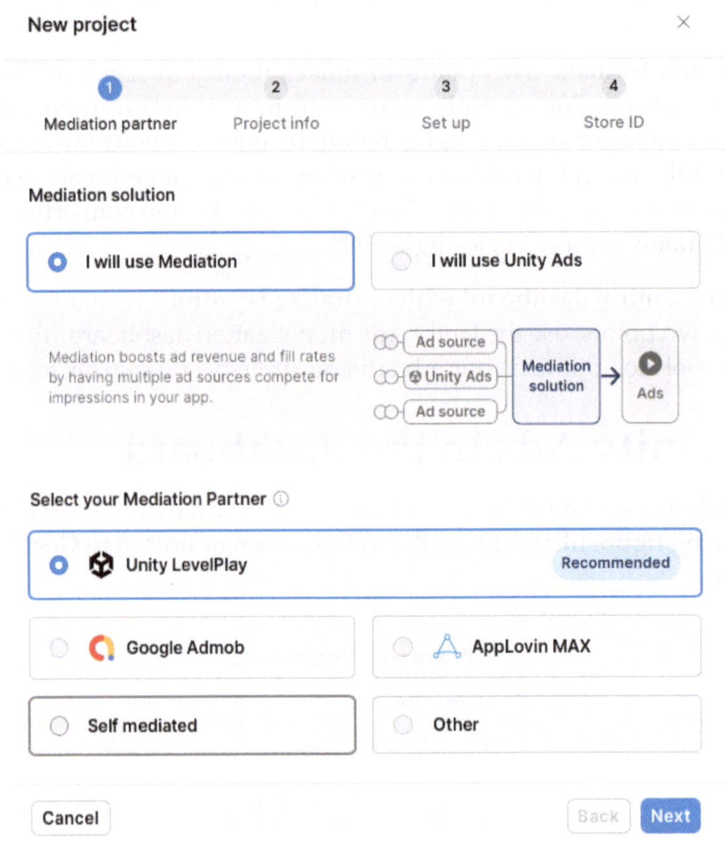

Figure 14.8: Selection of advertising model: Unity Ads or Mediation

The first big choice is to know if you will use only Unity Ads, where all the management of advertising goes through Unity, or if you want to use more advertising sources (mediation). If you choose the latter, you can add other advertising sources, such as **Google Admob** or **AppLovin MAX**. You can even develop a mediation to your liking.

The following figure further illustrates the selection of advertising sources when choosing the mediation model in Unity Ads:

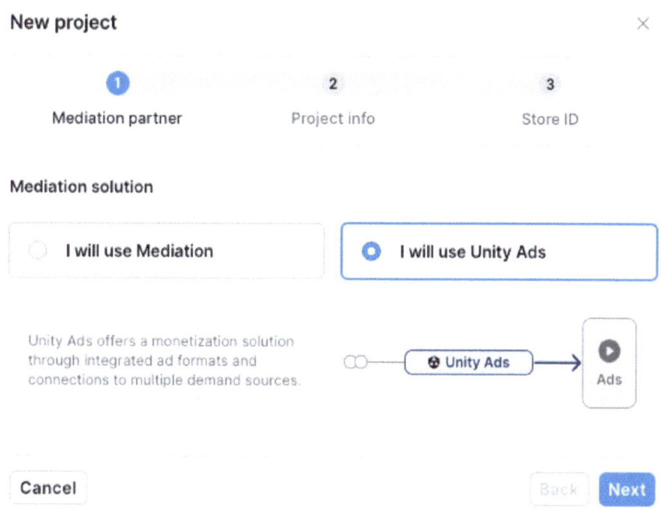

***Figure 14.9**: Choosing additional advertising sources through Mediation*

The selection you make here is important. You will have to remember it and take it into account when you make the code to implement monetization because there are two different packages, one for Mediation and the other for Unity. The packages are described in the following table:

Integration method	Description	Notes
Ads Mediation package	Use the Package Manager in the Unity Editor to install the Ads mediation package. This method allows you to integrate and manage your LevelPlay integration from within the Editor.	For more information, refer to Integrate LevelPlay through the Ads Mediation package.[2]
Unity Plugin	Download the **`.unitypackage`** file (the Unity Plugin) from the ironSource Knowledge Center. This is the original method for integrating the ironSource SDK.	For more information, refer to Unity plugin integration in the ironSource knowledge center.[3]

***Table 14.1**: Types of Ad integration*

Finally, we will be asked if we want to import advertising data from another project (this is very useful when you already have several applications and want to take advantage of all the knowledge of your users) or start from scratch:

2 https://docs.unity.com/monetization-dashboard/en-us/manual/integrate-ads-mediation
3 https://developers.is.com/ironsource-mobile/unity/unity-plugin/#step-1

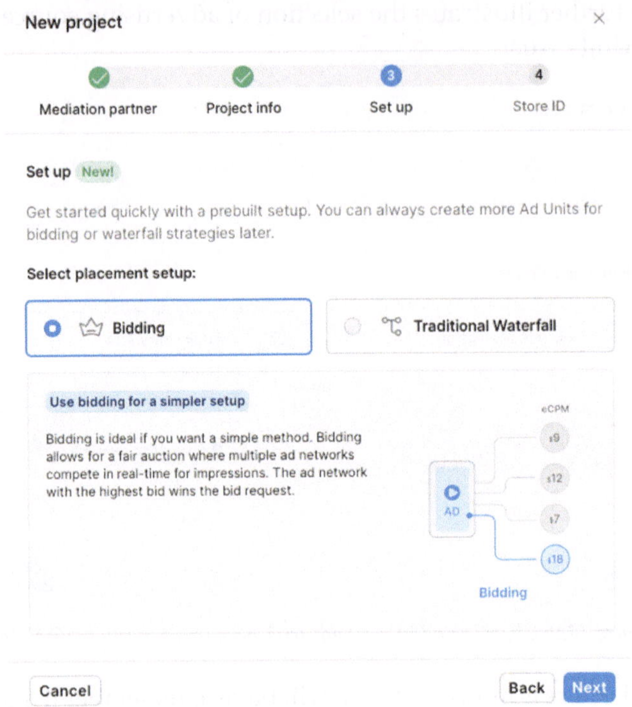

Figure 14.10: *You must select the type of integration*

Finally, you must choose the behavior system to place ads, and remember that you must comply with the laws for minors.

In order to avoid problems, the default behavior when there is no user-level age designation (we do not know how old the user is), Unity Ads will treat users as children and only serve contextual ads when they are not there is an age designation at the user level. This way, we will avoid many problems. [4]

The default behavior is only relevant for mixed audience applications and cannot be modified independently.

Let us look at the main types of ads.

Banners

Banner ads are probably the most popular (they are also common on websites). The banners appear in a designated part of the screen, specially for this purpose. They have a specified size, as shown in the following figure:

---

4 To go deeper into the legal aspects, visit the following a link to a very interesting guide from the Unity documentation where you can expand much more on the laws that must be complied with and how to do it: Child data law compliance, CARU compliance, and contextual ads

***Figure 14.11**: Sample of Unity Ads banner on the bottom of the screen*

The following is the example code needed to implement a banner using the SDK, considering the basic functionalities. It is divided into three parts to facilitate readability.

Part one: Class definition, button references, ad unit IDs, and initialisation (**`Start`** method):

```
using UnityEngine;
using UnityEngine.UI;
using UnityEngine.Advertisements;
public class BannerAdExample : MonoBehaviour
{
    // These [SerializeField] attributes make the Button variables
visible in the Unity Inspector
    // so you can link them to the corresponding UI Buttons in your scene. [1]
    [SerializeField] Button _loadBannerButton;
    [SerializeField] Button _showBannerButton;
    [SerializeField] Button _hideBannerButton;
    // This variable determines where on the screen the banner ad will be
displayed. [2]
    [SerializeField] BannerPosition _bannerPosition = BannerPosition.BOTTOM_
CENTER;
    // These strings hold the unique Ad Unit IDs for Android and iOS platforms.
    // You will get these IDs from the Unity Ads dashboard. [2]
    [SerializeField] string _androidAdUnitId = "Banner_Android";
    [SerializeField] string _iOSAdUnitId = "Banner_iOS";
    // This string will store the Ad Unit ID that is relevant for the
current platform. [2]
    string _
adUnitId = null; // This will remain null for unsupported platforms.
    void Start()
    {
        // This preprocessor directive checks if the current platform is iOS. [3]
```

```
#if UNITY_IOS
        _adUnitId = _iOSAdUnitId;
        // This preprocessor directive checks if the current platform is
Android. [3]
#elif UNITY_ANDROID
        _adUnitId = _androidAdUnitId;
#endif
        // Initially, the Show and Hide buttons are disabled
until an ad is successfully loaded. [3]
        _showBannerButton.interactable = false;
        _hideBannerButton.interactable = false;
        // Sets the position of the banner ad on the screen using the _
bannerPosition variable. [3, 9]
        Advertisement.Banner.SetPosition(_bannerPosition);
        // This line adds a listener to the Load Banner
button. When clicked, it will call the LoadBanner() method. [3, 10, 11]
        _loadBannerButton.onClick.AddListener(LoadBanner);
        // The Load Banner button is enabled at the start,
allowing the user to attempt loading an ad. [3, 12]
        _loadBannerButton.interactable = true;
    }
```

Part two: Loading the banner ad and handling load events (**LoadBanner**, **OnBannerLoaded**, **OnBannerError** methods):

```
// This method is called when the Load Banner button is clicked. [4]
    public void LoadBanner()
    {
        // BannerLoadOptions is used to set up
callbacks for load events. [4, 6]
        BannerLoadOptions options = new BannerLoadOptions
        {
            // This callback will be executed when the banner ad is
successfully loaded. [4, 8]
            loadCallback = OnBannerLoaded,
            // This callback will be executed if there is an
error during the banner ad load. [4, 13]
            errorCallback = OnBannerError
        };
```

```
        // This function initiates the process of loading a banner ad
using the determined _adUnitId and the specified options. [14, 15]
        Advertisement.Banner.Load(_adUnitId, options);
    }
    // This method is executed when the banner ad has been
successfully loaded. [16, 17]
    void OnBannerLoaded()
    {
        // A debug message is logged to the Unity console
indicating that the banner has loaded. [18, 19]
        Debug.Log("Banner loaded");
        // This adds a listener to the Show Banner
button, which will call the ShowBannerAd() method when clicked. [20, 21]
        _showBannerButton.onClick.AddListener(ShowBannerAd);
        // This adds a listener to the Hide Banner
button, which will call the HideBannerAd() method when clicked. [22, 23]
        _hideBannerButton.onClick.AddListener(HideBannerAd);
        // Now that an ad is loaded, the Show and Hide buttons are
enabled, allowing the user to interact with the banner. [24-26]
        _showBannerButton.interactable = true;
        _hideBannerButton.interactable = true;
    }
    // This method is executed if there is an error while
loading the banner ad. [27-29]
    void OnBannerError(string message)
    {
        // An error message, including the specific
error, is logged to the Unity console. [30, 31]
        Debug.Log($"Banner Error: {message}");
        // You can optionally add more code here, such as
attemptng to load another ad or informing the user about the issue. [32]
    }
```

Part three: Showing and hiding the banner ad and cleanup (**ShowBannerAd**, **HideBannerAd**, callback methods for interactions, and **OnDestroy** method):

```
    // This method is called when the Show Banner
button is clicked. [41, 42]
    void ShowBannerAd()
    {
```

```
        // BannerOptions is used to set up
callbacks for show events. [43-45]
        BannerOptions options = new BannerOptions
        {
            // This callback will be executed when the
banner ad is clicked. [46]
            clickCallback = OnBannerClicked,
            // This callback will be executed when the banner ad is
hidden. [47]
            hideCallback = OnBannerHidden,
            // This callback will be executed when the banner ad is
successfully shown. [48]
            showCallback = OnBannerShown
        };
        // This function displays the loaded banner ad using the
determined _adUnitId and the specified options. [49-51]
        Advertisement.Banner.Show(_adUnitId, options);
    }
    // This method is called when the Hide Banner
button is clicked. [33, 34, 52]
    void HideBannerAd()
    {
        // This function hides the currently visible banner ad. [36, 37]
        Advertisement.Banner.Hide();
    }
    // These empty methods are the callbacks for banner ad
interactions. [38-40]
    void OnBannerClicked() { }
    void OnBannerShown() { }
    void OnBannerHidden() { }
    // This method is called when the script component is being
destroyed. It's important to clean up any event listeners to
prevent memory leaks.
    void OnDestroy()
    {
        // These lines remove all listeners that were added to the
onClick events of the buttons.
        _loadBannerButton.onClick.RemoveAllListeners();
        _showBannerButton.onClick.RemoveAllListeners();
        _hideBannerButton.onClick.RemoveAllListeners();
```

```
    }
}
```

Interstitial ads

As mentioned previously, there is a type of ad that is usually placed when the player is on the menu or has just completed a mission. These are interstitials, also called display ads. They are basic full-screen interstitials that stay until the player dismisses them (sometimes, they have a backlog until they can be dismissed), as shown in the following figure:

Figure 14.12: *An interstitial ad on full screen*

Playable ads

Another well-known model is ads where you can interact. It is usually a simple and reduced version of the game or app that is advertised, but where it is shown in a very clear and direct way what it consists of, like:

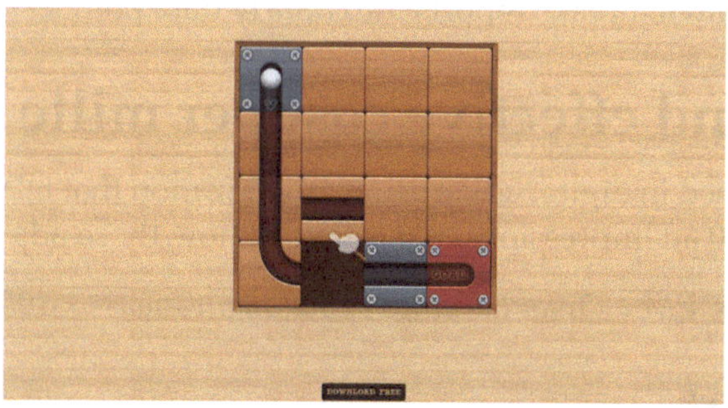

Figure 14.13: *A playable advertisement let you test the game*

Rewarded video ads

Video ads are the most common form of advertising. If the user watches the complete video, or at least a minimum amount of time, the players receive incentives (more points, stars, a surprise gift), as shown in the following figure:

Figure 14.14: Sample of a rewarded video ad

Understanding finances

The following are some basic concepts to understand and interpret the graphs and tables that will help us know when we are winning with our strategy and where we are producing more and less profit:

- **Revenue**: The total revenue collected to date.
- **Impressions/DAU**: Shows the average number of impressions per daily active user.
- **Effective cost per mille or eCPM**: Average revenue earned per 1,000 impressions.
- **Fill rate**: How often the waterfall can fulfill an ad request.
- **Hourly breakdown**: Breaks reports into hourly data points.

Placements and effective cost per mille targets

eCPM is a key metric used in digital advertising monetization that tells you how much money you earn for every 1,000 ad impressions, regardless of how those ads are priced:

$$eCPM = (Total\ Earnings\ /\ Total\ Impressions) \times 1000$$

Unity ads report

When you finally have your ad system up and running, and users are generating revenue, you can control the entire system from the dashboard. The report is designed to provide information at an organizational level and allows us to see graphically and clearly the profits with your monetization strategies and the factors that affect these profits:

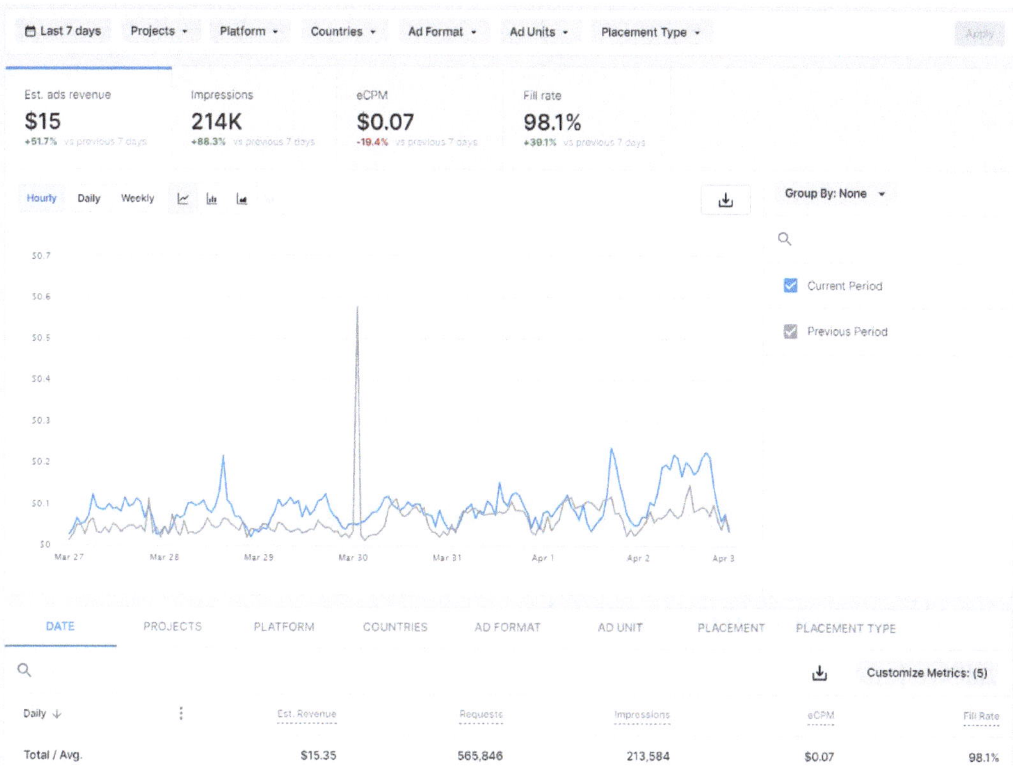

***Figure 14.15**: Unity Ads report show your earnings*

It is important to note that various filters can be applied that will allow us to segment the information according to what we need to know. The filters can be combined (turning on and off) and are as follows:

- **Date**: Select predefined dates (for example, last 3 days, last 7 days, last 14 days, or last 31 days) or choose a custom date range. The default selection is the last 7 days.
- **Projects**: Select projects to find out which ones provide the most and least profit. So, you can focus on the ones that suit you best.
- **Platform**: Select from different platforms to find out which one is working best.
- **Ad Formats**: Select banner, interstitial, or rewarded ad types.
- **Countries**: Select one, several, or all countries applicable to your application.

Another synthesized way to see the information about the benefits produced by the ads is in table mode, where the data appears in a very summarized form:

DATE PROJECTS PLATFORM COUNTRIES AD FORMAT AD UNIT PLACEMENT PLACEMENT TYPE

Customize Metrics: (5)

Daily	Est. Revenue	Requests	Impressions	eCPM	Fill Rate
Total / Avg.	**$15.35**	**565,846**	**213,584**	**$0.07**	**98.1%**
Apr 2, 2023	$3.48	109,974	46,062	$0.08	98%
Apr 1, 2023	$2.26	75,104	29,644	$0.08	97.9%
Mar 31, 2023	$1.99	84,933	32,114	$0.06	97.7%
Mar 30, 2023	$1.94	79,038	28,213	$0.07	97.8%
Mar 29, 2023	$1.90	77,074	27,245	$0.07	98.3%
Mar 28, 2023	$1.93	70,728	26,123	$0.07	98.7%
Mar 27, 2023	$1.85	68,995	24,183	$0.08	98.7%

Figure 14.16: *Unity Ads report show your comingsin*

Generating maximum profits

Now that we know what data we can recover, it is important to understand how to generate the most profit.

Every time your game requests an ad, Unity Ads holds an open auction for advertisers to bid on your impression. The highest bidder offers an ad. Advertisers can bid on different types of impressions to provide a diverse source of revenue. The following types are listed in ascending order of expected potential income:

- The player triggers an ad to start the ad.
- The player observes an advertisement until its conclusion in its entirety.
- The player clicks on the ad and leads to an external product link.
- The player clicks on the product's external page to install the product.

The effective cost per 1,000 impressions represents your overall combined revenue across these streams. The key to optimizing your eCPM is to design your ads to consistently generate the highest quality impressions.

To make the most of it, a technique called **Waterfalls** is used. It works as follows:

The most likely characteristics to place an ad are defined, but if the user where it is run does not meet the conditions, it tries to fill the next most likely network, and so on.

In the following figure, you can see the Waterfall technique for maximising ad revenue, a technique used to maximise ad placement by trying different ad networks based on defined characteristics and bid prices to fill ad requests:

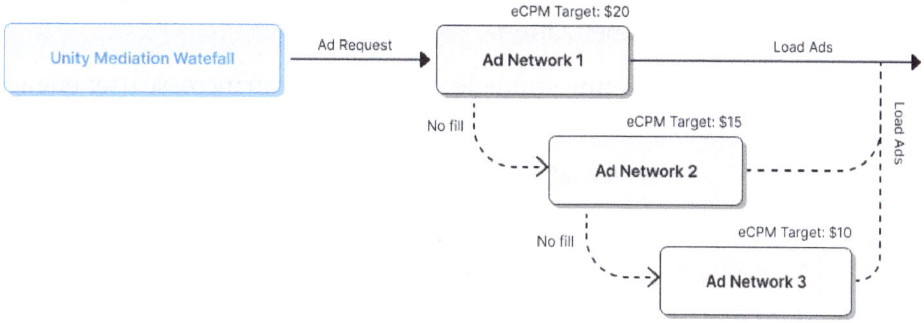

***Figure 14.17**: This figure visually explains the concept of Waterfalls*

Basically, the intent is to place an ad whenever possible. You can play with the conditions to try to always generate the ads and therefore the relevant income.

The best way to encourage users to pay more attention to ads is to personalize them whenever possible and allow players to opt-in to seeing ads, so they can choose to skip them or receive a reward.

When players voluntarily watch an advertisement, they are more likely to pay attention and show interest in the advertised product. This, in turn, enhances the standard of your impressions.

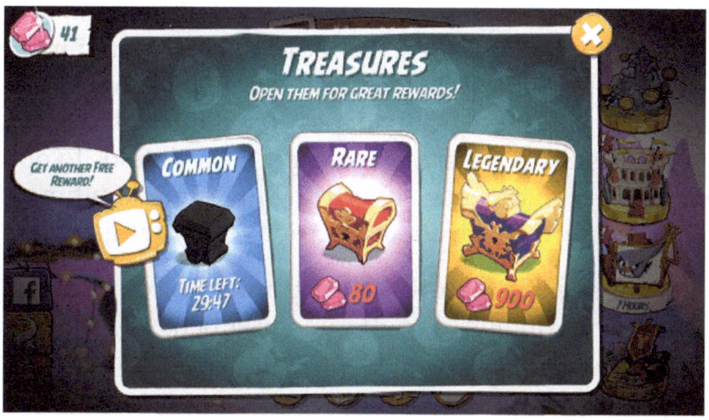

***Figure 14.18**: Example of monetization using Waterfalls*

Social networks

Social media platforms offer app developers many opportunities to attract new users, promote their apps, and ensure long-term monetization.

By using different social media marketing strategies, developers can increase user engagement and ultimately increase revenue over time.

In this section, we will look at how social media marketing can maximize user engagement and monetize your app.

We will look at five key strategies you can use to achieve these goals:

- **Identify the right platform**: Before diving into social media marketing, it is important to identify the right platform that best suits your target audience. By focusing on the platforms where users spend the most time, you can increase your chances of reaching and engaging them effectively.
- **Create engaging content**: To capture users' attention and encourage them to interact with your app, you need to create high-quality, visually appealing content that highlights your app's most important features and benefits. This includes images, videos, and other multimedia elements that will help your app stand out from the crowd.
- **Interact with potential users**: Actively engaging with potential users through comments, direct messages, and other interactions can help build relationships, increase trust, and ultimately increase app downloads and revenue.
- **Targeted advertising:** This strategy focuses on utilizing the robust advertising capabilities of social media platforms like *Facebook*, *Instagram*, and *TikTok*. It involves carefully defining your target audience based on demographics, interests, and behaviors. Then, you create compelling ad creatives – often utilizing eye-catching visuals and concise messaging – and strategically deploy them through these platforms. Crucially, this strategy emphasizes A/B testing different ad variations to optimize performance and maximize the return on your advertising investment, ultimately allowing you to reach potential players who are already receptive to your game's genre and style.
- **Utilizing platform-specific features**: This approach recognizes that each social media platform operates with unique strengths and user behaviors. Instead of a one-size-fits-all approach, it involves adapting your promotional efforts to leverage the distinctive features of each platform. For example, short, engaging gameplay videos are ideal for TikTok, while high-quality screenshots and interactive polls thrive on Instagram. Utilizing platform-specific tools, contests, and trends helps you maximize your reach and engagement within the most effective channels for your game's target audience.

Conclusion

In conclusion, this chapter has provided an overview of various advertising strategies employed to monetise mobile games or apps, such as interstitial ads, playable ads, rewarded video ads, and in-app purchases. We explored how to monitor and track the performance of these ad strategies using tools like the Unity Ads dashboard report. Furthermore, we covered fundamental financial concepts essential for understanding your monetisation performance, including revenue, eCPM, fill rate, and impressions, and examined some approaches to improve and optimise your ads to enhance their appeal to users. Hopefully, this chapter serves as a solid foundation for understanding and utilising the available monetisation tools.

Looking ahead, the next chapter will shift its focus to enhancing your projects with Unity, specifically within the realm of **virtual reality** (**VR**). You will explore stereoscopic images in VR and learn about techniques and strategies related to this technology. This will include topics such as projecting a 360 video on a sphere, using materials to change the normals, and implementing layer filters. The next chapter will delve into the principles of stereoscopic vision, explaining how it creates a sense of depth and three-dimensional space, thereby enhancing the overall VR experience. You will also learn practical methods for implementing stereoscopic images and videos in Unity, including working with 360 videos and employing techniques like dual cameras and rendering different perspectives for each eye.

Multiple choice questions

1. **Which monetization strategy is described as allowing players to opt to view an advertisement in exchange for in-game rewards, positioning it as a non-intrusive method?**
   a. Banner advertisements
   b. Subscription-based models
   c. Interstitial ads
   d. Rewarded advertisements
2. **In the context of IAPs, what is the key characteristic of a consumable product type?**
   a. Users can purchase the product only once.
   b. The product is available for a limited time only.
   c. Users have the option to purchase the product continuously.
   d. It typically includes items like a special sword or armor.

3. **What is the primary formula used to calculate eCPM?**
   a. (Total Impressions / Total Earnings) $\times$ 1000
   b. (Total Earnings / Total Impressions) $\times$ 1000
   c. (Total Revenue / Total Users) $\times$ 1000
   d. (Total Purchases / Total Users) $\times 1000$
4. **Which of the following Unity Ads formats are correctly defined as full-screen advertisements that remain visible until the player dismisses them?**
   a. Rewarded video ads
   b. Banner ads
   c. Playable ads
   d. Interstitial ads
5. **The Unity Ads monetization dashboard allows developers to optimize their advertising strategy by utilizing which powerful feature?**
   a. Centralized control over source code management
   b. Support for third-party game engine integration
   c. Advanced reporting tools to track income
   d. Automated server build pipelines
6. **A game studio plans to introduce special, time-limited holiday graphics and discounted virtual items, deploying them without requiring users to download a full new version of the app from the store. Which service enables this capability?**
   a. Unity version control system (VCS)
   b. Cloud Content Delivery service (CCD)
   c. Unity cloud diagnostics advanced
   d. Artifact center management
7. **Which key financial metric represents the average revenue earned for every 1,000 advertisement impressions?**
   a. Impressions/DAU
   b. Fill rate
   c. eCPM
   d. Hourly Breakdown

8. **When designing IAPs, what is the core reason why developers are advised against making the purchase of premium items a necessary condition to play the game?**
   a. It violates platform terms of service for most app stores.
   b. It is difficult to validate non-consumable items correctly.
   c. It may draw the ire of players who are frustrated at not being able to continue.
   d. It prevents the use of mediation for ad integration.
9. **The process of implementing an IAP system in Unity requires defining products based on which three primary types?**
   a. Premium, Standard, and Trial
   b. Consumable, Non-consumable, and Subscription
   c. Digital, Physical, and Service
   d. Local, Regional, and Global
10. **Which social media marketing strategy involves closely defining the target audience and using A/B testing to optimize ad performance on platforms like Facebook and TikTok?**
   a. Utilizing platform-specific features
   b. Interact with potential users
   c. Targeted advertising
   d. Create engaging content

Answers

1	d
2	c
3	b
4	d
5	c
6	b
7	c
8	c
9	b
10	c

Join our Discord space

Join our Discord workspace for latest updates, offers, tech happenings around the world, new releases, and sessions with the authors:

https://discord.bpbonline.com

CHAPTER 15
Enhancing Your Projects with Unity

Introduction

In this chapter, we cover different techniques to improve your projects. The Unity Animator engine is a powerful tool for creating complex character animations and controlling them in real-time within a Unity scene. It provides a visual interface for creating animation state machines and transitions between them.

In Unity3D, post-processing refers to a set of techniques used to enhance the visual quality of a game or application after the rendering process. These techniques can be applied to the final rendered image to create various effects like bloom, color grading, motion blur, and more. Overall, post-processing in Unity3D can be a powerful tool for enhancing the visual quality of a game or application. The post-processing stack makes it easy to apply and customize these effects, allowing developers to create stunning and immersive visuals with ease.

To simulate movement and interactions between objects in a game world, we use Unity Physics and Kinematics. Physics can simulate gravity, collisions, and other physical forces that affect the movement of objects, while Kinematics can be used to create a complex animation for a character performing a specific action. Unity lighting is a powerful tool for creating immersive and realistic game worlds. It enables developers to simulate the behavior of light and how it interacts with objects and surfaces. Directional lights, point lights, spotlights, backed lights. Each type of light source has different properties that can be adjusted to create the desired lighting effect.

Structure

In this chapter, we will cover the following topics:

- Animator engine
    - Object hierarchy
    - Creating animations
    - Mixamo

    - Animatric
- Animator
- Post-processing
    - Ambient Occlusion
    - Anti-aliasing
    - Bloom
    - Depth of Field
    - Color Grading
    - Tonemapping

Objectives

The chapter covers different techniques to improve projects. These include the Animator engine and post-processing. Readers will learn how the Animator engine can be used to make animations and situations where it is not advisable to use this system. The Animator component enables control of character movements and actions. They will also learn post-processing techniques to enhance the visual quality of a game or application after rendering. The post-processing stack allows the customization of effects, allowing developers to create immersive visuals. Some of the effects that can be applied include Ambient Occlusion, anti-aliasing, and Bloom. Other effects include Depth of Field, Colour Grading, and Tonemapping.

Animator engine

One of the most used features in any game engine is, without a doubt, the animation system. Unity is constantly reinventing itself, and for that reason, it has had several animation systems that have coexisted over time. The one that is most used today is Animator because of its great flexibility and because it adapts very well to 3D artists.

We are going to see how it can be used to make animations in your project, and at the end, we will see a case in which it is advisable not to use this system.

Object hierarchy

For this example, we are going to animate a robotic arm downloaded from *Sketchfab*. The first thing we must do is have the moving parts perfectly structured in a hierarchical way so that when we move an upper part, all the lower ones are affected. If it were a human arm, we could say that when you move the shoulder, the entire arm must move. When you move the elbow, only the forearm will move, and when you move the wrist, only the hand will move.

In the example, the moving parts are selected so that it can be seen clearly. They are **Arm01**, **Arm02** and **Arm03**, as shown in the following figure:

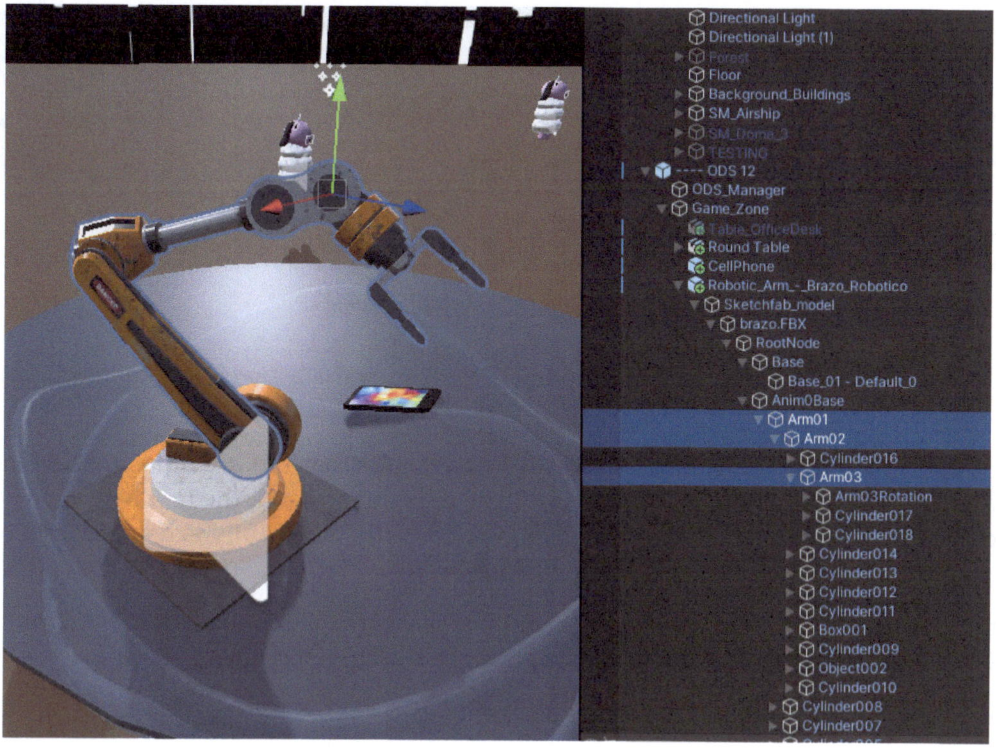

***Figure 15.1**: A correct hierarchy is fundamental to animate correctly*

The hierarchy is also important because the animations must hang from the main object of the tree in the **Robotic_Arm** example.

That way, we can animate any descendant in the structure, and when we do variant prefabs, the animations will be edited.

We also attach the scripts to the main object for the same reason.

Creating animations

For this example, we are going to animate a robotic arm that we downloaded from Sketchfab. The first thing we must do is open the animation editor by selecting **Window | Animation** from the menu.

With the main object selected (to which the animations will be assigned), in the new animation window, click on the **Create** button and indicate the name of your animation and the folder where you want to store the animations.

If everything is correct up to this point, the tool to create animations within the window will have been activated:

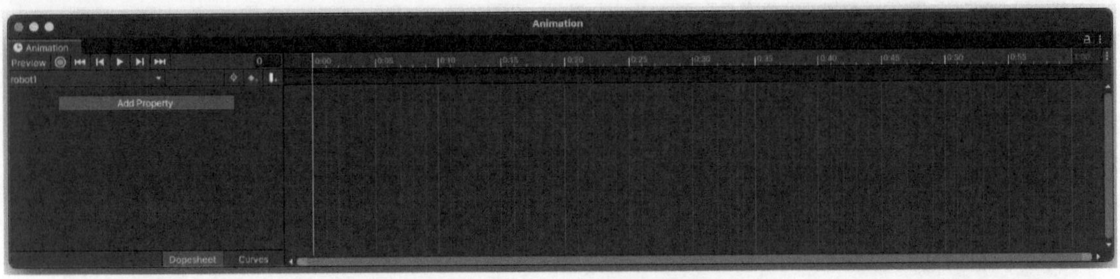

Figure 15.2: This is the Animation window

To start recording, we must click on the red circle icon and start creating keyframes on the timeline.

According to the *Oxford* reference[1], *keyframe,* in animation, are the drawings that define the start and end of an action: for example, if a figure raises their hand, the first keyframe would be the hand by the figure's side, and the next would be the hand fully extended. In-between frames are the frames that fill in all the points between.

In computer special effects, a set of programmable markers that define a point in a transition between two states so that the computer can generate in-between frames: see also interpolation.

The definition can be found on the following link:

https://www.oxfordreference.com/display/10.1093/acref/9780198841838.001.0001/acref-9780198841838-e-1465?rskey=HhGE8u&result=1

So, an animation is made up of the state of objects over a period of time.

At the moment it is being recorded, we can go to the moment that interests us on the timeline and move, rotate, scale, activate/deactivate objects, particle emitters, etc., so that all the changes in each keyframe are recorded.

With this button , you create the keyframe at the timeline position:

While we are recording, we can also press play to see how the animation we are creating is turning out:

1 **https://www.oxfordreference.com/display/10.1093/acref/9780198841838.001.0001/acref-9780198841838-e-1465?rskey=HhGE8u&result=1**

***Figure 15.3**: An animation with multiple keyframes*

On many occasions, the time is not what one expected and has to be adjusted. To do this, you must select the keyframes with the diamond at the top (when selected, it turns blue). If we press the *Shift* key, we can select several keyframes and move them around the timeline. When we select like this, the sidebars appear so that we can clearly see the selection:

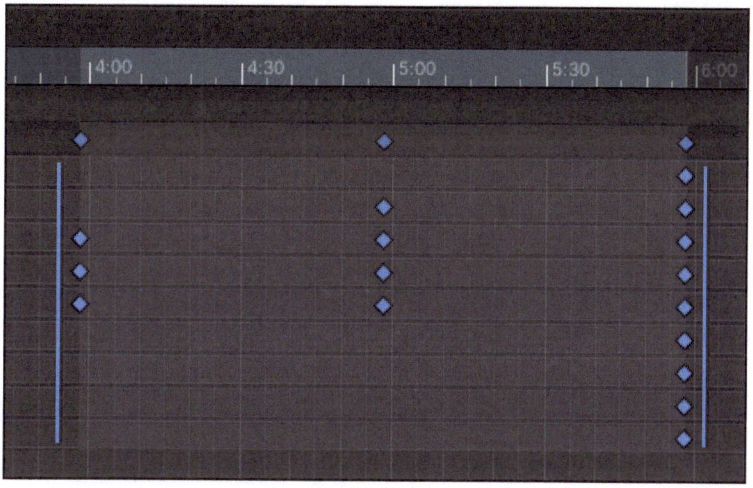

***Figure 15.4**: You can select and move a sequence of keyframes to adjust times*

Let us go one step further. How can we make something happen at a certain moment in the animation?

For this purpose, there is another button with which we can create an event in a specific frame of the animation. In that event, we can call a Unity script and do whatever we want there. In our example, we activate a particle emitter and launch a powerful sound to improve the immersive experience:

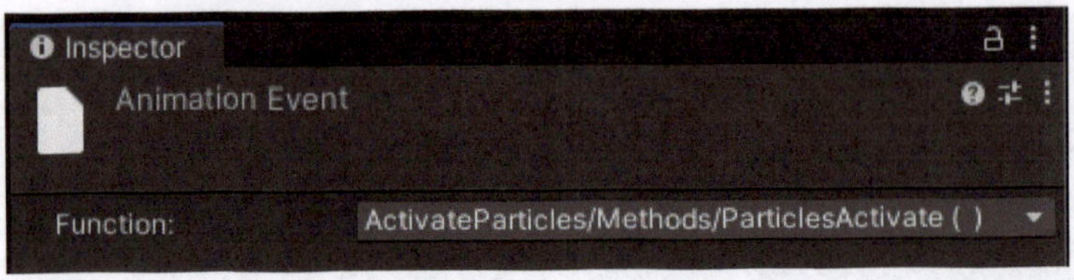

Figure 15.5: You will see this on the inspector when you select an Animation Event

Refer to the following code written for this simple animation.

There is a particle emitter that we only want to activate for a few seconds in the animation, so there are two methods created for activating or deactivating it.

In the animation, two events have been created, and in each of them, the corresponding method is called:

```
using UnityEngine;

public class ActivateParticles : MonoBehaviour
{
 [SerializeField] private GameObject _particleSystem;
 private AudioSource _audioSource;

 private void Start()
 {
  _audioSource = gameObject.GetComponent<AudioSource>();
  ParticlesDisActivate();
 }

 public void ParticlesActivate()
 {
  _particleSystem.gameObject.SetActive(true);
  _audioSource.Play();
 }

 public void ParticlesDisActivate()
 {
  _particleSystem.gameObject.SetActive(false);
  _audioSource.Stop();
 }
}
```

Making animations requires skill, time, and attention to detail. Adding small complementary movements to the main animation adds verisimilitude and greatly improves the animations. It is also important to accompany it with sound and effects (light, particles, etc.) that reinforce the action we want to highlight. The following figure shows an animation with keyframes:

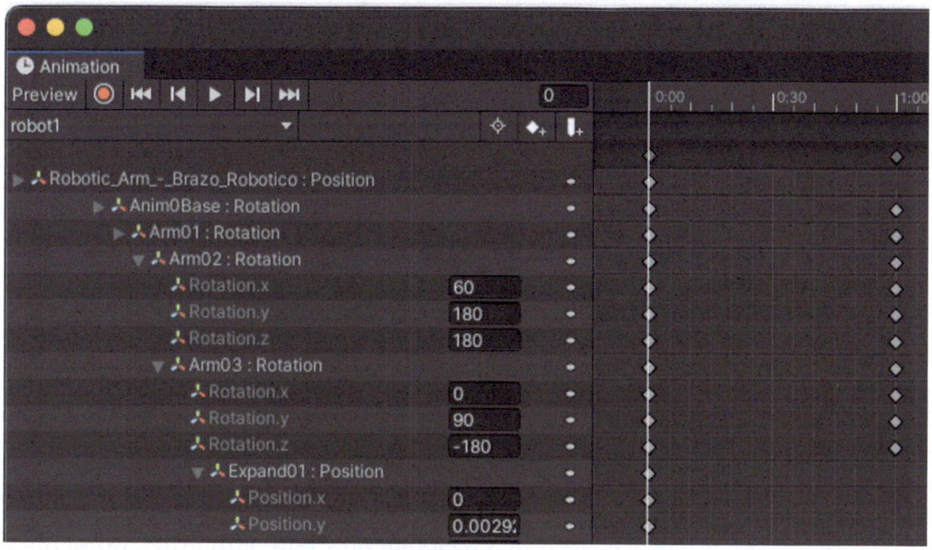

***Figure 15.6**: Final animation with events created and all structure*

Animations of robots or mechanical elements are easy to do, but the animations become much more complicated when we try to move characters, like humanoids. Fortunately, there are some tools that can help us a lot in this task.

Mixamo

On the mixamo.com website, we can find many animations of bipedal characters in multiple situations. This repository is searchable, and all the animations are of great quality, as shown in the following figure:

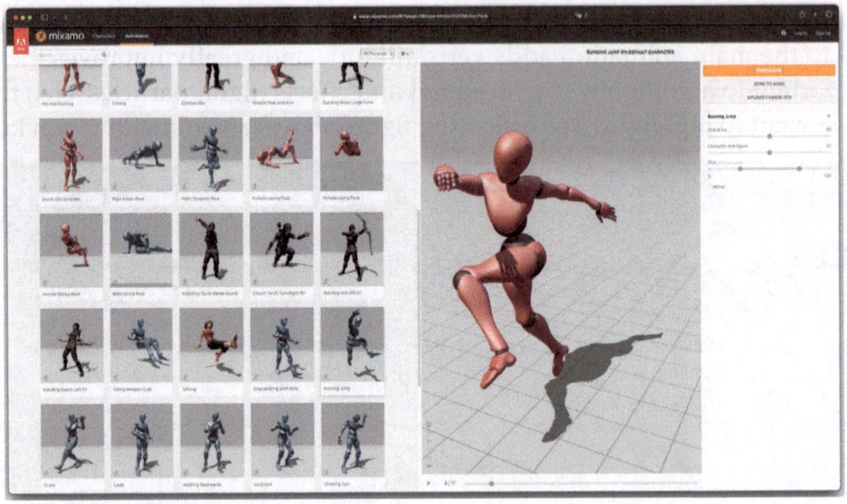

Figure 15.7: Mixamo is one of the best animation repositories for bipedal characters

The operation has the following simple steps:

- We look for the animation we need.
- By double-clicking, we can see it in a preview window with much more detail.
- We then download the animation (normally in FBX format for Unity).
- In the preview, we can choose if the animation is in place or if it moves. If a character is running, for example, we can do the entire animation, but without him moving forward.
- We can also indicate more configuration parameters (not too many), as seen in the following figure:

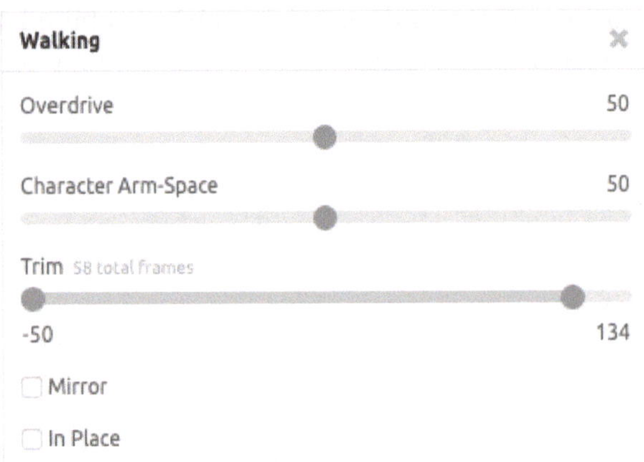

Figure 15.8: Some parameters could be ajusted

When we click on the download button, another window will appear with some drop-down menus that allow us to choose the format, the number of frames, if we want to reduce the number of keyframes or if we also want the skin to be exported (if you are going to use it with a character yours, you are not going to want the looks, just the movements), as shown in the following figure:

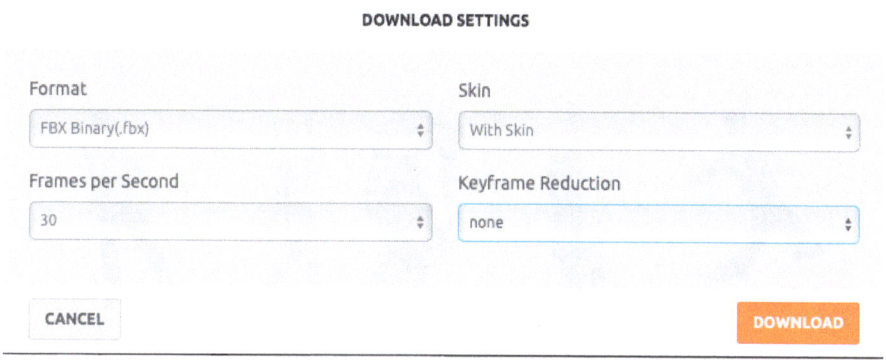

***Figure 15.9**: The download pop-up options are relevant*

Animating our characters

With those options alone, Mixamo is already an interesting platform to know and can solve the behavior of many characters thanks to the great variety of animations, but there is still one more functionality that we think can be very interesting: you will be able to upload your own characters to animate them.

Let us see what the entire process is like to give life to a character different from those that are by default in Mixamo. The character who must climb should be in a T position (with arms open and legs together, seen from the front), as shown in the following figure:

***Figure 15.10**: Original character on T-pose*

We have selected a Sketchfab character because it is lowpoly and upload to Mixamo. You can find this character at the following address: **https://sketchfab.com/3d-models/casual-lowpoly-male-rig-t-pose-2f69be91f3044fe68881e354b220fc60**

The tool has an authoring system that usually does very well if the characters are humanoid. If you are not able to recognize it, a screen appears with our character, where we will have to locate where to place the bones and the rotation points in order to apply the animations correctly. In the following figure, you can see some frames of a dancing animation:

***Figure 15.11**: Animation sequence applied to our avatar*

When the animations look correct, you can download them in `*.fbx` format that Unity imports directly.

Animatric

In the age of artificial intelligence, it is not surprising that we have a tool that generates animations using generative artificial intelligence from a text message.

The documentation for this interesting proposal has just been released. The instructions say verbatim: *A prompt is a short text phrase that Animatric interprets to produce an animation. Our application breaks down the words and phrases in a prompt into smaller fragments that are compared to your training data and then used to generate an animation.*

The outcomes are quite satisfactory. In the prompt, the character was requested to perform a dance, and the subsequent figures showcase two frames of the resulting animation:

***Figure 15.12**: Sample frames of an animation generated with AI*

Although it still lacks variety and the animations are limited, it will surely be a great alternative over time.

Animatric.ai has a plugin for Blender and another for Unreal Engine (at the moment, it does not have one for Unity). Of course, when exporting, there are quite a few options, and among them, one is Unity. With which we can use it perfectly.

On its website, you can also find documentation on how to make prompts (simple and a little more complicated) to get more out of it. It also has an API that can be called to do the generation in an automated way. At the moment, only one example is published in Python, but it is not difficult to adapt it for C# or other programming languages.

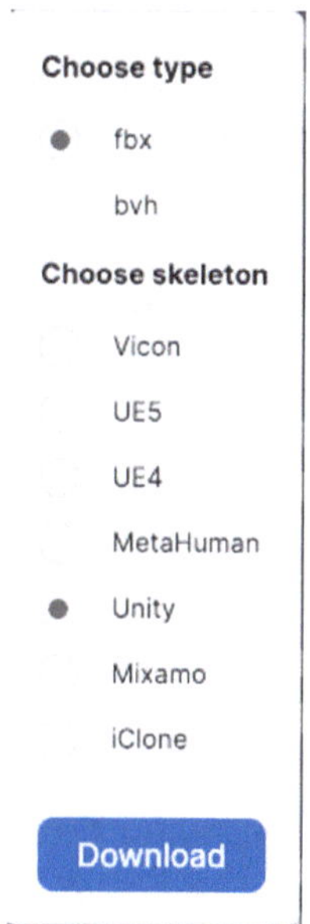

Figure 15.13: *Export form where select format and platform*

Animator

The Animator component enables artists to control character movements and actions in a user-friendly manner. It facilitates the creation of 3D character movements by specifying target positions, rotations, and scales through keyframes. This approach eliminates the need for manual adjustment of every value for each frame, facilitating the creation of intricate movements.

Furthermore, the Animator component facilitates the triggering of events based on specific conditions, such as characters reaching a designated point in space or, upon death, triggering corresponding animations. This functionality enables game logic to respond appropriately to gameplay events.

Lastly, the Animator component supports custom animations using custom data types, such as JSON files. This allows artists to create complex animations without the necessity of writing code or relying solely on pre-existing animations provided by Unity. While these pre-existing animations are also available, the option to create custom animations provides flexibility and artistic control.

You can set up the Animator through the following steps:

1. Create an Animator Controller:
   a. **Create an Animator Controller**: Right-click in the **Project** window, go to **Create | Animator Controller**. Name it (for example, **PlayerAnimator**).
   b. **Assign to a GameObject**: Select the **GameObject** (for example, your character), and in the **Inspector**, find the Animator component. Drag your new **Animator Controller** into the **Controller** field.
2. **Open the Animator window**:
   a. **Open Animator window**: Go to **Window | Animation | Animator**. This window allows you to create and manage animation states.

You can create animation clips through the following steps:

1. **Create animation clips**: In the **Project** window, right-click and choose **Create | Animation**. Create separate clips for each action (for example, **Walk, Run, Jump**).
   a. **Edit animation clips**: Double-click an animation clip to open the Animation window. Use this window to define the animation by manipulating the GameObject's properties over time.
2. You can add animations to the Animator through the following steps:
   a. **Add states**: we must be clear from the beginning about all the states that our characters will have and in which they will change.
   b. **Add animation clips**: Drag each animation clip into the Animator window. This creates states in the Animator.
   c. **Make transitions**: Right-click on a state and select **Make Transition**, then click on another state to create a transition between them. Define transitions for all required state changes.
3. Configuring transitions:
   a. Define transition conditions:
      i. **Select transition**: Click on a transition arrow between states.
      ii. **Set conditions**: In the **Inspector**, you can define conditions under which the transition occurs. Use parameters like **Bool**, **Float**, **Int**, or **Trigger** to control transitions based on conditions.

b. Adjust transition settings:

   i. **Transition duration**: Adjust the transition duration for smoother or faster transitions between states.

   ii. **Exit time**: Optionally set an exit time to control when a transition can occur relative to the current animation's progress.

4. Adding parameters:

   a. Create parameters:

      i. **Add parameters**: In the Animator window, under the **Parameters** tab, click the + icon to add parameters (e.g., **Speed, IsJumping**).

   b. Use parameters in transitions:

      i. **Apply parameters**: Use these parameters to control transitions. For example, a speed parameter might determine if the character transitions between idle and walking animations.

5. Controlling Animator via script:

   a. Access Animator Component:

      i. **Reference Animator**: In your script, get a reference to the Animator component, usually in **`Start`** or **`Awake`**.

```
Animator animator;
void Start() {
    animator = GetComponent<Animator>();
}
```

   b. Set parameters:

      i. **Set parameter values**: Use **`animator.SetBool`**, **`animator.SetFloat`**, **`animator.SetInteger`**, or **`animator.SetTrigger`** to control parameters.

```
csharp
void Update() {
    animator.SetFloat("Speed", currentSpeed);
}
```

6. Advanced features:

   a. Blend trees:

      i. **Create blend tree**: In the Animator window, right-click and select **Create State | From New Blend Tree**.

ii. **Configure blend tree**: Double-click the blend tree to edit it. Use blend trees to smoothly interpolate between multiple animations based on a parameter (e.g., transitioning between walking and running).

b. Layers:

i. **Add layers**: Use layers to handle complex animation systems (e.g., handling upper and lower body animations separately).

ii. **Blend layers**: Adjust the weight and blending of layers to achieve the desired animation combination.

7. Debugging and testing:

a. Test in Play Mode:

i. **Play Mode**: Test the animations in Play Mode to ensure they work as expected. Use the Animator window to monitor state transitions.

b. Debugging transitions:

i. **Debug transitions**: Check the Animator window for transition errors or unexpected behavior. Adjust conditions and parameters as needed.

Here is a simple script example for controlling a character's animation based on movement speed:

```
using UnityEngine;
public class PlayerController : MonoBehaviour {
   public float speed = 5.0f;
   private Animator animator;
   private Rigidbody2D rb;

   void Start() {
      animator = GetComponent<Animator>();
      rb = GetComponent<Rigidbody2D>();
   }

   void Update() {
      float move = Input.GetAxis("Horizontal");
      rb.velocity = new Vector2(move * speed, rb.velocity.y);

      animator.SetFloat("Speed", Mathf.Abs(move));
   }
}
```

In this example:

- The player's speed affects the **Speed** parameter in the Animator.
- The **Speed** parameter controls transitions between idle and moving states in the Animator.
- For further learning, you can check out:
- Unity's official Animator documentation.
- Unity Learn's Animation section.

This guide should give you a solid foundation for using Unity Animator. Feel free to explore more advanced features as you get comfortable.

This is a simple code to control the Animator component:

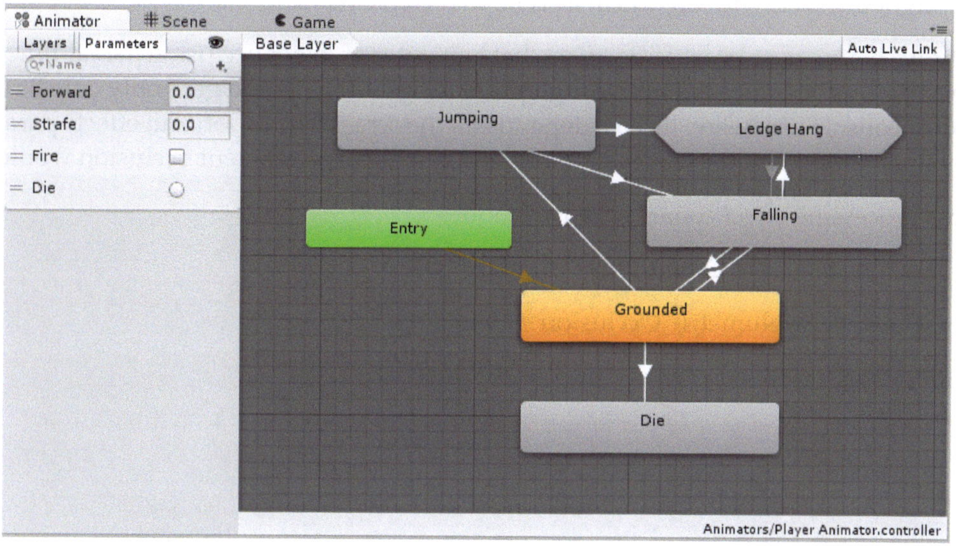

***Figure 15.14**: The Animator window let you control the transition between the animations*

Post-processing

Another important tool to make your projects look much more professional is post-processing.

This name comes from the world of cinema, where, after the film had been shot, different techniques were applied to improve the final result that was going to be reproduced in movie theaters.

Digital technology has completely changed the way films or audiovisual content are generated today, and postprocessing now has a much more important weight, since it is where special effects are often added.

The system that Unity uses is that once a frame has been completely rendered, a series of effects are applied (that we can define) before the image is displayed on the screen with the final result.

With postprocessing, we will achieve a much better result using relatively few resources since the system is very well optimized.

Some of the effects that we can apply are given in this section.

Ambient Occlusion

In real life, light does not arrive in the same way in folds, holes, intersections, and surfaces that are close to each other and tend to darken.

Ambient Occlusion (**AO**) is a technique used in multiple 3D rendering programs to simulate the way light interacts with objects in a scene to recreate realistic shadows and depth.

In Unity, we have a post-processing effect that generates ambient occlusion in real-time, giving a more natural appearance but with a high processing cost. It should generally only be used on desktop or console hardware. Its cost depends on the screen resolution and effects parameters, and does not depend on the complexity of the scene like true ambient occlusion would.

The post-processing effect comes with two modes:

- Scalable Ambient Obscurance
- Multi-scale Volumetric Occlusion

In the following figure, you can see the occlusion effect:

***Figure 15.15**: Sample of how Ambient Occlusion is generated*

Details of the form where the generation of ambient occlusion is parameterized are shown in the following figure:

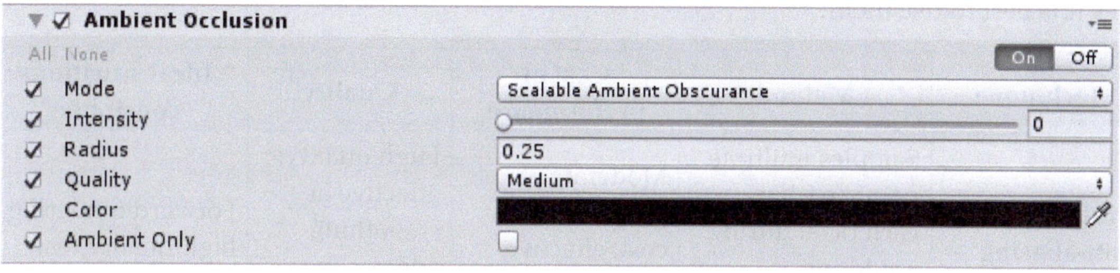

***Figure 15.16**: Detail of the Ambient Occlusion parameters*

Anti-aliasing

When computers had very low resolution, it was easy to see the pixels. In the games where 3D was simulated and we got very close to the 3D objects, the textures seen so closely allowed us to see the pixels as huge colored squares, as if they were tiles of a Roman mosaic.

To prevent them from looking bad, the developers used something similar to a painting technique (sfumato) that softens the edges.

Interspersing pixels of intermediate tones. If you had a black polygon and the other side was white, it was blurred with gray pixels, grading between them.

This technique is totally valid and helps to improve the visual quality of the final images when the adjacent textures have a lot of contrast, as shown in the following figure:

***Figure 15.17**: Anti-aliasing sample*

Although anti-aliasing reduces the jagged appearance of the lines, it also makes them blurry.

There are many techniques to do anti-aliasing. Each of them has advantages and disadvantages. In the following table, you can see a summary of the most important techniques and in which cases it is best to use them:

Technique	Method	Cost of performance	Quality	Ideal situations constrains
Multisample anti-aliasing (MSAA)	Samples multiple points within each pixel during rendering, averaging the results.	Moderate performance cost; effective on forward rendering paths.	High quality; effective at smoothing edges without much blurring.	Forward rendering, high-quality real-time applications.
Temporal anti-aliasing (TAA)	Uses multiple frames to smooth edges, reducing both spatial and temporal aliasing.	Moderate to high performance cost; depends on implementation.	High quality; reduces flickering and temporal artifacts.	Dynamic scenes with motion, deferred rendering.
Super-sample anti-aliasing (SSAA)	Renders at higher resolution and then downsamples to target resolution.	Very high-performance cost; often impractical for real-time.	Excellent quality; very effective at reducing aliasing and enhancing detail.	Offline rendering, high-quality screenshots, cinematics.
Subpixel morphological anti-aliasing (SMAA)	Edge detection and local blurring based on patterns found at subpixel level.	Moderate performance cost.	High quality; better at preserving detail compared to FXAA.	Real-time applications needing a balance between quality and performance.
Enhanced subpixel morphological anti-aliasing (SMAA T2X)	Combines SMAA with temporal component to reduce flickering.	Moderate to high performance cost.	Very high quality; combines benefits of SMAA and TAA.	Applications needing high quality with minimized temporal artifacts.

Technique	Method	Cost of performance	Quality	Ideal situations constrains
Supersampling (SS)	A generic term for techniques rendering at higher resolutions then downsampling.	Varies; generally high-performance cost.	Variable; high-quality output, similar to SSAA.	Cases where maximum quality is essential, such as rendering for offline use.
No anti-aliasing	Renders scene without any smoothing techniques applied.	No performance impact.	Low quality; results in visible jagged edges and aliasing artifacts.	Extremely performance-sensitive applications, basic prototypes.

***Table 15.1**: Table of anti-aliasing techniques*

You can select the anti-aliasing mode in the editor with this interface:

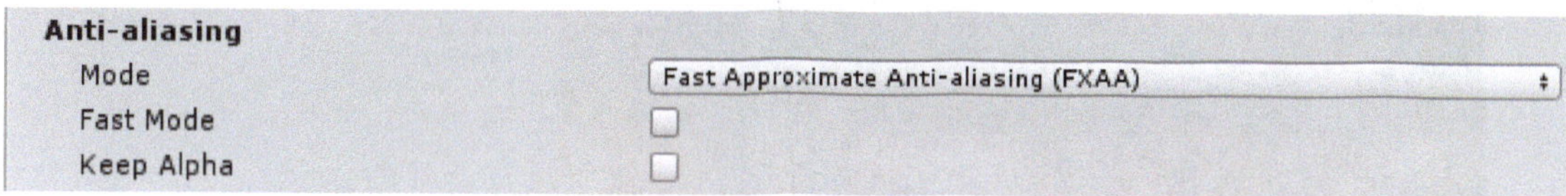

***Figure 15.18**: Detail of the form to select the type of anti-aliasing to be applied*

Bloom

The Bloom effect is a post-processing technique in Unity that simulates the way light spreads and scatters beyond the edges of bright areas of a scene. It is used to reproduce an image artifact from real-world cameras. The effect produces fringes of light that extend from the edges of bright areas of an image, contributing to the illusion of extremely bright light overwhelming the camera or eye capturing the scene. It creates a glow that enhances perceived brightness and adds a sense of realism, especially for high-intensity light sources such as lamps, sunlight reflections, or shiny objects.

Sometimes it is used to make neon lights, such as in TRON Legacy or Cyberpunk, as shown in the following figure:

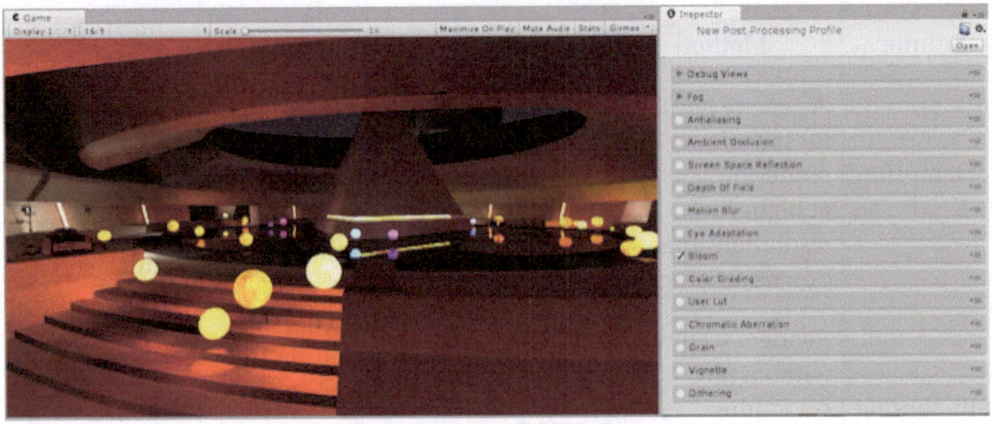

***Figure 15.19**: Scene without Bloom*

In the following figure, you can see the big difference when applying the Bloom effect:

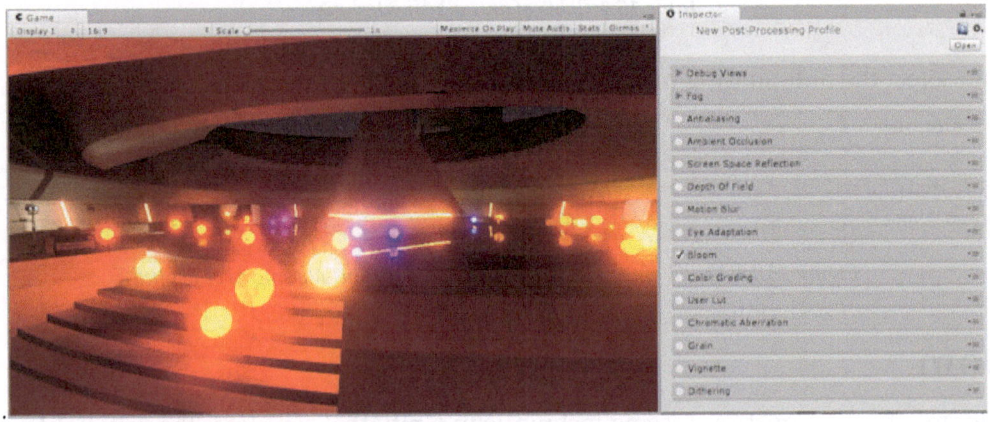

***Figure 15.20**: The same image with post-processing effects looks amazing*

In modern first-person shooters, a layer of spots or dust is often added to the full screen to diffract the Bloom effect. This is one of the parameters called *Lens Dirt*.

If you want to do these effects in a more precise way, it is possible to use C# to do it by code. An example of how we can use it with a Bloom effect is as follows, but it can be done with any of the post-processing effects:

```
using System.Collections;
using System.Collections.Generic;
using UnityEngine;
using UnityEngine.UI;
using UnityEngine.Rendering;
using UnityEngine.Rendering.Universal;
```

```
public class BloomControl : MonoBehaviour
{
    public Slider bloomSld;
    public Volume volume;
    private Bloom thisBloom;


    public void BloomByCode()
    {
        VolumeProfile proflile = volume.sharedProfile;


        volume.profile.TryGet(out thisBloom);
        thisBloom.intensity.value = bloomSld.value;

        if(bloomSld.value == 0)
            thisBloom.active = false;
        else
            thisBloom.active = true;
    }
}
```

Depth of Field

Depth of Field is an effect that has been widely used in cinema. It is very common to use the focus of the lens to focus on the closest or distant objects, creating a blur of those that are out of focus.

Blur not only gives a visual cue about the distance of an object, but also introduces the Bokeh effect, which is the term for the pleasing visual artifacts that appear around bright areas of the image when they are blurred.

An example of the Depth of Field effect can be seen in the following figure, showing the results of a focused mid-plane but a blurred background and foreground:

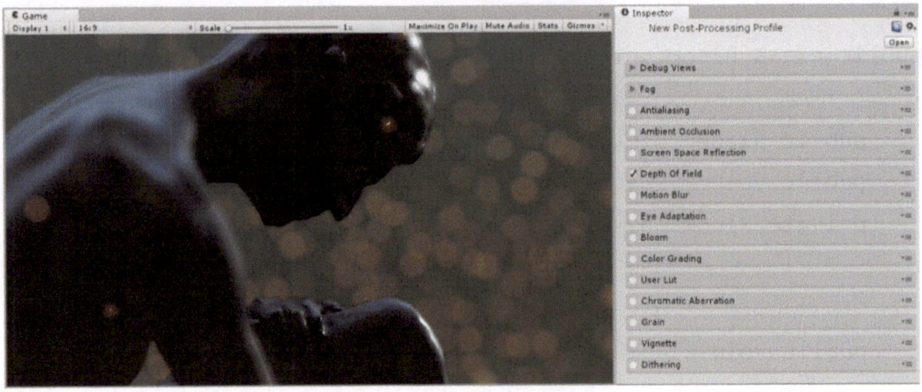

Figure 15.21: Depth of Field effect

It is very interesting to play with cinematic effects like these together with CineMachine. The results are spectacular.

The following are the parameters that Depth of Field uses. As you can see, they are all simulations of the real lenses in optical cameras:

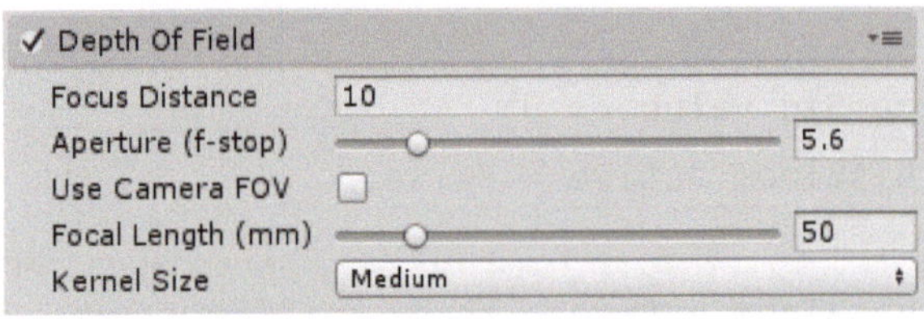

Figure 15.22: Detail of the form for Depth of Field

Color Grading

Color Grading is a process that involves modifying the color, contrast, and overall visual appearance of a scene. It enables the correction of undesirable color imbalances, the creation of artistic visual effects such as warm, cold, or sepia tones, and the adjustment of contrast, saturation, and highlights to highlight specific elements within the scene.

Lookup tables (**LUTs**) are pre-defined color grading profiles created in external tools like Photoshop or DaVinci Resolve. Unity supports LUTs for easy application of artistic looks.

To import and apply a LUT, you will need to perform the following steps:

1. Import a LUT texture by adding a LUT file (usually a **.png**) to your Unity project.
2. Apply the LUT
3. Add the Color Grading override.
4. Under the **Lookup Texture** section, assign your imported LUT texture.
5. Adjust the contribution slider to control the intensity of the LUT effect.

Tonemapping

Tonemapping is a technique employed to map **high dynamic range** (**HDR**) lighting into **low dynamic range** (**LDR**) displays. This ensures that scenes featuring bright highlights and deep shadows appear natural on monitors with limited dynamic range capabilities.

Types of tonemapping in Unity:

- **Linear (No Tonemapping):** Default for most scenes. Provides unaltered color and contrast but lacks visual pop.
- **Neutral:** A simple tonemapping curve that adjusts for HDR lighting but maintains realistic colors.
- **Academy Color Encoding System (ACES):** A professional film-like tonemapping curve. Widely used in the film and gaming industries for cinematic looks.
- **Custom curves:** Unity allows custom tonemapping curves if you need fine-tuned results.

Using the tonemapping component:

1. **Add the tonemapping override**: Go to your **Volume Profile**, click **Add Override**, and select **Post-processing** | **Tonemapping**.
2. **Choose a mode**: Select one of the modes: **None**, **Neutral**, or **ACES**.
3. **Fine-tuning tonemapping**: If you need more control, consider writing custom shaders or using HDRP's advanced tonemapping features.

Color Grading and tonemapping complement each other. Tonemapping ensures that HDR lighting and colors fit into the display's range. Color Grading adjusts the resulting tones to achieve the desired artistic or cinematic look.

Tips

These recommendations can enhance your post-processing workflow:

- **Utilize reference images:** Compare your scene against professional images or game assets to achieve consistent visual outcomes.
- **Enable HDR:** Activate HDR settings in your Unity project to maximize the impact of tonemapping and color grading.
- **Maintain subtle adjustments:** Excessive use of contrast, saturation, or hue can result in unnatural visuals. Subtle modifications often yield more aesthetically pleasing results.
- **Test on multiple displays:** Verify that your game renders correctly on various monitors or devices.

- **Integrate with lighting:** Color grading and tonemapping are most effective when your lighting setup is robust. Utilize baked or global illumination to complement post-processing effects.

In the following two figures, you can see a big difference between not using post-processing and using it:

Figure 15.23: *Image rendered without post-processing*

The visual quality of the same game has a more cinematic finish:

Figure 15.24: *The same image after aplying post-processing techniques*

Conclusion

In this chapter, we have explored several advanced techniques in Unity, including animation, post-processing, physics, cinematics, and advanced lighting. These features are crucial to improving the visual and functional quality of Unity projects.

We saw a small introduction to the use of these tools that contain enormous potential. This will allow you to create games and applications of a more professional quality. It is important to be able to integrate these elements to create immersive, engaging, and visually impressive experiences.

In the next chapter, you will learn about stereoscopic images in VR. You will explore techniques and strategies to maximize user engagement and monetization of your app or game. The chapter will cover topics such as projecting a 360 video on a sphere, materials to change the normals, and layer filters. The chapter will delve into the principles of stereoscopic vision, how it creates a sense of depth and three-dimensional space, and how it enhances the overall VR experience. You will learn how to implement stereoscopic images and videos in Unity, including 360 videos, using techniques like dual cameras and rendering different perspectives for each eye.

Multiple choice questions

1. **Why is a correct hierarchical structure of objects fundamental when setting up animations in Unity, particularly for complex assets like a robotic arm?**
   a. To enable the easy import of JSON animation files.
   b. To ensure that movements in the upper part (e.g., shoulder) affect all descendant parts (e.g., forearm).
   c. To guarantee that all animation scripts are attached only to leaf nodes.
   d. To allow animations to hang from the main object of the tree, ensuring inheritance in variant prefabs.
2. **In Unity3D, what is the process known as post-processing designed to achieve?**
   a. Optimizing code compilation time before deployment.
   b. Enhancing the visual quality of an image after the rendering process is complete.
   c. Simulating physical interactions like gravity and collisions in real-time.
   d. Creating a visual interface for managing animation state machines.
3. **What does the Unity Bloom effect primarily simulate in a rendered scene?**
   a. The lens focusing mechanism to create blur around distant objects.
   b. The way light spreads and scatters beyond the edges of bright areas, simulating a real-world camera artifact.
   c. The darkening of surfaces where light struggles to reach, such as folds or corners.
   d. The conversion of HDR lighting to LDR displays.

4. **The Unity Animator component offers which key functionalities for controlling character movements and actions?**
   a. Facilitating the creation of 3D movements by setting target positions and rotations through keyframes.
   b. Triggering events based on specific conditions, such as reaching a point in space.
   c. Automatically generating character geometry using artificial intelligence.
   d. Supporting custom animations using custom data types, such as JSON files.
5. **When creating an animation in Unity's Animation window, what function does a keyframe primarily serve?**
   a. It defines the start and end states of an action on a timeline, allowing the system to interpolate between them.
   b. It serves as a static marker that cannot store changes in position or rotation.
   c. It must be created using C# scripting, not the graphical interface.
   d. It automatically calls a method in a C# script without needing a separate Animation Event.
6. **What is the primary technical reason for using tonemapping in Unity's post-processing stack?**
   a. To introduce cinematic blur to objects outside the plane of focus.
   b. To map HDR lighting into LDR displays, ensuring natural appearance on limited-range monitors.
   c. To generate texture maps automatically using generative AI.
   d. To reduce jagged edges on high-contrast lines.
7. **For which specific task is Mixamo recommended as a valuable external resource for Unity developers?**
   a. Converting video formats like stereoscopic 360 video.
   b. Generating image textures from textual descriptions via AI.
   c. Providing a repository of high-quality, pre-made animations for bipedal characters.
   d. Allowing developers to upload their own humanoid characters (T-pose) to apply existing motion capture data.
8. **Anti-aliasing techniques in graphics rendering are used to address which visual artifact?**
   a. The blurring of background images due to lack of focus.
   b. The appearance of jagged or stair-step edges on lines and polygon boundaries in high-contrast areas.

c. Excessive light scattering causes bright areas to glow.

d. Incorrect rendering of lighting in shadowed corners and crevices.

9. **A developer is animating a dramatic explosion sequence for a cinematic. They want a powerful sound effect and a particle emitter to activate precisely when the animated explosion keyframe occurs. Which mechanism should the developer utilize in the Animation window to link this visual keyframe to a C# script function (`ParticlesActivate()`)?**

   a. A Blend Tree layer.

   b. An Animation Event.

   c. Ambient Occlusion.

   d. A custom JSON asset bundle.

10. **What is the fundamental goal of Color Grading in the Unity post-processing pipeline?**

    a. To adjust the device's graphics card clock speed based on thermal performance.

    b. To modify the color, contrast, and overall visual appearance of a scene to achieve artistic effects or correct imbalances.

    c. To ensure that animations transition smoothly between states.

    d. To automatically generate realistic depth effects without defining lens focus properties.

Answers

1	b, d
2	b
3	b
4	a, b, d
5	a
6	b
7	c, d
8	b
9	b
10	b

CHAPTER 16
Stereoscopic Images in VR

Introduction

This chapter delves into the utilization of stereoscopic images in **virtual reality** (**VR**), which are generated by presenting two slightly offset images to the left and right eye. When viewed through a VR headset, the brain merges these two images, thereby creating a perception of depth and three-dimensional space.

The incorporation of stereoscopic images in VR enhances the user experience by simulating depth and perspective. This augments the user's sense of presence and engagement within the virtual environment. Moreover, stereoscopic images can alleviate motion sickness and discomfort by providing a more accurate representation of depth and distance, thereby preventing disorientation and nausea. Furthermore, the utilization of stereoscopic images can augment the efficacy of training and educational applications by creating a more realistic and captivating environment, thereby facilitating information retention and skill development.

Structure

The chapter covers the following topics:

- The 3D success
  - Fusion Chamber system
  - Virtual camera
- Stereoscopic vision
- Stereoscopic projection
  - Anaglyph 3D
  - 3D polarization
- Stereoscopic capture
  - Acer SpatialLabs Eyes
  - Canon RF 5.2mm f/2.8 Dual Fisheye
  - Blackmagic URSA Cine Immersive
- Stereoscopic video formats and process
  - FFMPEG, the premier tool for video conversion

- Stereoscopic picture and video in Unity
- Stereoscopic 360 video in Unity
- 3D production for VR

Objectives

The objectives of this chapter are to provide a comprehensive understanding of stereoscopic vision and its applications in **virtual reality** (**VR**) using Unity 3D. The chapter aims to equip readers with the knowledge and skills to create immersive 3D experiences. Key areas of focus include understanding how stereoscopic vision works, including how the brain combines two images into a single 3D image, and exploring the techniques and technologies behind 3D filming, drawing on the innovations of *James Cameron* with his dual camera system, and how these can be applied within Unity.

The readers will also learn to use a virtual camera system to control a camera in a virtual environment and how this can be linked to real-time data from devices such as an iPhone. They will also understand and apply different methods of displaying 3D images, examine various 3D capture devices, and learning how to use FFMPEG for video conversion.

We will also learn to implement a stereoscopic view in Unity using the Meta SDK and how to project a 360 video onto a sphere with inverted normals by using a shader in Unity.

The 3D success

When *James Cameron* presented the movie AVATAR in 3D in 2009, few thought that the public would pay more to see the same movie in 3D; however, they were completely wrong. The technical innovations that *Cameron* had introduced allowed him to create images of beauty and spectacularity that made the most of adding depth, as shown in the following figure:

***Figure 16.1**: Avatar was a turning point in 3D recording techniques*

A 3D fever (even excessive) broke out. Television manufacturers incorporated 3D into their new products, and everyone wanted to sign up for the new goose that lays the golden eggs.

There were some other films that also took advantage of the features of 3D images, such as *Alfonso Cuarón's Gravity*. However, there were also some notable failures (usually films that had been shot in 2D and had been converted to 3D through post-processing).

The triumph of *James Cameron's* 3D was due to the creation of different technologies that revolutionized the way 3D movies were recorded.

Many of these techniques have become de facto standards in the film industry, and, best of all, we can use many of them today with Unity and especially in virtual reality development.

Fusion chamber system

This system finally allowed precise control over stereoscopic 3D filming and was based on the following techniques:

1. **Dual camera**: Two high-definition cameras are mounted together to simulate the perspective of the human eye, capturing detailed 3D images with minimal artifacts:

***Figure 16.2**: James Cameron with the famous dual camera*

2. **High resolution**: Filmed in full 1080p high definition, enhancing the clarity of 3D images.
3. **Frame rate**: A higher frame rate (48 frames per second) was used to reduce motion blur and make 3D action sequences smoother.

Other important techniques that allowed this qualitative leap in productions were the motion capture of actors in 3D, which were then integrated with CGI, ensuring realistic movements and expressions.

Virtual camera

Cameron also created an innovative system for recording shots called a *virtual camera*. The system used in *Avatar* combines elements of real-time computer graphics, motion capture, and camera operation. The renowned director was able to traverse Pandora's digital environment in real-world, framing the shots as if they were genuine scenes, resulting in a dynamic and immersive experience.

As incredible as it may seem, today we can use equal or superior technology with an iPhone and Unity 3D. The virtual camera[1] app will connect with our editor and provide us with real-time information about the following:[2]

- Position
- Rotation
- Focal length
- Focus distance
- Aperture

You can download the App to your mobile device from the App Store or Google Play. The icon of the app is as follows:

Figure 16.3*: Icon of the app Unity Virtual Camera*

In this way, we can precisely control a camera that will act as a bridge between the real and virtual worlds, as shown in the following figure:

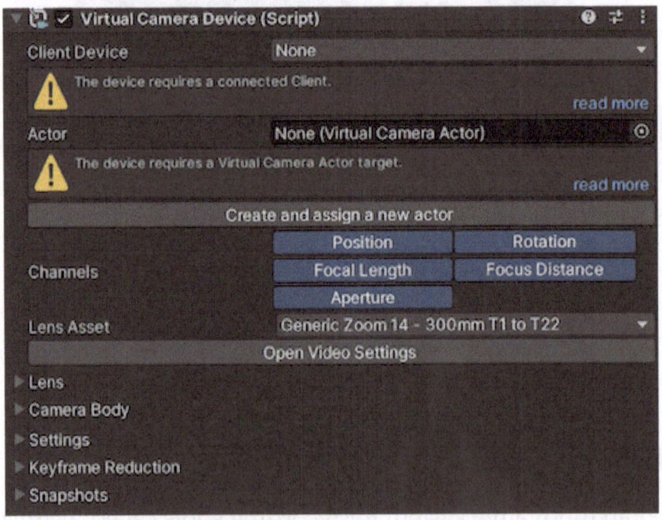

Figure 16.4*: Detail of the component where virtual camera is configured*

---

1 You can find a find all the technical information about Virtual Camera at this address: https://docs.unity3d.com/Packages/com.unity.live-capture@4.0/manual/virtual-camera-getting-started.html

2 The Unity Virtual Camera App is on the App Store: Unity Virtual Camera

Here, you can see all the camera shoot options:

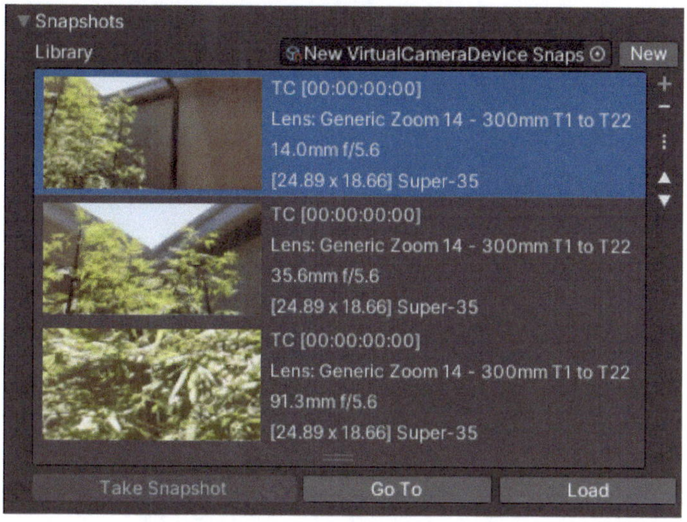

***Figure 16.5**: Different shots in the library*

Stereoscopic vision

Stereoscopic vision is a technique that combines two images, which the human brain is capable of integrating into one, resulting in a three-dimensional image. When both eyes adjust the lens to correctly focus on an object, both optical axes converge on the object being looked at. For the purpose of this procedure, binocular vision and stereoscopy are employed, as shown in the following figure:

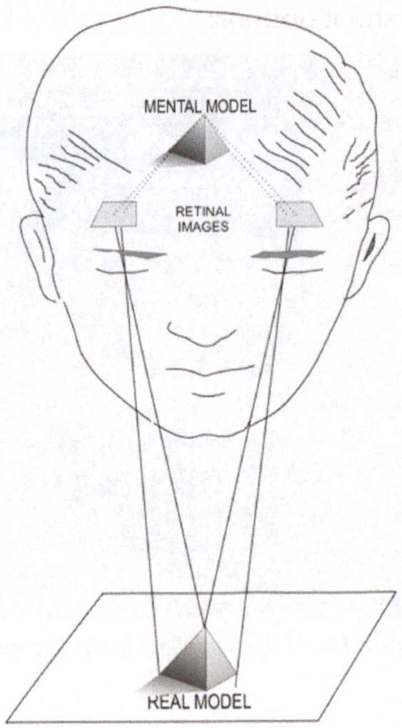

Figure 16.6: *Scheme of how the 3D mental model is formed from binocular vision*

Source: *Psychophysical Approach to the Measurement of Depth Perception in Stereo Vision:* ***https://www.researchgate.net/publication/221095819_Psychophysical_Approach_to_the_Measurement_of_Depth_Perception_in_Stereo_Vision***

This ability develops during childhood since it takes time for the brain to learn to combine all the information of a 3D world. It is generally believed that stereoscopic vision is not fully acquired until the age of 12.

James Cameron used two cameras, slightly separated and slightly rotated, to simulate the position of each of our eyes.

If, when the final movie is played, we get each eye to see only the playback of the video captured on the corresponding camera, we will get the brain to process the two images naturally, and we will see it in 3 dimensions.

Stereoscopic projection

Several techniques have been developed over time to display 3D images, taking advantage of different principles of stereoscopy, autostereoscopy, and holography. Let us look at some of the most widely recognized techniques.

Anaglyph 3D

Anaglyph 3D employs color filtering to produce a stereoscopic effect. Two images are juxtaposed and filtered with varying hues, typically red and cyan, as shown in the following figure:

Figure 16.7: *Gizmo reading a 3D's comic with 3D glasses*

Let us see how it is implemented:

- **Separate images**: Two slightly shifted images, one for each eye, are merged into one.
    - The red-cyan glasses filter the combined image so that each eye sees only one overlapping image.
    - The brain combines the two images to create a 3D effect: depth perception.

Some advantages are:

- It is economical because it only requires basic-colored glasses.
- Compatible with all standard screens and prints.

The negative aspects are:

- Color distortion affects the color of the image, reducing its quality.
- Ghosting can arise when the two images are incorrectly superimposed.
- Applications include the first 3D movies, educational materials, and 3D comics.

3D polarization

Polarized 3D uses polarization filters to separate the two images intended for each eye from the others.

It operates when two images are projected simultaneously on the screen, each of which has a different polarization (for example, one horizontal and one vertical).

Glasses, with their corresponding polarized lenses, filter images so that each eye only sees one image.

Figure 16.8: The polarized glasses are the most used

Its advantages are:

- Natural colors ensure the color consistency of images.
- High resolution provides higher image resolution than anaglyph.

The cons are:

- The use of a special silver screen is necessary to maintain polarization.
- The limited viewing angles may result in a decrease in image quality when viewed from extreme angles.
- Applications include contemporary 3D cinemas, 3D televisions, and virtual reality headsets.

Many other 3D projection and visualization systems (such as the parallax barrier used in the Nintendo 3DS) exist, but we are going to focus on these two because we can replicate something very similar in our virtual reality glasses.

As you can see, the technique consists of playing two videos at the same time in the same space. However, it is necessary to filter the frames that each eye can see.

In this chapter, we will play two videos in the 360 format in the same sphere, but taking advantage of the fact that we have a **virtual reality** (**VR**) helmet, we will filter what each eye sees to create a depth effect.

Stereoscopic capture

Currently, it is much more convenient to produce high-quality 3D captures, and there exists a diverse range of manufacturers and pricing options. We shall examine three recent examples.

Acer SpatialLabs Eyes

The Acer SpatialLabs Eyes is a small and portable camera, which weighs just over 200 grams. It is capable of offering a resolution of 4K per eye (3840 x 2160 at 30 fps), exceptional for 3D cameras in this price range (about €550). The camera is shown in the following figure:

Figure 16.9: You can find 3D cameras with surprising quality at very competitive prices

If you record at 60 fps, the resolution decreases, although you can always do software scaling or interpolation.

Some of the interesting additional features are electronic image stabilization, automatic or manual focus (touch), and software for real-time streaming or 3D calls.

On the website, you can download some examples of 3D photos and a short video. Apart from serving as advertising to show the quality that this camera offers, it may be very interesting for the project that we will do later in this chapter, where you will need some 3-dimensional video (they are not always easy to obtain).

Canon RF 5.2mm f/2.8 Dual Fisheye[3]

Canon's approach is different. This brand has developed a lens for its reflex camera, the Canon EOS R5, with very high-quality definition and lots of luminosity. The system is designed especially for the Apple Vision Pro, which has a resolution of around 14K (or around 100 megapixels):

3 You can find an interesting report about the Canon Dual Fisheye here: Dual Fisheye: https://global.canon/en/technology/interview/vrlens/index.html

***Figure 16.10**: Example of a 3D lens for a reflex camera*

In cameras of this type, as shown in the following figure, the viewfinder allows you to see perfectly what is being recorded for each eye. This will allow us to create the 3D effect later:

***Figure 16.11**: Detail of what the viewfinder looks like when capturing with the lens*

The main advantage of this system over others is that when two cameras are used, the final product is two files that must be post-processed (something quite slow and tedious) before being able to enjoy a 180° VR file, which is just what it offers us.

Blackmagic URSA Cine Immersive

On a professional level, we already find the recently presented Blackmagic camera, which is described as *the first commercial camera system for Apple Immersive Video.*

This camera features a built-in fixed lens system for recording in Apple Immersive Video. The lenses have the highest resolution in this small comparison: 8160 x 7200 for each eye, with pixel-level synchronization. Cinematographers will be able to record immersive stereoscopic 3D images at 90 fps in a single file.

***Figure 16.12**: The latest in cameras specially designed for the Apple Vision Pro*

This exceptional hardware has software to support it, and a future update to the prestigious DaVinci Resolve video editing program will incorporate amazing new tools that will allow the creation of complex workflows in order to achieve immersive images for Apple Vision Pro. The program will include a new immersive viewer that will give editors the ability to rotate images vertically and horizontally, and rotate them for viewing on 2D monitors or Apple Vision Pro devices, which will be an even more immersive experience. Transitions made on Apple Vision Pro devices can be removed using **Final Cut Pro XML** (**FCP XML**) file metadata.

In conclusion, this camera not only provides an exceptional image but also facilitates the post-production process, allowing content creators to take their productions to the next level using the Apple Vision Pro.

Stereoscopic video formats and process

In the following figure, you can see what a stereoscopic photo looks like. It is like a photo repeated to the right and left, but if you look closely, you can notice that some distances are smaller due to the distance between the two lenses that took the photo to simulate the interocular distance. Some reference points in red have been marked to make it easier to see the change in angle from one eye to the other, giving us the sensation of depth. It is possible that images appear up and down instead of right and left:

***Figure 16.13**: Notable differences in distances are highlighted in red*

In the preceding figure, you can observe what a stereoscopic photo looks like. It looks like a photo repeated to the right and left, but if you look closely, you can notice that some distances are smaller due to the distance between the two lenses that took the photo to simulate the interocular distance. Some reference points in red have been marked to make it easier to see. It is possible that images appear up and down instead of right and left.

Due to the large number of containers and codecs that exist, video can be much more complicated. Furthermore, we must also take into account the 180° and 360° formats that are widely used for VR.

Unity has attempted to simplify the file import process. When we drag and drop a file, it converts it to the format it uses internally. If we are downloading an audio file (mp3, wav), it automatically converts it to OggVorbis.

This is not always the case with video formats, as a result of the numerous video formats that exist between containers and codecs. When we ask for a special format like 360 stereoscopic. In numerous instances, it may be necessary to manually convert them into the format that is most suitable for our purposes.

For video conversion, there is a fantastic tool that is also free: **Fast Forward Motion Picture Expert (FFMPEG)**.

FFMPEG, the premier tool for video conversion

FFMPEG is a powerful open-source multimedia framework used for processing video, audio, and other multimedia files and streams. You use it as a command-line tool, but in reality, it is a complete set of libraries and tools.

For maximum optimization and portability, it is developed in C. It is compatible with most operating systems, including Windows, macOS, and Linux.

Some common useful functionalities of FFMPEG are their prompts:

- **Convert a video format**: `ffmpeg -i input.mp4 output.avi`
- **Extract audio from a video**: `ffmpeg -i input.mp4 -q:a 0 -map a output.mp3`
- **Resize a video**: `ffmpeg -i input.mp4 -vf scale=1280:720 output.mp4`
- **Add a watermark**: `ffmpeg -i input.mp4 -i watermark.png -filter_complex "overlay=10:10" output.mp4`
- **Stream a video**: `ffmpeg -i input.mp4 -f flv rtmp://streamingserver/live`

FFMPEG can be used for many tasks; in fact, Unity uses it internally to convert between different platforms. However, we are going to focus on Stereo3D[4] video content, which is the focus of this chapter.

4 If you want to go deeper, at this page will find all the FFMPEG related information: FFMPEG Stereo3D: https://ffmpeg.org/doxygen/trunk/group__lavu__video__stereo3d.html

These are some of the most useful commands when you have to convert a 3D video:

1. `ffmpeg -i input.m2ts -filter_complex "[0]crop=iw/2:ih:0:0[left];[0]crop=iw/2:ih:ow:0[right]" -map "[left]" -map 0:a left.mp4 -map "[right]" -map 0:a right.mp4`
2.
3.
4. `ffmpeg -i VG.mp4 -filter_complex "[0]crop=ih/2:ih:0:0[left];[0]crop=ih/2:ih:ow:0[right]" -map "[left]" -map 0:a leftVG.mp4 -map "[right]" -map 0:a rightVG.mp4`

Stereoscopic picture and video in Unity

We have already seen the principles of stereoscopic images. Now, we are going to port that into Unity to make a viewer that allows us to enjoy depth with a virtual reality headset.

We are going to do this example with the Meta SDK (although the concepts can be used in other systems). The first thing you will need to do is open the Unity editor, go to the package manager window, and install the Meta XR All-in-One SDK package:

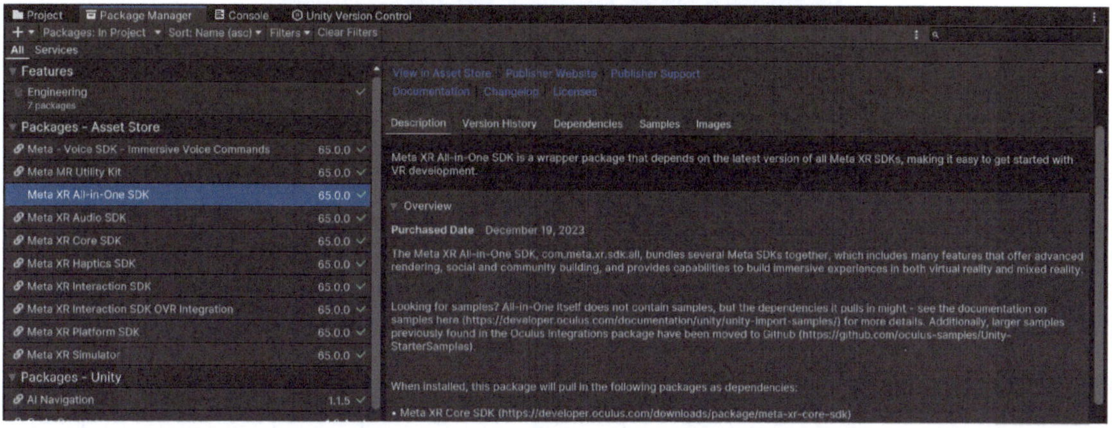

***Figure 16.14**: Package Manager installing Meta SDK*

Next, we will install the samples to have a scene to start with, and we will make sure that the project is correct from the window **Meta** | **Tools** | **Project Setup Tool**.

Click on **Fix all issues** to correct any possible problem.

If everything has gone correctly, we will be able to see and open the examples provided by Meta, so that we can experiment and learn how its SDK works. You will find them in the project folders.

Open some of the sample scenes and examine their structure in the Hierarchy window. Pay special attention to the nodes highlighted in the following image: **LeftEyeAnchor**, **RightEyeAnchor**:

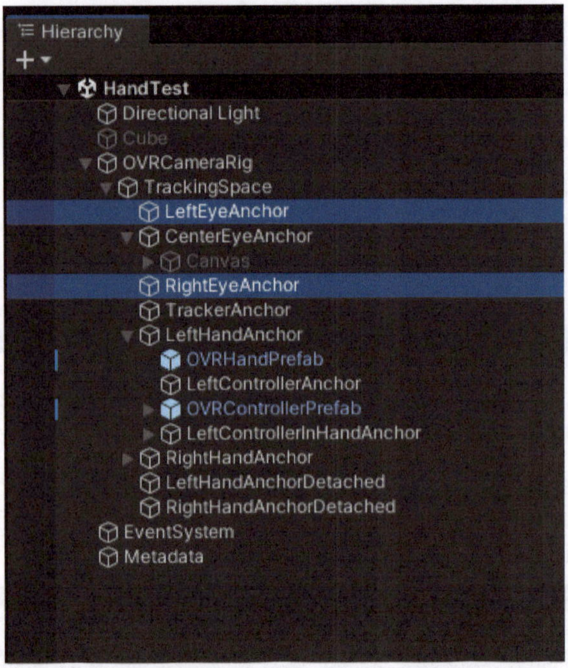

***Figure 16.15:** The two objects that we are going to use are selected*

By default, **CenterEyeAnchor** is activated, which generates the same image for both eyes (simply because it is more efficient to make one image than two), but what we want in this case is to create two different images for each eye. Therefore, we are going to proceed as follows: Each of these nodes contains a camera component; we must deactivate the CenterEyeAnchor camera and activate the two LeftEyeAnchor and RightEyeCamera cameras.

What we are going to achieve with this is to have two cameras, one for each eye, that will calculate and render what each eye sees separately. You must also make sure that the dropdown below (target eye) corresponds correctly with the eye and camera that we are configuring, as shown in the following figure:

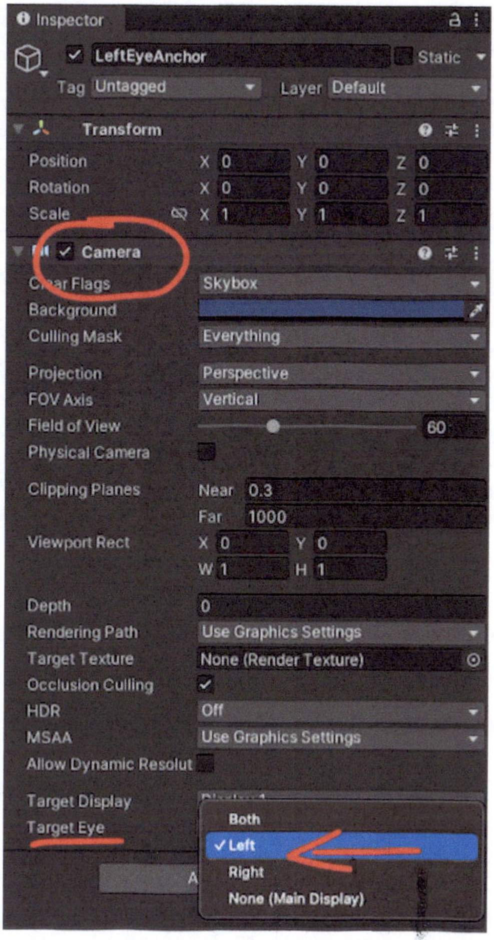

***Figure 16.16**: Select the target eye for the camera (left in this case)*

Now, the problem centers on what we project and how we get the camera to filter only what we want. Unity has a very simple way that allows us to select what each camera should render: the culling mask.

The culling mask is a drop-down menu from which we select which layers are rendered by the camera. So, for it to work, we will first have to create two layers that we are going to call leftEye and rightEye.

Select the layers drop-down (top right of the editor) and select the **Edit Layers...** option.

If you have followed the steps correctly up to this point, you should have the normal layers of the project, and you will have added two new ones, as seen in the following figure:

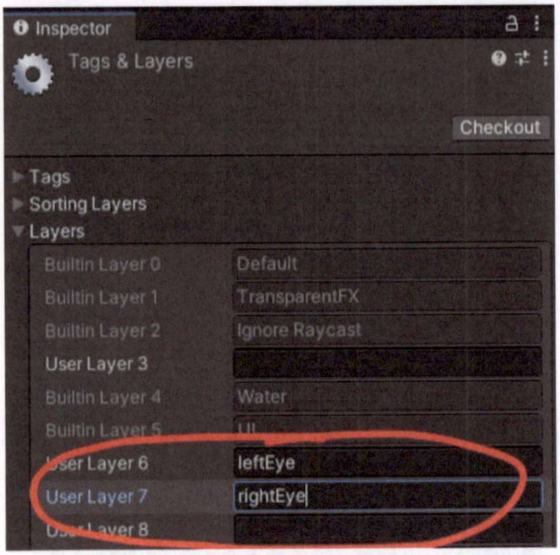

Figure 16.17: *Create a layer for each eye*

For everything to work well, we will have to return to the eye-facing camera and make it clear what it will see and what it will not.

In this camera (which corresponds to the right eye), the leftEye layer has been explicitly deselected to ensure that it will not be rendered, and rightEye has been selected. We will do the opposite in the left eye camera (deselect rightEye and select leftEye), as shown in the following figure:

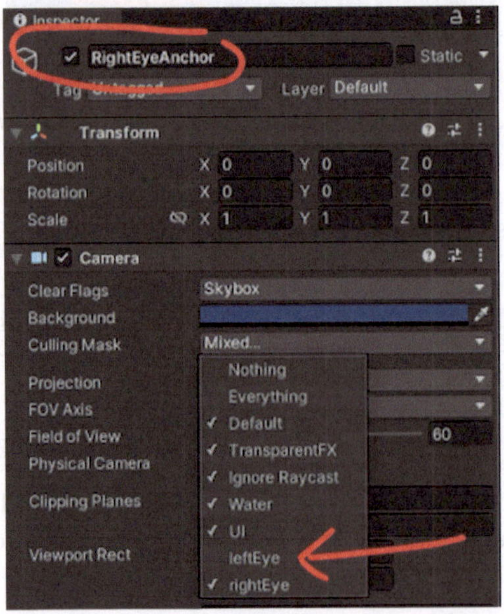

Figure 16.18: *We make sure that the Camera does not render the layer that we do not want*

With this configuration, we already have the base prepared. Now we just need to make sure the elements are on the right layer.

Let us look at a simple example. We will use one of the sample photos downloaded from the Acer camera. Using a photo editing program, we have split the original image precisely in half to create two separate images—one for each eye—which we then import into the Unity project's **Assets** folder:

***Figure 16.19**: The appearance of both images is similar but each one corresponds to an eye*

The original image was 7680x2160 pixels. So, we divided it to obtain two images of 3840 x 2160. Note that they are slightly different (the man's back is a good reference point with the house that can be seen in the background).

The following steps are simple:

- Create a plane (**Game Object** menu | **3D Object** | **Plane**).
- **Scale to the correct proportions**: We have scaled it so that it has the same proportion as the photo; otherwise, it would look deformed. If we divide the resolution x by y, we obtain the following proportion:

  3840/2160 = 1.77

  That is the scale we must set. To assign the image, we only have to drag and drop on the plane (remember that it is only visible on one side, and you may have to turn it around). Select the plane and change the scale:

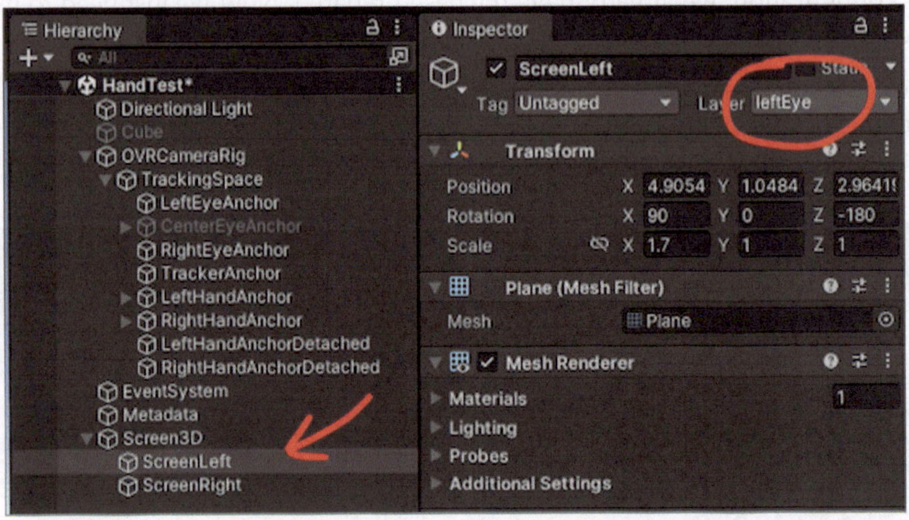

***Figure 16.20**: Creating a plane for left and another for right eyes*

- Once you have correctly located the plane in the 3D world, assign it the layer corresponding to the image.

The following figure shows that everything is already working correctly. You can see the Unity camera representing the user's head position, along with separate thumbnail previews for the left and right eyes—each displaying a slightly different image, as expected in a stereoscopic setup. When we put on the virtual reality headset, we will be able to see the image in depth as if we had it in front of us:

***Figure 16.21**: The Camera will render two different images that are projected to each viewer of the VR glasses*

This system works perfectly for both photos and rectangular videos, but let us see what happens if it is a 360 video.

Stereoscopic 360 video in Unity

For a 360 video to look good, it must be projected against a sphere (like when you go to the planetarium). The problem comes from the fact that Unity spheres are only rendered from the outside, not from the inside. For it to work, the normals of the polygons that make up the sphere must be inverted.

Figure 16.22: *A 360 video playing inside a Sphere*

This objective can be achieved by creating a geometry with inverted normals or with a shader specially designed for that purpose, as shown in the following figure:

```
Shader "Flip Normals" {
    Properties {
        _MainTex ("Base (RGB)", 2D) = "white" {}
    }
    SubShader {

        Tags { "RenderType" = "Opaque" }

        Cull Off

        CGPROGRAM
```

```

        #pragma surface surf Lambert vertex:vert
        sampler2D _MainTex;

        struct Input {
            float2 uv_MainTex;
            float4 color : COLOR;
        };

        void vert(inout appdata_full v) {
            v.normal.xyz = v.normal * -1;
        }

        void surf (Input IN, inout SurfaceOutput o) {
             fixed3 result = tex2D(_MainTex, IN.uv_MainTex);
             o.Albedo = result.rgb;
             o.Alpha = 1;
        }
        ENDCG
    }

    Fallback "Diffuse"
}
```

3D production for VR

The technique that we have seen in this chapter can reach truly incredible professional levels.

Surely, the most prestigious studio in the world is **https://www.felixandpaul.com**, which has created 360 3D content of a quality never seen before. A great example of this is the documentary series called *Meta Space Explorers*, where you can live the experience of being on the International Space Station in first person. This app can be found in the Meta App Store. It is free and one of the most incredible immersive experiences you can experience. You can see a frame of the series, as shown in the following figure:

Figure 16.23: Meta Space Explorers is a 3D 360 video documentary series

Conclusion

This chapter delved into the realm of stereoscopic vision, encompassing the entire process from capturing images to post-processing videos. It elucidated the implementation of this technique within Unity 3D, thereby achieving an immersive experience with virtual reality headsets. We also looked at *James Cameron's* groundbreaking innovations in 3D filmmaking, employing the dual camera system, which revolutionized the movie industry. The virtual camera system, which provides precise control over a camera within a virtual environment, utilizing real-time data from a connected device such as an iPhone, was also examined. The chapter elucidated the principles of stereoscopic vision, explaining how the brain merges two images into a single three-dimensional perception. Various methods for displaying 3D images were explored, including anaglyph 3D (utilizing color filtering with red and cyan glasses) and polarized 3D (utilizing polarized filters to separate images), and numerous 3D capture devices were presented, such as the Acer SpatialLabs Eyes camera, the Canon RF 5.2mm f/2.8 Dual Fisheye lens, and the Blackmagic URSA Cine Immersive camera. The chapter also covered the utilization of FFMPEG for video conversion, specifically for converting 3D videos into formats compatible with Unity. Finally, the chapter showcased how to project a 360 video onto a sphere with inverted normals using a shader within Unity. The chapter's objective was to establish a comprehensive foundation for the creation of immersive virtual reality experiences.

In the forthcoming chapter, the reader will delve into the realm of AI and its multifaceted applications within the Unity 3D platform. The chapter will elucidate the utilization of tools such as ChatGPT, DALL-E, and Whisper, empowering game developers to enhance their creations through text generation, image creation, and audio transcription. Furthermore, the chapter will provide insights into Unity Enterprises' implementation of AI solutions specifically tailored for Unity in the upcoming version of the editor. The chapter will demonstrate the indispensable role of AI as a pivotal ally in both technological and creative endeavors.

Multiple choice questions

1. **How is the perception of depth and three-dimensional space achieved when viewing stereoscopic images through a VR headset?**
   a. By utilizing the lens focusing mechanism of the headset.
   b. By applying a Tonemapping algorithm to the color profile.
   c. By merging two slightly offset images presented to the left and right eye.
   d. By rendering the scene at an ultra-high frame rate (48 frames per second).
2. **Which of the following are benefits explicitly attributed to the incorporation of stereoscopic images in a VR application?**
   a. Facilitating the creation of user-generated content (UGC).
   b. Augmenting the user's sense of presence and engagement.
   c. Alleviating motion sickness and user discomfort.
   d. Automatically adjusting graphical settings based on device temperature.
3. **The fusion chamber system, developed for films like Avatar, revolutionized 3D cinematography primarily through the use of which core technique?**
   a. Positional voice chat synchronization.
   b. Real-time data streaming from remote cloud servers.
   c. A dual camera setup to simulate a human binocular perspective.
   d. Automated server-side recording for content moderation.
4. **In Unity VR development using the Meta SDK to achieve a stereoscopic view, which component nodes must be activated to calculate and render distinct images for each eye?**
   a. MainCameraAnchor and FocusDepthAnchor
   b. LeftEyeAnchor and RightEyeAnchor
   c. CenterEyeAnchor and VirtualCamera
   d. PostProcessLayer and CullingMask
5. **When configuring a Unity scene for stereoscopic viewing, what specialized mechanism is used in conjunction with two distinct layers (e.g., leftEye and rightEye) to ensure each camera only renders the content intended for its corresponding eye?**
   a. The tonemapping effect in the post-processing profile.
   b. The Animation Event triggered by a Keyframe.

c. The Virtual Camera Follow/LookAt properties.

d. The Culling Mask property of the Camera component.

6. **Which display technique requires using glasses with distinct red and cyan filters to merge two slightly shifted images into a single perceived 3D image, while noting that a negative aspect is color distortion?**

   a. 3D Polarization

   b. Anaglyph 3D

   c. Parallax Barrier

   d. Holography

7. **Which open-source multimedia framework, usable as a command-line tool, is explicitly recommended for developers who need to manually convert 3D videos into formats suitable for Unity integration, such as separating combined stereoscopic video streams?**

   a. Unity Package Manager (UPM)

   b. FFMPEG

   c. Blender Video Sequence Editor (VSE)

   d. DaVinci Resolve

8. **When projecting a 360 stereoscopic video inside a Unity sphere for viewing in VR, what required geometric manipulation must be performed, often achieved using a specialized shader?**

   a. Applying the Bloom effect to the sphere's material.

   b. Inverting the normals of the sphere's polygons.

   c. Utilizing a blend tree to interpolate the video textures.

   d. Scaling the plane object to match the aspect ratio of the video.

9. **A developer is using the Unity Virtual Camera App on their iPhone during the rehearsal of a cinematic sequence. Which of the following data points is the App capable of providing in real-time to control the virtual camera in the Unity Editor?**

   a. Motion capture data for the actor's bone structure.

   b. Real-time network latency and bandwidth usage statistics.

   c. Focal length, position, and rotation of the device.

   d. The total number of GPU shader operations per frame.

10. **The Blackmagic URSA Cine Immersive camera system is noted for supporting the Apple Vision Pro by providing extremely high-resolution immersive stereoscopic 3D images. What technical feature related to image timing does this camera achieve to ensure quality?**

    a. Automated real-time deployment via Cloud Build pipelines.

    b. Pixel-level synchronization between the lenses for each eye.

    c. Compatibility with Intel-64 bit architecture using Rosetta.

    d. Dynamic adjustment of graphics settings based on device thermal status.

Answers

1	c
2	b, c
3	c
4	b
5	d
6	b
7	b
8	b
9	c
10	b

Join our Discord space

Join our Discord workspace for latest updates, offers, tech happenings around the world, new releases, and sessions with the authors:

https://discord.bpbonline.com

CHAPTER 17
Artificial Inteligence and Unity 3D

Introduction

Artificial intelligence (**AI**) has advanced significantly, influencing technology and society. This chapter explores AI's applications, focusing on its use within Unity 3D. **Large language models** (**LLMs**) like ChatGPT, Llama, Gemini, Gemma, and Phi-3 are AI designed to process and generate natural language. Choosing the correct model is important as models are trained to perform specific functions under certain conditions.

Ollama is an open-source LLM management system designed to simplify the process of running, tuning, and deploying language models locally.

AI tools such as ComfyUI for image generation and Udio for audio generation are also discussed. ComfyUI simplifies the image generation process using neural networks, with a focus on stable diffusion, using a node-based visual interface. Udio facilitates the creation of audio generation workflows.

Hugging Face, a platform for AI models and datasets, is covered. Hugging Face provides tools, libraries, and resources for AI model creation and collaboration.

The chapter discusses integrating AI tools like ChatGPT, DALL-E, and Whisper into Unity 3D to enhance game development. ChatGPT enables developers to quickly create dialogues and conversations between NPCs and players, saving time and resources. AI-powered conversational agents can understand and respond to natural language input, personalizing the game experience by adapting content based on players' preferences.

Structure

This chapter covers the following topics:

- Introduction to artificial intelligence
    - Large language model
    - Ollama

    - ConfUI
    - UDIO
    - Hugging Face
- ChatGPT
- Unofficial Unity package
    - Setting up the Unity package
    - DALL-E
    - Whisper
- Other LLMS
    - DeepSeek-R2
    - Qwen
    - Mistral

Objectives

In this chapter, readers will learn about the practical applications of AI in technology, specifically focusing on its use within Unity 3D. Readers will gain practical skills relating to key AI resources, including **large language models** (**LLMs**). They will learn how to use these models to process and generate natural language. They will also learn about Ollama, an open-source LLM management system for running and deploying language models locally. Readers will also explore Hugging Face, a prominent platform for AI models and datasets. A key focus will be on integrating AI in Unity 3D, using tools like ChatGPT for generating text, DALL-E for creating images, and Whisper for transcribing audio, therefore enhancing game development. Readers will learn how to use ChatGPT to create dialogues and conversations between NPCs and players, build conversational agents, and personalize game experiences.

Introduction to artificial intelligence

The following section will comment on several important resources to introduce the main AI resources that exist. It is intended as a general first approach, but it may be interesting to learn about other technologies external to Unity 3D.

Large language model

ChatGPT is a **large language model** (**LLM**). A large language model is a type of AI that is designed to process and generate natural language. It is trained on extensive data sets comprising text from books, articles, websites, and other sources, allowing it to acquire the patterns, structures, and nuances of human language.

There are many other LLMs. *Meta*, a very active company in AI, has a model called LLaMA, and it is one of the most used because its license is very open. Google has created Gemini and, recently, Gemma, Microsoft, Phi-3, and Florence.

There are various models, and it is important to choose the correct one because it has been trained with specific data to perform a specific function under certain conditions (for example, Phi3 is designed to be used with little memory).

ChatGPT, as shown in *Figure 17.1*, OpenAI's artificial intelligence based on LLMs, was the one that started the AI craze that is now spreading across all industries:

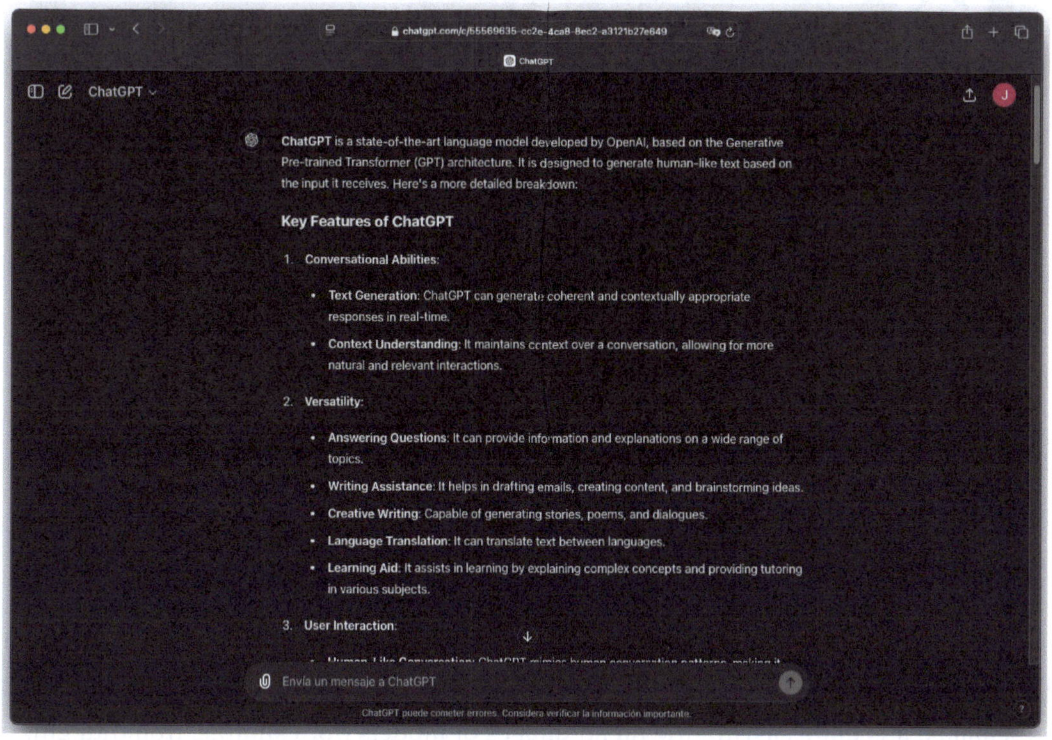

Figure 17.1: ChatGPT

Ollama

Once the models have been trained, they can be deployed for use. We normally use ChatGPT from their website, but it can also be done on a local computer/server.

Ollama is an open-source LLM management system designed to make it easier to run, tune, and deploy language models. Created by Ollama, it provides a set of tools to handle several large language models, including Meta's Ollama models and others, all within a scalable, easy-to-use environment.

Many times, this type of development is used from Docker images in containers. This makes it easier to have everything you need already perfectly configured and working with the correct versions within the container.

You can download a Docker image with Ollama preinstalled:

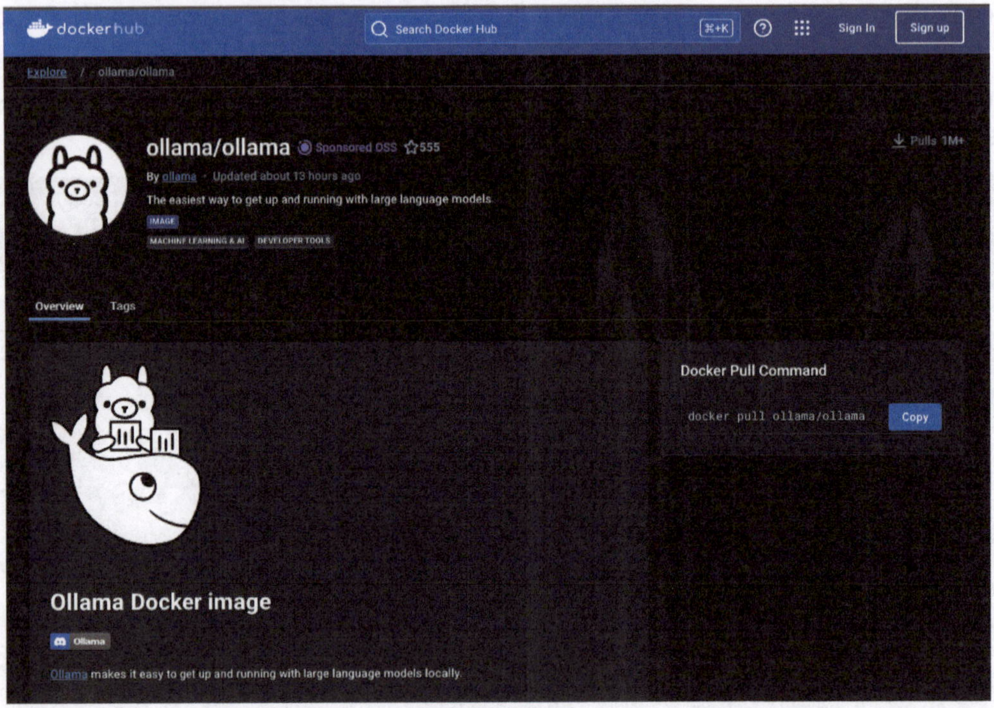

Figure 17.2: Ollama could be used from a Docker image

Ollama has aquite popular web interface that is normally used when installed locally. It is quite similar to ChatGPT but runs on your local server.

With Ollama, it is quite easy to download images of models (for example, from huggingface.co) and implement them on our computer.

It is very important to see the number of parameters and the memory they will occupy. Normally, the graphics card or **graphics processing unit** (**GPU**) is used for its great capacity to execute code in parallel. The latest **Reduced Instructions Set Computer** (**RISC**) technology processors also incorporate a **neural process unit** (**NPU**). This is the case of the Snapdragon Elite X. In the case of Apple's Silicon processors, it is called Neural Engine.

There is a feature of Apple processors that allows you to work with much more complex models: unified memory.

There are some models that are really heavy. As Apple's Silicon processors allow all memory to be accessible by its CPU, GPU, and the Neural Engine, it is capable of loading and operating models up to 128 GigaBytes. (The new M4 will be even more). In a PC environment with a graphics card, the models are limited to the memory size of the graphics card (about 24 Gbytes). Obviously, there are professional cards with more memory, but their cost can be that of the Mac multiplied by 10.

ComfyUI

Another of the star functions of AI is the generation of images and videos from a prompt.

There are many platforms and models, but we have selected ComfyUI since it can also be installed locally and is very popular.

ComfyUI is a flexible and modular tool designed to simplify the image generation process using neural networks, particularly focusing on stable diffusion. Provides a node-based visual interface that allows users to create complex imaging workflows. Here is an in-depth look at what ComfyUI offers.

ComfyUI is designed to make image generation accessible and intuitive, using a node-based approach where users can connect different components to create complex workflows. It is highly adaptable and caters to a wide range of imaging tasks, from artistic creations to practical applications. In the following figure, you can see the visual interface of ComfyUI:

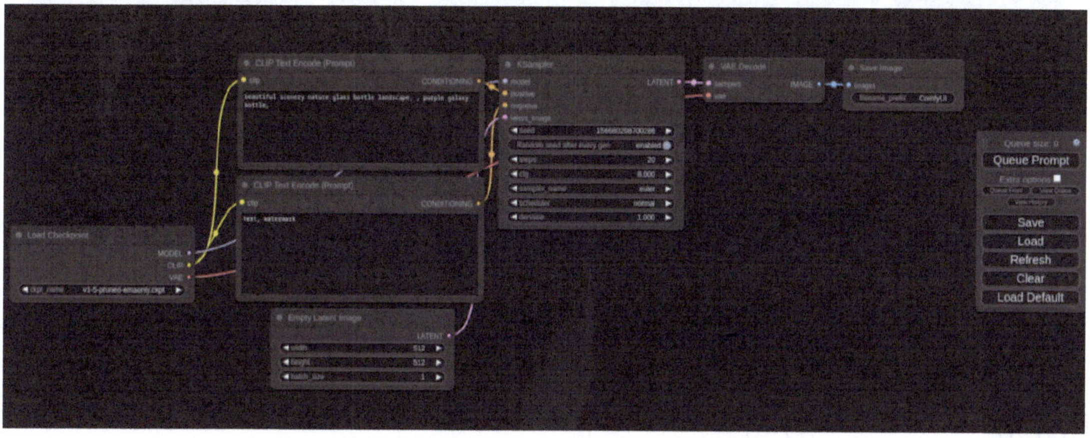

***Figure 17.3**: The ComfyUI use a node diagram style very easy to learn*

Udio

Since we have AI tools for generating images and video, they also exist for creating sounds, sound effects, and music.

This tool can be extremely useful for helping us create sound effects for our next graphic adventure or for playing a catchy melody that improves the experience of our new game.

Udio offers a visual interface based on nodes that facilitates the creation of audio generation workflows. It allows users to create, transform, and combine audio tracks and effects, making it suitable for various applications. The tool emphasizes simplicity of use, flexibility, and real-time feedback:

***Figure 17.4:** Audio helps a lot with musical creation through the selection of styles*

Hugging Face

Hugging Face (**www.huggingface.co**) is a prominent platform and community dedicated to the fields of **natural language processing** (NLP) and **machine learning** (ML). It provides a variety of tools, libraries, and resources for the creation, dissemination, and collaboration of AI models and applications:

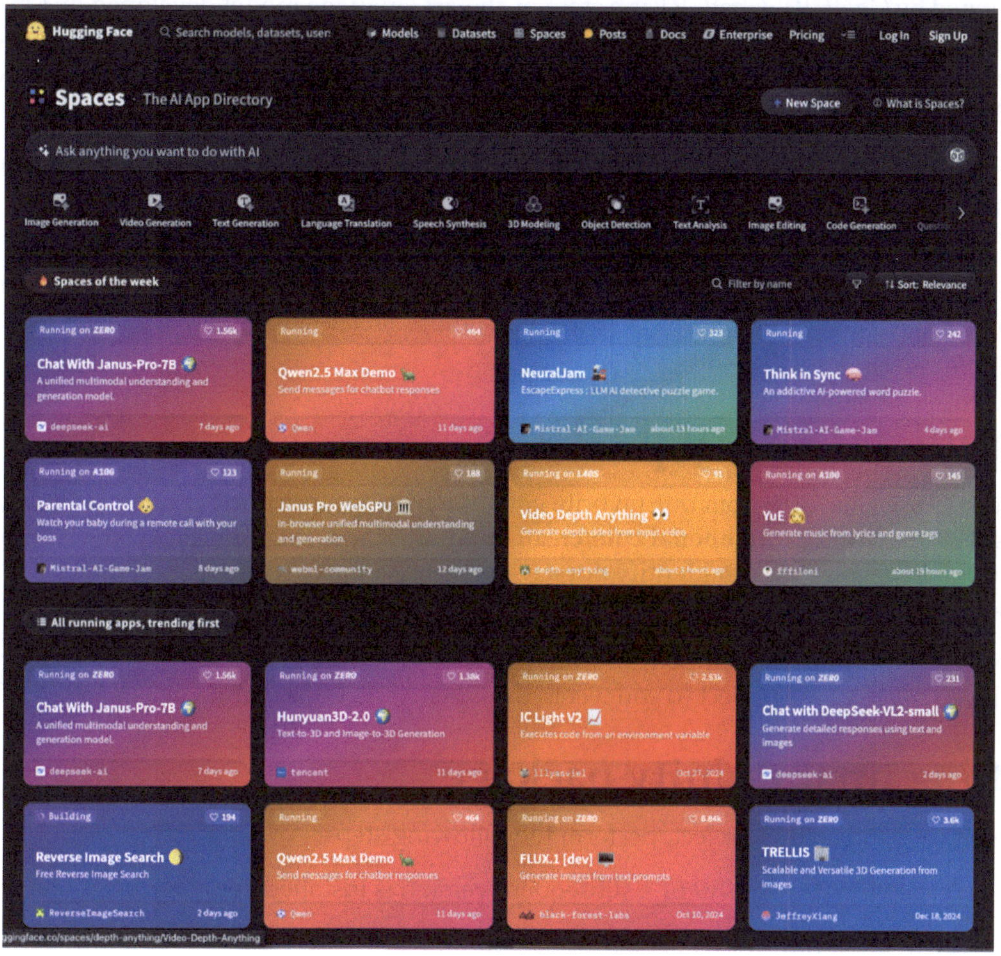

Figure 17.5: *The Hugging Face is one of the best repositories with models and datasets*

At the time of writing this page on Hugging Face, there are 25,150 trained models and 5815 Datasets.

ChatGPT

ChatGPT is, without a doubt, the most famous representative of AI and one of the most advanced and widely used in the world. OpenAI, the company that developed it, has signed a collaboration agreement with Microsoft and Apple to implement it in their operating systems. So, we are going to pay special attention to it, but it is not, by any means, the only one. There are currently more than 30,000 AI models that are very similar and, in some cases, better than ChatGPT.

As defined by ChatGPT, ChatGPT is a state-of-the-art language model developed by OpenAI, based on the **generative pre-trained transformer** (**GPT**) architecture. It is designed to generate human-like text based on the input it receives. You can find all the OpenAI documentation at this Address: **https://platform.openai.com/docs/api-reference/introduction**

ChatGPT is an LLM and is, therefore, able to *understand* and respond to questions asked in human language. We can ask it questions of any type, and it will be able to answer us in a coherent and structured way, although sometimes it makes things up.

Aside from its website, ChatGPT can be used via a **Representational Exchange State Transfer** (**REST**) API and can, therefore, be used on almost any modern development platform, including, unsurprisingly, Unity 3D.

Unofficial Unity package

In order to use ChatGPT from our favorite game's editor, we must first register as developers on its website: **https://auth.openai.com/create-account**. The most important thing is that they give us two codes so we can identify ourselves when we make requests. These codes are the API key and the organization ID.

Once we are officially developers, we are going to use a GitHub project that has already developed much of the project to connect to the OpenAI API (the company behind ChatGPT).

Setting up the Unity package

To begin working on this project, perform the following steps:

- Ensure that Unity 2019 or a subsequent version is installed.
- Go to the **Windows** | **Package Manager**.
- To add a package from the Git URL, click the + button.
- Copy the repository URL: **https://github.com/srcnalt/OpenAI-Unity.git** and click **Add**.

In the package details, you can find a samples section (to the far right, as seen in the following figure). Be sure to also import any examples you want to test or explore:

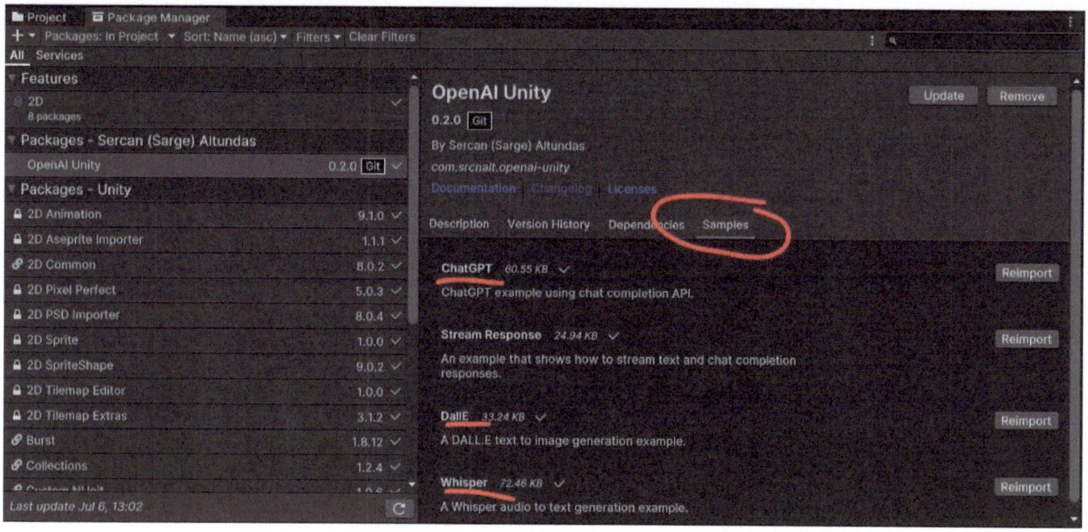

***Figure 17.6**: Details of how to install the package and the samples*

The package is already correctly installed, but it will require our credentials to make requests to the OpenAI API. This package requires us to store our keys in a JSON file in a specific location on our local computer.

- If you are developing for Linux or Mac, please go to the folder: **`~\`**
- If you are engaged in Windows development, kindly navigate to the folder named **`C:\Users\Username`**.

In the folder, create another folder called **`.openai`**, and inside it, create a file called **`auth.json`** with a code editor.

Add an **`api_key`** field and an organization field to the **`auth.json`** file and save it.

The values for these two fields, **`api_key`** and organization, can be found on the Open AI website, in the organization section: **https://platform.openai.com/settings/organization/general**

You can create also an **`api_key`** for each project: **https://platform.openai.com/settings/organization/api-keys**

The following is an illustration of how your **`auth.json`** file should appear:

```
{
    "api_key": "sk-...W4PF",
    "organization": "org-...JAF"
}
```

If you have done all the steps, you are now ready to use the OpenAI API within your Unity project. Let us see an example of what the code for a request would be like:

```
var req = new CreateChatCompletionRequest{
    Model = "gpt-3.5-turbo",
    Messages = new List<ChatMessage>
    {
        new ChatMessage()
        {
            Role = "Unity 3D developer",
            Content = "Write me a script to rotate objects on the 3 axis."
        }
    },
    Temperature = 0.7f,
};
private OpenAIApi openai = new OpenAIApi();
openai.CreateChatCompletionAsync(req,
    (responses) => {
        var result = string.Join("", responses.Select(response => response.Choices[0].Delta.Content));
        Debug.Log(result);
    },
    () => {
        Debug.Log("completed");
    },
    new CancellationTokenSource()
);
```

Now, you can use the power of ChatGPT AI to ask you all kinds of questions, write you some texts, or help you make some functions and some code.

Like most artificial intelligences, you get a few free credits and then have to pay for it. Make sure you have enough credits to keep everything running smoothly.

However, from the same package, you can also access other functionalities such as DALL-E or Whisper.

DALL-E

According to ChatGPT itself, *DALL-E is an advanced artificial intelligence model developed by OpenAI, designed to generate images from textual descriptions. Leveraging deep learning techniques, DALL-E creates unique and coherent images based on the entered text, allowing for creative and versatile image generation.*

This functionality is useful for any Unity developer. Imagine, for example, that you have just downloaded a 3D model, but its textures do not convince you once it is placed on the stage. We can ask DALL-E to make us a new texture that is also tileable so that it fits us perfectly.

Let us see it with an example. Open the Scene that comes in the example located in the folder **`Samples/OpenAi Unity/0.2.0/DallE`**:

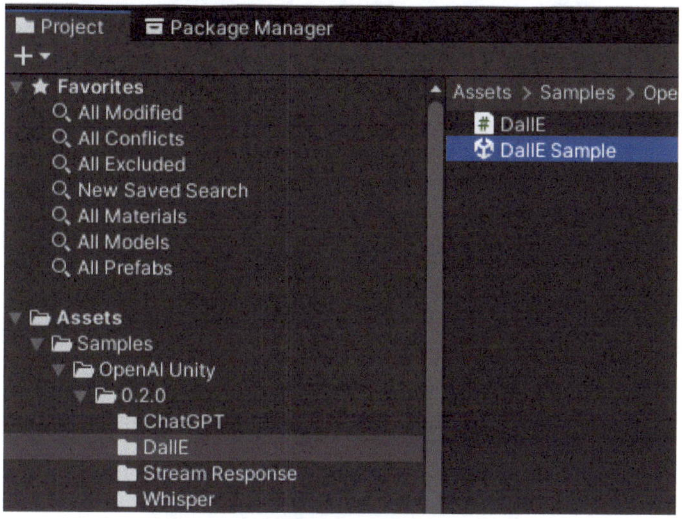

***Figure 17.7:** Detail of the installed package and its folders*

When you run this project, a blank square image will appear, and below it will be a field to send a prompt.

Write something similar to this prompt (although it is encouraged to test everything you want later): **`a Caribbean pirate with a parrot`**. As soon as you press the **Send** button, the following image will appear in the box:

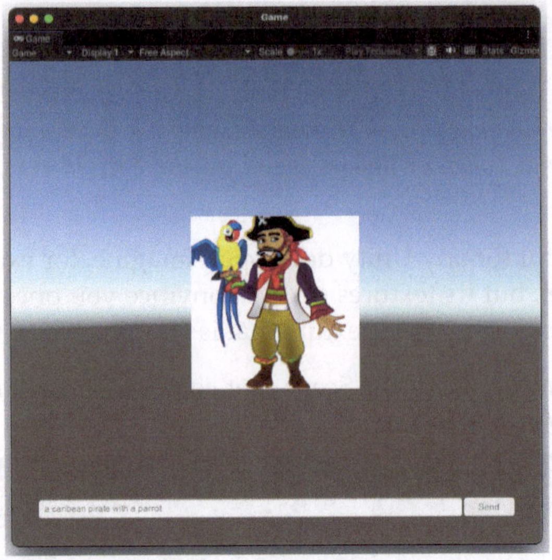

Figure 17.8: Sample of an image generated with DALL-E from the editor

Now, we are going to do something a little more adjusted to what is usually needed. A texture that we can apply to a 3D object that is tileable. The prompt is as follows:

`A tileable texture of metal brushed`

The result can be seen in the following figure:

Figure 17.9: This is a tileable texture

As you can see, this tool can save us a lot of work and help us be much more productive. If you are a developer, you should not see it as an adversary to beat but as an ally capable of giving you superpowers.

Whisper

Another OpenAI technology we have access to through this package is Whisper. Whisper is an advanced **Automatic Speech Recognition** (**ASR**) system designed specifically to transcribe and translate audio to text. Its main features include the following:

- Whisper is capable of accurately transcribing a wide range of audio inputs, including conversations, lectures, and multimedia content.
- It has multilingual capabilities, allowing you to transcribe audio in one language and translate it into another.
- It is designed to be used in the real world. Hence, it works well even with some adversities, such as background noise and changing accents, something that normally happens in many cases.

In the example project, we will be asked to choose a microphone.

Then, we must press the **Record Audio** button and say some words in English, as shown in the following figure:

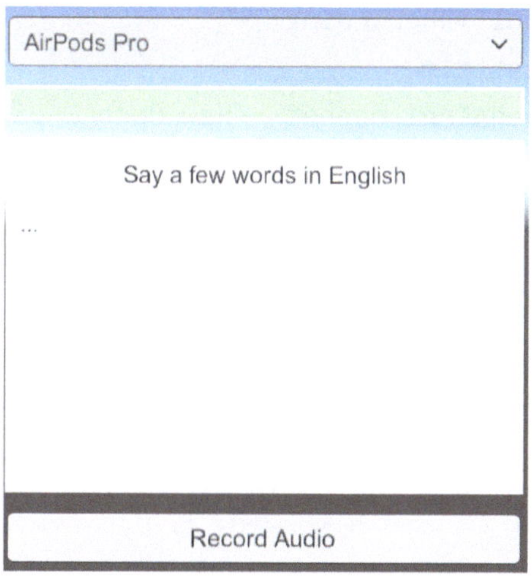

Figure 17.10: *Whisper transcribes the voice into text and translates to other languages*

The app will make a request with the recorded audio using the REST API that will be sent to the OpenAI server.

In the response, the text transcribed into text is returned and displayed on the screen.

Here is the code used. On line 71, you select the language to transcribe. You can change it if you need it:

```
1. using OpenAI;
2. using UnityEngine;
3. using UnityEngine.UI;
4.
5. namespace Samples.Whisper
6. {
7.     public class WhisperDemo : MonoBehaviour
8.     {
9.         [SerializeField] private Button recordButton;
10.        [SerializeField] private Image progressBar;
11.        [SerializeField] private Text message;
12.        [SerializeField] private Dropdown dropdown;
13.
14.        private readonly string fileName = "output.wav";
15.        private readonly int duration = 5;
16.
17.        private AudioClip clip;
18.        private bool isRecording;
19.        private float time;
20.        private OpenAIApi openai = new OpenAIApi();
21.
22.        private void Start()
23.        {
24.            #if UNITY_WEBGL && !UNITY_EDITOR
25.            dropdown.options.Add(new Dropdown.
   OptionData("Microphone not supported on WebGL"));
26.            #else
27.            foreach (var device in Microphone.devices)
28.            {
29.                dropdown.options.Add(new Dropdown.OptionData(device));
30.            }
31.            recordButton.onClick.AddListener(StartRecording);
32.            dropdown.onValueChanged.AddListener(ChangeMicrophone);
33.
34.            var index = PlayerPrefs.GetInt("user-mic-device-index");
```

```
            dropdown.SetValueWithoutNotify(index);
            #endif
        }

        private void ChangeMicrophone(int index)
        {
            PlayerPrefs.SetInt("user-mic-device-index", index);
        }

        private void StartRecording()
        {
            isRecording = true;
            recordButton.enabled = false;

            var index = PlayerPrefs.GetInt("user-mic-device-index");

            #if !UNITY_WEBGL
            clip = Microphone.Start(dropdown.options[index].text, false, duration, 44100);
            #endif
        }

        private async void EndRecording()
        {
            message.text = "Transcripting...";

            #if !UNITY_WEBGL
            Microphone.End(null);
            #endif

            byte[] data = SaveWav.Save(fileName, clip);

            var req = new CreateAudioTranscriptionsRequest
            {
                FileData = new FileData() {Data = data, Name = "audio.wav"},
                // File = Application.
```

```
persistentDataPath + "/" + fileName,
                Model = "whisper-1",
                Language = "en" // here you can change the language if you need it
            };
            var res = await openai.CreateAudioTranscription(req);

            progressBar.fillAmount = 0;
            message.text = res.Text;
            recordButton.enabled = true;
        }

        private void Update()
        {
            if (isRecording)
            {
                time += Time.deltaTime;
                progressBar.fillAmount = time / duration;

                if (time >= duration)
                {
                    time = 0;
                    isRecording = false;
                    EndRecording();
                }
            }
        }
    }
}
```

Other LLMS

While ChatGPT has achieved notable global fame, there are many other notable models, such as Claude 2 by Anthropic, DeepSeek, Qwen, or Mistral, that provide important, distinctive features and capabilities. Each model has its unique strengths, whether in specialized applications or advanced functionalities, contributing to the diverse toolset available in the AI landscape.

These models are not only revolutionizing the way we interact with technology but are also expanding into various industries through applications ranging from content creation and problem-solving to translation services. As research and innovation continue to drive improvements, LLMs promise further integration into our daily lives, improving efficiency and creativity across countless sectors. We will discuss some of the most notable ones in the following section.

DeepSeek-R2

DeepSeek, a pioneering artificial intelligence company established in 2023, positions itself as a leader in the field with a strong emphasis on precision, speed, and versatility. DeepSeek's strategic objective is to compete with global AI giants such as ChatGPT and Gemini AI by offering a more cost-effective solution. Notably, DeepSeek's approach typically requires less training costs, with Qwen requiring only 6 million compared to 12 million for ChatGPT.

One of DeepSeek's most distinctive features is the exceptional performance of its models in coding tasks. Specifically, DeepSeek's models excel in generating and fine-tuning techniques that enable them to comprehend and generate code in multiple languages. This versatility makes DeepSeek's models a highly effective and powerful tool in the generative model's landscape, particularly for developers and startups seeking robust yet cost-efficient AI solutions.

DeepSeek's models are also renowned for their multilingual capabilities and high inference efficiency, enabling them to operate seamlessly across diverse applications. The company's open-source stance presents an attractive option for developers and startups, offering a comprehensive yet affordable AI solution.

In the realm of security, DeepSeek implements robust encryption protocols to safeguard data both during transit and at rest. This ensures the confidentiality and security of user data throughout its lifecycle, addressing concerns raised about data security in other AI models.

DeepSeek's impact on the AI industry is profound, demonstrating significant advancements in various sectors. By providing real-time insights into customer trends, supply chain challenges, and market fluctuations, DeepSeek empowers businesses to proactively anticipate and respond to evolving market dynamics. This proactive approach grants businesses a competitive advantage in the highly competitive business landscape.

Furthermore, DeepSeek's models exhibit remarkable reasoning accuracy, exemplified by R1's ability to generate detailed and reasoned responses. This feature is crucial in the business realm, where companies require smarter, faster, and more cost-effective AI solutions.

Qwen

The Qwen series, developed by *Alibaba Cloud*, represents a substantial advancement in the field of LLMs. These models are renowned for their strong language processing capabilities, enabling them to effectively comprehend and analyze natural language inputs. The Qwen models, also referred to as *Tongyi Qianwen*, have undergone substantial development since their initial beta release in April 2023. The series has witnessed several iterations, with notable releases such as Qwen2.5 and its variants like Qwen-32B-Preview and Qwen-72B-Preview.

These models are pre-trained on extensive multilingual and multimodal datasets, ensuring their applicability across diverse languages and modalities. Furthermore, the models have been refined with high-quality data to align with human preferences, thereby enhancing their effectiveness in practical applications.

One of the most recent additions to the Qwen family is the Qwen2.5-VL, which signifies a significant advancement in vision-language capabilities. Building on the success of its predecessor, Qwen2-VL, the Qwen2.5-VL model has benefited from community feedback, resulting in the incorporation of novel features and optimization of its capabilities.

The Qwen2.5-VL model has substantially enhanced document parsing capabilities, surpassing basic text recognition to omnidocument parsing. This enhancement enables the model to excel in processing documents across multiple scenes and languages, including handling various built-in formats such as handwriting, tables, charts, chemical formulas, and music sheets.

Additionally, the Qwen2.5-VL presents precise object grounding capabilities across different formats. It achieves improved accuracy in detecting, pointing, and counting objects, accommodating both absolute coordinate and JSON formats for advanced spatial reasoning. These enhancements enable the model to effectively manage intricate real-world tasks with enhanced efficiency and precision compared to previous versions and other comparable generative models.

Mistral

Mistral AI stands out as a prominent player in the field of LLMs, prioritizing security and safety as fundamental principles in the development of its AI solutions. The company's models are meticulously designed to handle data with unwavering robustness and integrity, ensuring the utmost protection of user information from unauthorized access.

A cornerstone of Mistral's security approach lies in the comprehensive implementation of data encryption, both during transit and at rest. This ensures that user data remains highly confidential throughout its lifecycle, addressing the ongoing security concerns surrounding AI models. Mistral's encryption protocols are meticulously crafted, providing an additional layer of security that other AI models may not offer.

Beyond data security, Mistral's API empowers content moderation, capable of identifying and filtering harmful content across diverse categories, including hate speech, sexual content, violence, and sensitive information. This capability is underpinned by Mistral's LLM Ministral 8B, underscoring the seamless integration of advanced language models with rigorous security practices.

Mistral's unwavering commitment to safety is evident in its holistic approach, where security is paramount in the development of AI solutions. This distinction from competitors who may prioritize other aspects over safety has contributed to the trustworthiness and reliability of Mistral's AI offerings.

Conclusion

This chapter has explored the rapid advancement of AI and its growing impact on technology and society. It has introduced various AI models, including ChatGPT, Llama, and Gemini, all of which are trained on large datasets to understand and generate human-like text. It emphasized the importance of selecting the correct model for a specific function. The chapter also discussed Ollama, an open-source system for managing and deploying language models locally. It also covered AI tools such as ComfyUI for image generation and Udio for audio generation. The chapter examined the use of Hugging Face, a prominent platform for AI models and datasets, and the integration of AI in Unity 3D using tools such as ChatGPT, DALL-E, and Whisper. It showed how these tools can enhance game development by generating text, creating images, and transcribing audio. In the next chapter, we will explore how Unity has implemented AI solutions for the next version of the editor, explicitly designed for Unity.

The next chapter highlights how Unity's new tools and updates empower developers to push creative and performance boundaries, focusing on advancements in AI and rendering technologies.

Multiple choice questions

1. **What is the primary characteristic that defines a LLM like ChatGPT?**
    a. Its reliance on procedural generation techniques.
    b. Its design to process and generate natural language.
    c. Its architecture being limited exclusively to the RISC processor design.
    d. Its exclusive function is the generation of virtual camera paths.
2. **Which OpenAI model, accessible via the unofficial Unity package, is explicitly designed to generate images from textual descriptions (prompts)?**
    a. Whisper
    b. Mistral
    c. DALL-E
    d. Gemini

3. **What is Ollama defined as in the context of deploying LLMs?**

   a. A cloud-based platform for scalable AI model training across multiple regions.

   b. An open-source management system designed to simplify running, tuning, and deploying language models locally.

   c. A centralized dashboard for managing authentication tokens and user IDs.

   d. The architecture used by Apple Silicon processors for Neural Engine tasks.

4. **What is the core function of Whisper, the advanced ASR system provided by OpenAI?**

   a. Generating dynamic, royalty-free background music for games.

   b. Compressing audio files for optimized network transmission.

   c. Transcribing and translating audio inputs to text.

   d. Analyzing device temperature to adjust graphics performance.

5. **ComfyUI is described as a flexible and modular tool utilizing a node-based visual interface primarily to simplify the process of:**

   a. Creating complex audio generation workflows using real-time feedback.

   b. Managing Unity services in the cloud via the command line interface (CLI).

   c. Generating images using neural networks, specifically focusing on stable diffusion.

   d. Authenticating users via REST APIs and generating session tokens.

6. **The integration of ChatGPT into Unity 3D is primarily noted for enhancing game development productivity by enabling developers to rapidly créate which of the following**:

   a. High-fidelity skeletal mesh character animations.

   b. Dialogues and conversations between non-player characters (NPCs) and players.

   c. Custom shaders using complex GLSL or HLSL language.

   d. Automated server build pipelines for Continuous Integration.

7. **To connect the unofficial Unity package to the OpenAI API (for ChatGPT, DALL-E, etc.), where must the required credentials (API key and organization ID) be stored on the local development machine?**

   a. In the Project Settings window under 'External Services'.

   b. In a JSON file named \`auth.json\` located within the \`.openai\` folder in the user's home directory.

c. Directly in the C# script's private serialized fields.

d. In the Unity Editor's Package Manager settings for the OpenAI package.

8. **Scenario: A game studio wants to use an AI model specifically known for its high efficiency and strong performance in generating and refining complex code structures in multiple languages. Which LLM, often highlighted for excelling in coding tasks, should the developers prioritize for investigation?**

    a. Mistral

    b. DeepSeek

    c. Phi-3

    d. UDIO

9. **In the context of deploying large-scale LLMs locally, which technical advantage allows Apple Silicon processors to handle models up to 128 GigaBytes, overcoming the memory limitations typical of consumer-grade graphics cards (GPU)?**

    a. The use of specialized Docker images preinstalled with Ollama.

    b. The unified memory accessible by the CPU, GPU, and Neural Engine.

    c. The inherent architecture of the RISC processors.

    d. The mandated use of the XorEncrypt algorithm for security.

10. **Hugging Face serves as a prominent platform and community dedicated primarily to which area?**

    a. Providing analytics dashboards for player retention metrics.

    b. Offering tools for server-side recording and toxic behaviour analysis (Safe Voice).

    c. Offering a repository of trained models, datasets, libraries, and resources for NLP and ML.

    d. Managing cloud-based identity and access management for enterprise systems (Active Directory).

Answers

1	b
2	c
3	b
4	c
5	c
6	b
7	b
8	b
9	b
10	c

Join our Discord space

Join our Discord workspace for latest updates, offers, tech happenings around the world, new releases, and sessions with the authors:

https://discord.bpbonline.com

Chapter 18
Last Features of Unity 6

Introduction

In recent years, advancements in **artificial intelligence** (**AI**) and rendering technologies have significantly transformed game and application development. Unity, a leading platform, has consistently evolved to meet developer needs, introducing cutting-edge tools and updates that enhance creativity, performance, and immersive experiences.

Unity has integrated AI tools such as Unity Muse and Sentis, streamlining content creation and enabling real-time AI interactions. Unity 6 Preview further elevates rendering with improvements such as the GPU Resident Drawer and Adaptive Probe Volumes, boosting visual fidelity and runtime efficiency. For immersive realities, features like the foveated rendering API and XR Interaction Toolkit 3.0 simplify development, enhancing VR/AR experiences.

Additionally, the render graph API and WebGPU early access promise efficient workflows, while native support for Arm-based Windows devices and DirectX 12 backend improvements expand hardware compatibility. Unity's commitment to multiplayer services and experimental features underscores its dedication to innovation.

This chapter highlights Unity's leadership in shaping the future of game development, empowering creators to push boundaries and create transformative interactive experiences.

Structure

The chapter covers the following topics:

- Unity AI
    - Unity Muse
    - Unity Sentis
- Unity 6 LTS
    - Performance improvement
    - Lights improvements
    - Render graph

- Improvements for immersive realities:
    - Foveated rendering API
    - XR input and interactions
    - Unique hand gestures
    - XR Interaction Toolkit
- DirectX 12 backend improvements
    - Microsoft GDK packages
- Memory profiler
- Multiplayers center
- Peer-to-peer sessions
- WebGPU early access
- Supporting Arm-based Windows devices through Unity Editor

Objectives

The objectives of this chapter are to explore the cutting-edge advancements introduced in Unity 6 LTS, focusing on how they transform game development through AI and high-performance rendering. Readers will learn to leverage Unity Muse to streamline asset creation and Unity Sentis to integrate runtime AI models directly into their projects for dynamic interactions. The chapter aims to equip developers with the knowledge to utilize advanced rendering optimizations, including the GPU Resident Drawer, **Adaptive Probe Volumes** (**APVs**), and **Spatial-Temporal Post-Processing** (**STP**), ensuring superior visual fidelity and runtime efficiency. Furthermore, readers will gain insights into enhancements for immersive realities, such as Foveated Rendering and the XR Interaction Toolkit 3.0, alongside critical backend improvements like DirectX 12 support, WebGPU early access, and native support for Arm-based Windows devices. Finally, the objectives include mastering new multiplayer workflows through the Multiplayer Center and effectively implementing **peer-to-peer** (**P2P**) sessions.

Unity AI

In the preceding chapter, we explored several AI solutions that can be highly beneficial in the development of our applications. Unity Enterprises recognized the substantial potential of artificial intelligence to enhance the capabilities of artists and developers, leading them to create two additional tools that offer a unique advantage: seamless integration within the Unity ecosystem. These tools are Sentis and Muse.

Artificial intelligence's solutions in Unity: **https://assetstore.unity.com/ai-hub**

Unity Muse

Unity Muse is a set of artificial intelligence tools designed to help game and application developers create assets. With Muse, you can generate textures, animations, and scripts in a simpler and more efficient way. This allows a great increase in productivity since many of the steps necessary for creating new content are eliminated, and these, in addition, adapt perfectly to what we need.

In the next figure, we can see the Muse window where we can ask questions such as: **`How can I do a reverse cinematic?`** or **`We teach how to configure the controller so that the character can walk, run, and jump`**. Undoubtedly, the new tools are of great help and will change the way we develop:

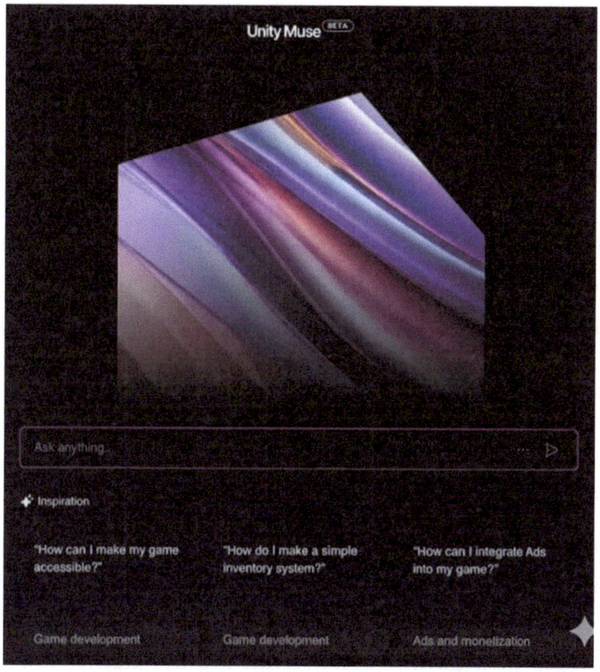

***Figure 18.1:** Unity Muse is like having a ChatGPT trained and integrated within the Unity editor*

Unity Sentis

Unity Sentis is another AI-related tool introduced by Unity. It comes from a package formerly called Barracuda. Unity Sentis is focused on empowering developers to deploy and run ONNX's models directly within their Unity applications. The **Open Neural Network Exchange** (**ONNX**) is an open-source file format that captures trained deep learning models in a framework-agnostic manner, allowing you to move the same model between different tools.

Some of its main features are:

- Allows developers to take AI models in ONNX format, which are typically trained outside of Unity using frameworks like TensorFlow or PyTorch, and integrate them into their Unity projects. This integration facilitates real-time AI inference within the Unity environment. Thanks to the fact that Unity can create applications for more than 20 different platforms, we can import the already trained neural network and use it on all those platforms!
- Sentis enables the execution of AI models on-device, enabling the real-time processing of data. This capability is crucial for applications that necessitate prompt responses, such as interactive gaming, **augmented reality** (**AR**), **virtual reality** (**VR**), and other immersive experiences.
- Sentis is designed to maximize the performance of AI models when they are running within Unity applications. It ensures that the models are efficient and have minimal impact on the overall performance of the application.
- The last Unity Editor now provides support for AI model weight quantization (FP16 or UINT8), allowing for a reduction in model size of up to 75%. That is a significant savings when it comes to shipping games to mobile. The model scheduling speed was also improved by 2x, along with reduced memory leaks and garbage collection. Lastly, Unity has expanded our support for additional ONNX operators.
- To make it easier to find the right AI model for your project, the Unity Sentis model[1] can now be found on Hugging Face, the world's largest AI model hub (over 600,000 models).

Some use cases could be:

- **Object identification**: Use an in-game or on-device camera to detect, classify, and segment objects using computer vision.
- **Trained neural network:** A neural network trained on the rules of a game to determine the probability of winning after each move. That way, you can make opponents much smarter and create custom difficulty curves to improve gameplay.
- **To occlude objects in a game scene**: Estimate the depth of real-world objects in an augmented reality view.
- **Text recognition:** Due to the detection capabilities of artificial intelligence, it is possible to identify numerical values, letters, and handwritten symbols or convert live speech into text by means of a machine learning language model. Significant enhancements can be made in the interactions with users.
- **Intelligent characters:** Create truly intelligent **non-player character** (**NPCs**) who are able to understand what you tell them in real-world and respond without waiting times. You will finally be able to develop meaningful interactions between players and NPCs that do not feel cookie-cutter.

1 All the Unity Sentis models now could be found at the Hugging Face.

In the following figure, you can see an NPC that responds intelligently and quickly to interactions with the player. Thanks to Sentis' AI integration, interactions with non-player characters can become increasingly natural and lifelike:

***Figure 18.2**: Sample of an interaction with voice with an NPC using Sentis*

- **Deploying AI models**: Unity Sentis allows developers to take AI models, which are typically trained outside of Unity using frameworks like TensorFlow or PyTorch, and integrate them into their Unity projects. This integration facilitates real-time AI inference within the Unity environment.

***Figure 18.3**: This is the new Unity home screen with the numbering change*

Unity 6 LTS

Just a few months ago, the latest version of Unity was presented: Unity 6, which has changed its numbering after many years. The latest version right now is 6000.0.31f LTS. This version incorporates important improvements that will allow us, as developers, to make better games and applications.

Performance improvement

The news of enhanced performance is always favorable for developers. Unity has consistently been characterized as a contained game engine that is capable of running on multiple platforms due to its ability to adapt and utilize resources sparingly.

Due to the efforts of developers and the use of optimized techniques, Unity 6 Preview, Universal Render Pipeline, and High Definition Render Pipeline see significant performance improvements that accelerate production on all platforms. Depending on the content, the enhancements outlined herein have the potential to reduce CPU workload by 30% to 50% while simultaneously delivering smoother and faster rendering across multiple platforms.

Unity needed to give optimization a boost to be able to create huge open worlds with complex scenes. They have achieved important improvements with two new technologies:

GPU Resident Drawer

The new GPU Resident Drawer allows you to efficiently render larger, richer worlds without the need for complicated manual optimizations. You can optimize your games with up to 50% CPU frame time reduction for GameObjects when rendering large, complex scenes on all platforms, including mobile devices, PCs, and high-end consoles.

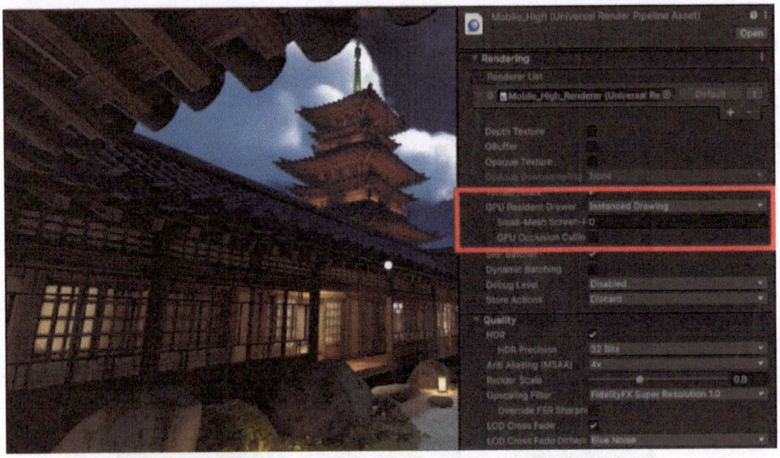

Figure 18.4: In the inspector we can see the parameters that allow us to use the new optimizations

GPU Occlusion Culling

Important advances have been made in the detection of those objects that should not be drawn since they are covered by other objects and, therefore, which means the renderer is not wasting resources drawing things that are not seen.

How it works:

1. **Depth pre-pass:** The GPU renders a simplified version of the scene, prioritizing depth information.
2. **Occlusion queries:** The GPU determines which objects are completely occluded by others based on depth testing.
3. **Visibility results:** The results are returned, and only visible objects are rendered in the final frame.

Since the GPU is highly parallel and optimized for handling large amounts of data, this method is generally faster and more scalable than CPU-based approaches.

Spatial-Temporal Post-Processing

Another technique that can be used to significantly improve visual quality and runtime performance is known as **Spatial-Temporal Post-Processing** (**STP**).

Traditional post-processing effects, such as motion blur, Depth of Field, bloom, and anti-aliasing, typically rely solely on the current frame (spatial data). However, STP enhances these effects by employing:

- **Spatial processing**: Samples and processes data from neighboring pixels within the same frame.
- **Temporal processing**: Incorporates information from preceding frames to generate smoother and more accurate effects.

By combining these techniques, STP mitigates noise, flickering, and aliasing artifacts, resulting in more stable and aesthetically pleasing outcomes.

STP is designed to take frames at a lower resolution and upscale them without loss of fidelity, delivering consistently high quality. Content is distributed to platforms with varying levels of performance capabilities and screen resolutions. STP provides support for both **Universal Render Pipeline** (**URP**) and **High Definition Render Pipeline** (**HDRP**) on desktops, consoles, and, in particular, computing-capable mobile devices.

In the following figure, we can see how the rendering engine of Unity 6 has improved a lot thanks to the optimizations that have been made by combining the rendering with the CPU and the GPU, which will allow us to be able to include many more polygons and improve the quality of our applications, games or simulations:

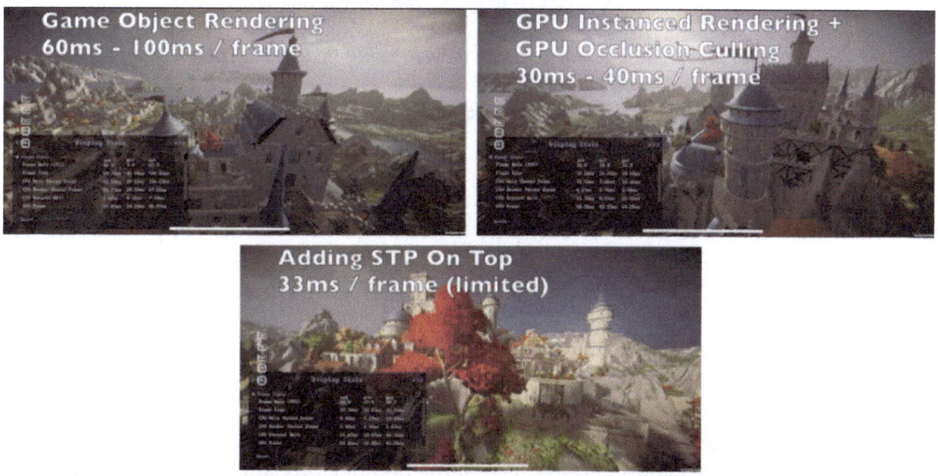

***Figure 18.5**: The improvement in the times used to render each frame are remarkable*

Lights improvements

On many occasions, we have seen assets that simulate the solar lighting cycle, how the light changes from dawn through the peak hours of the day, and how it becomes more reddish at the end of the day to reach night with only the light of the moon.

Adaptative Probe Volumes

This simple process greatly affects the entire system of calculating global lights in a 3D environment. A new way to create global illumination has been created in Unity 6: **Adaptive Probe Volumes** (**APVs**)[2] that enable more optimized creation and iteration times for objects illuminated by light probes and open up new possibilities, such as time of day and streaming scenarios.

Figure 18.6: *Sample of the time of the day cycle using new lights enhancements*

Without a doubt, one of the most laborious tasks of development in Unity is the creation of baked lighting.

The lightmaps precomputation process is often time-consuming; You need to create Lightmap UVs, deal with huge textures (which can put a heavy load on your applications' execution memory), and place probes so that dynamic objects light up correctly, adjusting to the environment in a sneaky way.

In Unity 6, a novel method has been introduced for creating illuminated environments utilizing light probes, which are considerably more automated and yield superior results

2 You can find the latest documentation about Adaptative Probe Volumes in Universal Render Pipeline at this address: https://docs.unity3d.com/Packages/com.unity.render-pipelines.universal@17.0/manual/probevolumes.html

through APVs. Additionally, fundamental enhancements are being made to the light baking backend, improving its stability.

***Figure 18.7**: Detail of the new APV lighting method*

Depending on our interests, we will want the lighting to be calculated, seeking maximum performance or the lowest possible memory usage. That is why a new baking profile has been included that allows you to choose the appropriate workflow intent:

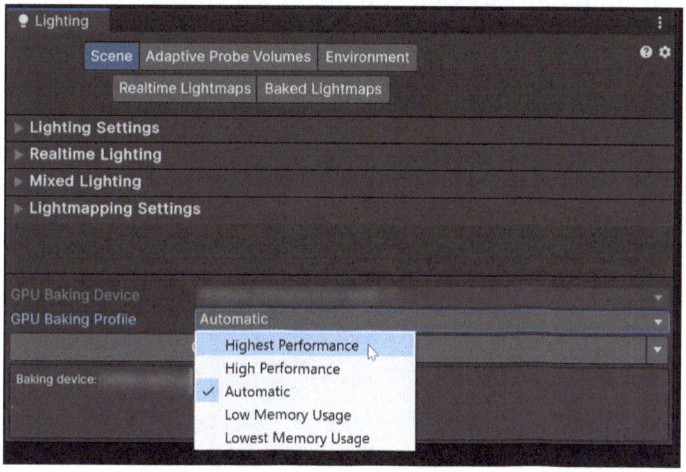

***Figure 18.8**: Detail of the rendering profiles that allow us to work at different levels of quality*

Debug probe sampling and masks

If you have experience working with light probe data, you may be familiar with the common challenges presented by light leaks. When developing APV, we introduced a complete toolbox to help address light leak issues, such as virtual offset, dilation, probe adjustment volumes, rendering layers, and performance and quality light leak prevention modes.

To investigate this issue, you can use the **Debug Probe Sampling** option to display each sampled probe along with its relevant weights. In our case, we can see that the result is interpolated between the brightest probes on the outside and the darkest ones on the inside. Ideally, only the interior of the store should sample the interior probes.

Render layers for APV allow you to create up to four different masks and restrict sampling to those specific masks for certain objects (landed in 6000.1f.1). This can be incredibly useful for preventing interior objects from sampling exterior probes or vice versa.

Render graph

In addition to the enhancements made in the rendering and lighting process, significant advancements have been made in the new render graph API, which streamlines the custom pass injection workflow. This enables users to augment the render pipeline with their own raster and customized passes. It is also possible to access all necessary channel resources reliably using the new context container.

The render graph for URP is a new rendering framework and API that simplifies the maintenance and extensibility of the render pipeline and improves rendering efficiency and performance. The new system introduces several key optimizations, such as automatic blending and creation of native render passes, in order to reduce memory bandwidth usage along with power consumption, especially on tile-based GPUs.

With the new **Render Graph Viewer** tool, you can now analyze engine render pass creation and frame resource usage directly in the editor. This will simplify render pipeline debugging and optimization:

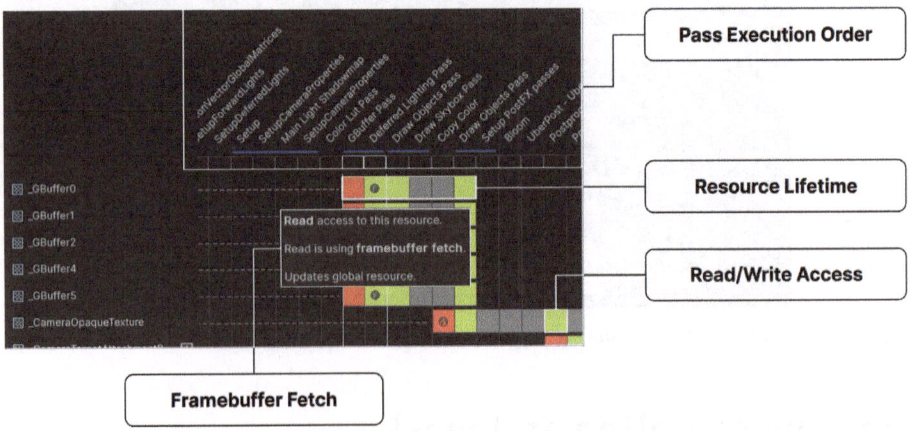

Figure 18.9: Render graph viewer tool detects problems and optimizes apps

Improvements for immersive realities

For VR/AR/XR developers, there have also been some performance improvements and a couple of important changes added that simplify development using the **XR Interaction Toolkit 3.0** (**XRI Toolkit 3.0**).

Foveated rendering API

This is a performance improvement intended especially for VR developers. The technique consists of taking into account how human vision works: we see the place where we are focusing more clearly, and lose sharpness of vision as we move away from that focused central point.

Foveated rendering generates with higher quality the area where we are supposed to be looking (if our VR viewer has eye tracking, this can be done with precision) and renders with lower quality everything that is in the periphery. In this way, the quantity and quality of what must be calculated is reduced, and therefore, we achieve greater and better performance.

The foveated rendering API is supported by the *Sony PlayStation®VR2* and *Meta Quest* plug-in via the Oculus XR plug-in and will soon be supported by the Open XR plug-in.

In the following figure, you can clearly see how the central part of the circle (where we are directing the gaze) is rendered with the highest quality, but what runs to the peripheral vision looks blurrier, with less sharpness:

***Figure 18.10**: Notice the difference in quality in the image rendered in the center of the circle and the one around it*

By concentrating rendering efforts on the user's focal point, this method improves performance where it matters most. As eye-tracking becomes mainstream, its benefits will grow substantially.

XR input and interactions

The way objects are used in XR has been simplified with a new Near-Far interactor that works differently depending on how far away objects are. That simplifies the entire process.

Regarding gesture (hand) recognition, more platforms are now supported, and the example project allows you to start working sooner. They also included tools to create, adjust, and refine your hand shapes and gestures to make your content accessible to more people.

Unique hand gestures

This system uses hand detection to allow us to interact with VR and AR apps. It works now on more platforms. You will be able to define custom hand gestures (such as thumbs up, thumbs down, pointing) as well as common Open XR hand gestures with this system. Included are examples to help you get started quickly. It also includes tools to create, adjust, and refine your hand shapes and gestures in order to make your content accessible to more people.

XR Interaction Toolkit

The Unity **XR Interaction Toolkit** (**XRI**) is designed to streamline the creation of immersive VR and AR applications. This framework incorporates pre-built components that facilitate intuitive user interactions, such as grabbing objects and teleportation, making it accessible for developers with varying levels of expertise.

The toolkit supports multiple platforms, including major VR and AR devices like Oculus, HTC Vive, and HoloLens, ensuring seamless cross-platform compatibility.

DirectX 12 backend improvements

Both the editor and the Windows editor are now able to work with DirectX 12 (as long as your system supports it). Developers will benefit from all the new features it implements, such as significant improvements in CPU performance through the use of split graphics jobs. Performance gains are expected to increase based on the complexity of the scene and the number of draw calls sent.

The DX12 graphics API provides support for a wide range of modern graphics capabilities, such as Unity's ray tracing pipeline. Future features will make use of DX12's advanced capabilities, including graphics and machine learning, to enable an unprecedented level of fidelity and performance.

Some performance improvements are also due to the adoption of the new version 12 of DirectX. It is not an optimization made directly by Unity, but as you can see in the following figure, we will obtain superior performance just by changing versions:

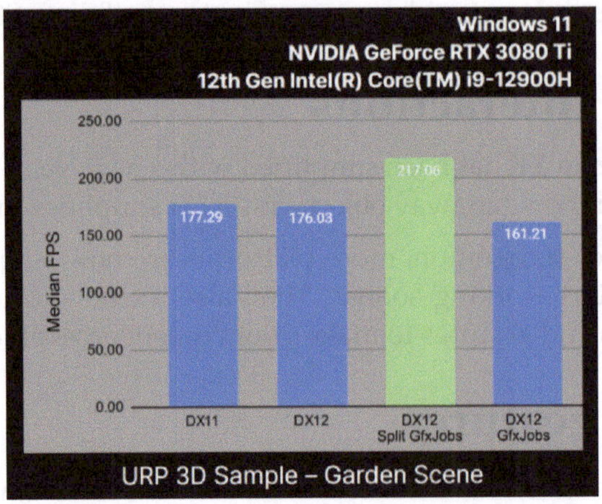

Figure 18.11: *You will improve the performance on Windows only for the use of DirectX12*

Microsoft GDK packages

There are now two new Microsoft GDK packages available with Unity 6 Preview: 2022 LTS and 2021 LTS. The Microsoft GDK tools and Microsoft GDK API packages can be used on Microsoft gaming platforms with an identical configuration and code base. These packages facilitate the development of Microsoft gaming platforms, such as Windows and Xbox, by using identical code to use Xbox services such as user identity, player data, social networks, and cloud storage, among others.

Memory Profiler

Unity 6 Preview introduces two significant enhancements pertaining to the Memory Profiler. Graphics memory that was previously uncategorized is now measured and reported per resource, such as render textures and compute shaders. Secondly, the reporting of resident memory is more precise, as memory that is switched to disk is no longer counted towards this. These updates address direct feedback regarding the problem of understanding native memory usage in particular.

In the following figure, you can clearly see the distribution and use of memory in a device. Knowing in depth how it works is essential to be able to optimize your applications for each device. Undoubtedly, the new Memory Profiler will be of great help to all developers:

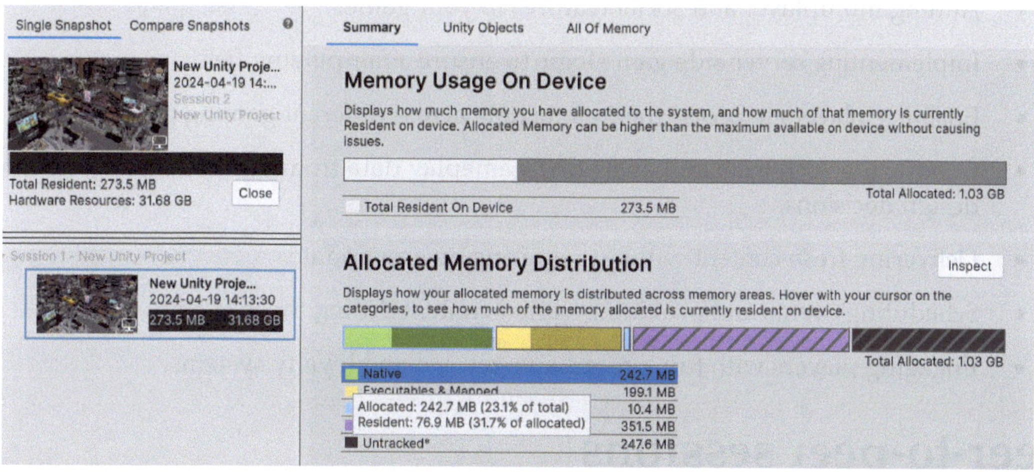

***Figure 18.12**: The new Memory Profiler is your best friend to develop for mobile devices*

Multiplayers Center

We dedicated a chapter to seeing the multiplayer tools that Unity Enterprises offered us. In this version, we will be able to test the latest developments that are being carried out to continue improving multiplayer services. Some of them are not yet ready for production environments, but it is interesting to know what new functionalities they will offer us when they are consolidated.

Multiplayer Center provides a comprehensive list of all relevant multiplayer tools and services, accessible whenever you need them. It simplifies the process of choosing which multiplayer feature technology to implement by recommending the best options for your project. The Multiplayer Widgets are pre-assembled UI elements—small, configurable, and customizable templates—that enable you to easily add multiplayer features, such as a lobby, session connection, or voice chat.

Multiplayer Center further streamlines the process by allowing you to instantly validate your gameplay. It launches up to four independent, lightweight editor processes from the same assets on disk. For the most ambitious server-hosted projects, Play Mode Scenarios enables you to configure deployment steps, including the build of your dedicated server and its direct upload to your Multiplay Hosting servers.

Unity Gaming Services is an all-inclusive platform that simplifies game development, engagement, and growth. It eliminates the need to worry about maintaining or scaling your back-end infrastructure, allowing you to focus on building and improving your game.

UGS simplifies various game development tasks and challenges, including:

- Adding multiplayer and social features to your game.
- Implementing server-side game logic to ensure a fair playing field.
- Enabling players to access their game data across different gaming platforms.
- Conducting A/B tests and analyzing gameplay data from various services to inform design decisions.
- Delivering fresh content without requiring an app update.
- Scheduling events and providing varied content during those events.
- Engaging players with fun, progressive reward and loyalty systems.

Peer-to-peer sessions

Peer-to-peer (P2P) sessions in Unity 6 represent a significant advancement in multiplayer game development, enabling players to connect directly without the need for a centralized server. This architecture enhances the gaming experience by reducing latency and simplifying setup processes, which is particularly beneficial for fast-paced and interactive games. Unity 6 incorporated improved networking features that facilitated P2P connectivity, allowing developers to create more immersive and responsive gameplay experiences across various platforms.

The transition to P2P architecture has garnered attention as games like *Beetle Brigade* and *Spidey Party* showcased its capabilities, encouraging developers to overcome challenges related to **network address translation** (**NAT**) and connection stability. Prominent discussions in industry events, such as *Michal Buras'* presentation at the *2024 Live Service Game Summit*, highlighted the growing importance of understanding networking technologies to optimize game performance and player engagement.

While P2P architecture offers advantages such as decentralization and scalability, it also presents challenges such as managing cheating and ensuring reliable connections, which can complicate the player experience.

The evolution of P2P sessions in Unity underscores their critical role in shaping the future of multiplayer gaming. As developers increasingly adopt this model, they leverage Unity's built-in tools for profiling and network management, which are essential for maintaining smooth gameplay in dynamic environments. Furthermore, the ongoing integration of advanced technologies and third-party services is anticipated to enhance the efficiency and security of P2P networks, addressing both player concerns and technical challenges. This ongoing development reflects the vibrant landscape of multiplayer gaming, where the demand for responsive, engaging, and secure gaming experiences continues to grow.

WebGPU early access

With the introduction of the WebGPU backend, we are now able to make apps for web browsers with graphics acceleration that was previously impossible.

WebGPU aims to leverage and expose modern GPU capabilities, such as compute shader support, on the web. This new web API will achieve this by providing a modern graphics acceleration interface that is implemented internally through native GPU APIs such as DirectX 12, Vulkan, or Metal, depending on which desktop device you use:

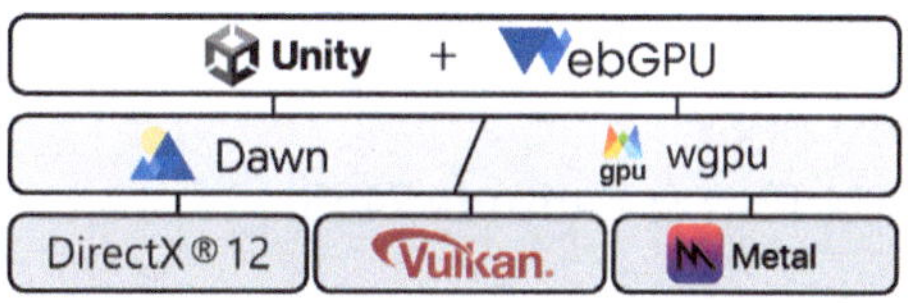

***Figure 18.13**: The WebGPU architecture brings us the GPU hardware potential*

It should be noted that the WebGPU graphics backend is still in an experimental state, so we do not recommend using it for production use. However, it promises a bright future.

WebGPU's support varies across different browsers and platforms. While major browsers like *Chrome* and *Edge* provide support, others, such as *Firefox*, are still in the development phase.

This inconsistency can create challenges for developers aiming for a wide audience, as they must account for varying levels of support and may need to implement fallbacks for unsupported environments.

It is important to remember that this feature works only in some desktop browsers and only in two mobile browsers.

If your browser does not yet support it, you can opt for the older WebGL2 feature (much less powerful but more widely used):

Mobile OS	Browser
iOS	Safari 15 or higher
Android	Chrome version 58 or higher

Table 18.1*: Browser version to use in mobile devices*

Supporting Arm-based Windows devices through Unity Editor

On July 18, 2024, new laptop models arrived on the market that have changed the **Complex Instruction Set Computer** (**CISC**) technology of Intel and AMD processors for a processor design based on **Reduced Instruction Set Computer** (**RISC**).

The laptops presented have a Snapdragon Elite X as a processor. The models that can currently be purchased are the following:

- Microsoft Surface Laptop 7th Edition and Surface Pro 11th Edition
- Asus Vivobook S 15 (S5507)
- Lenovo Yoga Slim 7x and ThinkPad T14s Gen 6
- Samsung Galaxy Book4 Edge
- Dell XPS 13, Inspiron 14 Plus & Latitude 7455
- Acer Swift 14 AI
- HP OmniBook X 14 and HP EliteBook Ultra G1q

Apple made the jump to this technology about three or four years ago, and although sometimes the performance may be a little lower, energy consumption and heat are greatly reduced. For this reason, ARM processors have until now been used for mobile devices, but the time has come to be able to use them in our laptops.

Unity, which always tries to be available for all platforms, now offers native Unity Editor support for Arm-based Windows devices in Unity 6. This means you can now take advantage of the performance and flexibility that Arm-powered devices can offer to create your Unity games.

***Figure 18.14**: Lenovo Yoga Slim Arm-based Laptop*

Conclusion

This chapter has highlighted the latest advancements within the Unity platform, demonstrating its continued evolution to meet the needs of game and application developers. Key innovations include the integration of AI tools like Unity Muse and Sentis, which streamline content creation and enable real-time AI interactions within the Unity ecosystem. Furthermore, Unity 6 Preview introduces significant rendering improvements, such as the GPU Resident Drawer and Adaptive Probe Volumes, leading to enhanced visual fidelity and runtime efficiency.

The chapter also covered improvements for immersive realities, with the foveated rendering API and XR Interaction Toolkit 3.0 simplifying the development of VR/AR/XR experiences. Additionally, the chapter detailed advancements in hardware compatibility through native support for Arm-based Windows devices and DirectX 12 backend improvements. Tools like the render graph API and WebGPU early access promise more efficient workflows and expanded capabilities. Finally, the chapter touched upon updates to the Memory Profiler and Multiplayer Center, showcasing Unity's ongoing commitment to providing comprehensive tools for developers. Overall, Unity is presented as a leading platform that is actively integrating AI, optimizing rendering pipelines, and expanding its reach into immersive and web-based experiences, empowering creators to push the boundaries of interactive content creation.

Multiple choice questions

1. **What core advantage does the GPU Resident Drawer technology offer developers using Unity 6 Preview?**
   a. Enabling the deployment of high-memory LLMs locally.
   b. Achieving automated conversion of 3D videos into stereoscopic formats.
   c. Efficiently rendering larger, richer worlds with up to 50% reduction in CPU frame time.
   d. Implementing advanced latency concealment and reconciliation techniques in multiplayer games.
2. **Which functionality is specifically attributed to Unity Muse as an artificial intelligence tool for content creators within the Unity ecosystem?**
   a. Deploying externally trained ONNX models directly within Unity applications.
   b. Automating shader code generation using complex GLSL language.

c. Generating textures, animations, and scripts based on text prompts.

d. Providing pixel-level synchronization for stereoscopic rendering.

3. **GPU Occlusion Culling is a technique in Unity 6 that optimizes rendering performance primarily by fulfilling which objective?**

   a. Reducing GPU clock speed based on device temperature thresholds.

   b. Calculating complex global illumination paths using Light Probes.

   c. Preventing the rendering of objects that are completely covered by others (unseen objects).

   d. Upscaling lower-resolution frames without loss of fidelity using temporal data.

4. **What significant enhancement do Adaptive Probe Volumes (APVs) introduce in Unity 6's lighting system?**

   a. Simplified management of version control repositories for Lightmaps.

   b. Optimized creation of global illumination, supporting features like time-of-day cycles and streaming scenarios.

   c. Dynamic adjustment of graphical settings based on network bandwidth consumption.

   d. Automated merging of work from multiple sources into a central repository.

5. **A developer integrates a neural network model, trained externally in TensorFlow using the ONNX format, into their Unity mobile game to predict player win probability after each move. Which Unity AI tool is essential for deploying and running this model on the target device?**

   a. Unity Muse

   b. Adaptive Probe Volumes

   c. GPU Resident Drawer

   d. Unity Sentis

6. **The foveated rendering API enhances VR performance by utilizing which principle derived from human vision?**

   a. Rendering both the central gaze area and the periphery with uniform, high quality.

   b. Prioritizing high-quality rendering only for the area directly focused on, and using lower quality for the periphery.

   c. Utilizing a multi-instance editor mode for simultaneous client testing.

   d. Calculating depth pre-pass information to optimize visibility.

7. **Unity 6 introduces native Editor support for Arm-based Windows devices, reflecting a hardware shift toward processors designed based on which architectural standard?**

   a. Complex Instruction Set Computer (CISC)

   b. Reduced Instruction Set Computer (RISC)

c. Distributed Authority (DA)

d. Neural Process Unit (NPU)

8. **What is the primary characteristic that defines a LLM like those utilized for generating text within the Unity context?**

    a. Their reliance on physics-based simulation engines.

    b. Their primary function is to calculate depth buffer information.

    c. Their design is to process and generate natural language.

    d. Their architecture is limited exclusively to the ARM processor design.

9. **Spatial-Temporal Post-Processing (STP) improves visual quality and runtime performance by mitigating noise and artifacts through the use of which information sources?**

    a. Data sampled from neighboring pixels within the same frame and information incorporated from preceding frames.

    b. The device's battery consumption rate and CPU utilization percentage.

    c. The server's network latency and bandwidth capacity.

    d. The shader cache and the memory allocation patterns of the application.

10. **Which feature, available in Unity 6 Preview, is designed to streamline multiplayer development and iteration by enabling the simultaneous execution of multiple instances of client-side logic on the same server?**

    a. A multi-instance editor mode

    b. P2P session architecture

    c. WebGPU Early Access

    d. The Foveated Rendering API

Answers

1	c
2	c
3	c
4	b
5	d
6	b
7	b
8	c
9	a
10	a

Index

Symbols

A

D

E

F

G

H

I

L